IB DIPLOMA PROGRAMME

Economics

Course Companion

Jocelyn Blink
Ian Dorton

OXFORD
UNIVERSITY PRESS

IBO

OXFORD
UNIVERSITY PRESS

Great Clarendon Street, Oxford OX2 6DP

Oxford University Press is a department of the University of Oxford.
It furthers the University's objective of excellence in research, scholarship,
and education by publishing worldwide in

Oxford   New York

Auckland Cape Town Dar es Salaam Hong Kong Karachi
Kuala Lumpur Madrid Melbourne Mexico City Nairobi
New Delhi Shanghai Taipei Toronto

With offices in

Argentina Austria Brazil Chile Czech Republic France Greece
Guatemala Hungary Italy Japan Poland Portugal Singapore
South Korea Switzerland Thailand Turkey Ukraine Vietnam

British Library Cataloguing in Publication Data

Data available

ISBN: 978-0-19-915124-0

10 9

Printed in China by Printplus.

Acknowledgements

We are grateful to the following for permission to reprint copyright material:
Canadian Broadcasting Corporation for 'Unemployment rate edges up to
6.4%', CBC News, 5 May 2006; **Cartoonstock Ltd** for Harley Schwadron cartoon,
www.cartoonstock.com; **The Economist** for extracts from 'Snapped', *The
Economist*, 16 December 1999, copyright © The Economist Newspaper Limited,
London 1999; 2 graphs, *The Economist* 15 July 2006, and 'The Big Mac Index', *The
Economist*, 26 May 2006, all copyright © The Economist Newspaper Limited,
London 2006; **The Financial Times** for 'Fed Chief believes inflation in retreat' by
Krishna Guha, *Financial Times*, 20 July 2006; **International Baccalaureate
Organization** for use of extracts from the IB Learner Profile and for example
questions from previous examination papers; **International Labour Office** for
information text from ILO website www.ilo.org, copyright © International Labour
Office 2006; **International Monetary Fund** for table; **Kingsport Publishing
Corporation** for editorial, 'Cigarette tax hike would benefit Tennessee residents',
The Kingsport Times, 20 March 2006; **Wangari Matthai** for quotation; **The New
York Times Agency** for 'Smoke Shifters' by Elisabeth Rosenthal, *The New York
Times*, 29 October 2006, copyright © 2006 The New York Times Co; **The New York
Times Syndicate** for 'The Japanese climate remains overcast' by Roger Buckley,
International Herald Tribune, 2 January 2001, copyright © 2001 IHT/iht.com; and 'EU
imposes long-term tariffs on Asian shoes' by Tom Rachman, *International Herald
Tribune*, 5 October 2006, copyright © 2006 IHT/iht.com; **News International
Syndication** for 'Public Investment aids growth as rising taxes hit customers' by
Gary Duncan, *The Times*, 23 December 2005, copyright © Gary Duncan/NI
Syndication Ltd, 2005; **OECD** for text from www.oecd.org, 13 June 2006, copyright
© OECD 2006, and tables and figures from ODA Statistics, copyright © OECD 2004;
Oxford University Press for extract from *Development as Freedom* by Amartya Sen
(OUP, 1999), and sections from Indicator Tables 1, 2, 5, 6, 7, 14 & 25 (adapted into
new tables with added columns) from the United Nations Development
Programme *Human Development Report 2005*; **Professor Friedrich Schneider** for
tables from Discussion Paper 1431, December 2004; **Telegraph Media Group Ltd**
for 'The bank of Italy shifts from dollars', including pie charts, *The Daily Telegraph*, 3
August 2006; **Transparency International** the Global Coalition Against
Corruption for tables from *Transparency International Global Corruption Barometer
2005*, (http://www.transparency.org/policy_research/surveys_indices/gcb/2005. To
read more about Transparency International go to www.transparency.org); **United
Nations** for tables from UNCTAD *World Investment Report* 2005, and from UNCTAD
secretariat estimates; **United Nations Development Programme** (UNDP) for
extract from *UNDP Annual Report 2006*; **Anup Shah** for tables using OECD data on
"The US and Foreign Aid Assistance", 7.10.06 at
www.globalissues.org/TradeRelated/Debt/USaid.asp/; **David Uren, News Limited
and The Australian** for 'Consumer Confidence on the Rise' by David Uren, *The
Australian*, 16 March 2006; **International Monetary Fund** via Copyright
Clearance Centre for table: "Real Primary Commodity Prices" and for table from

David Dollar and Art Kraay: "Trade, Growth and Poverty: A Selective Survey" (June
2001). Copyright © 2001 by the International Monetary Fund. P8:
Wikimedia/Oxford University Press; p9: Oxford University Press; p19:
Wikimedia/Oxford University Press; p23: Martial Trezzini/epa/Corbis; p31: Jaguar
Cars/Oxford University Press; p32: Bettmann/Corbis; p34: Oxford University Press;
p38: i-stock/Oxford University Press; p57: Wikimedia/Oxford University Press; p70:
Oxford University Press; p81: Oxford University Press; p97: Oxford University Press;
p109: Oxford University Press; p133: Wikimedia/Oxford University Press: p143:
INSADCO Photography/Alamy; p160: Touhig Sion/Corbis Sygma; p162: Oxford
University Press; p190: Bettmann/Corbis; p199: i-stock/Oxford University Press;
p209: Roger Ressmeyer/Corbis; p252: Bettmann/Corbis; p258: Steve Raymer/Corbis;
p276: i-stock/Oxford University Press; p319t: Simon Rawles/Alamy; p319m: Salient
Images/Alamy; p319b: Oxford University Press; p332: Jorgen Schytte/Still Pictures;
FAIRTRADE: p358; Fair Trade Trading: p359;

Barking Dog Artwork: pp341, 342, 367. All other technical artwork by Q2A.

We have tried to trace and contact all copyright holders before publication. If
notified the publishers will be pleased to rectify any errors or omissions at the
earliest opportunity.

Cover image © Image Source/Alamy.

Authors

Ian Dorton has been teaching IB Diploma Programme economics for
twenty years. He has taught in the UK and Singapore and is currently
teaching at the American International School in Vienna. He is an IB
deputy chief examiner for economics.

Jocelyn Blink has been teaching IB Diploma Programme economics
for fifteen years. She has taught in Canada, Nigeria and currently
teaches at the Vienna International School. She is an IB deputy chief
examiner for economics.

Consultants: Boyd Roberts has been engaged with the International
Baccalaureate for thirty years. He was head of the Amman Baccalaureate School
and of St Clare's, Oxford and is now consultant for international-mindedness
for the Course Companion series.

Manjula Solomon has taught in India, Iran, the US, and Indonesia, and has held
a variety of roles associated with the IBO, most recently as deputy chief assessor
for TOK. She is consultant for theory of knowledge for the Course Companion
series.

Dedication

We would like to thank our current and past Subject Area Managers,
Chris Mannix and Alison Doogan. We remember fondly our friend
and mentor, Tony Halsall.

We would like to dedicate this book to our children, Niki, Caroline,
Ben, and Nick.

Course Companion definition

The IB Diploma Programme Course Companions are resource materials designed to provide students with extra support through their two-year course of study. These books will help students gain an understanding of what is expected from the study of an IB Diploma Programme subject.

The Course Companions reflect the philosophy and approach of the IB Diploma Programme and present content in a way that illustrates the purpose and aims of the IBO. They encourage a deep understanding of each subject by making connections to wider issues and providing opportunities for critical thinking.

These Course Companions, therefore, may or may not contain all of the curriculum content required in each IB Diploma Programme subject, and so are not designed to be complete and prescriptive textbooks. Each book will try to ensure that areas of curriculum that are unique to the IB or to a new course revision are thoroughly covered. These books mirror the IB philosophy of viewing the curriculum in terms of a whole-course approach; the use of a wide range of resources; international-mindedness; the IB learner profile and the IB Diploma Programme core requirements; theory of knowledge; the extended essay; and creativity, action, service (CAS).

In addition, the Course Companions provide advice and guidance on the specific course assessment requirements and also on academic honesty protocol.

The Course Companions are not designed to be:

- study/revision guides or a one-stop solution for students to pass the subjects
- prescriptive or essential subject textbooks.

IBO mission statement

The International Baccalaureate Organization aims to develop inquiring, knowledgeable, and caring young people who help to create a better and more peaceful world through intercultural understanding and respect.

To this end the IBO works with schools, governments, and international organizations to develop challenging programmes of international education and rigorous assessment.

These programmes encourage students across the world to become active, compassionate, and lifelong learners who understand that other people, with their differences, can also be right.

The IB learner profile

The aim of all IB programmes is to develop internationally minded people who, recognizing their common humanity and shared guardianship of the planet, help to create a better and more peaceful world. IB learners strive to be:

Inquirers They develop their natural curiosity. They acquire the skills necessary to conduct inquiry and research and show independence in learning. They actively enjoy learning and this love of learning will be sustained throughout their lives.

Knowledgeable They explore concepts, ideas, and issues that have local and global significance. In so doing, they acquire in-depth knowledge and develop understanding across a broad and balanced range of disciplines.

Thinkers They exercise initiative·in applying thinking skills critically and creatively to recognize and approach complex problems, and make reasoned, ethical decisions.

Communicators They understand and express ideas and information confidently and creatively in more than one language and in a variety of modes of communication. They work effectively and willingly in collaboration with others.

Principled They act with integrity and honesty, with a strong sense of fairness, justice, and respect for the dignity of the individual, groups, and communities. They take responsibility for their own actions and the consequences that accompany them.

Open-minded They understand and appreciate their own cultures and personal histories, and are open to the perspectives, values, and traditions of other individuals and communities. They are accustomed to seeking and evaluating a range of points of view, and are willing to grow from the experience.

Caring They show empathy, compassion, and respect towards the needs and feelings of others. They have a personal commitment to service, and act to make a positive difference to the lives of others and to the environment.

Risk-takers They approach unfamiliar situations and uncertainty with courage and forethought, and have the independence of spirit to explore new roles, ideas, and strategies. They are brave and articulate in defending their beliefs.

Balanced They understand the importance of intellectual, physical, and emotional balance to achieve personal well-being for themselves and others.

Reflective They give thoughtful consideration to their own learning and experience. They are able to assess and understand their strengths and limitations in order to support their learning and personal development.

A note on academic honesty

It is of vital importance to acknowledge and appropriately credit the owners of information when that information is used in your work. After all, owners of ideas (intellectual property) have property rights. To have an authentic piece of work, it must be based on your individual and original ideas with the work of others fully acknowledged. Therefore, all assignments, written or oral, completed for assessment must use your own language and expression. Where sources are used or referred to, whether in the form of direct quotation or paraphrase, such sources must be appropriately acknowledged.

How do I acknowledge the work of others?

The way that you acknowledge that you have used the ideas of other people is through the use of footnotes and bibliographies.

Footnotes (placed at the bottom of a page) or endnotes (placed at the end of a document) are to be provided when you quote or paraphrase from another document, or closely summarize the information provided in another document. You do not need to provide a footnote for information that is part of a 'body of knowledge'. That is, definitions do not need to be footnoted as they are part of the assumed knowledge.

Bibliographies should include a formal list of the resources that you used in your work. 'Formal' means that you should use one of the several accepted forms of presentation. This usually involves separating the resources that you use into different categories (e.g. books, magazines, newspaper articles, Internet-based resources, CDs, and works of art) and providing full information as to how a reader or viewer of your work can find the same information. A bibliography is compulsory in the extended essay.

What constitutes malpractice?

Malpractice is behaviour that results in, or may result in, you or any student gaining an unfair advantage in one or more assessment component. Malpractice includes plagiarism and collusion.

Plagiarism is defined as the representation of the ideas or work of another person as your own. The following are some of the ways to avoid plagiarism:

- words and ideas of another person to support one's arguments must be acknowledged
- passages that are quoted verbatim must be enclosed within quotation marks and acknowledged
- CD-ROMs, email messages, web sites on the Internet, and any other electronic media must be treated in the same way as books and journals
- the sources of all photographs, maps, illustrations, computer programs, data, graphs, audio-visual, and similar material must be acknowledged if they are not your own work
- copying works of art, whether music, film, dance, theatre arts, or visual arts, and where the creative use of a part of a work takes place, must be acknowledged.

Collusion is defined as supporting malpractice by another student. This includes:

- allowing your work to be copied or submitted for assessment by another student
- duplicating work for different assessment components and/or diploma requirements.

Other forms of malpractice include any action that gives you an unfair advantage or affects the results of another student. Examples include, taking unauthorized material into an examination room, misconduct during an examination, and falsifying a CAS record.

Contents

Introduction

This book is designed to be a companion to you as you embark upon your study of the International Baccalaureate Diploma Programme in economics. Through its overarching emphasis on international economics and development economics, we hope that it will help you become, in the words of the IB learner profile, "internationally-minded people who, recognizing their common humanity and shared guardianship of the planet, help to create a better and more peaceful world".

Economics has a vital role to play in promoting international cooperation and mutual understanding because of its focus on global issues. To achieve this understanding, you need to learn to consider economic theories, ideas, and events from the points of view of different stakeholders in the world economy.

The Course Companion has been designed to facilitate this process in a number of ways.

- The study of the subject at both standard and higher level is encompassed and there is a focus toward the IB learner profile and international-mindedness. You will discover that many economic concepts and issues are closely linked to other disciplines, such as history, sociology, geography, and environmental studies.
- Opportunities are provided to learn and practise the skill of evaluation—a key skill needed to become an informed student of economics. As you expand your knowledge of economics and gain the ability to evaluate these ideas you will develop a balanced view of alternative viewpoints and become critical thinkers.
- The Student workpoints and Country investigations are intended to help you improve your research skills and gain a wider knowledge of the world.
- The importance of Theory of Knowledge (TOK) is emphasized, a core element of the IB Diploma Programme model. This will help you to understand that TOK exists in and applies to economics as it does in all academic areas. You will learn that economics is based on the collection of empirical evidence and the development of models which may differ,

depending on the assumptions upon which they are based. You will also become aware of the inherent biases in economics and that there are conflicting schools of thought within the discipline.

- *You be the journalist* is a feature designed to encourage you to write about economics in a creative way. In this role-playing exercise you will write in a journalistic style rather than the usual essay style. This will encourage you to be open to the perspectives of different stakeholders.
- Opportunities are created to discuss ethical issues, such as the causes and consequences of environmental damage, or the advantages and disadvantages of multinational investment in developing countries.
- There are biographies of several famous economists, which bring to light the fact that economic theory is devised by real people, people not unlike you.
- A number of data response exercises are included that are modelled on the final IB examination. Each exercise comprises a brief case study of economics in the real world.
- Sample examination questions are listed at the end of each chapter. These include examples of both the 10-mark short response questions that are on the higher level examination and the 25-mark essay questions that are on the standard level paper 2 and higher level paper 3 examinations.
- There is a valuable final chapter containing advice on internal assessment, examination technique, and extended essay writing. Tips on examination technique are also scattered through the Course Companion.

Economics is, by nature, a dynamic subject. As a result, theories evolve and change, and new theories are introduced to explain new evidence. It is not expected that you will rely entirely on this one Course Companion as your only resource. To benefit fully from an economics course at any level, you should draw on a variety of resources and approaches.

Jocelyn Blink and Ian Dorton
February 2007.

1 What is economics?

By the end of this chapter, you should be able to:

- define, and give examples of, a social science
- define, give examples of, and distinguish between, goods and services; needs and wants; economic goods and free goods
- define opportunity cost and understand its link to relative scarcity and choice
- explain the basic economic questions: "What to produce?", "How to produce?", and "How much to produce?"
- describe the factors of production
- explain, illustrate, and analyse production possibility curves.

Profile Adam Smith (1723–1790)

Often known as the "father of modern economics", Adam Smith was a Scotsman and wrote one of the first and most important books on the subject of economics, *An Inquiry into the Nature and Causes of the Wealth of Nations* (1776). It is no coincidence that the book was written during the beginning of the Industrial Revolution in Great Britain. This was the first period in which a country experienced industrialization. Prior to this economies had been fairly simple, agricultural systems, with most people involved in producing basic products, such as food and cloth, and just a few providing other necessities, such as farming equipment and leather goods. The coming of the steam engine, increased use of machinery, the emergence of banks for investment, and the birth of the stock exchange, made everything much more complex and in need of explanation.

Smith believed in the "free market". The free market is one where consumers may buy what they like and producers may produce what they like, with no government interference. Smith proposed that if everyone followed his or her own best interests, with as little state intervention as possible, then the public interest would be well served. He suggested that a laissez-faire (don't interfere) approach should be followed, leaving consumers and producers to make their own decisions and thus gaining maximum benefit for all from the market system. He believed that the "invisible hand" of competition would result in the most efficient outcome. He did not, however, advocate complete freedom and among other things, he identified possible problems relating to firms coming together and exploiting consumers. He also suggested that there might be problems if firms grew too large and so were able to dominate the market.

For the next 150 years the theories that originated with Adam Smith formed the basis of "classical economics". The overriding faith in the power of free markets to allocate resources efficiently was the orthodox (widely accepted) view of the time.

Economics is a social science, which is a study of people in society and how they interact with each other. Other social sciences include sociology, political science, psychology, anthropology, and history.

The Earth is, to all intent and purposes, finite. This means that we only have a finite amount of resources. We use these resources to produce the goods and services that we need or want, so the quantity of goods and services available is also finite. Goods are physical objects that are capable of being touched (tangible), such as vegetables, meat, or motorcars. Services are intangible things that cannot be touched, such as motorcycle repairs, haircuts, or insurance.

Human needs and wants are infinite. Needs are things that we must have to survive, such as food, shelter, and clothing. Wants are things that we would like to have but which are not necessary for our immediate physical survival, such as televisions and mobile phones.

student workpoint 1.1

1   Make a list of your own needs.

2   Make a list of the needs that your grandparents may have had. Explain the reason for any differences that you have suggested between your lists for questions 1 and 2.

3   Make a list of the needs of a person the same age as you, living in another continent. Explain the reason for any differences that you have suggested.

There is a conflict between the finite resources available and infinite needs and wants. People cannot have everything that they desire and so there must be some system for rationing the scarce resources. This is where economics comes in.

Economics is a study of rationing systems. It is the study of how scarce resources are allocated to fulfill the infinite wants of consumers.

Scarcity

To the economist, all goods and services that have a price are relatively scarce. This means that they are scarce relative to people's demand for them. It may seem that, in your town or city, cars are not scarce as there are a great number of them around. However, it is certain that not everyone who would like a car in your area has one, usually because they cannot afford to buy a car. Their ability to purchase a car is affected by the amount of money they have and the price of the car, so price is being used to ration the cars that are available. Any good or service that has a price, and is thus being rationed, is known as an economic good.

The term "scarcity" has a particular meaning in economics that is different from the way that the word is used in everyday life. A normal person would not say that cars were scarce in Mexico City, but an economist would be happy to state that they were relatively scarce.

Choice

Since people do not have infinite incomes, they need to make choices whenever they purchase goods and services. They have to decide how to allocate their limited financial resources and so always need to choose between alternatives. This leads to one of the key concepts of economics.

Opportunity cost

Opportunity cost is defined as *the next best alternative foregone when an economic decision is made*. This may sound quite complicated but simply means that opportunity cost is what you give up in order to have something else. For example, if you decide to buy a DVD for $15 rather than have a meal out, then the opportunity cost of the DVD is the meal out that you go without. It is not the $15, as opportunity cost is never expressed in monetary terms.

If a good or service has an opportunity cost then it must be relatively scarce, so it will have a price and be classified as an "economic good".

There are a few things, such as air and salt water, that are not limited in supply and so do not have an opportunity cost when they are consumed. We do not have to give up something else in order to breathe. These things are known as "free goods", as they are not relatively scarce and so will not have a price.

The basic economic problem

We have already seen that resources are relatively scarce and wants are infinite, which leads to choices to be made. These choices are often expressed in terms of three questions and represent the basic economic problem. The questions are:

● What should be produced and in what quantities? Using these scarce resources, how many computers should be produced, how many bicycles, how much wheat, and how much milk? This has to be decided for all economic goods.

● How should things be produced? There are many different ways of producing things and there are different combinations of resources that may be used in production. Should sports shoes be produced by an automated production line or by manual workers? Should crops be grown with high usage of fertilizer or organically?

● Who should things be produced for? Should they go to those who can afford them or be shared out in some "fair" manner? How will the total income (the national income) of the economy be distributed? Will teachers get higher incomes than nurses?

Whatever the system used to allocate resources, it needs to be able to answer these questions. There are two theoretical allocation (rationing) systems, the free market system and the planned economy. In reality, all economies are mixed economies, which are a combination of a free market system and a planned economy. We will look at these rationing systems in more detail in Chapter 2.

Factors of production

There are four resources that allow an economy to produce its output. These are known as factors of production.

Land

Land includes a large number of things. It is the land; everything that grows on the land or is found under it; the sea; and everything that is found in and under the sea. It therefore includes all natural resources. Some are basic raw materials, such as gold, coal, oil, and natural gas, and some are cultivated products, such as wheat, rice, and pineapples. Some natural resources are renewable, including all cultivated products, and some are non-renewable, including all fossil fuels like oil.

Labour

Labour is the human factor. It is the physical and mental contribution of the existing workforce to production.

Capital

Capital is the factor of production that comes from investment in physical capital and human capital. Physical capital is the stock of manufactured resources, such as factories, machinery, roads, and tools, that is used to produce goods and services in the economy. Human capital is the value of the workforce. Investment in human capital through education or improved health care may be a significant contributor to economic growth. Infrastructure (social overhead capital) is the large-scale public systems, services, and facilities of a country that are necessary for economic activity. This includes the stock of a nation's roads, railways, hospitals, schools, ports, airports, electricity plants, water plants, and telecommunications. These have been accumulated through investment, usually by the government. Improving infrastructure may lead to improved economic growth and development.

Management (entrepreneurship)

Management is the organising and risk-taking factor of production. Entrepreneurs organise the other factors of production, land, labour, and capital, to produce goods and services. They also use their personal money and the money of other investors to buy the factors of production, produce the goods and services, and, hopefully, make a profit. As a profit is never guaranteed and investment may be lost, this is the risk-taking part of the role of the entrepreneur.

Production possibility curves (production possibility frontiers)

These are used by economists to show the concepts of scarcity, choice, and opportunity cost, among other things. A production possibility curve (PPC) shows the maximum combinations of goods and services that can be produced by an economy in a given time period, if all the resources in the economy are being used fully and efficiently and the state of technology is fixed. This is known as potential output. An example of a PPC is shown in Figure 1.1, where only two things are being produced, schools or motorcars.

If all production is devoted to building schools, at point Y, then quantity Y of schools will be produced and no motorcars. Point X,

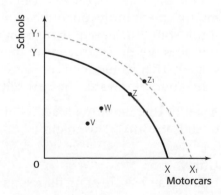

Figure 1.1 A production possibility curve

at the other end of the PPC, shows the situation where no schools are being built, only motorcars. At point Z resources are being shared between the production of motorcars and the building of schools. The points on the PPC show the possible combinations of school building and motorcar production. As you can see, it is impossible to build more schools without also producing fewer motorcars. The opportunity cost of more schools is the number of motorcars that are not produced.

The PPC is a curve because not all of the factors of production used to build schools and produce motorcars are equally good at both occupations. As we move towards point X, where few schools are being built, it is unlikely that the workers who usually build schools will be as productive as the workers who usually produce cars. In the same way, as point Y is approached, car workers will have to be involved in building schools and are unlikely to be as productive as the normal school builders. At point Z, the skilled workers in each industry will be specializing in the production at which they are best and so both sets of workers will be at their most productive.

It is possible to produce at any point inside the PPC, but it means that not all of the factors of production in the economy are being used or are being used inefficiently. In reality, economies are always producing within their PPCs, since there are always some unemployed factors of production in a country. For example, there is not a single economy in the world where the entire potential workforce is actually working at any given time—there will always be some unemployment in an economy.

Point V is inside the PPC and represents a combination of actual output. If there is a movement from point V towards the PPC, for example, to point W, then we say that there has been actual growth.

The point Z_1 is unattainable for an economy as it is outside the PPC. It could only be achieved if the PPC itself moved outwards. For example, if the PPC moved from YX to Y_1X_1, then the point Z_1 would be achievable. Any point on the PPC shows potential output, for example point Z. A PPC movement from YX to Y_1X_1 represents an increase in potential output and so a movement from Z to Z_1 would be potential growth.

An outward shift of the PPC can only be achieved if there is an improvement in the quantity and/or quality of factors of production. If this shift is achieved, there is an increase in potential output but this does not necessarily mean that there is an increase in actual output. That would require a movement of the current point of actual output towards the new PPC.

A fall in the quantity of factors of production would cause the PPC to shift inwards. This might be due to war or natural disasters.

Utility

Utility is a measure of usefulness and pleasure. It gives an idea of how much usefulness or pleasure a consumer receives when they consume a product. The two basic ways of measuring utility are total utility and marginal utility. Total utility is the total satisfaction gained from consuming a certain quantity of a product. If a person eats five ice creams the total utility would be a measure of the total pleasure gained from eating all of the ice creams. Marginal utility is the extra utility gained from consuming one more unit of a product. We could measure the extra utility that the consumer gains from each of the five ice creams consumed. It is believed that, in the majority of cases, the marginal utility gained from extra units of a product falls as consumption increases. If a person continues to eat ice cream after ice cream, the pleasure derived from each extra one will start to fall until, if the person continues eating for too long, they may be sick and a disutility may occur with marginal utility becoming negative.

 Theory of Knowledge

Social sciences

We have said that economics is a social science, a study of people in society and how they interact with each other. One of the important questions posed in TOK is whether or not it is possible to use a scientific approach effectively in a subject that deals with human beings. Noam Chomsky, the philosopher, has no doubts. He said in a television interview, "As soon as questions of will or decision or reason or choice of action arise, human science is at a loss."

There are a number of reasons why it is very difficult, if not impossible, to apply a scientific approach to the social (or human) sciences.

- Human beings are unique; they are all individuals, so there are no general laws that can be applied to them. They do not behave in a fully consistent manner.
- Social scientists are themselves human and so they are a part of the experiment that they are studying. It must be very difficult for them to suppress any bias that they may have, thus making any results open to question.

- Both objective and subjective concepts exist in social sciences and we know that subjective concepts are matters of opinion and so incapable of truly accurate scientific study.
- It is very difficult to measure data in the social sciences in numerical terms. How do we measure parental control or the satisfaction gained from eating a bar of chocolate?
- Predictions that are 100% certain are impossible to make in the social sciences.
- Social sciences are subjects where factors are always changing and so nothing is really constant. This makes measurement difficult and true prediction debatable.

1   Look at each of these reasons and consider whether the same problems do not exist, to some extent, in the natural sciences. Try to use examples to support your views.

2   "It is possible that the social sciences are in their infancy and that, just as with the natural sciences, they will become more dependable and accurate in their findings and predictions with time." Do you agree with this statement?

Examination questions

Short response questions

1   Using a diagram, explain the concept of opportunity cost.

2   Using an appropriate diagram, explain the difference between actual output and potential output.

3   With the help of examples, explain what is meant by the term "factors of production".

4   Using an appropriate diagram, explain the concept of potential growth.

You be the journalist

An international economics magazine has decided to include a new feature called The Student Corner. Each month it will include an article that presents economic analysis of a current issue to students, and they have hired you to be the journalist!

Each time you see the icon shown here, write an article using the information given. Each article should be between 250 and 350 words long and should include definitions of key terms and at least one diagram. Wherever possible consider all possible consequences of the issue, and any effect on possible stakeholders. Try to be creative—even inventive! You can make up interviews. You don't have to do it entirely on your own, however, as the headline and perhaps a few tips will be given.

You be the journalist

Headline: Hurricane Olesya devastates local economy

Economics concept: Production possibility curve + factors of production

Diagram: PPC curve

Here is an example

Hurricane Olesya devastates local economy

In November last year, powerful hurricane Olesya swept through the province of Kahlua, devastating factories and farms. The concept of the production possibility curve can be applied to this situation.

A production possibility curve (PPC) is a curve that shows the maximum combinations of goods and services that can be produced by an economy in a given period, if all the resources are being used fully and efficiently and the state of technology is fixed. The diagram shows the PPC for the

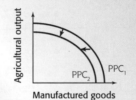

province of Kahlua before and after the hurricane. Before the hurricane, Kahlua had the possibility of producing anywhere on PPC_1. In reality, it is unlikely to have actually been producing on the curve, because there are always some resources that are not in use.

The hurricane destroyed some of the province's factors of production, therefore reducing the potential output of Kahlua and shifting the curve inwards to PPC_2. In this case, the factor

of production called land is no longer able to produce as much agricultural output as it could before because of the damage done to the fields. Sadly, this means that there will be none of those famous Kahlua oranges this summer. Damage to factories means that Kahlua has lost some of its factor of production known as capital. This means that Kahlua can currently produce fewer manufactured goods.

Although many people were displaced, fortunately there was no loss of lives and the labour force is keen to get things going. According to local entrepreneurs business will be back to normal by this time next year!

(260 words)

2 Rationing systems

By the end of this chapter, you should be able to:

- distinguish between microeconomics and macroeconomics; positive economics and normative economics; private sector and public sector
- explain that economists are model builders and that they employ the assumption of *"ceteris paribus"*
- explain and illustrate a basic model of an economy
- distinguish between different rationing systems
- compare and contrast the advantages and disadvantages of planned and free market economies
- define and give an example of a transition economy
- distinguish between economic growth and economic development
- define sustainable development.

Economics is a large subject area and so, to make things simpler, it is often split up into different sections. There are a number of ways of doing this.

Microeconomics and macroeconomics

Microeconomics deals with smaller, discrete economic agents and their reactions to changing events. For example, it looks at individual consumers and how they make their decisions about demand and expenditure; individual firms and how they make decisions, such as what to produce and how much; and individual industries and how they may be affected by such things as government action.

Macroeconomics takes a wider view and considers such things as measuring all the economic activity in the economy, inflation, unemployment, and the distribution of income in the whole economy.

Positive economics and normative economics

A positive statement is one that may be proven to be right or wrong by looking at the facts. For example, "The unemployment rate for China for 2004 was 9.8%". A normative statement is a matter of opinion and cannot be conclusively proven to be right or wrong. It is usually easy to spot because it uses value-judgment words such as "ought", "should", "too much", and "too little". For example, "The Chinese government put too little emphasis on curing unemployment in 2004".

Positive economics deals with areas of the subject that are capable of being proven to be correct or not. Normative economics deals with areas of the subject that are open to personal opinion and belief. While it is easier to be confident in matters of positive economics, it is often more interesting to deal with questions in normative economics, even though a conclusive outcome is very unlikely.

15

For example, many economists have put forward theories to suggest exactly why economies tend to move from periods of high economic activity to periods of depressed activity, but no one has been able to do so completely—they are all opinions. Indeed, it is often said that if 10 economists are locked in a room, they will come out with 12 conclusions!

Economists and model building

Economists, like all social scientists, tend to build theoretical models in order to test and illustrate their theories. These models may then be manipulated in order to see what the outcome will be if there is a change in one of the variables. This method of holding all but one of the variables constant is known as *ceteris paribus*. In Latin, this literally means "all other things being equal". When economists want to test the effect of one variable on another, they need to be able to isolate the effect of the one variable by assuming that there is no change in any of the other variables. For example, if they want to know how a change in wages will affect people's desire to work, they have to assume that there is no change in another variable, such as taxes. Economists are very famous for making assumptions, and it is always important to be aware of such assumptions.

To illustrate the idea of model building, look at the simple model of an economy in Figure 2.1. It is known as a circular flow model.

Theory of Knowledge

1 How reliable is the statistic that China's unemployment rate in 2004 was 9.8%?

2 How do economists "know" what is true?

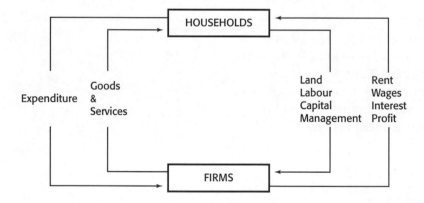

Figure 2.1 The circular flow of income

In the model, households represent the groups of individuals in the economy who perform two functions. They are the consumers of goods and services and they are the owners and providers of the factors of production that are used to make the goods and services. Firms represent the productive units in the economy that turn the factors of production into goods and services. This sector is known as the private sector. This is the part of production in the economy that is owned by private individuals.

Goods are tangible products. They may be split into durable goods, which are consumed over time, such as cars and washing machines, and non-durable goods, which are consumed over a short period of time, such as an ice cream or a bottle of mineral water.

Services are intangible products, such as a haircut or insurance, and, again, may be consumed immediately or over time.

The simple model ignores two other important sectors of the economy: the government and international trade. (The model will be developed more fully in Chapter 14.) The government has a number of roles in the economy. It is normally responsible for law and order, national defence, adjusting the economy in order to achieve agreed economic aims, and directly providing certain goods and services, which might include things such as water, public transport, electricity, or even cigarettes in some economies. The state-owned sector of the economy that provides goods and services is known as the public sector.

Rationing systems: planned economies v free market economies

Economics is a study of rationing systems. Since the resources in an economy: are relatively scarce, there must be some way of rationing those resources and the goods and services that are produced by them.

In theory, there are two main rationing systems.

1   *Planned economies:* In a planned economy, sometimes called a centrally planned economy or a command economy, decisions as to what to produce, how to produce, and who to produce for, are made by a central body, the government. All resources are collectively owned. Government bodies arrange all production, set wages, and set prices through central planning. Decisions are made by the government on behalf of the people and, in theory, in their best interests.

    The quantity of decisions to be made, data to be analysed, and factors of production to be allocated are immense. This makes central planning very difficult. If one then adds the need to forecast future events accurately in order to plan ahead, the task becomes almost impossible to achieve with any decent level of efficiency.

    In the 1980s, almost one third of the population of the world lived in planned economies, mainly in the USSR and China. These days, with the changes in Eastern Europe that have taken place, there are very few countries that rely solely on planning. Also, in China, which operates a predominantly planned system, elements of the free market are becoming very common and are, indeed, being encouraged in many market segments, such as textiles and clothing.

2   *Free market economies:* In a free market economy, sometimes called a private enterprise economy or capitalism, prices are used to ration goods and services. All production is in private hands and demand and supply are left free to set wages and prices in the economy. The economy should work relatively efficiently and there should be few cases of surpluses and shortages.

Individuals make independent decisions about what products they would like to purchase at given prices and producers then make decisions about whether they are prepared to provide those products. The producers' decisions are based upon the likelihood of profits being made. If there are changes in the pattern of demand, then there will be changes in the pattern of supply in order to meet the new demand pattern. For example, let us assume that producers have been making both roller skates and skateboards and find that they are equally profitable, in the quantities currently supplied. Now assume that tastes change and skateboards are seen to be more "cool". There will be an increased demand for skateboards and a fall in the demand for roller skates. Shops will experience a shortage of skateboards to sell and a surplus of roller skates that are not being sold. In order to rectify this, they will raise the price of skateboards, reducing the quantity demanded, and lower the price of roller skates in order to clear the surplus. Producers, whose costs have not changed, will realise that there is now more profit to be made in producing skateboards than there is in producing roller skates and will increase their production of skateboards and reduce their production of roller skates. Resources will be moved from producing roller skates to producing skateboards. Thus we can see that a change in the demand of consumers sends "signals" that bring about a chain of events that re-allocates factors of production and makes sure that the wishes of the consumers are met. The free market system is a self-righting system.

When consumers and producers work to their own best interest, the market functions to produce the "best" outcome for both. As Adam Smith (see Chapter 1) said, "Every individual...generally, indeed, neither intends to promote the public interest, nor knows how much he is promoting it...he intends only his own gain, and he is in this...led by an invisible hand to promote an end which was no part of his intention." This is often used as a justification for arguing that there should be minimal government interference in the economy.

In a market economy, it is said that resources will be allocated efficiently. However, sometimes it takes a long time for resources to be re-allocated from the production of one good or service to another. This is likely to create negative consequences for the stakeholders involved.

> ### Did you know?
>
> As a result of planning problems and an emphasis on industrial production, there were chronic shortages of consumer goods, and in the Soviet Union queues were a part of daily life. It is estimated that a Russian woman would spend two hours every day lining up to buy essential goods.

In reality, all economies are mixed economies. What is different is the degree of the mix from country to country. Some countries, such as China, have high levels of planning and government involvement in the economy. Even in the seemingly free economies, such as the USA, the UK, or even Hong Kong, government intervention is very much a part of the economic system. Government involvement is deemed essential, since there are some dangers that will exist if the free market is left to operate without interference. Some of the disadvantages of planned and free market economies are shown in Table 2.1.

Disadvantages of a free market economy	Disadvantages of a planned economy
1 Demerit goods (things that are bad for people, such as drugs or child prostitution) will be over-provided, driven by high prices and thus a high profit motive.	**1** Total production, investment, trade, and consumption, even in a small economy, are too complicated to plan efficiently and there will be misallocation of resources, shortages, and surpluses.
2 Merit goods (things that are good for people, such as education or health care) will be underprovided, since they will only be produced for those who can afford them and not for all.	**2** Because there is no price system in operation, resources will not be used efficiently. Arbitrary decisions will not be able to make the best use of resources.
3 Resources may be used up too quickly and the environment may be damaged by pollution, as firms seek to make high profits and to minimise costs.	**3** Incentives tend to be distorted. Workers with guaranteed employment and managers who gain no share of profits are difficult to motivate. Output and/or quality will suffer.
4 Some members of society will not be able to look after themselves, such as orphans, the sick, and the long-term unemployed, and will not survive.	**4** The dominance of the government may lead to a loss of personal liberty and freedom of choice.
5 Large firms may grow and dominate industries, leading to high prices, a loss of efficiency, and excessive power.	**5** Governments may not share the same aims as the majority of the population and yet, by power, may implement plans that are not popular, or are even corrupt.

Table 2.1 Disadvantages of free market and planned economies

Profile Karl Marx (1818–1883)

Best known not as an economist or philosopher but as a revolutionary communist, Karl Marx's works inspired the foundation of many communist regimes in the twentieth century. He had a massive influence upon the shape of the world in that century. Although he was originally trained as a philosopher, Marx eventually turned more towards economics and politics. He attempted to prove his theories using mathematics. He felt that this was important, since he said that his book, *Das Kapital*, was not a descriptive work but a "scientific description" of the course that history would take.

Marx saw "capitalism", the free market system, as being only one of a series of methods of production. Marx predicted that there would be an inevitable breakdown of capitalism, for economic reasons, and that communism would be the natural end result. He issued the rallying cry, "Workers of the world unite. You have nothing to lose but your chains!"

Marx predicted that, eventually, society's ability to produce would grow faster than its ability to consume, causing growing unemployment. Thus the free market could not be depended upon to serve the best interests of workers and there would be a need for the government to take over the means of production—communism.

Although his ideas are still influential in some quarters, it could be argued that in the twenty-first century, the movement towards free markets and away from planning in many of the former communist countries suggests that the days of Marxism are numbered. Clearly the desirability of such a situation is very much a subjective question.

Transition economies

Some countries, which were predominantly centrally planned, such as Hungary, Poland, and Russia, have been moving towards a more market-oriented balance in their economic systems. These economies are known as transition economies. The movement mostly began in the late 1980s, although for some it did not begin to take place until the next decade. The best way to learn about the concept of transition economies is to carry out a case study, as instructed in workpoint 2.1.

"MAKING A PROFIT WAS A LOT EASIER BEFORE SO MANY COUNTRIES ABANDONED SOCIALISM AND STARTED COMPETING!"

Student workpoint 2.1

Be an inquirer—conduct an investigation

Transition economy report

Write a report on a transition economy of your choice. The best way to do this is to gather figures from the Internet and then write a brief report, using some of the figures, identifying the main problem areas that the country has faced in its transition, and explaining the extent to which it is solving such problems. You might end with some predictions for the future.

Useful websites may be:

- http://hdr.undp.org/
- www.bized.ac.uk/
- www.oecd.org/home/
- www.worldbank.org/

Areas you should consider, if the information is available, are:

- *economic trends:* real GDP per capita, inflation, unemployment, balance of payments, types of goods and services produced, taxation structure, debt levels, levels of foreign investment
- *political structure:* type of political system, civil and political rights, corruption patterns and intensity
- *health and educational factors*
- *infrastructure:* level and quality of infrastructure

- *demographic trends:* population size, birth rates, death rates, migration rates
- *environmental issues:* e.g. long-term warming, pollution.

If possible, you should try to get figures for more than one year, so that you can identify movements (trends) in the figures, rather than just report on a "snapshot" set of figures from one year.

You may not be able to get information on all of the above and some of the factors will not be applicable to the country that you choose.

Structure of the report

The report should be word-processed. It should have a section showing all of the data that you have collected and then a separate section where you give a written report of the main problems that you feel the country in question is experiencing and assess the extent to which it is solving the problems. There should then be a concluding section where you attempt to say what you feel the future holds for the country. Don't worry about your relative lack of knowledge at this point—it is a good opportunity to investigate economics and find out some of the issues.

The written part of the report should not be more than 1000 words.

Economic growth

National income is the value of all the goods and services produced in an economy in a given time period, normally one year.

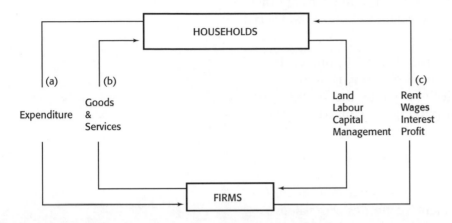

Figure 2.2 The different methods of measuring national income

National income can be measured by adding up all the activity along any one of the three routes, (a), (b), or (c), in the model in Figure 2.2. Thus it can be measured by looking at the value of the output of the goods and services (b), or the expenditure on the goods and services (a), or the total incomes of the households for letting the firms use their factors of production (c). It is too difficult to measure the value of the factors of production used, so that method is not attempted.

In order not to overstate the value, any increase caused by rising prices (inflation) is ignored and the national income after this has been done is known as real national income. The term "real", in economics, simply means having allowed for the effects of inflation.

If there is an increase in the level of real national income between one year and another, then we could say that the economy has grown. However, if the population has grown by the same percentage, then income per head of the population will not have grown. Thus, in order to be accurate, we measure increases in real national income per capita (per head). This measure of the increase in economic activity is known as economic growth.

Because it is purely a money measurement and an average, economic growth does not tell us very much about the actual welfare of the people in a country. A country's economy may grow because the military armaments sector grows, but this does not mean that the average person is better off. We will look at national income in much greater detail in Chapter 14.

We learned in Chapter 1 that potential growth is where there is an improvement in the quantity and/or quality of the factors of production and an outward shift of the production possibility curve. Economic growth is actual growth, a movement from a point inside the production possibility curve to a point that is nearer to the curve.

1 Introduction to Economics

21

Economic development

Unlike economic growth, economic development is a measure of welfare, a measure of well-being. It is usual to measure economic development not just in monetary terms, but also in terms of other indicators, such as education indicators, health indicators, and social indicators.

For example, the Human Development Index (HDI), one of the most commonly used development measures, weighs up real national income per head, the adult literacy rate, the average years of schooling, and life expectancy in ranking the countries of the world in terms of "development".

The HDI is calculated for a country and then gives the country an HDI value between zero and one. The nearer the value is to one, the more developed the country is said to be. A country with a value above 0.8 is said to have "high human development"; countries with values between 0.5 and 0.8 are said to have "medium human development"; and countries with values below 0.5 are said to have low human development. An example of HDI values for a selection of different countries in 2005 is shown in Table 2.1.

HDI rank	Country	HDI value
1	Norway	0.963
57	Trinidad & Tobago	0.801
58	Libya	0.799
145	Zimbabwe	0.505
146	Madagascar	0.499
177	Niger	0.281

Table 2.1 Selected HDI values

We can see that Norway is the most "developed" country. The line between high human development and medium human development separates Trinidad and Tobago from Libya, and the line between medium human development and low human development separates Zimbabwe from Madagascar. These lines are arbitrary and do not really mean that there is a noticeable difference between the countries on either side. Niger had the lowest HDI value in 2005. (Economic growth and economic development are considered in much greater detail in Chapter 15.)

Student workpoint 2.2

An investigation

1 Go to the website http://hdr.undp.org and find the HDI value for your own country.

2 Look at the countries that are classed as having low human development and identify which continents they come from.

3 Identify any pattern in 2.

Sustainable development

The World Commission on Environment and Development was formed by the United Nations in 1983, and in 1987 the report, *Our Common Future*, was published. The Commission was of the opinion that economic growth cannot be sustained into the future if environmental degradation is taking place and non-renewable resources are being used up at too fast a rate. The term "sustainable development" was introduced and defined as "development that meets the needs of the present without compromising the ability of future generations to meet their own needs". This really means that countries should not use up resources too quickly and should not harm the environment, since this will stop growth taking place in the future. Countries should limit their growth, and the way that they attempt to achieve it, right now in order to have prospects of healthy growth in times to come.

Profile Dr Gro Harlem Brundtland (1939–present) ●●●●●●●●●●●●●●●●●●●●

Gro Brundtland was born in Oslo, Norway in 1939. At the age of 7, she followed in the shoes of her political activist father by becoming enrolled as a member of the Norwegian Labour Movement and she has been a member ever since. When she was 10 years old, her family moved to New York where her father had been granted a Rockefeller Scholarship. It was there that she learned English. Her commitment to social issues and the fact that she was always encouraged to be independent and outspoken meant that she had a mature sense of global awareness at a young age.

Brundtland received a medical degree in Oslo in 1963, when she was 24. After receiving a Master's degree at Harvard, she returned to Oslo to work in public health. This, along with her active role in promoting women's rights, led her into politics and she became environment minister in 1975. An oil spill caused by an explosion on an oil-drilling platform in the North Sea was her first big test as environment minister and she became a strong advocate of measures to prevent future environmental disasters.

She was elected as the first woman Prime Minister of Norway in 1981. In 1983, she was asked by the Secretary General of the United Nations to chair the World Commission on Environment and Development, whose mandate was to evaluate the planet's critical environmental and developmental problems and to provide possible solutions. To staff this commission, Brundtland selected 21 representatives from around the world, ensuring that half of the representatives came from developing nations.

The Brundtland Commission released its report, *Our Common Future*, in April 1987. It was in this widely-distributed book that the concept of "sustainable development" was identified and promoted. The recommendations of the commission led to the Earth Summit in Rio de Janeiro in 1992, attended by almost 200 world leaders.

In 1986, Brundtland was elected as Prime Minister of Norway once again, and served until 1989. She was re-elected in 1990 for the next six-year term. In 1998, she was appointed as Director General of the World Health Organization.

Dr Brundtland was trained as a scientist and physician. She has worked as a politician and a diplomat. As an advocate for the environment, sustainability, women's rights, poverty alleviation, and public health, she is a role model for students in all disciplines.

Student workpoint 2.3

Be caring about the world's future

1 Explain why the debate about global warming suggests that current economic growth is not sustainable.

2 Can you think of any other threats to sustainable development?

Student workpoint 2.4

An investigation

In this chapter you have read about different types of economic systems, and have been introduced to the concepts of economic growth and economic development. All of these factors result in the grouping of the world's economies into different categories.

In the past, we simply used the terms First World, Second World, and Third World, but today there are many different names and categories.

1 The **UNDP** groups countries according to levels of development as shown by the HDI. List the groups, name five countries in each category and note the HDI for each.

2 The **World Bank** groups countries according to levels of national income. List the groups, name five countries in each category and note the national income for each.

3 Another group of countries are known as **newly-industrialised countries** (NICs). Name five countries in this category.

4 Find out how many countries are in the **Organisation for Economic Cooperation and Development** (OECD) and name five of these.

5 *The Economist* magazine identifies a group of countries known as **emerging markets**. Name five countries in this category, and explain what is meant by the term "emerging markets".

6 What are the G-8 countries?

Make sure that you can locate each of the countries you list in this exercise on a world map! Better yet, get a blank world map and label each one.

Sources:

● www.undp.org

● www.oecd.org

● www.worldbank.org

● www.economist.com

Examination questions

Short response questions

1 Using real world examples, explain the difference between positive and normative economics.

2 Explain **three** disadvantages of a planned economy.

3 Explain **three** disadvantages of a free market.

Brief response questions

Explain the difference between:

a macroeconomics and microeconomics

b positive economics and normative economics

c planned economies and free market economies

d economic growth and economic development.

3 Demand and supply

By the end of this chapter, you should be able to:

- define demand
- explain the Law of Demand, verbally, and using diagrammatic analysis
- explain the determinants of demand
- distinguish between a shift of a demand curve and a movement along a demand curve

HL
- explain the exceptions to the Law of Demand
- define supply
- explain the Law of Supply, verbally, and using diagrammatic analysis
- explain the determinants of supply
- distinguish between a shift of a supply curve and a movement along a supply curve.

Demand

Demand is the quantity of a good or service that consumers are willing and able to purchase at a given price in a given time period. For example, a group of people may buy 150 soft drinks, at a price of $1.20 each, in an afternoon. We would say that their demand for soft drinks at a price of $1.20 would be 150 units an afternoon.

The important phrase here is "willingness and ability". It is not enough for consumers to be willing to purchase a good or service, they must also be able to purchase it, i.e. they must have the financial means to buy the product, the ability to buy. This is known as effective demand and it is this that is shown on a demand curve.

The Law of Demand

This simply states that "as the price of a product falls, the quantity demanded of the product will usually increase, *ceteris paribus*". It is sometimes expressed even more simply as "the demand curve normally slopes downwards". *Ceteris paribus* is an assumption that means "all other things being equal". This assumes that when there are a number of different factors that determine something, only one is changing and all of the others are held constant. Thus, in this case, price is changing but any other determinants of demand are assumed to be unchanging.

The Law of Demand may be illustrated using either a demand schedule or a demand curve. The example in Table 3.1 illustrates the effective demand for soft drinks at a sports event.

Price of soft drinks ($)	Quantity demanded of soft drinks (cans)
2.00	100
1.20	150
0.80	225
0.40	400

Table 3.1 A demand schedule for soft drinks

The quantity of soft drinks demanded increases as the price falls. The table showing these changes is known as a demand schedule. The same information can be shown in graphical form, using a demand curve. This is a curve that shows the relationship between the price of a product, which is placed on the vertical axis, and the quantity demanded of the same product over time, which is placed on the horizontal axis. This is shown in Figure 3.1.

As we can see from the diagram, demand curves are normally convex to the origin. However, for ease of analysis, economists usually draw them as straight lines, although they still call them curves! We will do the same.

As we saw in the example, in the Law of Demand, a change in the price of the product itself will lead to a change in the quantity demanded of the product, i.e. a movement along the existing demand curve. The phrase "change in the quantity demanded" is important, since it differentiates a change in price from the effect of a change in any of the other determinants of demand. In Figure 3.1, a change in the price of soft drinks from $1.20 to $0.80 leads to an *increase in the quantity demanded* of soft drinks from 150 cans to 225 cans.

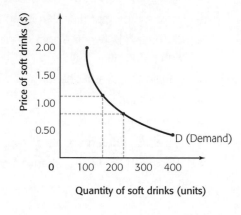

Figure 3.1 A demand curve for soft drinks

The increase in demand is for two reasons:

1 *Income effect:* When the price of a product falls, then people will have an increase in their "real income", which reflects the amount that their incomes will buy. With this increase in real income, the people will be likely to buy more of the product.

2 *Substitution effect:* When the price of a product falls, then the product will be relatively more attractive to people than other products, whose prices have stayed unchanged, and so it is likely that consumers will purchase more of the product, substituting it for products that were previously purchased.

The determinants of demand

There are a number of factors that determine demand and lead to an actual shift of the demand curve to either the right or the left. Whenever we look at a change in one of the determinants, we always make the *ceteris paribus* assumption. If we do not, then the analysis becomes too complicated and it is almost impossible to identify the effect of a change in any one of the determinants. The determinants of demand are outlined below.

1 Income

There are two types of products to consider when we are attempting to understand how a change in income affects the demand for a product. These are normal and inferior goods.

Normal goods

For most goods, as income rises, the demand for the product will also rise. Such goods are known as normal goods. As income rises, the demand curve for a normal good will shift to the right. The size of the shift in demand will depend upon the good itself. An increase in income may cause a small shift to the right in the demand curve for salt, but a larger increase in the demand for cinema tickets.

The demand curve for air travel is shown in Figure 3.2. In this case, an increase in income shifts the demand curve for air travel to the right, so more air travel is demanded at every price.

Inferior goods

If a product is considered to be inferior, then demand for the product will fall as income rises and the consumer starts to buy higher priced substitutes in place of the inferior good. Examples of inferior goods may be cheap wine or "own brand" supermarket detergents. As income rises, the demand curve for the inferior good will shift to the left. When income gets to a certain level, the consumer will be buying only the higher priced goods and the demand for the inferior good will become zero. Thus the demand curve will disappear.

2 The price of other products

There are three possible relationships between products. They may be substitutes for each other, complements to each other, or unrelated.

Substitutes

If products are substitutes for each other, then a change in the price of one of the products will lead to a change in the demand for the other product. For example, if there is a fall in the price of chicken in an economy, then there will be an increase in the quantity demanded of chicken and a fall in the demand for beef, which is a substitute.

This would lead to a movement along the demand curve for chicken and a shift to the left of the demand curve for beef. This is shown in Figure 3.3.

A fall in the price of chicken from p to p_1 leads to an increase in the quantity demanded of chicken from q to q_1. This change in the price of a substitute means that some consumers will switch from buying beef to buying chicken and there will be a fall in the demand for beef, at all prices, and the demand curve will shift to the left from D to D_1. Even though the price of beef has not changed, there is a fall in demand from q to q_1.

In the same way, an increase in the price of a substitute product will lead to a fall in the quantity demanded of that product and an increase in demand (shift of the demand curve to the right) for the substitutes whose prices have not changed.

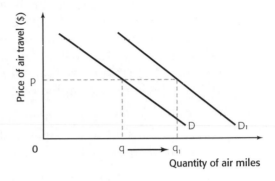

Figure 3.2 The market for air travel

Demand for chicken

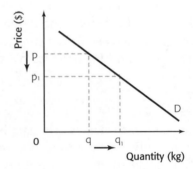

Demand for beef

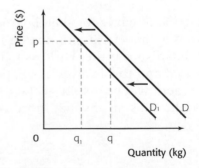

Figure 3.3 The markets for chicken and beef

Complements

Complements are products that are often purchased together, such as printers and ink cartridges. If products are complements to each other, then a change in the price of one of the products will lead to a change in the demand for the other product. For example, if there is a fall in the price of DVD players in an economy, then there will be an increase in the quantity demanded of DVD players and an increase in the demand for DVDs, which are a complement.

This would lead to a movement along the demand curve for DVD players and a shift to the right of the demand curve for DVDs. This is shown in Figure 3.4.

As we can see, a fall in the price of DVD players from p to p_1 leads to an increase in the quantity demanded of players from q to q_1. This change in the price of a complement means that some consumers will now buy more DVDs to go with the additional DVD players that they are buying and there will be an increase in the demand for DVDs, at all prices, and the demand curve will shift to the right from D to D_1. Even though the price of DVDs has not changed, there is an increase in demand from q to q_1.

In a similar fashion, an increase in the price of a complementary product will lead to a fall in the quantity demanded of that product and a fall in demand (shift of the demand curve to the left) for the complements whose prices have not changed.

Unrelated goods

If products are unrelated, then a change in the price of one product will have no effect upon the demand for the other product. For example, an increase in the price of toilet paper will have no effect upon the demand for pencils. We say that the two products are unrelated.

Tastes

To the economist, tastes are usually considered to be outside the scope of study. It is enough to know that marketing may alter tastes and that firms attempt to influence tastes so that they can shift the demand curve for their product to the right. A change in tastes in favour of a product will lead to more being demanded at every price.

The demand curve for skateboards is shown in Figure 3.5. If there is an advertising campaign to encourage the purchase of skateboards, or if the world skateboarding championships are televised and this leads to more people wishing to skateboard, then there will be a shift of the demand curve for skateboards to the right. This means that more skateboards will be demanded at every price.

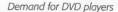

Demand for DVD players

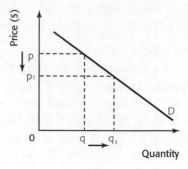

Demand for DVDs

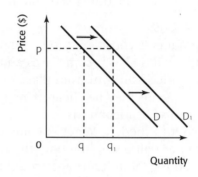

Figure 3.4 The markets for DVD players and DVDs

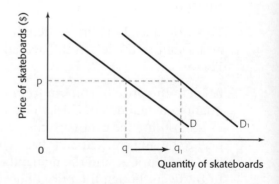

Figure 3.5 The market for skateboards

Other factors

There are a number of other, larger factors that affect the demand for a product, apart from the microeconomic ones named already. These would include the following.

● *The size of the population:* If the population begins to grow, then it is logical to assume that the demand for most products will increase and that their demand curves will start to shift to the right.

● *Changes in the age structure of the population:* If the age structure of the economy starts to alter, then this will affect the demand for certain products. For example, if the percentage of older people in an economy starts to increase, then there may be an increase in the demand for walking frames and the demand for them would shift to the right. At the same time, there may be a fall in demand for skateboards and the demand curve would shift to the left.

● *Changes in income distribution:* If there is a change in the distribution of income, such that the relatively poor are better off and the rich slightly worse off, then there may be an increase in the demand for basic necessity goods, such as meat, and a subsequent shift of the demand curve for meat to the right.

● *Government policy changes:* Changes in direct taxes, i.e. taxes on incomes, may affect the money that people have to spend, and thus their demand. Also, government policies such as compulsory seat belts, compulsory wearing of bicycle helmets, or a ban on smoking in public places, would all affect demand in the relevant markets.

● *Seasonal changes:* Changes in seasons may lead to changes in the pattern of demand in the economy. For example, there will be more demand for warm coats in the winter and less demand for swimsuits.

The distinction between a movement along a demand curve and a shift of the demand curve

Sometimes there are movements along the existing demand curve and sometimes the demand curve actually shifts to the left or the right. When these things occur is very simple.

A change in the price of the good itself leads to a movement along the existing demand curve, since the price of the good is on one of the axes. This is shown in Figure 3.6, where a fall in the price of soccer boots from p to p_1 leads to an increase in the quantity demanded from q to q_1.

A change in any of the other determinants of demand will always lead to a shift of the demand curve to either the left or the right. For example, as shown in Figure 3.7, a government policy requiring cyclists to wear safety helmets would lead to a shift to the right of the demand curve for safety helmets from D to D_1. Thus more would be demanded at each price and at the existing price of p, demand would increase from q to q_1.

2 Microeconomics

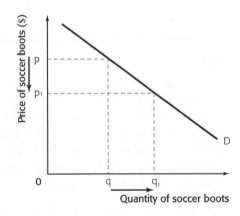

Figure 3.6 The market for soccer boots

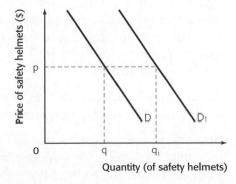

Figure 3.7 The demand for safety helmets

● ● ● ● ● ● ● ● ● ● ● ● ● ● ● ● ● ●

Student workpoint 3.1

Be a thinker—make some reasoned decisions

Using fully labelled diagrams, illustrate what may be the outcome in each of the questions given below.

1 What would happen to the demand for bicycles if there were a large increase in the tax on motor scooters?

2 What would happen to the demand for foreign holidays if there were an increase in incomes?

3 What would happen to the demand for DVDs if there were a significant fall in the price of DVD players?

4 What would happen to the demand for cars if there were a significant increase in the level of income tax?

5 What would happen to the demand for ice creams if the price of ice creams went up?

6 What would happen to the demand for a certain brand of bottled water if there was an article about the lack of purity of the source of the water in a national newspaper?

7 What would happen to the demand for carrots if there was an increase in the size of the population?

Important note
Whenever you draw a diagram, it is important to use a ruler to draw the axes and lines, and to be sure to label all lines as fully and accurately as possible. Thus, for each of the questions in workpoint 3.1, the axes should always indicate which market you are illustrating.

HL

Exceptions to the Law of Demand

Giffen goods

Giffen goods are a unique type of inferior good that was first identified by Sir Robert Giffen in the nineteenth century. He suggested that there was a tendency for the very poor to buy more of the basic foodstuffs on which they depended when the price of them rose and less when the price of them fell. In Giffen's case, the observation took place regarding peasants in Ireland and their reaction to changes in the price of potatoes, a staple good for them.

The key point here is poverty. When the price of a staple product falls for the very poor, then they are likely to buy less of the product and to use their increased real income to buy higher quality products, which they can now afford. In the same way, when the price of a staple good rises for the very poor, then they will buy more of it, because they cannot now afford the higher quality products and will consume more of the Giffen good, since it has no substitutes.

As we can see in Figure 3.8, at low prices, a typical Giffen good will experience an increase in quantity demanded as the price rises.

In modern times, most economists would agree that there are no real examples of Giffen goods in developed economies. Some economists, such as Jenson and Miller,[1] have shown that Giffen goods may exist

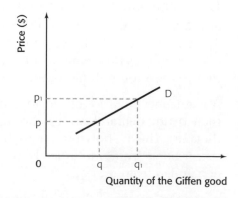

Figure 3.8 The demand for a Giffen good

---

[1] Jenson, R. and Miller, N. 2002. *Giffen Behaviour: Theory and Evidence.* KSG Faculty Research Working Papers Series RWP 02-014.

in the form of rice or noodles, in different parts of China, but they are very much a rarity and may soon disappear if poverty diminishes.

Veblen goods

Thorstein Veblen, another economist, identified a different situation where the quantity demanded rose as price rose. In his book, *The Theory of the Leisure Class*, he reported that some products become more popular as their price rises. Part of the reason for this he attributed to "conspicuous consumption": the fact that people get satisfaction from being seen by other people to consume expensive products. He said that "failure to consume in due quantity and quality becomes a mark of inferiority and demerit". As the price of a Veblen good rises, such as a Louis Vuitton handbag, people with high incomes begin to buy more of the product because it has a "snob value"; it is a "good of ostentation".

As we can see in Figure 3.9, at low prices, a typical Veblen good will have a normal demand curve, with the quantity demanded falling as the price rises. However, as the price continues to rise, the product eventually achieves "snob value status" and further price rises start to lead to increases in the quantity demanded.

The role of expectations (the "bandwagon" effect)

It is often argued that there are times when the quantity demanded of a product rises as the price rises, because of expectations of what is going to happen to prices in the future. In some cases, such as house prices, an increase in prices may lead to more people "jumping on the bandwagon", if they think that prices are going to rise even further in the future. The same sometimes occurs with the price of shares on the stock market. Some may argue that the increase in prices in these cases is caused by a shift of demand to the right, which then brings about the next increase in demand and so on. It is an area where economists, once again, disagree!

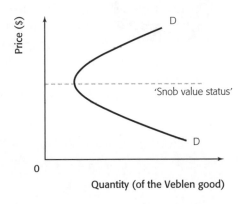

Figure 3.9 The demand for a Veblen good

Student workpoint 3.1

Be a thinker—explain the following.

1 Explain why a Jaguar car might be considered a Veblen good.

2 Try to think of three other examples and explain why they might be considered to be Veblen goods.

Profile **Thorstein Veblen** (1857–1929) ••••••••••••••••••••••

Thorstein Veblen was born in the USA, the son of Norwegian immigrants. He studied at Carlton College, Yale, Cornell, and John Hopkins universities. He was a true "social" scientist, arguing that "human nature" was too simplistic an explanation as a basis for economic actions and that economics must be shaped by culture.

His two most famous publications were *The Theory of the Leisure Class* (1899) and *The Theory of Business Enterprise* (1904). His main interest lay in such questions as: "What is the nature of economic man?", "Why does a community have a leisure class?", and "What is the economic meaning of leisure itself?" Unlike Karl Marx, Veblen did not believe that the lower classes would eventually want to overthrow the upper class; instead, he believed that the lower classes would work hard in order to move up the class structure. Veblen thought that the presence of the upper class set an example and gave the working class an aim.

Supply

Supply is the willingness and ability of producers to produce a quantity of a good or service at a given price in a given time period. For example, firms may produce 4000 frozen pizzas per week, at a price of $3 each. We would say that their supply of frozen pizzas at a price of $3 would be 4000 units each week.

The important phrase here is "willingness and ability", as it was in demand. It is not enough for producers to be willing to produce a good or service; they must also be able to produce it, i.e. they must have the financial means to supply the product, the ability to supply. This is known as effective supply and it is this that is shown on a supply curve.

The Law of Supply

The Law of Supply simply states that "as the price of a product rises, the quantity supplied of the product will usually increase, *ceteris paribus*". It is sometimes expressed even more simply as "the supply curve normally slopes upwards".

The Law of Supply may be illustrated using either a supply schedule or a supply curve. The example in Table 3.2 illustrates the effective supply for frozen pizzas in a small town.

Price of frozen pizzas ($)	Quantity supplied of frozen pizzas (per week)
3.50	4400
3.00	4000
2.50	3500
2.00	2750
1.50	1750

Table 3.2 A demand schedule for soft drinks

As shown, the supply of frozen pizzas increases as the price increases. A table showing such changes is known as a supply schedule. The same information can be shown in graphical form, using a supply curve. This is a curve that shows the relationship between the price of a product, which is placed on the vertical axis, and the quantity supplied of the same product over time, which is placed on the horizontal axis. This is shown in Figure 3.10.

Supply curves are normally curved and get steeper as price rises. However, for ease of analysis, economists usually draw them as straight lines, and so shall we from now on.

As we have seen, in the Law of Supply a change in the price of the product itself will lead to a change in the quantity supplied of the product, i.e. a movement along the existing supply curve. The phrase "change in the quantity supplied" is important, since it differentiates a change in price from the effect of a change in any of the other determinants of supply. In Figure 3.10, a change in the price of frozen pizzas from $2.50 to $3.00 leads to an increase in the quantity supplied of frozen pizzas from 3,500 pizzas per week to 4,000 pizzas per week.

This occurs because at higher prices there will be more potential profits to be made and so the producer will increase output. Indeed, other producers may also be attracted to enter the market supplying frozen pizzas.

The determinants of supply

There are a number of factors that determine supply and lead to an actual shift of the supply curve to either the right or the left. Whenever we look at a change in one of the determinants, we always make the *ceteris paribus* assumption. If we do not, then the analysis becomes too complicated and it is almost impossible to identify the effect of a change in any one of the determinants. The determinants of supply are now outlined.

The cost of factors of production

If there is an increase in the cost of a factor of production, such as a wage increase in a firm producing textiles, which is labour-intensive, then this will increase the firm's costs, meaning that they can supply less, shifting the supply curve to the left. This is shown in Figure 3.11.

A rise in the level of wages in the textile firm means that the firm must now supply fewer textiles at all prices and the supply curve will shift to the left from S to S_1. A fall in the cost of factors of production will enable firms to increase their supply, shifting the supply curve to the right.

The price of other products, which the producer could produce instead of the existing product

Often, producers have a choice as to what they are going to produce. For example, a producer of roller skates may also be able to produce skateboards with a minimal change in production facilities. In this case, if the price of skateboards rises, because there is more demand

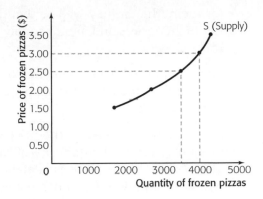

Figure 3.10 A supply curve for frozen pizzas

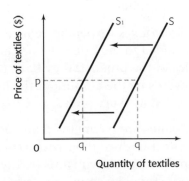

Figure 3.11 The supply of textiles

for them, then it may well be that the producer will be attracted by the higher prices and aim to supply more skateboards and fewer roller skates.

This would lead to a movement along the supply curve of skateboards and a shift to the left of the supply curve of roller skates. This is shown in Figure 3.12.

As you can see, a rise in the price of skateboards from p to p_1 leads to an increase in the quantity of skateboards supplied from q to q_1. This change in the price of skateboards means that some producers will now supply fewer roller skates, since they are manufacturing skateboards; there will be a fall in the supply of roller skates, at all prices, and the supply curve will shift to the left from S to S_1. Even though the price of roller skates has not changed, there is a fall in the supply from q to q_1.

The state of technology
Improvements in the state of technology in a firm or an industry should lead to an increase in supply and thus a shift of the supply curve to the right. In the unlikely event of a backward step in the state of technology, the supply curve would shift to the left. Although this is unlikely, natural disasters, such as hurricanes or earthquakes, may have the effect of moving technology backwards in an area or country.

Government intervention
In many cases, governments intervene in markets in ways that alter the supply. The two most common ways are indirect taxes and subsidies.

Indirect taxes (expenditure taxes) are taxes on goods and services that are added to the price of a product. Because these taxes force up the price of the product, they have the effect of shifting the supply curve upwards by the amount of the indirect tax. Less of the product will be supplied at every price.

Subsidies are payments made by the government to firms that will, in effect, reduce their costs. This then has the effect of shifting the supply curve downwards by the amount of the subsidy. More of the product will be supplied at every price. We will look at indirect taxes and subsidies in much more detail in Chapter 6.

The distinction between a movement along a supply curve and a shift of the supply curve
As you may have noticed above, sometimes there are movements along the existing supply curve and sometimes the supply curve actually shifts to the left or the right. When these occur is very simple.

A change in the price of the good itself leads to a movement along the existing supply curve, since the price of the good is on one of the axes. This is shown in Figure 3.13, where a fall in the price of soccer boots from p to p_1 leads to a fall in the quantity supplied from q to q_1.

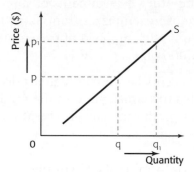

Supply of skateboards

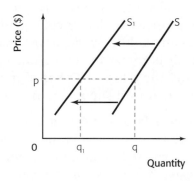

Supply of roller skates

Figure 3.12 The supply of skateboards and roller skates

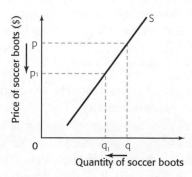

Figure 3.13 The supply of soccer boots

A change in any of the other determinants of supply will always lead to a shift of the supply curve to either the left or the right. For example, as shown in Figure 3.14, an increase in the cost of the rent of the land occupied by a large car firm will have the effect of shifting the supply curve to the left from S to S_1. Thus less will be supplied at each price and at the existing price of p, supply will fall from q to q_1.

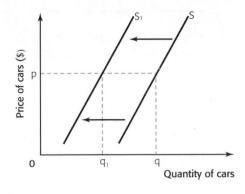

Figure 3.14 The supply of cars

Student workpoint 3.3

Be a thinker—make some reasoned decisions

Using fully labelled diagrams, illustrate what may be the outcome in each of the questions given below (remember to use a ruler and include accurate labels).

1 What would happen to the supply of bicycles if there were a large increase in the tax on bicycles?

2 What would happen to the supply of foreign holidays if there were a fall in the price of foreign holidays?

3 What would happen to the supply of DVDs if there were a significant increase in the price of the components used to make DVDs?

4 What would happen to the supply of cars if the government were to subsidise car production in order to protect employment?

5 What would happen to the supply of white bread if a firm were to discover that there has been a large increase in the demand for brown bread, which they could also produce?

6 What would happen to the supply of a certain brand of bottled water if there were an improvement in the technology used to produce it?

7 What would happen to the supply of carrots if the farmer decided to preserve the environment by farming in a more traditional manner, instead of making more profits?

Theory of Knowledge

Utilitarianism

Utilitarianism is a philosophy stemming from the late English philosophers and economists, Jeremy Bentham (1748–1832) and John Stuart Mill (1806–1873). It has applications in economics. Utilitarianism tries to answer the question, "What should a person do?" The utilitarian answer is that the person should act to try to produce the best consequences from his or her actions.

In terms of consequences, a utilitarian person attempts to evaluate all of the good things and bad things produced by an act, whether they happen after the act has been performed or during its performance. Utilitarians believe that an action is right if the happiness produced by it is greater than the unhappiness. They believe that if all individuals were to follow this ethos, then the outcome would be the greatest good for the greatest number of people.

Happiness is sometimes referred to as utility and attempts to measure positive and negative happiness are often calculated in utils, which are measures of happiness, and negative utils, which are measures of unhappiness.

The consumption of products can be measured in utils and it is assumed that the marginal utility, the extra utility gained from consuming an extra unit of a product, will decrease as consumption increases.

People will get less happiness from eating a second ice cream than they did from consuming the first one.

It is this theory that has been used in economics, in a simplistic sense, to explain why the demand curve slopes downwards. Consumers will only purchase more of a product if it is cheaper, since they receive less extra utility as they increase their consumption, and so will not pay as much for it.

Questions

1 Research the basic concept of utilitarianism.
2 You have $20 and are considering going out for the evening or giving the money to the World Wildlife Fund. Consider who would benefit from the two options and try to give util values to the options in order to decide the right course of action. (Itemise all those who would benefit and lose from each option.)
3 Drink five glasses of mineral water and attempt to give a marginal utility value to each glass. How does your marginal utility change as you consume each extra glass of water? How would this affect the amount that you are prepared to pay for a glass?
4 Does utilitarianism assume rational consumer behaviour?

Examination questions

Short response questions

1 Distinguish between a shift of the demand curve for a product and a movement along the product's demand curve. *[10 marks]*

2 With reference to two different determinants of demand, explain why the demand curve for bicycles might increase. Use a diagram to support your answer. *[10 marks]*

3 Distinguish between a shift of the supply curve for a product and a movement along the product's supply curve. *[10 marks]*

4 With reference to two different determinants of supply, explain why the supply of coffee beans might decrease. Use a diagram to support your answer. *[10 marks]*

HL 5 Explain two exceptions to the Law of Demand. *[10 marks]*

Assessment advice: short response questions

On HL Paper 2, students are expected to answer three questions in 60 minutes. As such, each question is designed to be answered in 20 minutes. These questions are referred to in this companion as "short response questions" to differentiate them from the longer essays written on HL Paper 1 and SL Paper 1. Each question is worth ten marks.

You should refer to Chapter 34 for more information on this type of assessment, but it is worth mentioning

a few key points. Answers tend to resemble each other structurally. Each should start with a written explanation in which the key economics terms are defined. This would usually be followed by a diagram to illustrate the theory, followed by a further explanation in which the diagram is explained in the context of the specific question.

It is always recommended that you use examples to support your response. For example, in question 3 of the short response questions included here, when you explain that a change in the costs of production will cause a shift in the supply

curve, you could elaborate by giving an example such as "a decrease in the cost of grapes will cause an increase in the supply of wine".

Bear in mind that the majority of short response questions will be enhanced by the use of the diagram, even if the question does not specifically ask for one.

While SL students do not answer these questions on their final exam, the short response questions included in this Course Companion are very good practice, and unless indicated as a HL extension topic, are very useful for all students.

Data response exercise

Read the following article and answer the questions below.

Smoke shifters

Learning to Love the Ban by Elisabeth Rosenthal

On Jan. 10, 2005. Italy enacted a law that banned smoking in public places like offices, restaurants, cafes and bars. Smokers declared—basta!—they would never comply. Restaurant owners were certain business would suffer. And politicians worried that an essential pleasure of Italy would be lost.

Nearly two years later the result is that people in Italy smoke a lot less and are exposed to far less secondhand smoke. In fact, the law has become very popular, with support for smoking bans increasing yearly among nonsmokers and smokers alike. Business in bars is up. A study in Turin found that the number of people brought to hospital emergency rooms after suffering heart attacks decreased after the ban (secondhand smoke could be a trigger), a finding that echoes studies in the United States.

In the three months after the ban, demand for cigarettes dropped 8 per cent, Italian tobacco sales data indicate. Among young people ages 15 to 24 the drop was most pronounced: 23 per cent. In 2004, more than 26 per cent of the Italian population smoked. That dropped to 24.3 per cent in 2006, although it is not clear how much of the drop can be attributed to the ban, since the numbers had been decreasing slightly anyway.

Violations are enforced with fines of more than $250. The Italian law gives restaurants and bars the option of creating sealed and independently ventilated smoking rooms, but only a tiny number of them have taken that expensive step. Smoking is still permitted in outdoor seating areas.

Ireland, New Zealand, Norway, Scotland and Uruguay have enacted total bans, as have Australia and Canada and many jurisdictions of the United States.

The New Year Times, 29 October 2004

1 Define "demand". [2 marks]

2 With the help of a diagram, explain what has happened to the demand for cigarettes. [4 marks]

3 To what extent can it be argued that the fall in demand for cigarettes is due to the smoking ban? [2 marks]

4 Which groups of stakeholders have been affected by the government policy? How have they been affected? [4 marks]

5 Explain two other policies that the government might use to reduce the demand for cigarettes. [4 marks]

Assessment advice: data response

This is the first of many data response questions that you will be doing in this course. On your final exam, the data response questions will all follow exactly the same pattern, which you will come to recognize. This first question does not follow that pattern exactly, but serves as a good introduction to the task of answering data response questions. Key skills involve writing clear and succinct definitions, drawing neat and well-labelled diagrams and using the information from the text to support your analysis. Soon, you will add the skill of evaluation to this list. For further information about answering data response questions, see Chapter 34.

2 Microeconomics

4 The interaction of, and applications of, demand and supply

By the end of this chapter, you should be able to:

- explain the concept of equilibrium
- explain the effect of changes in demand and supply upon the equilibrium
- explain the concepts of excess demand and excess supply
- explain, distinguish between, and give examples of, maximum and minimum price controls
- discuss the consequences of price controls
- explain how a buffer stock scheme works
- discuss the consequences of a buffer stock scheme
- define a commodity pricing agreement.

Now that we have looked at demand and supply, it is time to put them together and to consider what will happen when they are together in the same diagram.

Equilibrium

The concept of equilibrium is very important in economics. Equilibrium may be defined as "a state of rest, self-perpetuating in the absence of any outside disturbance". For example, a book is in equilibrium if it is lying on a desk. Unless someone comes along and moves it (an "outside disturbance"), then it will continue to lie there ("a state of rest"). If someone does move it, then it is in disequilibrium until it is put down somewhere else, at which time it is in a new equilibrium situation.

Economists spend a lot of time considering situations where equilibriums change and the reasons why the change has taken place. They then use the information to begin to predict changes in equilibrium situations that may be caused by a certain action. They can begin to formulate economic policy.

Let us look at demand, supply, and the equilibrium for coffee.

In Figure 4.1, both the demand and supply curves for coffee are in the same diagram and we see that, at the price P_e, the quantity Q_e is both demanded and supplied. We would say that the market is in equilibrium at the price P_e, since the amount of coffee that people wish to buy at that price, Q_e, is equal to the amount of coffee that suppliers wish to sell at that price. The price P_e is sometimes known as the market-clearing price, since everything produced in the market will be sold. The market is in equilibrium, since it will stay like this, in each time period, until there is an "outside disturbance" to change the equilibrium.

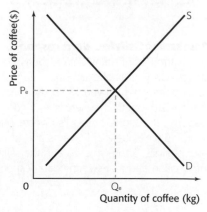

Figure 4.1 The market for coffee

The equilibrium in this situation is "self-righting", i.e. if you try to move away from it, without an outside disturbance, it will return to the original position. This is best explained through diagrams.

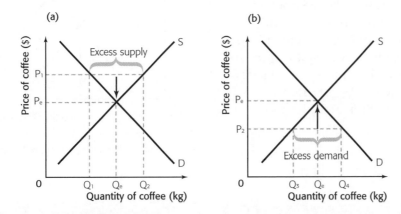

Figure 4.2 The market for coffee

In Figure 4.2, we can see what will happen if the producers try to raise or lower the equilibrium price. In diagram (a), the producers have tried to raise the price to P_1. However, at this price, the quantity demanded will fall to Q_1 and the quantity that producers supply rises to Q_2. We now have excess supply of Q_1–Q_2. More is being supplied than demanded at the price P_1. In order to eliminate this surplus, producers will need to lower their prices. As they do so, the quantity demanded will increase and the quantity supplied will fall. This process will continue until the quantity demanded once again equals the quantity supplied. This will be back at the equilibrium price and so the situation is self-righting if price is raised for no external reason.

In diagram (b), the producers have tried to lower the price to P_2. However, at this price, the quantity demanded will rise to Q_4 and the quantity that producers supply falls to Q_3. We now have excess demand of Q_3–Q_4. More is being demanded than supplied at the price P_2. In order to eliminate this shortage, producers will need to raise their prices. As they do so, the quantity demanded will fall and the quantity supplied will increase. This process will continue until the quantity demanded once again equals the quantity supplied. This will be back at the equilibrium price and so, once again, the situation is self-righting.

The effect of changes in demand and supply upon the equilibrium

As we know, the equilibrium may be moved by any "outside disturbance". In the case of demand and supply, this would be a change in one of the determinants of demand or supply, other than the price of the product, which would lead to a shift of either of the curves.

Take the example of an increase in income for consumers of foreign holidays, which is a normal good. When income increases, then there will be an increase in the demand for holidays and the demand curve for holidays will shift to the right, *ceteris paribus*, as shown in Figure 4.3.

When the demand curve shifts from D to D₁, price initially remains at P$_e$ and so we find that Q$_e$ continues to be supplied, but demand now increases to Q₂. This means that at the old equilibrium price, there is now a situation of excess demand. In order to eliminate this excess demand, it is necessary for price to rise until the quantity demanded once again equals the quantity supplied. Thus price will rise until it reaches P$_{e1}$, the new equilibrium price, where Q$_{e1}$, the new equilibrium quantity, is both demanded and supplied.

Whenever there is a shift of the demand or supply curve, the market will, if left to act alone, adjust to a new equilibrium, market-clearing, price.

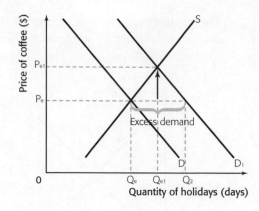

Figure 4.3 The market for foreign holidays

Student workpoint 4.1

Be a thinker—illustrate and explain

Using fully labelled diagrams, illustrate what will happen to the equilibrium price and quantity in each of the situations below, and then explain what has happened.

1 There has been a health scare relating to the consumption of chicken.

2 There has been an increase in the costs of production in the motorcycle industry.

3 There has been an improvement in production technology in the textile industry.

4 Manufacturers in the sportswear industry have decided to raise the price of training shoes.

Did you know?

Although demand was already strong, "World Cup fever" led to a surge in sales of liquid-crystal display (LCD) televisions in 2006. One British retailer claimed that it was selling a flat-screen TV once every 15 seconds in the run-up to the World Cup.

Although demand was strong, prices are about half of what they were a year ago as global supply increased by 135% from the same period the previous year. Manufacturers were well prepared for the eager football fans!

Assessment advice: being evaluative
Whenever you see the scales sign in this Course Companion, it indicates a point in the text where evaluation is taking place. Evaluation takes place when a value is placed upon something and its worth is judged. It often involves comparing the values of different things. Evaluation is a skill that you are expected to

show when you write essays and when you write your commentaries in the internal assessment. The highest mark bands are reserved for students who can illustrate the skill of evaluation. To ensure that you have an idea of what constitutes evaluation, you should now go to Chapter 34 and read the section on evaluation.

Price controls
Although it may seem to be an optimum situation, the free market does not always lead to the best outcomes for all producers and consumers, or for society in general, and so governments often

2 Microeconomics

choose to intervene in the market in order to achieve a different outcome. There are a number of situations where this occurs:

● maximum prices

● minimum prices

● price support/buffer stock schemes

● commodity agreements.

We now look at each of these situations in turn.

Maximum (low) price controls

This is a situation where the government sets a maximum price, below the equilibrium price, which then prevents producers from raising the price above it. These are sometimes known as ceiling prices, since the price is not able to go above "the ceiling".

Maximum prices are usually set to protect consumers and they are normally imposed in markets where the product in question is a necessity and/or a merit good (a good that would be underprovided if the market were allowed to operate freely). For example, governments may set maximum prices in agricultural and food markets during times of food shortages to ensure low-cost food for the poor, or they may set maximum prices on rented accommodation in an attempt to ensure affordable accommodation for those on low incomes.

Figure 4.4 shows the situation that may exist if the government were to implement a maximum price in the market for bread.

Without government interference, the equilibrium quantity demanded and supplied would be Q_e, at a price of P_e. The government imposes a maximum price of P_{Max} in order to help the consumers of bread. However, a problem now arises. At the price P_{Max}, Q_2 will be demanded because the price has fallen, but only Q_1 will be supplied. Thus we have a situation of excess demand. If the government does not intervene further, they will find that consumption of bread actually falls from Q_e to Q_1, even though it is at a lower price.

 The excess demand creates problems. The shortages may lead to the emergence of a black market (an illegal market), where the product is sold at a higher price, somewhere between the maximum price and the equilibrium price. There may also be queues developing in the shops and producers may start to decide who is going to be allowed to buy. Since these problems are not really "fair" for the consumers, the government may now need to make attempts to eliminate, or at least reduce, the shortage.

There are a number of ways in which the government may try to do this. Essentially, it would have two options. First, it could attempt to shift the demand curve to the left, until equilibrium is reached at the maximum price, but this would limit the consumption of the product, which goes against the point of imposing the maximum price.

Second, the government can attempt to shift the supply curve to the right, until equilibrium is reached at the maximum price, with more being supplied and demanded. There are a number of ways of doing this.

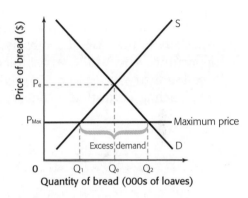

Figure 4.4 The market for bread

1 The government could offer subsidies to the firms in the industry to encourage them to produce more.

2 The government could start to produce the product themselves, thus increasing the supply.

3 If the government had previously stored some of the product (see buffer stocks later in this chapter), then they could release some of the stocks (stored goods) onto the market. However, if the product were perishable, like bread, this would not be possible.

As we can see in Figure 4.5, if the government is able to shift the supply curve to the right, by subsidising, direct provision, or using stored bread, then equilibrium will be reached at P_{Max}, with Q_2 loaves of bread being demanded and supplied. However, it is fair to say that this may well mean that the government incurs a cost, especially in the case of a subsidy, and that this will have an opportunity cost. If the government spends money supporting the bread industry, it may have to reduce expenditure in some other area, such as education or health care.

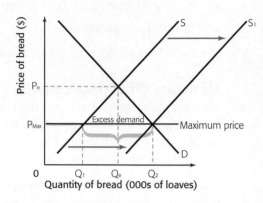

Figure 4.5 Government action to solve the problem of excess demand

---

Student workpoint 4.2

Be a thinker—illustrate, explain, and suggest solutions

A government wishes to keep the cost of cheap rented accommodation low in a city, by imposing legal maximum rents on properties of a certain size. In doing this, they aim to:

● provide low-cost rented accommodation for people on low incomes

● provide more rented accommodation for people on low incomes.

1 Draw a diagram to show the effect of the maximum rent legislation on the market for rented accommodation.

2 Explain the situation facing those people who rent out their properties.

3 Explain the situation facing those people who wish to rent properties.

4 Suggest measures that the government might take to ensure that they achieve both of their stated aims above.

Minimum (high) price controls

This is a situation where the government sets a minimum price, above the equilibrium price, which then prevents producers from reducing the price below it. These are sometimes known as floor prices, since the price is not able to go below "the floor".

Minimum prices are mostly set for one of two reasons.

1 To attempt to raise incomes for producers of goods and services that the government thinks are important, such as agricultural products. They may be helped because their prices are subject to large fluctuations, or because there is a lot of foreign competition.

2 To protect workers by setting a minimum wage, to ensure that workers earn enough to lead a reasonable existence.

Figure 4.6 shows the situation that might exist if the government were to implement a minimum price in the market for wheat.

Without government interference, the equilibrium quantity demanded and supplied would be Q_e, at a price of P_e. The government imposes a minimum price of P_{Min} in order to increase the revenue of the producers of wheat. However, a problem now arises. At the price P_{Min}, only Q_1 will be demanded because the price has risen, but Q_2 will be now be supplied. Thus we have a situation of excess supply. If the government does not intervene further, they will find that consumption of wheat actually falls from Q_e to Q_1, albeit at a higher price.

The excess supply creates problems. Producers will find that they have surpluses and will be tempted to try to get around the price controls and sell their excess supply for a lower price, somewhere between P_{Min} and P_e.

In order to maintain the minimum price, it is likely that the government will have to intervene. This is shown in Figure 4.7.

The government would normally eliminate the excess supply by buying up the surplus products, at the minimum price, thus shifting the demand curve to the right and creating a new equilibrium at P_{Min}, with Q_2 being demanded and supplied. The new demand curve would be D + government buying.

The government could then store the surplus, destroy it, or attempt to sell it abroad. However, storage tends to be rather expensive and destroying products is considered to be wasteful. Selling abroad is always an option, but it often causes angry reactions from the foreign governments involved, who claim that products are being dumped on their markets and will harm their domestic industries. In some cases, such as the European Union agricultural policy, farmers are guaranteed a minimum price and are then paid to "set aside" land that they would have used to produce the product in question. They are then paid the price for an estimated harvest and nothing is actually grown. This costs the same for the government, but avoids storage costs or destroying produce.

There is bound to be an opportunity cost whenever governments spend money in any given area. In this case, the cost of buying up and storing surpluses must be paid and so the government may well have to cut back on expenditure in some other area, such as funding for teacher training, or raise taxes.

There are two other ways that the minimum price can be maintained. First, producers could be limited by quotas, restricting supply so that it does not exceed Q_1. This is shown in Figure 4.8. This would keep price at P_{Min}, but would mean that only a limited number of producers would receive it.

Second, the government could attempt to increase demand for the product by advertising or, if appropriate, by restricting supplies of the product that are being imported, through protectionist policies, thus increasing demand for domestic products.

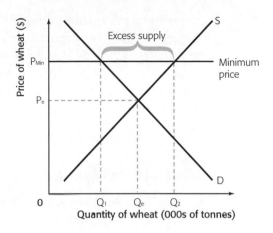

Figure 4.6 A minimum price in the market for wheat

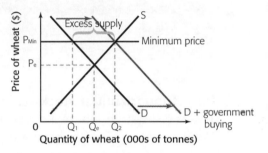

Figure 4.7 Government action to solve the problem of excess supply

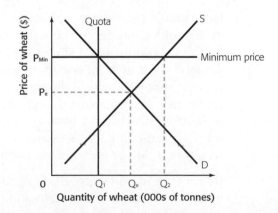

Figure 4.8 A quota to maintain a minimum price

If governments do protect firms by guaranteeing minimum prices, problems are likely to occur. Firms may think that they do not have to be as cost-conscious as they should be and this may lead to inefficiency and a waste of resources. It may also lead to firms producing more of the protected product than they should and less of other products that they could produce more efficiently.

●●●●●●●●●●●●●●●●●●●●●●●●●●●●●●●●●

Student workpoint 4.3

Be a thinker—illustrate and explain

A government wishes to increase earnings for those workers who are on low wages, by introducing minimum wage legislation in order to raise wage levels above the equilibrium wage. In doing this, they aim to:

● ensure higher wages for low-paid workers

● increase the number of workers employed.

1 Draw a diagram to show the effect of the minimum wage legislation on the market for low-paid workers.

2 Explain the consequences of the minimum wage for the workers.

3 Explain the situation facing the employers.

4 Suggest measures that the government might take to ensure that they achieve both of their stated aims above.

Price support/buffer stock schemes

This is a situation where a government intervenes in a market to stabilise prices. This has been attempted in markets for commodities (raw materials), whose prices are often unstable. Consider agricultural commodities first of all; producers of agricultural commodities such as wheat, coffee, or cocoa are very much at the mercy of the weather and also other dangers, such as insects and crop diseases. If conditions are excellent, i.e. the perfect amount of sun and rain, then there might be what is known as a bumper crop, which is an abundant supply. This will drive the price of the product down, and affect the incomes of the producers. If there is poor weather, such that the supply of the crop falls, this will drive the price up, but this will only be for the benefit of the farmers who have the crops. Thus producers of agricultural commodities are in a situation where they face volatile prices.

Another category of raw materials is industrial, or mineral, commodities such as copper, rubber, or tin. These producers also face volatile prices, but mainly due to factors that cause big swings in demand. Changes in the world economy are likely to have a large impact on producers of such commodities. As world income grows, demand for industrial commodities rises as industries expand output to meet increased world demand, leading to a positive situation where price increases lead to greater income for commodity producers. However, a slowdown in the world economy has a similarly large impact, as demand for industrial commodities falls, resulting in lower incomes for commodity producers.

Both demand and supply-side factors create instability in commodity markets. Producers, uncertain about the future, will find planning difficult. Unstable incomes may result in lower standards of living, with negative consequences for commodity producers and their communities. As a result, governments may attempt to intervene to protect prices from extreme fluctuations by operating a buffer stock scheme. To do this, the "buffer stock manager" sets a price band with a highest possible price and a lowest possible price. It then intervenes in the market whenever free market forces push the price either above the top price or below the bottom price. This is illustrated in Figure 4.9.

If there is a bumper crop, then supply will increase. Consider the example shown in Figure 4.10, where the increase in supply from S_1 to S_2 would push the price below the acceptable bottom price of \$2 per kilo. At the bottom price, there would be an excess supply of Q_1 to Q_2. In order to maintain the price at \$2, the buffer stock manager would have to buy up this excess supply (surplus). This surplus would then have to be stored.

On the other hand, if there is poor weather or a problem with pests, such that supply were to fall considerably from S_1 to S_2, then this would push the price above the acceptable top price of \$4. At the top acceptable price, there would be excess demand (shortage) of Q_1 to Q_2. As part of its commitment, the buffer stock manager would have to intervene to prevent the price from going above the price band. The manager would do this by selling coffee from the stored stocks, i.e. sell quantity Q_1 to Q_2 from the buffer stocks. This is shown in Figure 4.11.

There are many problems associated with a buffer stock scheme. Most of the problems are similar to the problems discussed above in the maintenance of guaranteed minimum prices. It is only suitable to use such a scheme with non-perishable goods, but even goods that are non-perishable must be stored in appropriate containers with the right temperature, degree of moisture, and cleanliness. Thus storage costs are likely to be high. Given the massive improvement in technologies, it is highly likely that there will be persistent surpluses that must be bought by the authorities. This puts financial pressure on the scheme, especially if there are few "bad" seasons to release the stocks. Choosing the appropriate price band can be problematic; producers are likely to want it to be as high as possible, and this results in a situation of persistent surpluses.

Commodity agreements

When different countries work together to operate a buffer stock scheme for a particular commodity, it is known as a "commodity price agreement". These were pioneered in the 1960s through the United Nations Conference on Trade and Development (UNCTAD) to try to support commodity producers in developing countries. There are many cases where developing countries are dependent on the export of a few commodities for their export revenues, and some countries have seen slow growth and little development as a result of low commodity prices. There have been attempts to set up commodity agreements for several commodities, including coffee, copper, tin, and rubber, but none of these has experienced any long-term success due to the problems mentioned above and the lack of agreement among members of such agreements. See the accompanying case study on the International Natural Rubber Organisation.

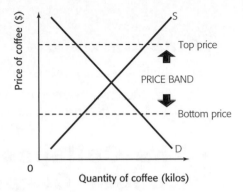

Figure 4.9 The price band set in a buffer stock scheme

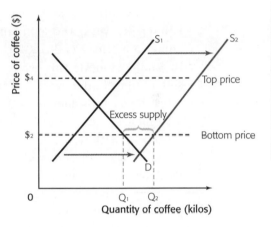

Figure 4.10 A surplus in a buffer stock scheme

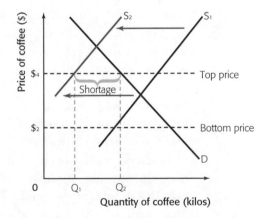

Figure 4.11 A shortage in a buffer stock scheme

2 Microeconomics

○ ○

Student workpoint 4.4

Be a thinker—read and explain

Read the following article and explain how it highlights the problems that
are likely to face the members of a commodity price agreement.

The Collapse of the International Natural Rubber Organisation

"FOR SALE: 140,000 tonnes of rubber. One slightly careless owner." Such could be the epitaph for the International Natural Rubber Organisation (INRO), the association of rubber-growers and consumers, which has come to a sticky end. Its former members met in Kuala Lumpur this week to decide how to sell a huge "buffer stock" of natural rubber left after the cartel's demise in October. When that disappears, the final traces of INRO will disappear with it.

Rubber was introduced into Asia by the British, whose traders smuggled seedlings out of Brazil in 1876 and brought them to plantations in colonial Malaya. By 1900, a "rubber revolution" on the Malay peninsula saw the trees replace almost all other cash crops.

More recently, lower-cost countries such as Thailand and Indonesia have taken most of the market, while Malaysia has begun to grow higher-value crops, such as palm oil. Its government turned against INRO because it thought that the nation's development would be hindered by making rubber planting more lucrative than it deserved to be. Malaysian interests also shifted from producers to consumers, as it became the world's biggest maker of surgical gloves.

But INRO had more fundamental problems. Like most of the buffer stock schemes that preceded it, including sugar, tin and tea, it failed to keep the market at bay. INRO was leaky, because hundreds of "smallholder" plantations and other producers operated outside the organisation. And rubber consumption is slowing as more passenger-car tyres are made of synthetic rubber, leaving truck and aircraft tyres (which need the tougher natural product) as the main markets. Because INRO contained both producers and consumers, there was also conflict between its members. Although all agreed that the aim was price stability, importers and exporters in INRO wanted to push prices in opposite directions. The price band could not stretch enough to accommodate both.

This tension, which had existed for years, finally became unbearable during the Asian financial crisis, which began in 1997. Thailand, the biggest producer, and Malaysia, a major consumer, both quit INRO, killing the cartel by depriving it of most of the fees it needed to intervene in the market.

The collapse of INRO is no tragedy. When it was created in 1979 rubber prices were rising fast, as the price of synthetic rubber climbed because of the oil crisis. Importers wanted to bring order to the market. For a while it worked, but at a cost. By limiting the amount by which prices later fell, INRO encouraged over-production and the perpetuation of nearly half a million small, inefficient rubber plantations where workers earn some of the lowest wages for the drudgery of collecting tiny latex dribbles from each tree.

The Economist, 16 December 1999

Examination questions

Short response questions

1 Using demand and supply analysis, explain how resources are allocated through changes in price in a market economy. *[10 marks]*

2 Using an appropriate diagram, explain the likely consequences of an increase in the legislated minimum wage. *[10 marks]*

Essay questions

1 a Explain the role of prices in allocating resources in a market economy. *[10 marks]*

   b Evaluate the consequences of government intervention in the market in setting maximum prices. *[15 marks]*

2 a Explain how a buffer stock scheme is expected to work. *[10 marks]*

   b Evaluate the likely success of an international buffer stock scheme in the coffee industry. *[15 marks]*

2 Microeconomics

Assessment advice: essay questions

The first examination paper you will write in your final IB Diploma Programme economics exam will be the essay paper, paper 1. You will find more information about this paper in Chapter 34, but we introduce you to the topic here.

In paper 1, you will be given four questions and have to answer one of them. Each of the four questions has a part (a), worth 10 marks, and part (b), worth 15 marks. You will have one hour for this paper.

Part (a) resembles a HL paper 2 question and, as such, you are encouraged to define key terms, provide examples, and illustrate theory with an appropriate diagram. Remember to use the diagram in your answer. Don't just stick it on at the end!

Part (b) invites you to use the skill of evaluation. For example, as in the part (b) questions you are given here, you may be asked to evaluate the ways in which governments solve particular economic problems. Alternatively, you may be asked to evaluate the likely consequences of a change in economic policy. Evaluation is a higher order skill and one that you will practise a great deal. Evaluation is a process that involves the careful consideration of a topic or issue, with a view to forming a balanced conclusion.

Data response exercise

This data response exercise follows the exact pattern that you will encounter on your IB examination, in standard level paper 2 or higher level paper 3.

Read the following article and answer the questions on the next page.

Oil prices climb to record high levels: Hurricane damage still seen as threat to winter supplies

Crude oil prices climbed above $51(US) a barrel for the first time following concerns about hurricane damage in the Gulf of Mexico. The US pumped 27% less oil than normal yesterday because of damage from Hurricane Ivan three weeks ago. The storm has cut a total of 15.3 million barrels of oil production since 13 September. "With the hurricane disruption to Gulf of Mexico production and the heating-oil season approaching, there's a great deal of concern," said an oil executive. "Prices could definitely continue to climb."

Last week, oil prices hit the previous record of $50.12 a barrel due to concerns that the damage in the Gulf of Mexico and threats against production facilities in Nigeria would cut global **supply**. **Demand** is at a record high this year, with the biggest consumption increases taking place in the US and China, which together consume one-third of the world's crude oil.

The price for natural gas has also risen sharply. Gas competes with oil in almost 10% of US factories and power plants. Demand reaches its highest peaks in the winter, when US homeowners increase their consumption of the fuel. Recently, the price for natural gas increased by 43.9 cents (per million thermal units) to finish at $7.16.

Bloomberg News, 6 October 2004

Data response exercise

1 Define the following terms, highlighted in the text:

   a supply *[2 marks]*

   b demand *[2 marks]*

2 Using a supply and demand diagram, explain how Hurricane Ivan has affected the price of oil. *[4 marks]*

3 Using a supply and demand diagram, explain why the price of natural gas has been affected. *[4 marks]*

4 Using evidence from the text and your knowledge of economics, evaluate what is likely to happen in the oil market in the upcoming months. *[8 marks]*

Assessment advice: data response

Whenever you can, in all diagrams, you should use values from the text on your axes and label the axes accordingly, e.g. in (2), the axes would be "price of oil ($)" and "quantity of oil (millions of barrels)". In part (4) of this question, evaluation may be best achieved by considering the short- and long-run effects and also by looking at how the various stakeholders are affected. For more advice on evaluation, see Chapter 34. Where appropriate, diagrams should also be used in (4). In order to achieve the top marking level (above 5 marks) it is necessary to make direct reference to the text.

You be the journalist

Headline: Warm temperatures heat up several local businesses, but others suffer

Economics concept: Changes in demand

Diagram: Demand and supply diagrams

Hints: Make up a community and think of at least two markets that would benefit from hot weather and two that would suffer.

Assessment advice: internal assessment (IA)

Having covered basic demand and supply, you are now able to start preparing for the task of writing your IA commentaries. However, it would not be advisable to attempt a proper commentary at this stage, as you don't really have enough conceptual knowledge to write a sufficiently sophisticated piece. Nonetheless, you can do a basic commentary using demand and supply analysis to explain the movement of the price of a particular good or service. In this chapter, for example, there have been references to a number of markets such as LCD televisions, rubber and oil.

To find an article, go to a search engine that specifically finds news items and type in the words "price" plus the name of a good you might want to research. Commodities such as oil and copper are possibilities, as are any currently popular items. Entering "supply" and "demand" is also a possibility. Make sure that you get an actual news item that comes from a media source.

An appropriate article will explain why the market is changing, and you have to turn this into economic analysis. That is, you have to identify any determinants of demand and supply that might be changing and explain why they are changing. You should support your answer with neatly-labelled and accurate diagrams. Also remember to note the *ceteris paribus* assumption where appropriate.

It is difficult to evaluate a great deal at this stage, but you could attempt to do so by:

- explaining how different stakeholders might be affected by possible price changes
- explaining the most important reasons for any changes in the market
- looking at how the market might change in the long run.

You will find more information about internal assessment in Chapter 34.

5 Elasticities

By the end of this chapter, you should be able to:

- explain the concept of elasticity
- define elasticity of demand
- define and calculate price elasticity of demand
- illustrate different values of price elasticity of demand using demand curves
- explain the determinants of price elasticity of demand
- define and calculate cross elasticity of demand
- explain the possible range of values for cross elasticity of demand
- define and calculate income elasticity of demand
- explain the possible range of values for income elasticity of demand
- define elasticity of supply
- define and calculate price elasticity of supply
- illustrate different values of price elasticity of supply using supply curves
- explain the determinants of price elasticity of supply.

Elasticity is a measure of responsiveness. It measures how much something changes when there is a change in one of the factors that determines it. We now look at elasticity in terms of demand and supply.

Elasticity of demand

Elasticity of demand is a measure of how much the demand for a product changes when there is a change in one of the factors that determine demand. There are three elasticities of demand to consider:

1 price elasticity of demand [PED]

2 cross elasticity of demand [XED]

3 income elasticity of demand [YED].

Price elasticity of demand [PED]

Formula and definition

Price elasticity of demand is a measure of how much the quantity demanded of a product changes when there is a change in the price of the product. It is usually calculated by using the following equation:

$$PED = \frac{\text{Percentage change in quantity demanded of the product}}{\text{Percentage change in price of the product}}$$

Take an example. A publishing firm discovers that when they lower the price of one of their monthly magazines from $5 to $4.50, the number of magazines that are bought by customers each month rises from 200,000 to 230,000. With this information, we can calculate the price elasticity of demand for the magazine in question:

1 The price has fallen by 50¢ from an original price of $5, which is a change of –10%. This is calculated by the equation

$$PED = \frac{-50}{100} \times 100 = -10\%.$$

2 The quantity demanded has increased by 30,000 from an original demand of 200,000, which is a change of 15%. This is calculated by the equation

$$\frac{30,000}{200,000} \times 100 = 15\%.$$

3 If we put the two values above into the equation for PED, we get $\frac{15\%}{-10\%}$, which gives a value of –1.5.

4 The negative value indicates that there is an inverse relationship between price and the quantity demanded. However, in order to simplify matters, economists usually ignore the negative value that comes from the equation and simply give the answer as a positive figure. Thus, in this case, the PED for the monthly magazine would be 1.5.

The range of values of price elasticity of demand
The possible range of values for price elasticity of demand usually goes from zero to infinity. The two extreme values are theoretical and the real values lie in between.

If PED is equal to zero, then a change in the price of a product will have no effect on the quantity demanded at all. The percentage change in quantity demanded would therefore be zero and so would the value on the top of the PED equation. Since zero divided by anything is zero, no matter what the percentage change in price, the PED value will be zero. A demand curve with a PED value of zero is shown in Figure 5.1 and, in this case, demand is said to be perfectly inelastic—it is completely unresponsive to price changes. Whether price is P_1, P_2, or any other price, the quantity demanded will be Q.

A PED value of infinity is best explained by using a diagram and the situation is shown in Figure 5.2. In this case, demand is said to be perfectly elastic. At the price P_1, the demand curve goes on for ever and so the quantity demanded is infinite. However, if price is raised above P_1, even by the smallest amount, demand will fall to zero, an infinite change. Because of this, the value on the top of the PED equation would be infinity. Since infinity divided by anything is infinity, no matter what the percentage change in price, the PED value will be infinity.

As stated before, it must be remembered that the extreme values of PED are simply theoretical and there are no single products that would possess a PED value of zero or infinity. Normal products have values of PED between the two and we will now look at those values. The range of values of PED is normally split into three categories.

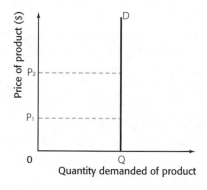

Figure 5.1 A perfectly inelastic demand curve

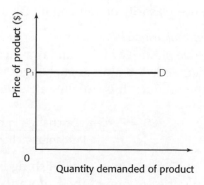

Figure 5.2 A perfectly elastic demand curve

1   *Inelastic demand:* The value of PED is less than one and greater than zero. If a product has inelastic demand, then a change in the price of the product leads to a proportionally smaller change in the quantity demanded of it. This means that if the price is raised, the quantity demanded will not fall by much in comparison, and so the total revenue gained by the firm (the number of units sold **x** the price of the product) will increase. This may be shown by an example.

When the price of a carton of strawberry yoghurt is raised from $1 to $1.20, the firm finds that quantity demanded per week falls from 12,000 cartons to 10,800 cartons. Thus a 20% increase in price is causing a 10% fall in the quantity demanded. We can work out the PED by using the equation:

$$PED = \frac{\% \Delta \text{ in Quantity Demanded}}{\% \Delta \text{ in Price}} = \frac{10\%}{20\%} = 0.5$$

As we can see, the PED is 0.5, less than one, so the demand for the yoghurt is inelastic. Before the price increase, the total revenue gained by the firm was 12,000 **x** $1 = $12,000. After the increase, the total revenue becomes 10,800 **x** $1.20 = $12,960. The firm has increased revenue by lowering the price. This is shown in Figure 5.3.

The "revenue boxes" in the diagram clearly show why a price increase causes an increase in total revenue, when the demand for a product is inelastic. In this case, before the price rise, the firm was getting revenue equal to "revenue box b" + "revenue box c". After the price increase, the firm loses "revenue box c", because quantity demanded falls to 10,800 cartons, but gains "revenue box a", because the remaining cartons are now sold at $1.20 each. Since "revenue box a" (10,800 **x** 0.20 = $2,160) is clearly larger than "revenue box c" (1,200 **x** $1 = $1,200), the firm's total revenue rises by $960.

Thus, if a firm has inelastic demand for its product and wishes to increase total revenue, it should raise the price of the product.

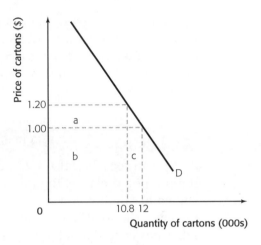

Figure 5.3 The demand for strawberry yoghurt

2 Microeconomics

Student workpoint 5.1

Be a thinker—calculate, illustrate, and explain

A firm producing decorative candles lowers the price of one of its scented candles from $4 to $3.60 and finds that the weekly quantity demanded of the candles goes up from 600 per week to 630.

a   Calculate the percentage changes in price and quantity demanded.

b   Calculate the price elasticity of demand for the scented candles.

c   Calculate the change in total revenue that the firm will experience following the fall in price.

d   Draw a "revenue box" diagram to illustrate the effect on quantity demanded and total revenue following the price change for the scented candle.

e   Was the firm sensible to lower the price of the scented candles? Explain your answer.

2 *Elastic demand:* The value of PED is greater than one and less than infinity. If a product has elastic demand, then a change in the price of the product leads to a greater than proportionate change in the quantity demanded of it. This means that if price is raised, the quantity demanded will fall by more in comparison, and so the total revenue gained by the firm (the number of units sold **x** the price of the product) will fall. This may be shown by an example.

When the price of a hot dog is raised from $2 to $2.10, a hot dog seller finds that quantity demanded per week falls from 200 hot dogs to 180 hot dogs. Thus a 5% increase in price is causing a 10% fall in the quantity demanded. We can work out the PED by using the equation:

$$\text{PED} = \frac{\%\ \Delta\ \text{in Quantity Demanded}}{\%\ \Delta\ \text{in Price}} = \frac{10\%}{5\%} = 2$$

As we can see, the PED is 2, greater than 1, so the demand for the hot dog is elastic. Before the price rise, the total revenue gained by the hot dog seller was 200 **x** $2 = $400. After the increase, the total revenue becomes 180 **x** $2.10 = $378. The seller has caused a fall in revenue by raising the price. This is shown in Figure 5.4.

The "revenue boxes" in the diagram clearly show why a price increase causes a decrease in total revenue, when the demand for a product is elastic. In this case, before the price rise, the hot dog seller was earning revenue equal to "revenue box b" + "revenue box c". After the price increase, the hot dog seller loses "revenue box c", because quantity demanded falls to 180 hot dogs, but gains "revenue box a", because the remaining hot dogs are now sold at $2.10 each. Since "revenue box a" (180 **x** $0.10 = $18) is clearly smaller than "revenue box c" (20 **x** $2 = $40), the hot dog seller's total revenue falls by $22.

Thus, if a firm has elastic demand for its product and wishes to increase total revenue, it should not raise the price of the product.

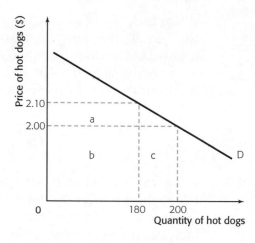

Figure 5.4 The demand for hot dogs

Student workpoint 5.2

Be a thinker—calculate, illustrate, and explain

A pizzeria lowers the price of its most popular takeaway pizza, the Margherita, from $5 to $4.50 and finds that the weekly quantity demanded of the pizzas goes up from 60 per week to 72.

a Calculate the percentage changes in price and quantity demanded.

b Calculate the price elasticity of demand for the pizzas.

c Calculate the change in total revenue that the pizzeria will experience following the fall in price.

d Draw a "revenue box" diagram to illustrate the effect on quantity demanded and total revenue following the price change for the Margherita.

e Was the firm sensible to lower the price of the Margherita? Explain your answer.

3 *Unit elastic demand:* The value of PED is equal to one. If a product has unit elastic demand, then a change in the price of the product leads to a proportionate, opposite, change in the quantity demanded of it. This means that if price is raised by a certain percentage, then the quantity demanded will fall by the same percentage, and so PED is equal to 1 and the total revenue gained by the firm (the number of units sold **x** the price of the product) will not change. A curve that has unit elasticity at every point is shown in Figure 5.5. It is known as a rectangular hyperbola.

The rectangular hyperbola is drawn in such a way that price times quantity at any point is constant. This means that the "revenue boxes" always have the same area and if the revenue does not change when price changes, then PED must be unity. Thus, in Figure 5.5, the two rectangles a and b have the same area, and a+b is equal to b+c.

A mathematical note about elasticity

It is a common mistake for students to assume that elasticity is a measure of the slope of the demand curve and that the value is always the same at any point on the curve. This is not the case. For a straight-line, downward-sloping demand curve, the value of PED falls as price falls. This is shown in Figure 5.6.

When price falls from $20 to $18, quantity demanded increases from 60 to 80 units. Thus the PED value is:

$$\text{PED} = \frac{\% \ \Delta QD}{\% \ \Delta P} = \frac{33.3\%}{10\%} = 3.3$$

The value of PED is 3.3, elastic, when we move from point a to point b.

When price falls from $10 to $8, quantity demanded increases from 160 to 180 units. Thus the PED value is:

$$\text{PED} = \frac{\% \ \Delta QD}{\% \ \Delta P} = \frac{12.5\%}{20\%} = 0.625$$

The value of PED is 0.625, inelastic, when we move from point c to point d.

Thus we can see that the value of PED falls as we move down a demand curve. It is logical that this should happen. Low-priced products have a more inelastic demand than high-priced products, because consumers are less concerned when the price of an inexpensive product rises than they are when the price of an expensive product rises.

Determinants of price elasticity of demand

Different products will have different values for PED. For example, the demand for a restaurant meal may have a PED value of 3, i.e. it is elastic, whereas the demand for petrol may have a PED value of 0.4, which is inelastic. What actually determines the value of PED for a product? There are a number of determinants:

1 *The number and closeness of substitutes:* The number and closeness of substitutes that are available is certainly the most important determinant of PED. It is fair to say that the more substitutes

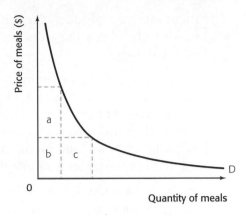

Figure 5.5 A rectangular hyperbola, where PED = 1 at every point

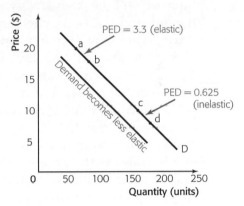

Figure 5.6 PED values for a normal demand curve

there are for a product, the more elastic will be the demand for it. Also, the closer the substitutes available, the more elastic will be the demand.

For example, there are many different brands of butter available on the market and so an increase in the price of one brand will lead to a large number of customers changing their demands to another brand. Thus the demand for products with lots of substitutes, such as brands of household products, types of meat, and types of fruit, will tend to have elastic demand.

Products with few substitutes, such as oil, will tend to have relatively inelastic demand, with the demand falling relatively little as the price goes up.

2 *The necessity of the product and how widely the product is defined:* Food is a necessary product. Indeed, if we do not have food, then we will die, so it is very necessary. Thus we would expect the demand for food to be very inelastic, which it is. However, if we define food more narrowly and consider meat, we would expect the demand to be less inelastic, since there are many alternatives, such as vegetables. Once again, if we then define meat more narrowly and consider chicken, beef, lamb, and pork, we could once again reasonably assume that the demand for each would be relatively elastic, since the consumer can easily change from one type of meat to another, if the price of one rises. As the product is defined even more narrowly, into chicken products and then identical, but branded, chicken products, demand becomes even more elastic. This is shown in Figure 5.7.

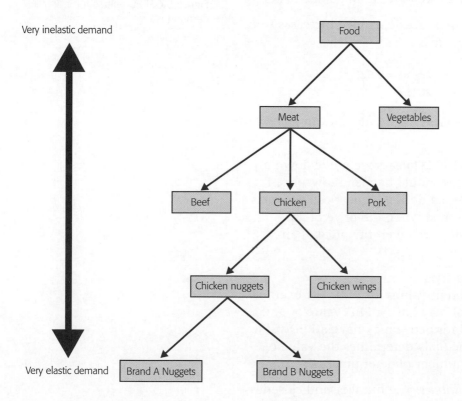

Figure 5.7 Level of definition

It is worth remembering that for many goods, necessity will change from consumer to consumer, since different people have different tastes and necessity is often a subjective view.

For example, in Malaysia, chicken is very popular among the population and so the demand for it is less elastic than it would be in Italy, where it is not valued as highly.

Necessity may go to extremes when individuals consider products to be very "necessary", such as habit-forming goods, like cigarettes, alcohol, or hard drugs. Such products tend to have inelastic demand.

3 *The time period considered:* As the price of a product changes, it often takes time for consumers to change their buying and consumption habits. PED thus tends to be more inelastic in the short term and then becomes more elastic, the longer the time period it is measured over.

For example, when heating oil prices rose sharply in Austria, the demand for oil that winter changed by a proportionately smaller amount than the change in price. Demand was relatively very inelastic, since people did not really have many alternative products that they could switch to. They still needed heating oil for their central heating. However, over the next few years, the demand for heating oil began to fall as people started to change their heating systems to ones that used gas, coal, or wood. The PED, when measured over a longer time period, was certainly more elastic.

Student workpoint 5.3

Be a thinker—calculate, illustrate, and explain

For each of the following pairs of goods, identify the one that would you expect to have the higher price elasticity of demand and explain your choice by referring to at least one of the determinants of elasticity.

1	Heineken beer	Beer
2	A prescription tablet to reduce blood pressure	A tablet to reduce headache pain
3	Milk	Orange juice

Price elasticity of demand and taxation

Governments need to be aware of the possible consequences when they impose indirect taxes, such as sales taxes, on products. If a government puts a tax on a product, then its price will usually rise. (This is dealt with in more detail, for higher level students, in Chapter 6.) This means that the quantity demanded of the product in question is likely to fall and this will have consequences for employment in the industry concerned. If the demand for the product is very elastic, then a price increase as a result of the imposition of a tax on the product will lead to a relatively large fall in the demand for the product. This means that the demand for production workers in the industry is likely to fall significantly, increasing unemployment in the economy.

Since governments are not usually keen to increase unemployment, they normally place taxes on products where demand is relatively inelastic, so that the demand for the product will not fall by a significant amount, and will not thus lead to high unemployment.

Student workpoint 5.4

Be a thinker—calculate, consider, and explain

Estimates based on studies of the US population suggest that a 10% increase in the price of cigarettes would reduce overall consumption by adults by 3% to 5%. The same 10% increase would reduce the consumptions by youths by 13%.

1 Calculate the price elasticity of demand for cigarettes among US adults and among US youths.

2 Suggest possible reasons for the different magnitude of elasticity between the two groups.

3 Explain two possible reasons why a government would place a tax on cigarettes.

Cross elasticity of demand (XED)

Formula and definition

Cross elasticity of demand is a measure of how much the demand for a product changes when there is a change in the price of another product. It is usually calculated by using the equation below:

$$XED = \frac{\text{Percentage change in quantity demanded of the product X}}{\text{Percentage change in price of the product Y}}$$

For example, the owners of a pizza stand find that when their competitor, a hamburger stand, lowers the price of a burger from $2 to $1.80, the number of pizza slices that they sell each week falls from 400 to 380, because of the lower priced burger. With this information, we can calculate the cross elasticity of demand for the pizza slices from the stand.

1 The price of the competitor's burgers has fallen by 20¢ from an original price of $2, which is a change of −10%. This is calculated by the equation

$$\frac{-20}{200} \times 100 = -10\%.$$

2 The quantity demanded of the pizza slices has fallen by 20 from an original demand of 400, which is a change of −5%. This is calculated by the equation

$$\frac{-20}{400} \times 100 = -5\%.$$

3 If we put the two values above into the equation for XED,

we get $\frac{-5\%}{-10\%}$, which gives a value of +0.5.

The range of values for cross elasticity of demand

XED explains the relationship between products. Unlike price elasticity of demand, where the vast majority of products have a positive value for PED, the value of XED may be positive or negative and the sign is important, since it tells us what the relationship between the two goods in question is.

If the value of XED is positive, then the two goods in question may be said to be substitutes for each other. Products that are very close substitutes will have a higher positive value than products that are not so close. Two types of margarine may be very close substitutes in the view of consumers and so a rise in the price of one will lead to a significant fall in the demand for it and a large increase in the demand for the competitor's margarine. Thus there would be a high positive value for XED.

If the value of XED is negative, then the two goods in question may be said to be complements for each other. Products that are very close complements will have a lower negative value than products that are not so close. A computer gaming machine and the games that are played on it may be very close complements for consumers. A rise in the price of the gaming machine may lead to a significant fall in the quantity demanded of it and so a large fall in the demand for the games. Thus there would be a strong negative value for XED.

Some products, such as matchsticks and houses, are not connected. Thus an increase in the price of matchsticks would have no effect on the demand for housing and so the value of XED for the two products would be zero. We say that the two goods are unrelated.

Firms need to be aware of the XED for the products that they produce. It is essential that firms are aware of the possible impact on the demand for their products that may arise if there is a change in the price of a close rival's products. In the same way, they need to be aware of the impact of any change in price that they make on the demand for their close rival's products.

In addition, firms that produce complementary products, such as power tools and accessories, need to be aware of the effect that any price change they make on one product might have on the demand for complementary products that they also produce.

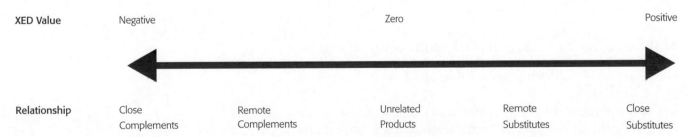

XED Value	Negative		Zero		Positive
Relationship	Close Complements	Remote Complements	Unrelated Products	Remote Substitutes	Close Substitutes

Figure 5.8 XED values and the strength of the relationship between products

Student workpoint 5.5

Be a thinker—calculate and explain

"Light-Bites", a sandwich shop, finds that when its rival, "Super-Snack", reduces the price of its chicken wraps from $5 to $4.60, the demand for "Light-Bites" sandwiches falls from 400 sandwiches a week to 340 sandwiches a week. In addition, "Super-Snack" finds that following the fall in price of their chicken wraps, the demand for soft drinks rises from 600 cans to 630 cans per week.

a Calculate the cross elasticity of demand between "Light-Bite" sandwiches and "Super-Snack" sandwiches.

b Explain the relationship above in terms of cross elasticity of demand.

c Calculate the cross elasticity of demand between "Super-Snack" sandwiches and the "Super-Snack" soft drinks.

d Explain the relationship above in terms of cross elasticity of demand.

Income elasticity of demand (YED)

Formula and definition

Income elasticity of demand is a measure of how much the demand for a product changes when there is a change in the consumer's income. It is usually calculated by using the equation below:

$$YED = \frac{\text{Percentage change in quantity demanded of the product}}{\text{Percentage change in income of the consumer}}$$

Take an example. A person has an increase in annual income from $60,000 per year to $66,000. She then increases her annual spending on holidays from $2,500 to $3,000. With this information, we can calculate her income elasticity of demand for holidays.

1 Her income has risen by $6,000 from an original income of $60,000, which is a change of +10%. This is calculated by the equation

$$\frac{+6,000}{60,000} \times 100 = +10\%.$$

2 The quantity demanded of holidays has increased by $500 from an original demand of $2,500, which is a change of +20%. This is calculated by the equation

$$\frac{500}{2,500} \times 100 = +20\%.$$

3 If we put the two values above into the equation for PED,

we get $\frac{+20\%}{+10\%}$, which gives a value of +2.

The range of values for income elasticity of demand

Like XED, the sign obtained from the equation is important. In this case, the sign of YED tells us whether the product we are looking at is a normal good or an inferior good. Remember that the demand for a normal good rises as income rises and the demand for an inferior good falls as income rises.

For normal goods, the value of YED is positive, i.e. the demand increases as income increases. If the percentage increase in quantity demanded is less than the percentage increase in income, then a YED value between zero and one is obtained and the demand is said to be income-inelastic. If the percentage increase in quantity demanded is greater than the percentage increase in income, then a YED value greater than one is obtained and the demand is said to be income-elastic.

Necessity goods are products that have low income elasticity. The demand for them will change very little if income rises. For example, the demand for bread does not increase significantly as income rises, because people feel that they already have enough bread and so will not increase consumption.

Superior goods are products that have high income elasticity. The demand for them changes significantly if income rises. As people have more income and have satisfied their needs, they begin to purchase products that are wants, i.e. non-essential, in greater number. For example, the demand for holidays in foreign countries is likely to be income-elastic.

For inferior goods, the value of YED is negative, because the demand decreases as income increases. People start to switch their expenditure from the inferior goods that they had been buying to superior goods, which they can now afford. For example, the demand for inexpensive jeans falls as income rises because people switch to buying branded jeans.

An *Engel Curve* shows the relationship between income and the demand for a product over time. It is named after Ernst Engel, a nineteenth-century German economist. Such a curve is shown in Figure 5.9. We can see that as the income in a country rises over time, the demand for potatoes may increase, then become constant, and then begin to fall as people begin to buy superior products instead, such as pasta.

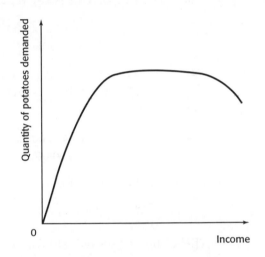

Figure 5.9 An Engel Curve showing the relationship between income and the demand for potatoes

Student workpoint 5.6

Be a thinker—calculate and explain

A consumer had an increase in income, following a salary rise, from $80,000 per year to $100,000 per year. In the following year, her expenditure on holidays increased from $8,000 to $10,000, her expenditure on gym membership remained the same, and her expenditure on locally produced clothes fell from $2,000 to $1,500.

a Calculate her income elasticity of demand for holidays.

b Explain what the value of her income elasticity of demand for holidays means.

c Calculate her income elasticity of demand for gym membership.

d Explain what the value of her income elasticity of demand for gym membership means.

e Calculate her income elasticity of demand for locally produced clothes.

f Explain what the value of her income elasticity of demand for locally produced clothes means.

Price elasticity of supply (PES)

Formula and definition
Price elasticity of supply is a measure of how much the supply of a product changes when there is a change in the price of the product. It is usually calculated by using the equation below.

$$\text{PES} = \frac{\text{Percentage change in quantity supplied of the product}}{\text{Percentage change in price of the product}}$$

For example, a publishing firm realises that they can now sell their monthly magazine for $5.50 instead of $5.00. In light of this, they increase their supply from 200,000 to 230,000 magazines per month. With this information, we can calculate the price elasticity of supply for the magazine in question.

1 The price has risen by 50¢ from an original price of $5, which is a change of +10%. This is calculated by the equation

$$\frac{50}{500} \times 100 = -10\%.$$

2 The quantity supplied has increased by 30,000 from an original supply of 200,000, which is a change of 15%. This is calculated by the equation

$$\frac{30,000}{200,000} \times 100 = 15\%.$$

3 If we put the two values above into the equation for PES, we get $\frac{15\%}{10\%}$, which gives a value of 1.5.

4 The value of PES will almost always be positive.

The range of values of price elasticity of supply
The possible range of values for price elasticity of supply usually goes from zero to infinity. Unlike PED, we will come across examples of both extreme values as we continue our study of economics.

If PES is equal to zero, then a change in the price of a product will have no effect on the quantity supplied at all. Thus the percentage change in quantity supplied would be zero and so would the value on the top of the PES equation. Since zero divided by anything is zero, no matter what the percentage change in price, the PES value will be zero. A supply curve with a value of zero is shown in Figure 5.10 and, in this case, supply is said to be perfectly inelastic—it is completely unresponsive to price changes. Whether price is P_1, P_2, or any other price, the quantity supplied will be Q.

In the very short run, sometimes known as the immediate time period, it is impossible for firms to increase their supply straight away, no matter what happens to price, and so the supply curve would look like the one in Figure 5.10, until new factors of production could be employed. Thus a perfectly inelastic supply curve is a possibility.

A PES value of infinity is best explained by using a diagram and the situation is shown in Figure 5.11. In this case, supply is said to be

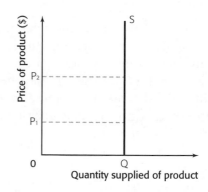

Figure 5.10 A perfectly inelastic supply curve

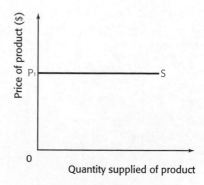

Figure 5.11 A perfectly elastic supply curve

perfectly elastic. At the price P_1, the supply curve goes on forever and so the quantity supplied is infinite. However, if price falls below P_1, even by the smallest amount, supply will fall to zero, an infinite change. Because of this, the value on the top of the PES equation would be infinity. Since infinity divided by anything is infinity, no matter what the percentage change in price, the PES value will be infinity.

In international trade, it is often assumed that the supply of commodities, such as wheat, available to a country for import is infinite. The consumers in the country can have all that they want as long as they are prepared to pay the current world market price. Thus the market in the country will have a "world supply" curve that is perfectly elastic at the current world market price. (We will deal with this in more detail in Chapter 24.)

Normal products have values between zero and infinity and we will now look at those values. The range of values of PES is normally split into three categories:

1 *Inelastic supply:* The value of PES is less than one and greater than zero. If a product has inelastic supply, then a change in the price of the product leads to a less than proportionate change in the quantity supplied of it, and so the value of PES is greater than zero and less than one.

2 *Elastic supply:* The value of PES is greater than one and less than infinity. If a product has elastic supply, then a change in the price of the product leads to a greater than proportionate change in the quantity supplied of it, and so the value of PES is greater than one and less than infinity.

3 *Unit elastic supply:* The value of PES is equal to one. If a product has unit elastic supply, then a change in the price of the product leads to a proportionate change in the quantity supplied of it and so the value of PES is equal to one.

Examples of supply curves with different values of PES are shown in Figure 5.12.

In Figure 5.12, curves S_1 and S_2 have a PES value of one along their entire length. This is because the percentage change in price is always equal to the percentage change in quantity supplied. For mathematical reasons, it is correct to say that any straight-line supply curve, passing through the origin, has an elasticity of supply of one.

Curve S_3 has a PES value of less than one along its entire length. This is because the percentage change in price is always greater than the percentage change in quantity supplied. For mathematical reasons, it is correct to say that any straight-line supply curve starting from the x-axis has a PES value less than one.

Curve S_4 has a PES value of greater than one along its entire length. This is because the percentage change in quantity supplied is always greater than the percentage change in price. For mathematical reasons, it is correct to say that any straight-line supply curve starting from the y-axis has a PES value greater than one.

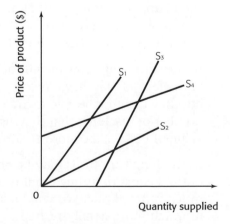

Figure 5.12 Supply curves with different values of PES

● ●

Student workpoint 5.7

Be a thinker—illustrate, explain, and calculate

A firm producing stuffed toys experiences an increase in the demand for its main product, a cuddly dog, because of an increase in its popularity. The price of the toy rises from $15 to $18. In response, the firm increases its output of the toy from 5,000 per week to 5,500 per week.

a Using a demand and supply diagram, explain why the price of the toy dog has increased.

b Calculate the elasticity of supply for the toy dog.

Determinants of price elasticity of supply

Different products will have different values for PES. For example, the supply of cans of a soft drink may have a PES value of 2, i.e. it is elastic, whereas the supply of electricity may have a PES value of 0.5, which is inelastic. What actually determines the value of PES for a product? There are a number of determinants.

1 *How much costs rise as output is increased:* If total costs rise significantly as a producer attempts to increase supply, then it is likely that the producer will not raise the supply and so the elasticity of supply for the product will be relatively inelastic. It would take large price rises to make increasing the supply worthwhile.

If, however, total costs do not rise quickly, then the producer will raise the supply and take advantage of the slow increase in costs to benefit from the higher prices, thus making more profits. Total costs will not rise quickly if the firm has a lot of spare capacity and if the costs of factor inputs do not rise quickly as the firm uses more of them.

2 *The time period considered:* The amount of time over which PES is measured will affect its value. In general terms, the longer the time period considered, the more elastic will be supply.

In the immediate time period, firms are not really able to increase their supply very much, if at all, if price increases, since they cannot immediately increase the number of factors of production that they employ. The value of PES will be very inelastic.

In the short run, firms may be able to increase the quantity of some of the factors that they employ, such as raw materials and labour, but they may not be able to increase all of their factors, such as the number of machines that they use or the size of their factory. The value of PES will be more elastic than the immediate time period.

In the long run, firms may be able to increase the quantity of all of the factors that they employ and so the value of PES will be much more elastic. We will look at time periods and production in much more detail in Chapter 7.

Assessment advice: using the language of economics

Whenever you are discussing any type of elasticity in an examination question, you must try to be very precise with language. Elasticity measures the responsiveness of change, and it is the percentage change or proportionate change that is significant. Never say that a small change in price (or income) causes a large change in the quantity. Be specific—say that a given price change causes a proportionately smaller (or proportionately larger) change in quantity. Or say that a given percentage change in price leads to a smaller (or larger) percentage change in quantity. Or you could give values. For example, say that a 10% increase in price leads to a change in quantity that is greater (or less) than 10%. The adjectives "small" and "big" are just too imprecise.

2 Microeconomics

Examination questions

Short response questions

1 With the help of examples, explain the determinants of price elasticity of demand. [10 marks]

2 A businessperson wants to increase her revenues. Using appropriate diagrams, explain why knowledge of price elasticity of demand would be useful. [10 marks]

3 With the help of examples, explain the concept of cross elasticity of demand. [10 marks]

4 With the help of examples, explain the determinants of price elasticity of supply. [10 marks]

5 Using income elasticity of demand, explain the difference between normal, necessity, and inferior goods. [10 marks]

Essay question

1 a Explain the concept of elasticity of demand. [10 marks]

b Discuss why it may be important for a firm to have a knowledge of elasticity of demand. [15 marks]

You be the journalist

Headline: Pharmaceutical giant Paladol misjudges its market by raising the price on its best-selling headache relief tablet.

Economics concept: PED, substitute goods, XED.

Diagram: Revenue box diagram.

Hint: What do you think Paladol was assuming about the elasticity of demand for its tablet? Who might gain from this decision?

Assessment advice: essay writing

When a question does not state a specific type of a concept, then you need to address all of the possible types. For example, in part (b) of the essay question given here, it would be necessary to cover price, income, and cross elasticity of demand. For further information about answering essay questions, see Chapter 34.

6 Indirect taxes, subsidies, and elasticity

By the end of this chapter, you should be able to:

- define and give examples of an indirect tax
- explain the difference between a specific tax and a percentage tax
- explain the importance of elasticity in understanding the effect of an indirect tax on the demand for, and supply of, a product
- explain how the imposition of an indirect tax may affect consumers, producers, and the government
- define a subsidy
- explain the importance of elasticity in understanding the effect of a subsidy on the demand for, and supply of, a product
- explain how the granting of a subsidy may affect consumers, producers, and the government.

When governments impose taxes on products, or give subsidies to firms, there are bound to be effects upon demand and supply and we now need to consider those possible effects and how they are influenced by the relative price elasticities for the product.

The effect of an indirect tax on the demand for, and supply of, a product

An indirect tax is one imposed upon expenditure. It is placed upon the selling price of a product, so it raises the firm's costs and shifts the supply curve for the product vertically upwards by the amount of the tax. Because of this shift, less product will be supplied at every price.

There are two types of indirect taxes to consider:

1 *A specific tax:* This is a specific, or fixed, amount of tax that is imposed upon a product, for example, a tax of $1 per unit. It thus has the effect of shifting the supply curve vertically upwards by the amount of the tax, in this case, by $1. This is shown in Figure 6.1(a). S is the original supply curve and S+tax is the curve after the tax is imposed.

2 *A percentage tax (also known as an* ad valorem *tax):* This is where the tax is a percentage of the selling price and so the supply curve will shift as shown in Figure 6.1(b). It is clear from this that the gap between S1 and S+tax will get bigger as the price of the product rises. If the percentage tax is 20%, then at a price of $5, the tax on the product will be $1. If the price of the product is $10, then the tax becomes $2. The gap between the supply curves widens because it is a percentage tax.

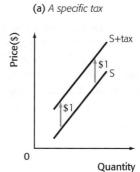

(a) *A specific tax*

(b) *A percentage tax*

Figure 6.1 The effect on a supply curve of different types of indirect taxes

When an indirect tax is imposed on a product, we need to consider what the effect will be on consumers, producers, the government, and the market as a whole. In order to do that, add the demand curve to the graph and consider the following questions.

- What will happen to the price that the consumers pay?
- What will happen to the amount received by the producer?
- How much tax will the government receive?
- What will happen to the size of the market, and so employment?

If we take a normal demand and supply curve and then assume that the government imposes a specific tax on a product, we get the diagrams shown in Figure 6.2(a), (b), and (c).

The market is in equilibrium, with Q_e being supplied and demanded at a price of P_e. After the tax of XY per unit is imposed, the supply curve shifts vertically upwards from S_1 to S_1+tax. The producers would like to raise the price to P_2 and so pass on all of the cost of the tax to the consumers. However, as we can see in Figure 6.2(a), at that price, there is an excess supply and so price has to fall until a new equilibrium is reached, which is at a price of P_1, where Q_1 is both demanded and supplied.

We can now address the questions that we asked previously. From Figure 6.2(a), we can see that the price of the product for the consumers rises from P_e to P_1, which is their share of the tax, and is about half of the whole tax of XY. Producers now receive C per unit, after paying the tax of XY to the government. Thus they contribute the rest of the tax, P_eC per unit. The revenue for producers falls from $0P_eWQ_e$ to $0CYQ_1$. This is shown in the blue striped section in the diagram.

From Figure 6.2(b), we can see that the government will receive tax revenue equal to CP_1XY and that the market falls in size from one producing Q_e units to one producing Q_1 units. This may well have implications for the level of employment in the market, as firms might employ fewer people.

Figure 6.2(c) shows us that, in this case, the burden of the indirect tax is shared fairly evenly between the consumers and the producers.

However, the share of the tax burden for consumers and producers will vary with the relative values of price elasticity of demand and supply for the product, as will government revenue, and the effect on the size of the market.

Let us look at two different situations. In the first case, consider a market where the price elasticity of demand is relatively elastic and the price elasticity of supply is relatively inelastic, i.e. where the value of PED is greater than the value of PES. This is shown in Figure 6.3.

The market is in equilibrium with Q_e being supplied and demanded at a price of P_e. After the tax of XY per unit is imposed, the supply curve shifts vertically upwards from S_1 to S_1+tax. The producers would like to raise the price to P_2 and so pass on all of the cost of the tax to the consumers.

(a) *Producer revenue*

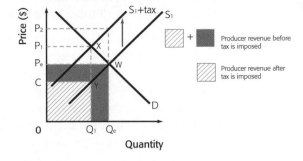

(b) *Government tax revenue*

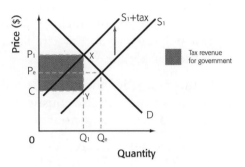

(c) *The tax burden*

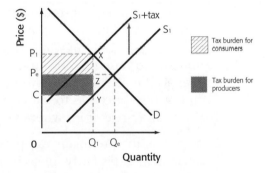

Figure 6.2 The imposition of a specific tax on a product

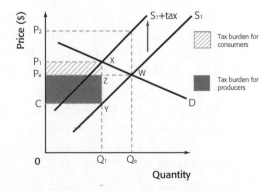

Figure 6.3 The imposition of a specific tax on a product where PED is greater than PES

2 Microeconomics

65

However, at that price, there is an excess supply and so price has to fall until a new equilibrium is reached, which is at a price of P_1, where Q_1 is both demanded and supplied.

However, in this case, the producers cannot pass on a lot of the burden of the tax, because demand is very elastic and too many of the consumers would stop buying the product. Thus the producers have to bear most of the burden of the tax themselves. The price of the product for the consumers rises just a little from P_e to P_1. Producers now receive C per unit, after paying the tax of XY to the government. Thus they contribute the majority of the tax, P_eC per unit. The income of producers falls a great deal, from $0P_eWQ_e$ to $0CYQ_1$. The consumers' share of the tax is P_eP_1XZ. The government will receive high tax revenue equal to CP_1XY and the market falls in size from one producing Q_e units to one producing Q_1 units. This will once again have implications for the level of employment in the market.

In this case, the burden of the indirect tax is much heavier on the producers than on the consumers. This is because of the difference in the values of the elasticities.

In the second case, consider a market where the price elasticity of demand is relatively inelastic and the price elasticity of supply is relatively elastic, i.e. where the value of PED is less than the value of PES. This is shown in Figure 6.4.

The market is in equilibrium with Q_e being supplied and demanded at a price of P_e. After the tax of XY per unit is imposed, the supply curve shifts vertically upwards from S_1 to S_1+tax. The producers would like to raise the price to P_2 and so pass on all of the cost of the tax to the consumers. However, at that price, there is an excess supply and so price has to fall until a new equilibrium is reached, which is at a price of P_1, where Q_1 is both demanded and supplied.

In this case, the producers can pass on a lot of the burden of the tax, because demand is fairly inelastic and few of the consumers would stop buying the product. Thus the consumers have most of the burden of the tax passed on to them. The price of the product for the consumers rises substantially from P_e to P_1. Thus they contribute the majority of the tax, P_1P_e per unit. Producers now receive C per unit, after paying the tax of XY to the government. The income of producers falls a small amount, from $0P_eWQ_e$ to $0CYQ_1$. The government will receive high tax revenue equal to CP_1XY and the market falls in size from one producing Q_e units to one producing Q_1 units. This will once again have implications for the level of employment in the market.

In this case, the burden of the indirect tax is much heavier on the consumers than on the producers. We can use the examples above to derive a set of rules relating to the incidence of indirect taxes on producers and consumers:

1 Where the value of PED is equal to the value of PES for a product, then the burden of any tax imposed will be shared equally between the consumers and producers of the product.

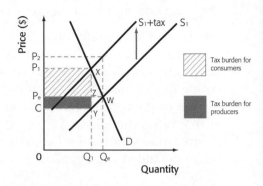

Figure 6.4 The imposition of a specific tax on a product where PED is less than PES

2 Microeconomics

2 Where the value of PED is greater than the value of PES for a product, then the burden of any tax imposed will be greater on the producers of the product than on the consumers.

3 Where the value of PED is less than the value of PES for a product, then the burden of any tax imposed will be greater on the consumers of the product than on the producers.

This is why governments tend to place indirect taxes on products that have relatively inelastic demand, such as alcohol and cigarettes. By doing this, demand changes by a proportionately smaller amount than the change in price and so the government will gain high revenue and yet not cause a large fall in employment. You should be able to think of some other good reasons why governments put taxes on such goods. These will be addressed further in Chapter 13.

Student workpoint 6.1

Be a thinker—illustrate and explain

1 A product has relatively inelastic demand and also relatively inelastic supply. Draw a diagram to show this and then show the effect of the imposition of a **percentage tax** on the product. Label the diagram carefully and state the areas corresponding to:

a the original revenue of the producer

b the revenue of the producer after the tax is imposed

c the tax revenue received by the government

d the amount of the tax paid by the consumers

e the amount of the tax paid by the producers.

Would it be sensible for a government to tax a product with such elasticities? Explain your answer.

2 A product has relatively elastic demand and also relatively elastic supply. Draw a diagram to show this and then show the effect of the imposition of a **specific tax** on the product. Label the diagram carefully and state the areas corresponding to:

a the original revenue of the producer

b the revenue of the producer after the tax is imposed

c the tax revenue received by the government

d the amount of the tax paid by the consumers

e the amount of the tax paid by the producers.

Would it be sensible for a government to tax a product with such elasticities? Explain your answer.

The effect of a subsidy on the demand for, and supply of, a product

A subsidy is an amount of money paid by the government to a firm, per unit of output. There are a number of reasons why a government may give a subsidy for a product and the main ones are:

1 To lower the price of essential goods, such as milk, to consumers. In this way, the government hopes that the consumption of the product will be increased, encouraged by the lower price.

2 To guarantee the supply of products that the government thinks are necessary for the economy. This may be because the goods are essential for the economy, such as a basic food supply or a power source like coal. It may also be that the industry creates a lot of employment that would be lost, thus causing economic and social problems.

3 To enable producers to compete with overseas trade, thus protecting the home industry. (This is dealt with in more detail in Chapter 24.)

If a subsidy is granted to a firm on a certain product, then the supply curve for the product will shift vertically downwards by the amount of the subsidy, because it reduces the costs of production for the firm, and more will be supplied at every price. As with indirect taxes, the amount of the subsidy that is passed on to the consumers in the form of lower prices, and the amount that is retained by the producers, will depend upon the relative elasticities of demand and supply.

Although percentage subsidies are sometimes granted, they are rare and so we will concentrate on specific subsidies. A specific subsidy is a specific amount of money that is given for each unit of the product, for example, a subsidy of $2 per unit. It thus has the effect of shifting the supply curve vertically downwards by the amount of the subsidy, in this case by $2, at every price. This is shown in Figure 6.5. S_1 is the original supply curve and S_1–subsidy is the curve after the subsidy is granted.

If we take a normal demand and supply curve and then assume that the government grants a specific subsidy on a product, we get the diagrams shown in Figure 6.6(a), (b), and (c).

The market is in equilibrium with Q_e being supplied and demanded at a price of P_e. After the subsidy of WZ per unit is granted, the supply curve shifts vertically downwards from S_1 to S_1 – subsidy. As we can see in Figure 6.6(a), the producers lower their prices and increase output until a new equilibrium is reached, which is at a price of P_1, where Q_1 is both demanded and supplied.

From Figure 6.6(a), we can see that the price to consumers falls from P_e to P_1, not the whole amount of the subsidy, which would need a fall to P_2. The income of the producers rises from the original amount of $0P_eXQ_e$ to $0DWQ_1$. The consumers pay $0P_1ZQ_1$ for their purchases and P_1DWZ is paid to the producers by the government as the subsidy on the Q_1 units.

From Figure 6.6(b), we can see that the consumers get to buy the original Q_e units at a lower price, P_1, thus saving the expenditure P_1P_eXY. However, they do purchase more units, Q_eQ_1, because the price is lower, spending Q_eYZQ_1 extra. Total consumer expenditure may increase or fall, depending upon the relative savings and extra expenditure.

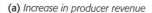

Figure 6.5 The effect on a supply curve of a specific subsidy

(a) *Increase in producer revenue*

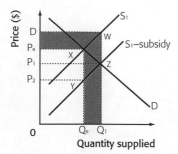

(b) *Change in consumer expenditure*

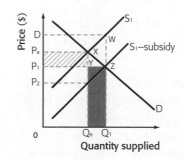

(c) *Amount of government subsidy*

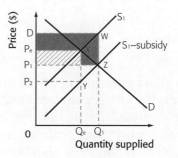

Figure 6.6 The granting of a specific subsidy on a product

2 Microeconomics

Figure 6.6(c) shows us that the total cost of the subsidy to the government is P₁DWZ. This money has to be found from somewhere and so there is an opportunity cost here. Once again, the government must either take money away from other areas of expenditure, such as building infrastructure or providing public amenities, or it must raise taxes.

Now consider a market where the price elasticity of demand is relatively elastic and the price elasticity of supply is relatively inelastic. This is shown in Figure 6.7.

The market is in equilibrium with Q_e being supplied and demanded at a price of P_e. After the subsidy of YW per unit is granted, the supply curve shifts vertically downwards from S_1 to S_1 – subsidy. The producers lower their prices and increase output until a new equilibrium is reached, which is at a price of P_1, where Q_1 is both demanded and supplied.

The price to consumers falls from P_e to P_1, a small part of the subsidy. If the whole subsidy was passed on, price would need to fall to P_2. The income of the producers rises from the original amount of $0P_eXQ_e$ to $0DYQ_1$. The consumers pay $0P_1WQ_1$ and P_1DYW is paid to the producers by the government as the subsidy.

Once again, consumption of the product is increased and so is the revenue of the producers. The consumers do not benefit from a great price fall but, because their demand is relatively elastic, they increase their consumption by a significant amount.

Finally, consider a market where the price elasticity of demand is relatively inelastic and the price elasticity of supply is relatively elastic. This is shown in Figure 6.8.

The market is in equilibrium, with Q_e being supplied and demanded at a price of P_e. After the subsidy of YW per unit is granted, the supply curve shifts vertically downwards from S_1 to S – subsidy. The producers lower their prices and increase output until a new equilibrium is reached, which is at a price of P_1, where Q_1 is both demanded and supplied.

The price to consumers falls from P_e to P_1, a significant part of the subsidy. If the whole subsidy were passed on, price would need to fall to P_2. The income of the producers rises from the original amount of $0P_eXQ_e$ to $0DYQ_1$. The consumers pay $0P_1WQ_1$ and P_1DYW is paid to the producers by the government as the subsidy.

Consumption of the product is increased and so is the revenue of the producers. The consumers benefit from a relatively large price fall but, because their demand is relatively inelastic, their consumption does not increase by a great amount.

We can use these examples to derive a set of rules relating to the granting of subsidies on producers and consumers:

1 Where the value of PED is equal to the value of PES for a product then the price of the product will fall by half of the subsidy.

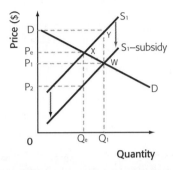

Figure 6.7 The granting of a specific subsidy to a product where PED is greater than PES

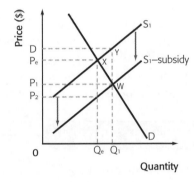

Figure 6.8 The granting of a specific subsidy to a product where PED is less than PES

2 Where the value of PED is greater than the value of PES for a product then the price of the product will fall by less than half of the subsidy.

3 Where the value of PED is less than the value of PES for a product then the price of the product will fall by more than half of the subsidy.

 In all cases, however, consumption will rise and the income of producers will be increased.

There are a number of things that need to be evaluated when a government is considering the granting of a subsidy:

● The opportunity cost of government spending on the subsidy in terms of other alternative government spending projects

● Whether the subsidy will allow firms to be inefficient, if they do not have to compete with foreign producers in a "free market"

● Although a subsidy allows consumers to buy products at a lower price, they may also be the taxpayers who are funding the subsidy. Who is paying the taxes?

● What damage will it do to the sales of foreign producers who are not receiving subsidies from their governments? There is a great deal of international debate concerning the billions of dollars of subsidies that high-income countries give to their farmers. These subsidies lead to over-production and it is argued that this is highly damaging to small-scale farmers in developing countries who do not receive subsidies themselves and then have to compete with the low prices charged by the farmers who do receive subsidies. High-income country farmers are accused of dumping their products in developing countries. That is, they are accused of selling such products at prices beneath their costs of production. This is a major issue of contention at the World Trade Organization (WTO).

Did you know?

It is estimated that every cow in the European Union receives a subsidy equivalent to $2.20 per day! When approximately 3 billion people (half the world's population) earn less than $2 a day, these subsidies have recently been questioned. In addition, the milk and powdered milk that is being sold in developing countries at subsidised prices can make it even more difficult for local farmers to survive. Governments in higher-income countries are now under pressure to reform their agricultural support systems.

For more information on this issue, go to http://oxfam.org and follow links to the "Make Trade Fair" site. Here you will find a wealth of information, along with interesting and informative activities.

2 Microeconomics

Student workpoint 6.2

Be a thinker—illustrate and explain

1 A product has relatively inelastic demand and also relatively inelastic supply. Draw a diagram to show this and then show the effect of the granting of a specific subsidy on the product. Label the diagram carefully and state the areas corresponding to:

 a the original revenue of the producer

 b the revenue of the producer after the subsidy is granted

 c the total subsidy paid by the government.

 Would it be sensible for a government to subsidise a product with such elasticities? Explain your answer.

2 A product has relatively elastic demand and also relatively elastic supply. Draw a diagram to show this and then show the effect of the granting of a percentage subsidy on the product. Label the diagram carefully and state the areas corresponding to:

 a the original revenue of the producer

 b the revenue of the producer after the subsidy is granted

 c the total subsidy paid by the government.

 Would it be sensible for a government to subsidise a product with such elasticities? Explain your answer.

Examination questions

Short response questions

1 Explain the effect on consumers and producers when a specific tax is placed on a product that has relatively elastic demand and relatively inelastic supply. *[10 marks]*

2 Explain the effect on consumers and producers when a government grants a subsidy to the producers of a product that has relatively elastic demand and supply. *[10 marks]*

Essay questions

1 a Explain the possible effects of granting a subsidy to a producer. *[10 marks]*

 b Evaluate the reasons why a government might grant a subsidy to an agricultural product. *[15 marks]*

2 a Explain the possible reasons why a government might impose an indirect tax on a product. *[10 marks]*

 b Evaluate the possible outcomes of imposing such a tax. *[15 marks]*

You be the journalist

Headline: Drivers and petrol station owners protest angrily against a recent increase in petrol taxes

Economics concept: The effect of an indirect tax, elasticity of demand

Diagram: The effect of an indirect tax.

Hints: Work out whether you think the demand for petrol is relatively elastic or inelastic. The diagram should show a tax and then show the consequences of an increase in the tax. As before, set up a hypothetical community and consider the stakeholders.

Data response exercise

Read the text below and answer the questions that follow.

Cigarette tax hike would benefit Tennessee residents

THOUGH southern states like Tennessee traditionally suffer from the highest incidence of youth and adult smoking in the nation, the indirect taxes the state and its neighbours impose on cigarettes are among the lowest.

It is felt that increasing Tennessee's **indirect tax** on cigarettes would help immensely in the fight to keep teenagers from beginning the habit. That's one of the advantageous aims of identical pieces of legislation in the House and Senate that propose to increase state taxes on cigarettes in this session, while decreasing the tax on groceries by the same amount.

While a tax increase of any kind tends to be highly unpopular, this proposal deserves serious consideration.

It has been calculated that the state has the country's highest average food tax at 8.4%, but one of the lowest cigarette taxes. The **specific tax** is set at 20 cents per pack, or one cent a cigarette. The national average for cigarette taxes is 91 cents per pack.

The legislation seeks to decrease the state sales tax rate on food, while increasing the tax on cigarettes to 3.25 cents per cigarette on 1 July 2006, with further increases each year of .15 cents or the amount needed to balance the loss in revenue created by the decrease in the sales tax on food.

The increase in the per-pack tax on cigarettes proposed in this legislation is admittedly a huge increase. But the decrease in sales tax on grocery items would obviously benefit the majority of Tennesseans. And no one seriously disputes the disastrous health consequences of cigarette smoking. The evidence is all around us.

In Tennessee, studies show 14,500 youths become regular smokers every year. Yet, according to recent data from the Department of Health and Human Services, Tennessee only spends about $1.5 million on smoking prevention and treatment programs annually. That's the lowest amount budgeted among all states except for Pennsylvania. Tennessee has one of the highest percentages of smokers in the nation. That obviously needs to change.

This is legislation that will reduce the effective price of food, save lives and decrease the long-term health care costs associated with tobacco use. This sounds like a winning proposition for everyone.

Kingsport Times-News
Monday, 20 March 2006

1 Define the following terms highlighted in the text:

   a indirect tax   *[2 marks]*

   b specific tax   *[2 marks]*

2 If we assume that the demand for cigarettes is inelastic, draw a diagram to show how the proposed change in the tax on cigarettes will affect the market for cigarettes in Tennessee.   *[4 marks]*

3 If we assume that the demand for food is elastic, draw a diagram to show how the proposed change in the tax on food will affect the food market.   *[4 marks]*

4 Evaluate the effects of the changes to the taxes on food and cigarettes.   *[8 marks]*

Assessment advice: data response

Whenever you are drawing diagrams in a data response answer, always try to use actual numbers on the diagram, if they are given in the text. Also, make sure that you label the axes fully.

7 Costs, revenues, and profit

By the end of this chapter, you should be able to:

- define, explain, and compare the concepts of the short run and the long run
- define, explain, illustrate, and calculate total, average, and marginal product
- define and explain the law of diminishing returns
- explain the different ways of measuring costs
- define, explain, illustrate, calculate, and give examples of, short-run costs
- define, explain, illustrate, and give examples of, long-run costs
- define and give examples of economies and diseconomies of scale
- explain the relationship between long-run costs and returns to scale
- define, explain, illustrate, and calculate total, average, and marginal revenue
- explain and illustrate the relationship between average revenue, marginal revenue, total revenue, and price elasticity of demand
- define and explain the measurement of profit
- distinguish between normal and abnormal profit
- define and distinguish between the shutdown price in the short and the long run
- define, explain, and illustrate the concepts of break even and profit maximisation.

In the next six chapters, we address the topic known as "The Theory of the Firm". We look at the different types of behaviour of firms in relation to the markets in which they operate and the nature of competition in different markets. In this first chapter, we cover the fundamental concepts necessary to carry out an analysis of the four different theoretical market structures that exist. These fundamental concepts are costs, revenues, and profits

Cost theory

The short run and the long run
When a firm is producing some of its factors of production will be fixed in the short run, i.e. the firm will not be able to quickly increase the quantity of them that it has. Often the fixed factor is some element of capital or land, but this is not always the case. It could be a type of highly skilled labour, such as a specialist machine worker. Therefore, if a firm wishes to increase output in the short run, it may only do so by applying more units of its variable factors to the fixed factors that it possesses, while it plans ahead to change the number of fixed factors that it has.

Definitions

The **short run** is that period of time in which at least one factor of production is fixed. All production takes place in the short run.

The **long run** is that period of time in which all factors of production are variable, but the state of technology is fixed. All planning takes place in the long run.

The length of the short run for a firm will be determined by the time it takes to increase the quantity of the fixed factor. This will vary from industry to industry. For example, a small firm involved in gardening may find that its fixed factor is the number of lawn mowers that it has available and that it takes a week to order and get delivery of a new lawn mower. Thus its short run is one week. On the other hand, a national electricity provider is constrained by its fixed factor, the number of electricity generating plants that it has. Building a new electricity generating plant may take up to two years (more if a nuclear plant is built) and so its short run is a lot longer.

If a firm plans ahead to change its fixed factors then all factors of production are variable as the plans are being made. The firm is planning in the long run. However, as soon as the fixed factors are changed the firm is once again in the short run; it simply has a different number of fixed factors. Once again, the only way that output can be increased is to apply more units of the variable factors to the new quantity of the fixed factors. As we said earlier, all production takes place in the short run and all planning takes place in the long run.

Student workpoint 7.1

Be knowledgeable

Improve your knowledge of the short run and the long run by considering the following scenario.

A small firm sets up a plant making teddy bears. The firm has a small production unit, two teddy bear making machines and two operators. There is one manager, who owns the firm, and carries out all non-production activities. There is also an unlimited amount of the materials needed to make the teddy bears.

Answer the following questions.

1 What are the fixed factors?

2 What is the variable factor?

There is an increase in the demand for teddy bears and the firm decides to satisfy this demand with the existing factors.

3 What will the firm do?

The increase in demand persists and so the firm now decides to expand the production unit, bring in two extra machines and employ two more workers.

4 The planning takes place in which time period?

5 What time period is the firm in once the changes to the plant have taken place and the firm is producing again?

6 What are the fixed factors now?

The following short section provides you with some important definitions and equations. They may initially seem puzzling, but will become clearer when used in an example.

Total, average and marginal product

Total product (TP) is the total output that a firm produces, using its fixed and variable factors in a given time period. As we have already said, output in the short run can only be increased by applying more units of the variable factors to the fixed factors.

Average product (AP) is the output that is produced, on average, by each unit of the variable factor. $AP = \frac{TP}{V}$, where TP is the total output produced and V is the number of units of the variable factor employed.

Marginal product (MP) is the extra output that is produced by using an extra unit of the variable factor. $MP = \frac{\Delta TP}{\Delta V}$, where ΔTP is the change in total output and ΔV is the change in the number of units of the variable factor employed.

Take an example. A firm has four machines (fixed factors) and increases its output by using more operators to work the machines. Production figures for each week are given in Table 7.1.

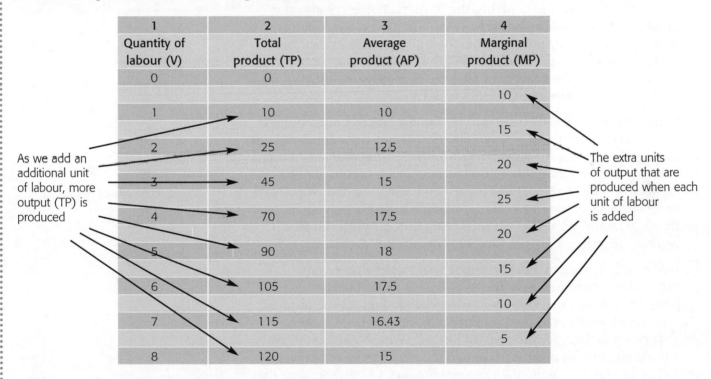

1 Quantity of labour (V)	2 Total product (TP)	3 Average product (AP)	4 Marginal product (MP)
0	0		
			10
1	10	10	
			15
2	25	12.5	
			20
3	45	15	
			25
4	70	17.5	
			20
5	90	18	
			15
6	105	17.5	
			10
7	115	16.43	
			5
8	120	15	

As we add an additional unit of labour, more output (TP) is produced

The extra units of output that are produced when each unit of labour is added

Table 7.1 Total, average, and marginal product per week

Now we can plot these curves.

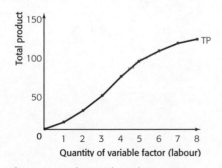

Figure 7.1 The total product curve

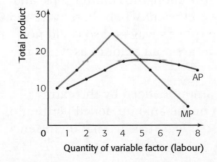

Figure 7.2 Average and marginal product curves

The law of diminishing returns

From the table, we can deduce the following definitions.

Definitions

The hypothesis of eventually diminishing marginal returns

As extra units of a variable factor are added to a given quantity of a fixed factor, the output from each additional unit of the variable factor will eventually diminish.

The hypothesis of eventually diminishing average returns

As extra units of a variable factor are added to a given quantity of a fixed factor, the output per unit of the variable factor will eventually diminish.

The two hypotheses look at the same relationship from different angles. The whole concept is really a matter of common sense. Consider an example.

A young entrepreneur named Ben sets up a new business, which is a small hamburger stand on a busy street corner. The stand consists of a very small shop, containing a refrigerator, a grill, and some countertops for preparing the burgers. There are also the implements for making burgers. These are all the fixed factors. When he starts out, Ben works alone and prepares everything himself. He makes the burgers, cuts the onion, lettuce, and tomatoes, heats the buns, and sells the hamburgers to the customers. He can make 20 burgers per hour.

Ben finds demand to be high and he cannot make enough burgers, so he hires his friend, Caroline, to help. They divide up the jobs and manage to produce 50 burgers each hour. The hamburgers become even more popular and Ben and Caroline agree that they need another worker, so Nick joins them. They divide up the work again, with each specialising in a task, and produce 90 burgers each hour. Demand continues to rise, so they bring in Niki. With the four working together, they produce 124 burgers per hour.

When Ben worked alone, his output was 20 burgers per hour. When Caroline joined him, the total output was 50 burgers per hour. This means that Caroline's marginal product was 30 burgers. When Nick joined, the total number of burgers per hour rose to 90, so Nick's marginal product was 40 burgers. When Niki joined (we are adding units of a variable factor), the total output of burgers rose to 124 per hour, making the marginal product 34 burgers. Note that the marginal product fell when Niki was added to the workforce. Why was this? Well, it was efficient to add extra people up to three workers, but because the space in the shop, the counter tops, and the grill, are all fixed, it became less efficient when there were more people. They started to get in each other's way and so could not increase the output of burgers by as great an amount as when the previous worker was added.

Whether we measure it from the amount added by the extra variable factor (marginal product) or the amount added per unit of the variable factor (average product), logic tells us that inefficiency must eventually begin to occur.

Short-run costs

Firms have many different costs when producing whatever good or service they provide. We need to be able to understand the different types of costs that firms face and to understand where those costs originate.

We can start by looking at the example from Table 7.1, and adding some costs. We will assume that the cost of a machine per week is $100 (there are four machines) and that the cost of a worker is $200 per week. The outcome of this on the costs of a firm are shown in Table 7.2.

1	2	3	4	5	6	7	8	9
Quantity of labour (V)	Total product (TP) or Output (q)	Total fixed cost (TFC)	Total variable cost (TVC)	Total cost (TC)	Average fixed cost (AFC)	Average variable cost (AVC)	Average total cost (ATC)	Marginal cost (MC)
0	0	400	0	400	-	-	-	
								20
1	10	400	200	600	40	20	60	
								13.33
2	25	400	400	800	16	16	32	
								10
3	45	400	600	1,000	8.89	13.33	22.22	
								8
4	70	400	800	1,200	5.71	11.43	17.14	
								10
5	90	400	1,000	1,400	4.44	11.11	15.55	
								13.33
6	105	400	1,200	1,600	3.81	11.43	15.24	
								20
7	115	400	1,400	1,800	3.48	12.17	15.65	
								40
8	120	400	1,600	2,000	3.33	13.33	16.67	

Table 7.2 Total, average, and marginal costs per week

Using the figures above, we can explain the different ways of measuring costs. We tend to separate costs into two groups:

1 *Total costs:* Total costs are the complete costs of producing output. We use three measures:

   a *Total fixed cost (TFC):* TFC is the total cost of the fixed assets that a firm uses in a given time period. Since the number of fixed assets is, by definition, fixed, TFC is a constant amount. It is the same whether the firm produces one unit or one hundred units.

   TFC is equal to the number of fixed assets times the cost of each fixed asset. In the example in Table 7.2, TFC per week is $400 (four machines costing $100 each) at every level of output.

b *Total variable cost (TVC):* TVC is the total cost of the variable assets that a firm uses in a given time period. TVC increases as the firm uses more of the variable factor.

TVC is equal to the number of variable factors times the cost of each variable factor. So in the current example, TVC is $200 when one worker is being employed and $1,200 when six workers are being used.

c *Total cost (TC):* TC is the total cost of all the fixed and variable factors used to produce a certain output. It is equal to TFC plus TVC.

So in the current example the total cost of producing 105 units of output per week is $1,600. It is the fixed cost of $400 plus the variable cost of $1,200.

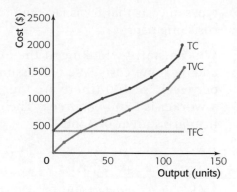

Figure 7.3 Total cost, total variable cost, and total fixed cost

The different total cost curves are shown in Figure 7.3.

2 *Average costs:* These are costs per unit of output. We use three measures:

a *Average fixed cost (AFC):* AFC is the fixed cost per unit of output. It is calculated by the equation $AFC = \dfrac{TFC}{q}$, where q is the level of output.

Because TFC is a constant, AFC always falls as output increases. In the current example, AFC is $40 per unit when output is 10 units and falls to $3.33 per unit when output increases to 120 units.

b *Average variable cost (AVC):* AVC is the variable cost per unit of output. It is calculated by the equation $AVC = \dfrac{TVC}{q}$, where q is the level of output.

AVC tends to fall as output increases, and then to start to rise again as the output continues to increase. This is explained by the hypothesis of eventually diminishing average returns. As more of the variable factors are applied to the fixed factors, the output per unit of the variable factor eventually falls, and so the cost per unit of output eventually begins to rise. In the current example AVC is $20 per unit when output is 10 units, falls to $11.11 per unit when output rises to 90 units and then increases to $13.33 when output continues to rise to 120 units.

c *Average total cost (ATC):* ATC is the total cost per unit of output. It is equal to AFC plus AVC. It is calculated by the equation
$ATC = \dfrac{TC}{q}$, where q is the level of output.

As with AVC, ATC tends to fall as output increases, and then to start to rise again as the output continues to increase. In the current example ATC is $60 per unit when output is 10 units, falls to $15.24 per unit when output rises to 105 units and then increases to $16.67 when output continues to rise to 120 units.

3 *Marginal cost (MC):* MC is the increase in total cost of producing an extra unit of output. It is calculated by the equation:

$$MC = \frac{\Delta TC}{\Delta q}$$, where ΔTC is the change in total cost and Δq is the

change in the level of output.

MC tends to fall as output increases, and then to start to rise again as the output continues to increase. This is explained by the hypothesis of eventually diminishing marginal returns. As more of the variable factors are applied to the fixed factors, the extra output from each additional unit of the variable factor added eventually falls, and so the extra cost per unit of output eventually begins to rise. In the current example MC is $20 when output rises from 0 to 10 units, falls to $8.00 when output rises from 45 to 70 units and then increases to $40.00 when output continues to rise and goes up from 115 to 120 units.

The average and marginal cost curves from our example are shown in Figure 7.4.

It is important to recognise the relationship between the ATC, AVC, and MC curves. Quite simply, the MC curve cuts the AVC and ATC curves at their lowest points. This is a mathematical relationship. AFC falls as output increases and, since it is the difference between ATC and AVC, the vertical gap between ATC and AVC gets smaller as output grows.

We have seen how to calculate the different types of average and marginal costs and draw the curves that represent the data. When economists draw costs curves to illustrate a general position, they draw them as shown in Figure 7.5:

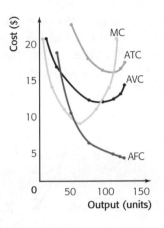

Figure 7.4 Short-run AFC, AVC, ATC, and MC curves

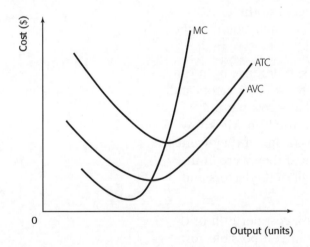

Figure 7.5 A general diagram showing short-run ATC, AVC, and MC

The long run

Definition
The long run is that period of time in which all factors of production are variable, but the state of technology is fixed. All planning takes place in the long run.

We have already said that the long run is the planning stage. When planning in the long run, an entrepreneur is free to adjust the quantity of all of the factors of production that are used and is only restrained by the current level of technology.

This means that in the long-run, we look at what happens to costs when all of the factors of production are increased in order to increase output. What we find is rather different in theory to practice. In theory, the long-run average cost curve (LRAC) is an "envelope" curve, i.e. it envelops an infinite number of short-run average cost (SRAC) curves. This relationship is shown below in Figure 7.6.

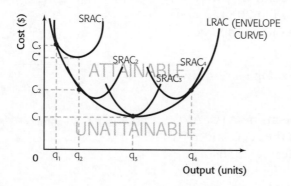

Figure 7.6 The LRAC curve and short-run average cost curves

Let us assume that the firm in Figure 7.6 is producing an output of q_1 at a cost per unit of c_1. They are operating on the short-run average cost curve $SRAC_1$. (Remember that all production takes place in the short run.) c_1 is the lowest possible cost of producing the output, since it is a point on the SRAC curve that is tangent to the LRAC curve. Thus this single point from $SRAC_1$ is also a single point on the LRAC curve.

If demand is increased and the firm now wishes to produce q_2, it can do so in the short run by simply employing more variable factors and moving along $SRAC_1$ until q_2 is being produced at a cost per unit of C^*. This is a lower cost per unit than before, but the firm will know that they could produce this output even more cheaply if they were able to alter all of their factors of production, i.e. if they were in the long run. Thus they will plan ahead to change all of the factors and will eventually move to $SRAC_2$.

Now they will be producing an output of q_2 at a cost per unit of C_2. They are operating on $SRAC_2$, where C_2 is the lowest possible cost of producing the desired output, q_2, since it is again a point on the SRAC curve that is tangential to the LRAC curve. This single point on $SRAC_2$ is another single point on the LRAC curve.

The whole LRAC curve is made up of an infinite number of single points from SRAC curves. These curves would represent all of the possible combinations of fixed and variable factors that could be used to produce different levels of output for this firm.

The LRAC curve is the boundary between unit cost levels that are attainable by the firm and unit cost levels that are unattainable. If possible, the firm would wish to produce different output levels at points on the LRAC curve in order to minimise their cost per unit of output. This may not, of course, always be possible in the short run.

When long-run unit costs are falling as output increases, we say that the firm is experiencing increasing returns to scale. This means that a given percentage increase in all factors of production will lead to a greater percentage increase in output, thus reducing long-run average costs.

When long-run average costs are constant as output increases, we say that the firm is experiencing constant returns to scale. This means that a given percentage increase in all factors of production will lead to the same percentage increase in output, thus leaving long-run average costs the same.

When long-run average cost is rising as output increases, we say that the firm is experiencing decreasing returns to scale. This means that a given percentage increase in all factors of production will lead to a smaller percentage increase in output, thus increasing long-run average costs.

We need to consider why the long-run costs may increase or decrease as output increases. There are two factors to be considered:

1 *Economies of scale:* Economies of scale are any decreases in long-run average costs that come about when a firm alters all of its factors of production in order to increase its scale of output. Economies of scale lead to the firm experiencing increasing returns to scale. There are a number of different economies of scale that may benefit a firm as it increases the scale of its output.

   a *Specialisation:* In small firms there are few, if any, managers and they have to take on many different roles, often roles for which they are not the best candidates. This may lead to higher unit costs. As firms grow they are able to have their management specialise in individual areas of expertise, such as production, finance, or marketing, and thus be more efficient.

   b *Division of labour:* This is breaking a production process down into small activities that workers can perform repeatedly and efficiently. As firms get bigger and demand increases, they are often able to start to break down their production processes, use division of labour, and reduce their unit costs. A good example of this would be workers on assembly lines, where they each have a position by a conveyor belt and add parts to a product as it moves down the conveyor belt. Motor cars and television sets, among other things, have been produced by this sort of method.

   c *Bulk buying:* As firms increase in scale they are often able to negotiate discounts with their suppliers that they would not have received when they were smaller. The cost of their inputs is then reduced, which will reduce their unit costs of production.

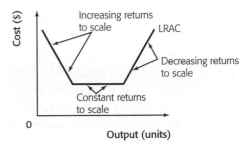

Figure 7.7 Increasing, constant, and decreasing returns to scale

d *Financial economies:* Large firms can raise financial capital (money) more cheaply than small firms. Banks tend to charge a lower interest rate to larger firms, since the larger firms are considered to be less of a risk than the smaller firms, and are less likely to fail to repay their loans.

e *Transport economies:* Large firms making bulk orders may be charged less for delivery costs than smaller firms. Also, as firms grow they may be able to have their own transport fleet, which will then cost less because they will not be paying other firms, who will include a profit margin, to transport their products.

f *Large machines:* Some machinery is too large to be owned and used by a small producer, for example a combine harvester for a small farmer. In this case, small farmers have to hire the use of the equipment from suppliers who will then charge a price that includes a profit margin for the supplier. However, once a farm can increase to a certain size it becomes feasible to have its own combine harvester, reducing the unit costs of production.

g *Promotional economies:* Almost all firms attempt to promote their products by using advertising, or sales promotion, or personal selling, or publicity, or a combination of the above. The costs of promotion tend not to increase by the same proportion as output. If a firm doubles its output, it is unlikely that it will double its expenditure on promotion methods, such as sales promotion and advertising. Thus the cost of promotion per unit of output falls. This situation also applies to other fixed costs, such as insurance costs or the costs of providing security for the production unit.

2 *Diseconomies of scale:* Diseconomies of scale are any increases in long-run average costs that come about when a firm alters all of its factors of production in order to increase its scale of output. Diseconomies of scale lead to the firm experiencing decreasing returns to scale. There are a number of different diseconomies of scale that may afflict a firm as it increases the scale of its output:

a *Control and communication problems:* As firms grow in scale, the management will find it harder to control and coordinate the activities of the firm and this is said to lead, eventually, to inefficiency and increases in the unit costs of production. In the same way, greater size leads to a huge increase in the need for effective communication and it is suggested that there will be more communication breakdowns as firms increase in size, eventually causing unit cost increases.

b *Alienation and loss of identity:* As firms grow, it is suggested that both workers and managers may begin to feel that they are only a very small part of a very big organisation. They begin to think that what they do does not matter and they start to lose a sense of belonging and loyalty. If this happens, then it is likely that the workers and managers will begin to work less hard and become less productive, and this will tend to force up the unit costs of production.

All of the above economies and diseconomies of scale relate to the unit cost decreases or increases that might be encountered by a single firm. They are known as internal economies and diseconomies of scale.

There is another group of economies and diseconomies that come about when the size of the whole industry increases and this has an effect on the unit costs of the individual firms. They are known as external economies and diseconomies of scale.

An example of external economies of scale might be where the growth of an industry in a certain geographical area leads to local universities and colleges starting up courses that relate to the skills required in the industry. The graduates of these courses would be ready trained for the firms in the industry, at no direct cost to the firms, and so would make the firms more efficient, reducing unit costs. An example of this could be colleges offering metallurgy courses in an area like Sheffield in the UK where one of the main industries is the large-scale production of cutlery.

An example of external diseconomies of scale might be where the rapid growth of an industry leads to more competition among individual firms to acquire raw materials, capital and qualified labour. Such competition may force up the prices of the factors so forcing up the unit costs of the firms in the industry.

● ● ● ● ● ● ● ● ● ● ● ● ● ● ● ● ● ●

Student workpoint 7.2

Be a thinker

On page 76 we looked at a burger stand run by a young entrepreneur called Ben. If demand for the burgers continues to be strong, and Ben is facing diminishing marginal returns, what should be his strategy in terms of the long run?

Final note on cost theory

You should always remember that:

- Short-run cost curves are U-shaped because of the hypothesis of diminishing returns. The existence of eventually diminishing average returns explains the shape of the short-run average variable cost curve and the existence of eventually diminishing marginal returns explains the shape of the short-run marginal cost curve.

- Long-run cost curves are U-shaped, in theory, because of the existence of economies and diseconomies of scale.

- In reality, economists have not yet found evidence of a firm becoming so large that the diseconomies of scale start to outweigh the economies of scale in the long run. Actual long-run cost curves may be drawn as shown in Figure 7.8.

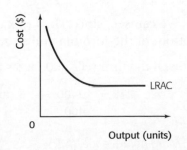

Figure 7.8 A long-run average cost curve in reality

Theory of Knowledge

Deductive and inductive logic

Empirical evidence suggests that firms benefit from economies of scale up to a certain level of output. Economies of scale reduce long-run unit costs. *Ceteris paribus*, firms will find that their profit per unit of output rises if they increase the amount of factors of production up to a certain level of output.

1 Distinguish between deductive reasoning and inductive reasoning.

2 Is the example above a piece of deductive reasoning or inductive reasoning?

3 Do you think that most economic reasoning is deductive or inductive? Why?

Revenue theory

Revenue is the income that a firm receives from selling its products, goods, and services, over a certain time period.

Measurement of revenue

Revenue may be measured in three ways:

1 Total revenue (TR)

TR is the total amount of money that a firm receives from selling a certain amount of a good or service in a given time period. It is calculated by using the formula:

$$TR = p \times q$$

where p is the price that the good or service sells for and q is the quantity of the good or service sold in the time period being considered.

If a firm sells 400 pizzas per week, at a price of $6 per pizza, then:

$$TR = \$6 \times 400 = \$2,400 \text{ per week}$$

2 Average revenue (AR)

AR is the revenue that a firm receives per unit of its sales. It is calculated using the formula:

$$AR = \frac{TR}{q} = \frac{p \times q}{q} = p$$

As we can see, since TR is (p **x** q), q is common to the top and bottom of the formula and so AR is the same as p.

Thus, if the firm sells 400 pizzas at a price of $6 per pizza, then:

$$AR = \frac{\$2400}{400} = \$6 \text{ (the same as the price per unit)}$$

3 Marginal revenue (MR)

MR is the extra revenue that a firm gains when it sells one more unit of a product in a given time period. It is calculated by using the formula:

$$MR = \frac{\Delta TR}{\Delta q}, \text{ where } \Delta \text{ means "the change in".}$$

Thus, if our pizza firm lowered the price of a pizza to $5 and found

$$MR = \frac{\$2500 - \$2400}{100} = \frac{\$100}{100} = \$1$$

that their weekly sales rose to 500 pizzas, then:

The extra revenue gained from selling an extra unit is $1.

Revenue curves and output

We now need to consider what happens to a firm's revenue as output increases. We shall consider two different situations.

1 Revenue when price does not change with output (when elasticity of demand is infinite)

If a firm does not have to lower price as output increases and it wishes to sell more of its product, then it faces a perfectly elastic demand curve. This situation only happens in theory, but it is very useful to economists when they are building their models of how markets work and they start with the theoretical market form of perfect competition (see Chapter 8).

A firm that has a perfectly elastic demand curve might have the revenue figures shown in Table 7.3.

Price ($)	Quantity demanded	Total revenue ($)	Average revenue ($)	Marginal revenue ($)
5	1	5	5	5
5	2	10	5	5
5	3	15	5	5
5	4	20	5	5
5	5	25	5	5
5	6	30	5	5
5	7	35	5	5

Table 7.3 Possible revenue figures for a firm with a perfectly elastic demand curve

We can assume that the firm is very small in terms of the size of the whole industry, and that they can increase their output without affecting total industry supply, and thus price, in any significant way. Therefore the firm can sell all that it produces at the same price.

If we graph the revenues, we will get the curves shown in Figure 7.9(a) and (b).

In these graphs, we can see that, when price elasticity of demand is perfectly elastic, then price, average revenue, marginal revenue, and demand are all the same. In this case, they are all $5.

Total revenue increases at a constant rate as output increases, since each extra sale adds $5 to total revenue. Marginal revenue is constant at $5.

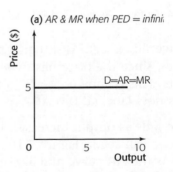

(a) *AR & MR when PED = infini*

Figure 7.9 Curves for PED = infinity

2 Revenue when price falls as output increases (when the demand curve is downward sloping, i.e. when elasticity of demand falls as output increases)
When we look at what happens to TR, AR, and MR as price falls when output decreases we get a very different set of curves from the ones above. If a firm wishes to sell more of its output and it can control the price at which it sells, then it will have to lower the price if it wants to increase demand. In simpler terms, it will face a downward-sloping demand curve. An example of this, and the revenue figures relating to it, is shown in Table 7.4.

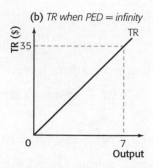

Figure 7.9 Curves for PED = infinity

Price ($)	Quantity demanded	Total revenue ($)	Average revenue ($)	Marginal revenue ($)	PED
50	0	0			
				45	
45	2	90	45		9.00
				35	
40	4	160	40		4.00
				25	
35	6	210	35		2.33
				15	
30	8	240	30		1.50
				5	
25	10	250	25		1.00
				-5	
20	12	240	20		0.67
				-15	
15	14	210	15		0.43
				-25	
10	16	160	10		0.25
				-35	
5	18	90	5		0.11
				-45	
0	20	0			

Table 7.4 Output, revenue, and PED figures for a firm with a normal demand curve

As we would expect, AR is equal to price and so it falls as output increases, since the price has to be lowered in order to sell more products. This is shown clearly in Figure 7.10, where the demand curve is now labelled D = AR.

MR also falls as output increases, but at a greater rate than AR. In fact, as we can see in Figure 7.10, the MR curve is twice as steeply sloping as the AR curve and also goes below the x-axis. This is a relationship that holds for all downward-sloping AR curves and the MR curves that relate to them.

MR is below AR because in order to sell more products the firm has to lower the price of all products sold, losing revenue on the ones that could have been sold at a higher price in order to get the revenue from the extra sales.

For example, in Table 7.4, when price is dropped from $40 to $35, the quantity demanded increases from 4 units to 6. Before the price drop, the TR was $160 ($40 **x** 4). After the price drop, TR becomes $210 ($35 **x** 6).

$$\text{The MR is } \$25 \; \left(\frac{\Delta TR}{\Delta q} = \frac{50}{2} = 25\right).$$

There are two events affecting the TR. First, two extra units of the product are sold at a price of $35 and so TR rises by $70. However, in order to do this, the price of the 4 units that could have been sold for $40 has been dropped to $35 and so there is a loss of revenue of $20 (4 **x** $5). The overall effect is an increase in revenue of $70 – $20 = $50.

For a normal, downward-sloping demand curve, TR rises at first but will eventually start to fall as output increases. This is because the extra revenue gained from dropping price and selling more units is outweighed by the loss in revenue from the units that were being sold at a higher price and now have to be sold at the lower price.

For example, in Table 7.4, when price is dropped from $15 to $10, the quantity demanded increases from 14 units to 16. Before the price drop, the TR was $210 ($15 **x** 14). After the price drop, TR becomes $160 ($10 **x** 16).

$$\text{The MR is } -\$25 \; \left(\frac{\Delta TR}{\Delta q} = \frac{-50}{2} = -25\right).$$

The negative MR means that TR will fall. MR is negative because, when the price is lowered, two extra units of the product are sold at a price of $10 each, but the price of the 14 units that could have been sold for $15 has been dropped to $10, and so there is a loss of revenue of $70 (14 **x** $5). The overall effect is a fall in total revenue of $20 – $70 = –$50.

There are some very important relationships between price elasticity of demand, MR, AR, and TR that we can identify from Figure 7.10. They are most easily explained by a logic tree, using information already discovered in the study of price elasticity and revenue.

This knowledge of the relationship between the value of PED for a demand curve and TR is very useful for firms when they are trying to assess the impact that a change in the price of their product will have upon the total revenue that they receive.

If the firm raises price and demand is inelastic then the firm will find that total revenue will increase, because the increase in price will see a relatively smaller fall in the quantity demanded.

However, if the firm raises price and demand is inelastic then the firm will find that total revenue will decrease, because the increase in price will cause a relatively larger fall in the quantity demanded.

So, if a firm knows whether their demand is elastic or inelastic, they will know what pricing policy to adopt to increase their revenue.

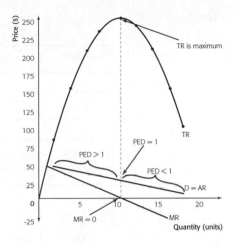

Figure 7.10 The relationship between D, AR, MR, TR, and PED for a normal demand curve

2 Microeconomics

The basic rules are:

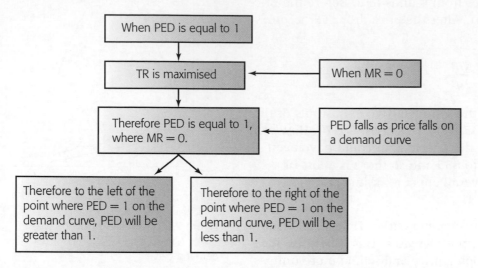

Figure 7.11 A logic tree explaining the varying values of PED on a demand curve

1 When PED is elastic any firm wishing to increase revenue should lower its price.

2 When PED is inelastic any firm wishing to increase revenue should raise its price.

3 When PED is unity then any firm wishing to increase revenue should leave the price unchanged, since revenue is already maximised.

Student workpoint 7.3

Be a thinker—solve the problems and illustrate the outcomes

Here are some figures for the price and quantity demanded of a product:

Price ($)	Quantity demanded	Total revenue ($)	Average revenue ($)	Marginal revenue ($)	PED
20	1				
				+16	
18	2				
16	3				
14	4				
12	5		12		
10	6				
8	7				
6	8				
4	9	36			

2 Microeconomics

Student workpoint 7.3

1 Copy out the table and fill in the missing values in the other columns.

2 On a piece of graph paper, draw a vertical axis, labelled Price ($), going from −12 to +60. Then add a horizontal axis, labelled Quantity Demanded, going from 0 to 10.

3 Plot the demand curve on the graph (i.e. plot price against quantity demanded). Label the curve D. Plot the Average Revenue curve. What do you notice? Now add "= AR".

4 Plot the Total Revenue curve.

5 Plot the Marginal Revenue curve, remembering to plot it at the half-way marks on the horizontal axis.

6 Using the PED figures that you have calculated, try to identify:
- the elastic region of the demand curve
- the inelastic region of the demand curve
- the point where PED = 1.

7 Complete the following sentences:
- In the elastic region of the demand curve, as price falls, total revenue _____.
- In the inelastic region of the demand curve, as price falls, total revenue _____.
- Total revenue is maximized where PED is equal to _____ and where the marginal revenue is _____.

Assessment advice: the use of diagrams

In workpoint 7.3, you drew an important diagram showing the relationship between demand, average revenue, marginal revenue, total revenue, and PED. It should look much like Figure 7.10.

It is very helpful if you are confident in your understanding of these relationships and if you can draw the diagram showing the relationships without any figures. This is worth practising!

Profit theory

An economist and an accountant were talking about the accounts of a company. The accountant said that the owner of the firm, Nermin, would be very happy, because the profit for the year was $80,000. The economist, however, looked at the same set of figures and said that the owner would be satisfied, but only just.

"Why is that?" asked the accountant. "Profit is total revenue minus total cost and when I work that out, the profit figure is very healthy."

"Yes," said the economist, "I agree with your definition of profit, but what you need to understand is that we do not take the same view on how to calculate costs. As an economist, I include one cost, the most important one that the firm faces, that you do not."

"Which cost is that?" asked the accountant.

"I include the opportunity cost of the owner of the firm, the entrepreneur," said the economist. "If an owner does not manage to cover his or her opportunity cost in the long run, then they will close the firm down and move on to their next best alternative occupation. Thus the opportunity cost is the most important one for the firm to cover. It is the difference between survival and non-survival."

"In Nermin's case," said the economist, "I know that she expects to make $80,000 per year, since she could earn the same amount if she closed down the firm and went back to her old job as a marketing manager. That means that she is satisfied with what she has made this year, but no more."

The conversation above explains how economists measure profit.

Total profit = Total revenue − total cost (fixed, variable, and opportunity cost)

From this point forward, we will assume that we are now economists and that when we discuss total cost we are including opportunity cost.

If total revenue is equal to total cost, we say that a firm is making normal profit. If total revenue is greater than total cost, then we say that the firm is making abnormal profit. If total revenue is less than total cost, then we say that the firm is making losses.

In Table 7.5, we can see the three situations.

	Firm A	Firm B	Firm C
Total revenue ($)	200,000	200,000	200,000
Total fixed cost ($)	40,000	40,000	40,000
Total variable cost ($)	80,000	100,000	120,000
Opportunity cost ($)	60,000	60,000	60,000
Total cost ($)	180,000	200,000	220,000

Table 7.5 Revenue and cost information for one year for firms A, B, and C

Firm A is making abnormal profit of $20,000. This means that the revenue earned by the firm is not only covering all the costs, but is in fact $20,000 more. This will make the entrepreneur happy, as she was expecting to cover her opportunity costs of $60,000 and in fact gets $80,000.

Firm B is making normal profit. The revenue earned by the firm exactly covers all of the costs. The entrepreneur will be satisfied.

Firm C is making losses. Although an accountant would say that the firm is making a profit of $40,000 ($200,000 − $160,000), the entrepreneur will not be happy since fixed and variable costs are covered, but opportunity cost is not being covered. The entrepreneur will close down the firm, moving to the entrepreneur's next best occupation.

We now need to consider three different scenarios:

1 the shut-down price

2 the break-even price

3 the profit-maximising level of output.

The shut-down price

It is not unusual to see firms continue to operate, in the short run, even if they are making a loss. It is also not unusual to see firms shut down for a short period of time and then open up again. Let us look at these two situations.

If it wants to, a firm may close down, temporarily, in the short run and produce nothing. If it does this, then it will only lose its total fixed costs, the costs that are unavoidable, such as rent or interest repayments on loans. To make things easier, we will now include opportunity cost as a fixed cost and not show it on its own, so it is also not being covered. This may be better than producing and not getting enough revenue to cover the variable costs, thus losing the fixed costs and the part of the variable costs that have not been covered.

This can be best explained by using an example. Suppose that there are three firms, all producing comics, and all making losses at the moment. The firms are called Archie, Batcat, and Charlie. Their monthly revenue and cost figures are given in Table 7.6.

	Archie	Batcat	Charlie
Total revenue ($)	80,000	120,000	150,000
Total fixed costs (inc opportunity cost) ($)	100,000	100,000	100,000
Total variable costs ($)	100,000	120,000	140,000
Total costs ($)	200,000	220,000	240,000
Loss ($)	120,000	100,000	90,000

Table 7.6 Revenue and cost figures for Archie, Batcat, and Charlie

Archie would be better not producing at all in the short run and closing down temporarily. This is because the revenue gained has failed to cover all of the variable costs, so Archie loses the $20,000 of variable costs that are not covered by the total revenue and all of the $100,000 of fixed costs. So by producing, Archie has lost $120,000, whereas it would only lose $100,000 of fixed costs if it did not produce.

Batcat loses $100,000 whether it produces or not. The revenue gained means that the variable costs are just covered, so they will lose the fixed costs, $100,000, whether they produce or not. In this situation, it is likely that Batcat will continue to produce in order to maintain the continuity of production, thus pleasing customers, and to maintain the employment of workers and the usage of inputs, thus pleasing the workforce and the suppliers.

Charlie loses $90,000 by producing, since their total revenue covers their variable costs and also contributes $10,000 towards their fixed costs. If they did not produce then Charlie would lose their fixed costs of $100,000. So Charlie will produce in the short run.

However, all three firms are making losses in the short run and they cannot do this for ever. Whether they produce or not in the short run, the firms need to plan ahead in the long run in order to change their combinations of factors and to devise a situation where they are able to cover all of their costs and make normal profits. If they cannot do this then they will have to close down permanently.

From this example, we can derive a definition for the shut-down price.

Definition

The shut-down price is the level of price that enables a firm to cover its variable costs in the short run, i.e. it is the price where price = average variable costs. If price does not cover average variable costs, then the firm will shut down in the short run.

2 Microeconomics

In Figure 7.12, the shut-down price is P. At this price, the firm is able to cover its variable costs in the short run, because P = avc, and so is only losing its fixed costs. At any price below P, the firm will shut down in the short run.

Although this may seem like theory, there are in fact many real examples of this behaviour. In Vienna, Austria, there is an ice cream store that shuts down each October, because the demand for its products is low over the winter and so the revenue earned would not be enough to cover even its variable costs. In April each year, it opens up again, when demand is beginning to rise and it makes impressive profits until the end of September. The act of temporarily closing down, because it cannot cover its variable costs, is a good example of a firm that is not reaching its shut-down price in the short run.

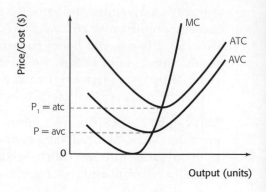

Figure 7.12 A general diagram showing short run ATC, AVC, and MC

The break-even price

The break-even price is the price at which a firm is able to make normal profit in the long run. This means that it will break even, covering all of its costs, including the opportunity cost.

The break-even price is the level of price that enables a firm to cover all of its costs in the long run, i.e. it is the price where price = average total costs. If price does not cover average total costs in the long run, then the firm will shut down for good.

In Figure 7.12, the break-even price is P_1. At this price, the firm is able to cover its total costs, because P_1 = atc, and so all costs are covered.

The profit-maximising level of output

Economists usually assume that the main aim of a firm is to maximise profits. If this is the case, then firms need to know what level of output they have to produce in order to achieve maximum profits.

If a firm finds that at its present level of output the cost of producing another unit (MC) is less than the revenue that the unit would bring in (MR), it is clear that the firm could increase its profits by producing more. Wherever the firm finds that MR>MC, it should increase production.

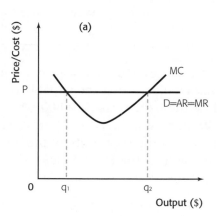

We can see the marginal cost and marginal revenue situation for a firm with a perfectly elastic demand curve in Figure 7.13.

As we can see in Figure 7.13(a), the MC curve cuts the MR curve at two points. The first point where MC = MR, q_1, is the point of profit minimisation (loss maximisation). The firm has made a loss on every unit produced up to this level of output, because MC is greater than MR. From q_1 to q_2, the firm makes a profit on every extra unit produced, because the MR is greater than the MC. As long as the profit made between q_1 and q_2 is greater than the loss made on the first q_1 units, then the firm will be making abnormal profits. Any unit that is produced beyond q_2 will make a loss, because MC would again be above MR. So if the firm produces more than q_2, the level of abnormal profit will begin to fall. It is at q_2 where profits are maximised.

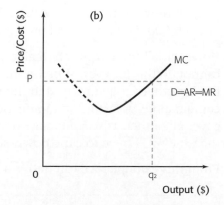

Figure 7.13 Revenue and costs for a firm with a perfectly elastic demand curve

Because profit minimisation is not what a firm would want, to avoid confusion the left hand part of the MC curve is normally omitted in diagrams. This means that only the profit maximising output, q_2, is shown, as in Figure 7.13 (b). As a general rule, we can say that:

If a firm wishes to maximise its profits, it should produce at the level of output where Marginal Cost (MC) cuts Marginal Revenue (MR) from below.

The profit-maximising output for a normal demand and MR curve is shown in Figure 7.14.

Profit is maximised by producing where MC = MR, at a level of output of q. To find the price, we look at what consumers are willing to pay for this quantity. This is shown on the demand curve. It is found by going from q up to the demand curve and then across to the y-axis.

In order to show a measurable amount of profit on a diagram, i.e. a simple shape like a rectangle, the average cost curve (AC) is added to the diagram.

You must remember to make sure that the MC curve cuts the AC curve at the lowest point on the AC.

This is shown in Figure 7.15.

The profit-maximising output is q and the price is p. The profit per unit of producing q is the difference between AR and AC. Thus the profit per unit is a – b. Since q units are produced, the total abnormal profit is the shaded area, ab **x** 0Q.

Whether an abnormal profit is made will depend upon the position of the AC curve. The AC curve is a student's best friend! This is because it can be moved around to show what we want, i.e. abnormal profit, normal profit, or losses. This is shown in Figure 7.16.

If the average cost is at AC, then the diagram shows an abnormal profit of pabc. If the average cost is represented by AC_1, then normal profit is being made, because $p = c_1$ and so there is no abnormal profit rectangle. If average cost is shown by AC_2, then a loss is being made and it is represented by the rectangle pc_2da.

Final note on profit theory
In reality, firms may not always have the main aim of maximising profits. Not everyone has studied economics! Other aims followed by entrepreneurs may be:

- *Revenue maximisation:* Entrepreneurs often measure success by the amount of revenue that they make. If this is the case, then they may attempt to maximise their sales revenue by producing where the marginal revenue is zero. They will actually produce above the profit-maximising level of output. (See Figure 7.9.)

- *Sales maximisation:* Entrepreneurs sometimes believe that the more they sell, the better they will do. If this is the case, then they will produce beyond the profit-maximising level of output and not realise that they could actually make more profit by charging a higher price and selling less. Another possibility may be that a

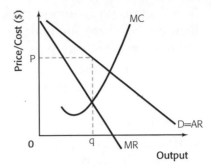

Figure 7.14 The profit-maximising level of output for a normal demand curve

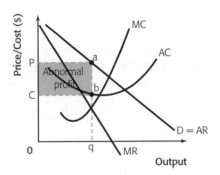

Figure 7.15 Showing an area of profit using the AC curve

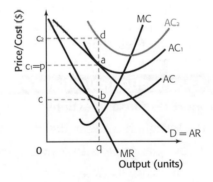

Figure 7.16 Using AC to show different profit and loss situations

firm attempts to maximise sales in the short run, in order to gain high market share and to drive other firms out of the industry. Having done this, they may then aim to maximise profits.

● *Maximising employment:* Entrepreneurs sometimes measure their success by the number of workers that they employ, losing sight of the fact that having a larger workforce does not necessarily mean that profits will be greater.

● *Environmental aims:* Entrepreneurs who are interested in protecting the environment will sometimes be prepared to pay higher prices for raw materials in order to ensure that their raw materials are from a source that is environmentally friendly or from a source that does not involve the exploitation of labour. For example, they may buy Fairtrade products, at a higher cost, in order to support suppliers from developing countries.

● *Satisficing:* There are now economic theories that doubt whether entrepreneurs ever, in reality, attempt to maximise profits. They claim that what entrepreneurs actually do is to "satisfice". They suggest that, if people own firms, they will work hard enough to make a reasonable living (cover their opportunity costs), but will not really, in most cases, push themselves further. They also suggest that, in many cases, firms are run by people who do not actually own them. An example of this would be a firm owned by shareholders, who are not involved in running the company, and so managed by employed non-owners. In this case, the managers do not have a great deal to gain if the firm makes the maximum profits possible. It is likely that the managers will make enough profit to keep the owners of the firm happy, so keeping their jobs, but no more. They will "satisfice".

Examination questions

Short response questions

1 Distinguish between the concepts of the short run and the long run. *[10 marks]*

2 Using an appropriate diagram, explain the concept of diminishing marginal returns. *[10 marks]*

3 Distinguish between an economist's definition of profit and an accountant's definition of profit. *[10 marks]*

4 Using a diagram, explain how a firm might be able to stay in business in the short run, even if it is not covering all of its costs. *[10 marks]*

5 Explain three sources of economies of scale. *[10 marks]*

6 Explain two goals of firms other than to maximise profits. *[10 marks]*

There are no examples of longer essay questions at this point as there is little evaluation that is possible at this stage.

8 Perfect competition

By the end of this chapter, you should be able to:

- explain the assumptions of perfect competition
- distinguish between the demand curve for the industry and for the firm in perfect competition
- explain how the firm maximises profit in perfect competition
- explain and illustrate short-run profit and loss situations in perfect competition
- explain and illustrate the long-run equilibrium in perfect competition
- explain and illustrate the movement from short run to long run in perfect competition
- define and illustrate productive efficiency
- define and illustrate allocative efficiency
- explain and illustrate productive and allocative efficiency in the short and long run in perfect competition.

As we already know, social scientists, especially economists, are model builders. We use models to try to explain how things work and what might be the possible outcomes of certain economic situations.

Perfect competition is a model used as the starting point to explain how firms operate. It is a theoretical model, based upon some very precise assumptions. However, although it is purely theoretical, it is very important because once we have built our model of a perfectly competitive market we can then begin to relax the theoretical assumptions that we have made and move towards models of markets that are much more realistic.

The assumptions of perfect competition

Perfect competition is based upon a number of assumptions.

- The industry is made up of a very large number of firms.
- Each firm is so small, relative to the size of the industry, that it is not capable of altering its own output to have a noticeable effect upon the output of the industry as a whole. This means that a firm cannot affect the supply curve of the industry and so cannot affect the price of the product. Individual firms have to sell at whatever price is set by demand and supply in the industry as a whole. We say that the individual firms are "price-takers".
- The firms all produce exactly identical products. Their goods are "homogeneous". It is not possible to distinguish between a good produced in one firm and a good produced in another. There are no brand names and there is no marketing to attempt to make goods different from each other.

● Firms are completely free to enter or leave the industry. This means that the firms already in the industry do not have the ability to stop new firms from entering it and are also free to leave the industry, if they so wish. We say that there are no barriers to entry or barriers to exit.

● All producers and consumers have a perfect knowledge of the market. The producers are fully aware of market prices, costs in the industry, and the workings of the market. The consumers are fully aware of prices in the market, the quality of products, and the availability of the goods.

Although we say that it is completely theoretical, there are some industries in the world that get quite close to being perfectly competitive markets. The industries most often used as examples by economists are usually agricultural markets.

For example, let us consider the growing of wheat in the European Union (EU). There are some large wheat farms in the EU, but they are very small in relation to the whole wheat-growing industry. An individual farm could increase its output many times over without having a noticeable effect on the total supply of wheat in the EU. Thus a single farm is not able to affect the price of wheat in the EU, since it cannot shift the industry supply curve. The farm has to sell at whatever the existing industry price is. In addition, wheat is wheat, and so there is no way to tell one farm's wheat from another.

So far so good for the assumptions of perfect competition. However, although firms are relatively free to enter or leave the wheat industry, there are significant costs in doing either and these may affect the decisions of firms. Also, although information is fairly open in the industry it is unlikely that producers and consumers will have "perfect knowledge". We can say that the wheat industry in the EU may be close to being a perfectly competitive market, but is not precisely one.

The demand curves for the industry and the firm in perfect competition
We have said that the individual firms in perfect competition will be price-takers, since they cannot affect the price of the industry and so must sell at whatever the market price is. This means that we can make certain assumptions about the demand curves for both the firm and the industry.

2 Microeconomics

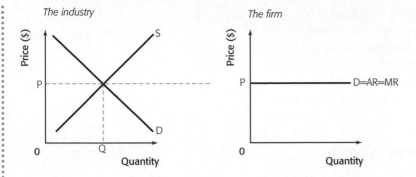

Figure 8.1 The demand curves for the industry and the firm in perfect competition

As we can see in Figure 8.1, the industry in perfect competition will face normal demand and supply curves. We would expect producers to wish to supply more at higher prices and we would expect consumers to demand less as price rises. We would expect demand to be downward sloping and supply to be upward sloping. The industry price would therefore be P and the quantity demanded would be Q.

For the individual firms we know that they will have to sell at the industry price, P, because they are price-takers. If they try to sell at a higher price then consumers will simply buy the product from another firm, since the goods are homogeneous and so there is no difference in looks or quality. If they sell at the industry price the firm can sell as much as it wants, because as it increases output it does not affect the industry supply curve and so it does not alter the industry price.

If the firm can sell all that it wishes at the price P then it must face a perfectly elastic demand at that price. In Figure 8.1 we can see that the firm derives its price of P from the equilibrium price in the industry, where the industry supply equals the industry demand. This is another explanation of the term "price-taker", because the firm has to take the price set in the industry.

Profit maximisation for the firm in perfect competition

Firms maximise profits when they produce at the level of output where MC = MR. For perfect competition, we now have to add the marginal cost curve, shown in Figure 8.2.

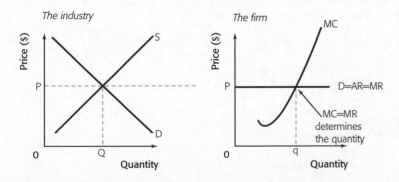

Figure 8.2 The profit-maximising level of output in perfect competition

We can see that the firm takes the price P from the industry and, because the demand is perfectly elastic, P=D=AR=MR. Profit is maximised where MC=MR, which is at the level of output q. We must remember that although the scale of the price axes is the same for the firm and the industry, this is not the case for output. The quantity q is very small in relation to the total industry output, Q, and it would not even register on the output axis for the industry. If it could, then it would be large enough to shift the supply curve and thus alter the industry price.

Possible short-run profit and loss situations in perfect competition

In the short run in perfect competition, there are two possible profit/loss situations:

1 *Short-run abnormal profits:* In this case, which is shown in Figure 8.3, the firms in the industry are making abnormal profits in the short run. This means that they are more than covering their total costs, including the opportunity costs.

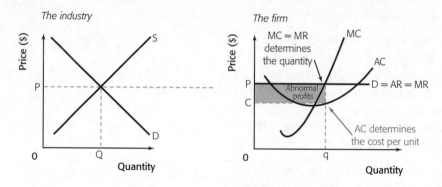

Figure 8.3 Short-run abnormal profits in perfect competition

As we can see in Figure 8.3, the firm is selling at the industry price, P, and is maximising profits by producing at the quantity q, where MC=MR. At q, the cost per unit, average cost, is C, and the revenue per unit, average revenue, is P, so average cost is less than average revenue and the firm is making an abnormal profit of P–C on each unit. The shaded area shows the total abnormal profit.

2 *Short-run losses:* In this case, shown in Figure 8.4, the firms in the industry are making losses in the short run. This means that they are not covering their total costs.

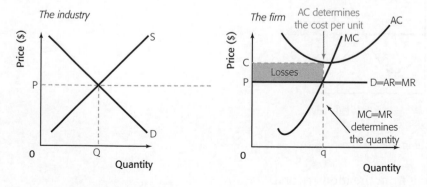

Figure 8.4 Short-run losses in perfect competition

In Figure 8.4 the firm is selling at the industry price, P, and is maximising profits by producing at the quantity q, where MC=MR. However at output q, the cost per unit is C, which is greater than the price and so the firm is making a loss of C–P on each unit. The shaded area shows the total loss. Although making a loss, the firm is still producing at the "profit-maximising" level of output, because any other output would create a greater loss. In effect, they are loss minimising.

The movement from short run to long run in perfect competition

If firms are making either short-run abnormal profits, or short-run losses, other firms begin to react and the situation starts to change until an equilibrium point is reached in the long run.

Short-run abnormal profits to long-run normal profits

Let us look first at the situation of short-run abnormal profits. The process is shown in Figure 8.5. The firm is making abnormal profits shown by the shaded area, but this situation will not continue for long.

Since there is perfect knowledge and no barriers to entry, firms outside of the industry that could also produce the good will start to enter the industry, attracted by the chance to make abnormal profits. At first, this will have no real effect, because the firms are relatively small. However, as more and more firms enter the industry, attracted by the abnormal profits, the industry supply curve will start to shift to the right.

As the industry supply curve starts to shift from S towards S_1, the industry price will begin to fall from P towards P_1. Because the firms in the industry are price-takers, the price that they can charge will start to fall and their demand curves will start to shift downwards. This means that the abnormal profits that they had been making will start to be "competed away".

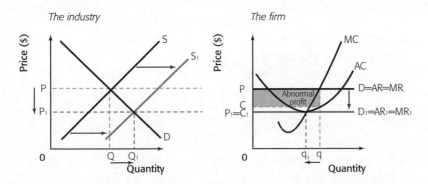

Figure 8.5 The movement from short-run abnormal profit to long-run normal profit

This process will continue as long as there are abnormal profits in the industry. Eventually the industry supply curve reaches S_1, where the price is P_1. At this point, the firms are "taking" the price of P_1 and the demand curve is $D_1 = AR_1 = MR_1$. We now find that the firms are making normal profits with the price per unit equal to the cost per unit, i.e. $P_1 = C_1$. The entrepreneurs of the firms in the industry are satisfied, because they are exactly covering their opportunity costs. However, there is now no abnormal profit to attract more firms into the industry and so the industry is in a long-run equilibrium situation. No one will now enter and no one will now leave. The outcome is a much bigger industry producing Q_1 units, with smaller firms, each producing q_1 units.

Short-run losses to long-run normal profits

Now take the situation of short-run losses. The process is shown in Figure 8.6. As we can see, the firm is making losses shown by the shaded area but this situation will not remain the same.

Some firms in the industry will, after a time, start to leave the industry. At first, this will have no real effect, because the firms are relatively small. However, as more and more firms leave the industry, unable to achieve normal profit, the industry supply curve will start to shift to the left.

As the industry supply curve starts to shift from S towards S_1, the industry price will begin to rise from P towards P_1. As the firms in the industry are price-takers, the price that they can charge will start to rise and their demand curves will start to shift upwards. This means that the losses that they had been making begin to get smaller.

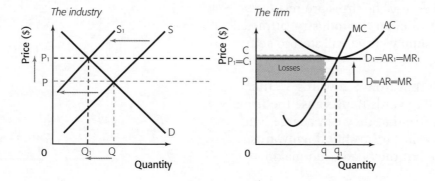

Figure 8.6 The movement from short-run losses to long-run normal profit

This process will continue as long as there are losses being made in the industry. Eventually the industry supply curve reaches S_1, where the price is P_1. At this point, the firms are "taking" the price of P_1 and the demand curve is $D_1=AR_1=MR_1$. We now find that the firms are making normal profits, with the price per unit equal to the cost per unit, i.e. $P_1=C_1$. Now the entrepreneurs of the firms in the industry are satisfied, because they are exactly covering all of their costs, including their opportunity costs. There would be no reason to leave the industry as the firm could not do better elsewhere. However, there is now no abnormal profit to attract more firms into the industry and so the industry is in a long-run equilibrium situation. No one will now enter and no one will now leave. The outcome will be a smaller industry producing only Q_1 units, with slightly larger firms, each producing q_1 units.

Long-run equilibrium in perfect competition

We can conclude that, in the long run, firms in perfect competition will make normal profits. This is because, even if they are making short-run abnormal profits or short-run losses, the industry will adjust with firms entering or leaving the industry until a normal profit situation is reached.

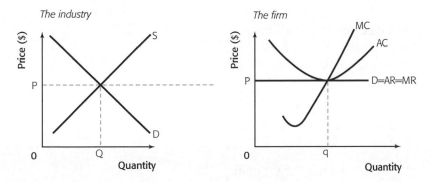

Figure 8.7 Long-run equilibrium in perfect competition

In Figure 8.7, the firms are making normal profits in the long run. They are selling at the price P, which they are taking from the industry. MC is equal to MR so they are maximising profits by producing q, and at that output P is equal to AC so they are making normal profits.

In this situation there is no incentive for firms to enter or leave the industry and so the equilibrium will persist until there is a change in either the industry demand curve or in the costs that the firms face. If this does happen, then firms will be making either short-run abnormal profits or short-run losses and the industry will once again adjust, with firms entering or leaving until long-run equilibrium is restored.

---

student workpoint 8.1

Be a thinker—explain and illustrate

1 Why is a firm in perfect competition a "price-taker"?

2 Draw the following diagrams. Be sure to use a ruler and include accurate labels. Also be sure that your MC curves cross at the minimum of AC.

  a A firm in perfect competition earning abnormal profits

  b A firm in perfect competition making economic losses

  c A firm in perfect competition in its long-run equilibrium earning normal profits

---

Productive and allocative efficiency in perfect competition

Productive efficiency

One of the efficiency measures used by economists is that of productive efficiency. A firm is said to be productively efficient if it produces its product at the lowest possible unit cost (average cost). This is shown in Figure 8.8.

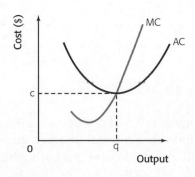

Figure 8.8 Productive efficiency

At the output q, the firm in Figure 8.8 is able to produce at the most efficient level of output, i.e. the lowest average cost of production. This is the cost c. So q is known as the productively efficient level of output.

We know from earlier in the chapter that MC always cuts AC at its lowest point, and so we can say that the productively efficient level is where:

$$MC = AC$$

Productive efficiency is important in economics, because if a firm is producing at the productively efficient level of output then they are combining their resources as efficiently as possible and resources are not being wasted by inefficient use.

Allocative efficiency
This measure of efficiency is sometimes also called the socially optimum level of output.

Allocative efficiency occurs where suppliers are producing the optimal mix of goods and services required by consumers.

Price reflects the value that consumers place on a good and is shown on the demand curve (average revenue). Marginal cost reflects the cost to society of all the resources used in producing an extra unit of a good, including the normal profit required for the firm to stay in business. If price were to be greater than marginal cost, then the consumers would value the good more than it cost to make it.
If both sets of stakeholders are to meet at the optimal mix, then output would expand to the point where price equals marginal cost. Similarly, if the marginal cost were to be greater than the price, then society would be using more resources to produce the good than the value it gives to consumers and output would fall.

Allocative efficiency occurs where marginal cost (the cost of producing one more unit) is equal to average revenue (the price received for a unit). Thus the allocatively efficient level of output is where:

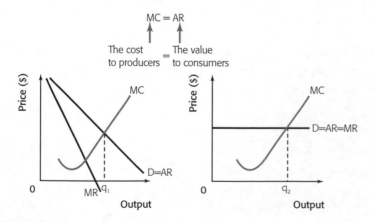

Figure 8.9 Allocative efficiency

In Figure 8.9, we can see the allocatively efficient level of output for a firm with a normal demand curve and for a firm with a perfectly elastic demand curve. In both cases we are looking for the output where $MC = AR - q_1$ for the firm with a normal demand curve and q_2 when the demand is perfectly elastic.

2 Microeconomics

Allocative efficiency is important in economics, because if a firm is producing at the allocatively efficient level of output there is a situation of "Pareto optimality" where it is impossible to make one person better off without making someone else worse off. We will look at this in more detail when we consider market failure in Chapter 13.

Productive and allocative efficiency in the short run in perfect competition

If a firm is making abnormal profits in the short run in perfect competition, we can see from Figure 8.10 that although they are producing at the profit-maximising level of output, q, (where MC=MR) and the allocatively efficient level of output, q_2, (where MC=AR), the firm is not producing at the most efficient level of output, q_1 (where MC=AC).

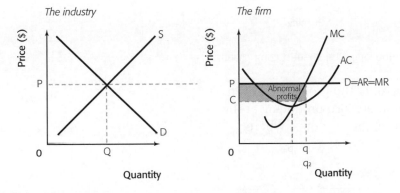

Figure 8.10 Productive and allocative efficiency with short-run profits in perfect competition

In the same way, if a firm is making losses in the short run in perfect competition, we can see from Figure 8.11 that although they are producing at the profit-maximising level of output, q, (where MC=MR) and the allocatively efficient level of output, q_2, (where MC=AR), once again the firm is not producing at the most efficient level of output, q_1 (where MC=AC).

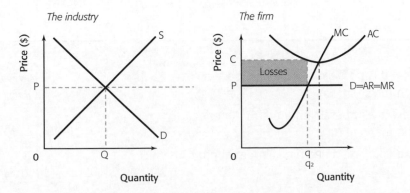

Figure 8.11 Productive and allocative efficiency with short-run losses in perfect competition

Productive and allocative efficiency in the long run in perfect competition

As we can see in Figure 8.12, profit-maximising firms in the long run in perfect competition all produce at the lowest point of their long-run average cost curves. Because we assume that there is perfect knowledge in the industry, all of the firms will face the same cost curves, and so they are all selling at the same price and minimising their average costs by producing where MC=AC.

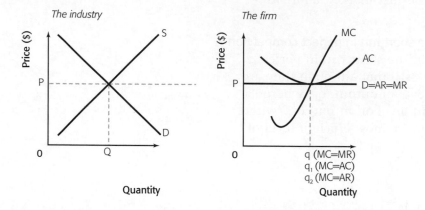

Figure 8.12 Productive and allocative efficiency in the long run in perfect competition

Also shown in Figure 8.12 is the fact that all of the profit-maximising firms in the long run in perfect competition are also producing at the allocatively efficient level of output, because they produce where MC=AR.

Student workpoint 8.2

Fill in the spaces in the table below with either a yes or a no.

Perfect competition	Abnormal profits possible?	Losses possible?	Allocatively efficient?	Productively efficient?
Short run				
Long run				

Examination questions

Short response questions

1 With the help of a diagram, explain how it is possible for a firm in perfect competition to earn abnormal profits in the short run.   *[10 marks]*

2 With the help of a diagram, explain how it is impossible for a firm in perfect competition to earn abnormal profits in the long run.   *[10 marks]*

3 Explain whether or not a firm in perfect competition earning abnormal profits is productively and allocatively efficient.   *[10 marks]*

Essay question

1 a Explain the characteristics of a perfectly competitive market structure.   *[10 marks]*

   b Evaluate the extent to which it is possible for a firm in perfect competition to earn abnormal profits.   *[15 marks]*

9 Monopoly

By the end of this chapter, you should be able to:

- explain the assumptions of monopoly
- define, explain, and give examples of, sources of monopoly power/barriers to entry
- define, explain, and illustrate a natural monopoly
- explain and illustrate the demand curve facing the monopolist
- explain and illustrate possible profit situations in monopoly
- explain and illustrate levels of efficiency in monopoly
- compare monopoly and perfect competition.

Assumptions of the model

In the theory of monopoly, we assume that:

- There is only one firm producing the product so the firm is the industry.
- Barriers to entry exist, which stop new firms from entering the industry and maintains the monopoly.
- As a consequence of barriers to entry the monopolist may be able to make abnormal profits in the long run.

However, whether a firm really is a monopoly depends upon how narrowly we define the industry. For example, Microsoft may be the only producer of a particular kind of software, but it does not have a monopoly of all software. The vegetable shop in your area may have a monopoly of the sale of vegetables in that area, but it is not the only seller of vegetables and if the area is widened then the shop loses its monopoly.

The important question here is not whether or not a firm is a monopoly, but rather how much monopoly power the firm has. To what extent is the firm able to set its own prices without worrying about other firms, and to what extent can it keep people out of the industry? The strength of monopoly power possessed by a firm will really depend upon how many competing substitutes are available. For example, the underground railway in a city may have the monopoly of underground travel, but it will face competition from other industries, such as buses, taxis, and private transport.

Student workpoint 9.1

Be reflective—use your own experience

In each case below, suggest which ones are monopolies and also define the width of the industry that you are assuming:

1 the canteen in your school

2 your doctor

3 the local refuse disposal service

4 your school

5 the national telephone service

6 the national postal service.

Sources of monopoly power/barriers to entry

A monopoly may continue to be the only producer in an industry if it is able to stop other firms from entering the industry in some way. These ways of preventing entry to the industry are known as barriers to entry. There are a number of possible barriers to entry as follows.

1 Economies of scale

As we have seen in Chapter 7, firms gain average cost advantages as their size increases: these are known as economies of scale. Things such as specialization, the division of labour, bulk-buying, and financial economies may lead to cost savings and lower unit costs. If a monopoly is large, then they will be experiencing economies of scale. Any firm wishing to enter the industry will probably have to start up in a relatively small way and so will not have the economies of scale that are enjoyed by the monopolist. Even if the new firm were able to start up with the same size as the monopolist, it would still not have the economies that come from expertise in the industry, such as managerial economies, promotional economies, and research and development.

Without equal economies of scale, a would-be entrant to the industry knows that it would not be able to compete with the existing monopolist, who would simply have to reduce price to the level of normal profits. At this level the new entrant would be making losses, because the average costs would be higher, so the lack of economies of scale acts as a deterrent to firms that might want to enter a monopoly industry.

2 Natural monopoly

Some industries are classified as natural monopolies. An industry is a natural monopoly if there are only enough economies of scale available in the market to support one firm. This is best shown by a diagram, such as Figure 9.1.

In this case, the monopolist is the industry and has the demand curve D_1. The long-run average cost curve faced by the monopolist is LRAC and its position and shape are set by the economies of scale that the firm is experiencing. The monopolist is able to make abnormal profits by producing an output between q_1 and q_2, because the average revenue is greater than the average cost for that range of output.

If another firm were to enter the industry, then the firm would take demand from the monopolist and the monopolist's demand curve

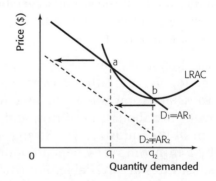

Figure 9.1 A natural monopoly

would shift to the left, in this case to D_2. Since we can assume that the situation will be the same for both firms, the two firms would now be in a position where it is impossible for them to make even normal profits. Their LRACs would be above AR at every level of output.

In this industry, the LRAC, which is shaped by the economies of scale experienced by the monopolist, will only give an abnormal profit if the monopolist is able to satisfy all of the demand in the market. The industry is a natural monopoly, because the market will only support one firm. Examples of natural monopolies include the industries that supply utilities such as water, electricity, and gas.

3 Legal barriers

In certain situations, a firm may have been given a legal right to be the only producer in an industry, i.e. the legal right to be a monopoly. This is the case with patents, which give a firm the right to be the only producer of a product for a certain number of years after it has been invented. Patents are usually valid for approximately 20 years. When a patent expires other producers will then be allowed to produce and sell the product. Patents exist as a means to encourage invention. If individuals or firms put time and money into inventions, only to find that they were copied as soon as they were successful, then there would be little incentive to do so. However, if a firm knows that, if its invention is successful, it will have a protected monopoly for a number of years, then it is more likely to invest in research and development.

Patents, along with copyrights and trademarks, are examples of intellectual property rights. Intellectual property refers to the creations of the mind. Just as private property rights allow people to own physical property, so patents guarantee the creators of ideas the rights to own their ideas. A very good example of patent protection is found in the pharmaceutical industry.

Another example of legal barriers is where the government of a country grants the right to produce a product to a single firm. It may do this by setting up a nationalised industry, such as a state postal service, and then banning other firms from entering that industry, or it may simply sell the right to be a sole supplier to a private firm, such as the right to be the only network provider for mobile phones, once again banning other firms.

4 Brand loyalty

It may be that a monopolist produces a product that has gained huge brand loyalty. The consumers think of the product as the brand. For example, in the early days of the vacuum cleaner they were simply known by their brand name, Hoover. If the brand loyalty is so strong then new firms may be put off from entering the industry, since they will feel that they are not able to produce a product that will be sufficiently different in order to generate such strong brand loyalty.

2 Microeconomics

Student workpoint 9.2

Be reflective—use your own experience

Can you think of any other products that dominate the market so heavily that the product is known by its brand name rather than its product name? Can you think of any products that have lost this market dominance to competitors?

Student workpoint 9.3

Be reflective

Use the information below to explain the possible advantages and disadvantages of pharmaceutical patents for the different stakeholders involved.

Discoveries of new drugs have led to significant improvements in health and longevity. None of this would have been possible if pharmaceutical companies hadn't had the incentive to carry out the research, development, and testing necessary to bring these drugs onto the market. Estimates of the costs of developing and testing new drugs in the US range from $800 million to $2 billion and it can take anywhere from 12 to 15 years to bring a new drug onto the market.

Given these figures, it is not surprising that drug developers want to have some guarantee that they will be able to be the exclusive providers so that they can recover their costs and maximize their profits. This is why patents are justified. In fact, pharmaceutical companies continually lobby governments to have increased patent protection for their products.

As soon as the patent on a drug expires, other pharmaceutical companies can produce and sell their own version of the drug. These are commonly known as generic drugs or simply generics. A generic drug is exactly the same as its patented version in terms of dosage, safety, strength, intended use, risks, and benefits. They are said to be "bio-equivalent".

The producers of the generic drug can develop the drug while the brand name drug is protected by its patent and release it as soon as the patent expires.

Generic drugs are vastly less expensive than the brand name drugs quite simply because the pharmaceutical companies that produce the generic drug do not have the huge development and testing costs. The generics have to meet the country's health and safety standards, but it takes much less time and money than the original. With lower costs, they can charge lower prices.

Drug companies spend a lot of money on advertising to try to make sure that the consumers of their drugs maintain brand loyalty. This is particularly important when a drug is facing its patent expiry. They hope that their consumers will stick with their drug even when cheaper generics are on the market. If the drug is a prescription drug, the pharmaceutical companies may find ways to convince doctors that they should keep prescribing the brand name drugs.

There are deep ethical issues involved in the question of patents on life-saving drugs. The fact that people die from preventable diseases because they cannot afford to buy the patented medicines, even though generic drugs may be made available at a fraction of the price is currently under debate.

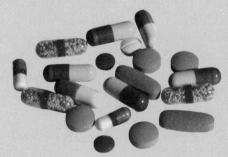

---

5 Anti-competitive behaviour

A monopolist may also attempt to stop competition by adopting restrictive practices, which may be legal or illegal. For example, an established monopoly should be in a strong position to start a "price war" if another firm enters the industry. The monopoly can lower its price to a loss-making level and should be able to sustain the losses for a longer time than the new entrant, thus forcing the new firm out of the industry. Indeed, knowledge of this possibility should be enough to dissuade new firms from even attempting to enter the industry.

Another example of anti-competitive behaviour can be found in the case against Microsoft. In 2004, the European Union Competition Commission fined Microsoft €497 million for bundling a media player and messaging technologies into its Windows operating system. The commission claimed that this prevented potential competitors from reaching consumers. It also ordered Microsoft to make public technical information to allow other companies the ability to produce goods that are compatible with Microsoft. As of July 2006, the fine remained unpaid, and Microsoft received an additional fine of €280.5 million for failure to comply with the 2004 fine. There continues to be much debate on the issue.

Student workpoint 9.4

Be an inquirer—conduct research and assess the outcomes

1 Make an annotated time line to briefly explain the series of events and decisions in the Microsoft legal battle with the European Union Competition Commission.

2 What are the arguments for and against the large fine?

The demand curve and the profit-maximising level of output in monopoly

As we know, the monopolist is the industry and so the monopolist's demand curve is the industry demand curve and is downward sloping. The monopolist can therefore control either the level of output or the price of the product, but not both. Students often assume that monopolists can charge whatever price they like and still sell their products, but this is not the case. In order to sell more they must lower their price.

The demand curve facing a monopolist is shown in Figure 9.2. The monopolist has a normal demand curve, with marginal revenue below it, and maximises profit by producing at the level of output where marginal cost is equal to marginal revenue.

We can see that in this case, the monopolist sells a quantity q at a price per unit of P.

Possible profit situations in monopoly

If a monopolist is able to make abnormal profits in the short run, and if the monopolist has effective barriers to entry, then other firms cannot enter the industry and compete away the profits that are being earned. In this situation, the monopolist is able to make abnormal profits in the long run, for as long as the barriers to entry hold out. This situation is shown in Figure 9.3.

The monopolist is maximising profits and is making abnormal profits shown by the shaded area, PabC. Without the entry of new firms to the industry this situation will continue.

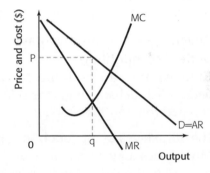

Figure 9.2 The demand curve facing a monopolist

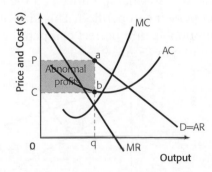

Figure 9.3 Abnormal profits in the long run in monopoly

It is sometimes assumed that a monopolist will always earn abnormal profits, but this is of course not true. If the monopolist produces something for which there is little demand, then it will not earn abnormal profits. If a monopolist were making losses in the short run, then it would have the option of closing down temporarily (if it was not covering its variable costs) or continuing production for the time being. However, it would plan ahead in the long run to see whether changes could be made so that normal profits, at least, could be earned. If this were not possible, then the monopolist would close down the firm and, since the firm is the industry, the industry would cease to exist. This situation is shown in Figure 9.4.

Here, the firm is not able to cover costs in the long run, since the average cost is greater than the average revenue at all levels of output. Since there is nothing that can be done to rectify the situation, this will be an industry in which no firm will be willing to produce. There will be no industry.

Efficiency in monopoly

Unlike perfect competition, the monopolist produces at the level of output where there is neither productive efficiency nor allocative efficiency. This is shown in Figure 9.5.

The monopolist is producing at the profit-maximising level of output, q. Output is being restricted in order to force up the price and to maximise profit. However, the most efficient level of output, q_1 and the allocatively efficient level of output, q_2, are not being achieved.

Advantages and disadvantages of monopoly in comparison with perfect competition

Although they are both theoretical market forms, there has always been much debate about the relative merits and demerits of perfect competition and monopolies.

The advantages of monopoly in comparison with perfect competition

Monopolies may be able to achieve large economies of scale simply because of their size. Monopolies do not have to be big, but if the industry is big, then the monopolist should gain substantial economies of scale. If this pushes the MC curve down, then it is possible that the monopolist may produce at a higher output and at a lower price than in perfect competition. This idea of relative price and output in monopoly and perfect competition is very debateable. The situation is shown in Figure 9.6.

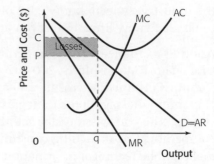

Figure 9.4 A monopolist making losses in the long run

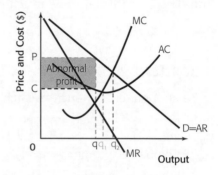

Figure 9.5 Productive and allocative efficiency in monopoly

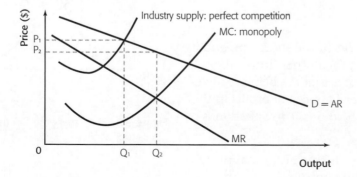

Figure 9.6 Economies of scale in monopoly

In perfect competition, the equilibrium price and quantity will be where demand is equal to supply. This means that the price will be P_1 and that a total output of Q_1 will be produced. However, if the industry is a monopoly, with significant economies of scale, then the MC curve may well be substantially below the MC curve in perfect competition, which is the industry supply curve.

If this is the case, then the monopolist will produce where MC=MR, maximising profits, and producing a greater quantity than perfect competition, Q_2, at a lower price, P_2.

A second advantage may be that there will be higher levels of investment in research and development in monopoly. Firms in perfect competition are, by definition, relatively small, and so may find it difficult to invest in research and development. However, a monopolist making abnormal profits is in a better situation to use some of those profits to fund research and development. This would, in the long run, benefit consumers, who would have better products and even more choice.

The disadvantages of monopoly in comparison with perfect competition

If significant economies of scale do not exist in a monopoly, then the monopoly may restrict output and charge a higher price than under perfect competition.

In Figure 9.7, there are no differences in costs for the monopolist and the perfectly competitive market. If this is the case, then the monopolist will produce Q_2 at a price of P_2, where MC = MR. The perfectly competitive market will, however, produce Q_1 at a price of P_1, where industry supply meets industry demand. Thus higher prices and lower output would exist under monopoly.

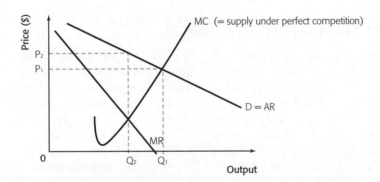

Figure 9.7 Monopoly v perfect competition without economies of scale

The high profits of monopolists may be considered as unfair, especially by competitive firms, or those on low incomes. The scale of the problem depends upon the size and power of the monopoly. The monopoly profits of your local post office may seem of little consequence when compared to the profits of a giant national company.

To summarise, there are three possible problems associated with monopolies in comparison with perfect competition.

● They are productively and allocatively inefficient.

● They can charge a higher price for a lower level of output.

2 Microeconomics

● They can exercise anti-competitive behaviour to keep their monopoly power.

These potential problems mean that monopolies can act against the public interest. As a result, all governments have laws and policies to limit monopoly power. This will be developed in Chapter 13.

Examination questions

Short response questions

1   Explain the level of output at which a monopoly firm will produce.   *[10 marks]*

2   Using a diagram, explain the concept of a natural monopoly.   *[10 marks]*

3   Using appropriate diagrams, explain whether a monopoly is likely to be more efficient or less efficient than a firm in perfect competition.   *[10 marks]*

Essay question

1   a   Explain three barriers to entry that allow a firm to be a monopoly.   *[10 marks]*

     b   Evaluate the view that governments should *always* prevent firms from being monopolies.   *[15 marks]*

Assessment advice: essay writing
In essay question 1 (b) the word "always" is in italics. This is a word that often appears in examination questions, but if you see it on your exam, it won't be in italics. It is in italics here in order to draw your attention to it to let you know that it is a key word. In your evaluation, you are likely to explain why governments should prevent firms from being monopolies, but then discuss any circumstances where they should not. That is, you will be arguing against the view that they should *always* do so.

Data response exercise

Read the article below and answer the questions that follow.

Bitter pill for pharmaceutical company Merck

Indian pharmaceutical companies Ranbaxy and Dr Reddy's Laboratories are expected to be major beneficiaries to take advantage of a multi-billion dollar sales vacuum created by the **patent** expiry of two popular drugs in the US. One of the drugs is a cholesterol-cutting drug called Zocor and the other is an antidepressant drug named Zoloft.

Merck earned huge profits from its sales of Zocor, whose patent expired on 23 June. Pfizer lost its patent on 30 June. When a company loses its exclusive patent for a branded drug, it is no longer a **monopoly** in the market, and the market opens to generic drugmakers. This can lead to a drop of nearly 80% in the drug's price, resulting in a major gain for consumers as well as the makers of generic version of these drugs.

Indian companies are in good shape to gain from the patent expiries in developed markets like the US and Europe. They have a tremendous ability to create, manufacture, and market generic drugs at low prices, aided by the availability of cheaper and skilled labour. Ranbaxy is planning to produce Simvastatin, a generic version of Zocor, after receiving the required approval from the US Food and Drug Administration. Including those from India, as billions of dollars' worth of drugs are scheduled to come off patent in 2006.

Data response exercise

1 Define the following terms, indicated in bold in the text:

   a patent   *[2 marks]*

   b monopoly.   *[2 marks]*

2 Using an appropriate diagram, explain why Merck was able to earn huge profits from its sales of Zocor. *[4 marks]*

3 Using an appropriate diagram, explain how cheaper labour allows India to manufacture generic drugs at low prices. *[4 marks]*

4 Using information from the text and your knowledge of economics, evaluate the effects of the Zocor patent expiry on the market for cholesterol-reducing medicines. *[8 marks]*

10 Monopolistic competition

By the end of this chapter, you should be able to:

- explain the assumptions of monopolistic competition
- define and give examples of product differentiation
- explain and illustrate the demand curve for the firm in monopolistic competition
- explain how the firm maximises profit in monopolistic competition
- explain and illustrate short-run profit and loss situations in monopolistic competition
- explain and illustrate the long-run equilibrium in monopolistic competition
- explain the movement from short run to long run in monopolistic competition
- explain and illustrate productive and allocative efficiency in the short and long run in monopolistic competition.

The theory of monopolistic competition was developed by Edward Chamberlin (1899–1967), an American economist. He was dissatisfied with the two extreme theories that existed at the time, perfect competition and monopoly, so wanted to devise something more realistic that would sit between the two existing theories. In simple terms, a monopolistically competitive market is one with many competing firms where each firm has a little bit of market power. This is why we have the term "monopolistic", as firms have some ability to set their own prices.

The assumptions of monopolistic competition

The assumptions for monopolistic competition are as follows.

- The industry is made up of a fairly large number of firms.
- The firms are small, relative to the size of the industry. This means that the actions of one firm are unlikely to have a great effect on any of its competitors. The firms assume that they are able to act independently of each other.
- The firms all produce slightly differentiated products. This means that it is possible for a consumer to tell one firm's product from another.
- Firms are completely free to enter or leave the industry. That is, there are no barriers to entry or exit.

The only difference from perfect competition is that in monopolistic competition, there is product differentiation. Product differentiation exists when a good or service is perceived to be different from other goods or services in some way. Products may be differentiated by brand name, colour, appearance, packaging, design, quality of service, skill levels, and many other methods. Examples of monopolistically competitive industries are nail (manicure) salons, car mechanics, plumbers, and jewellers.

Although it may appear to be a small difference from the assumptions of perfect competition, this leads to a markedly different market structure. As the products are differentiated there will be some extent of brand loyalty. This means that some of the consumers will be loyal to the product and continue to buy it if the price goes up a little. For example, it may be that the customers of a certain plumber will stay with that plumber when she raises her prices above local rivals, because they believe that she is slightly more skilled than her competitors.

This brand loyalty means that producers have some element of independence when they are deciding on price. They are, to an extent, price-makers, and so they face a downward sloping demand curve. However, demand will be relatively elastic since there are many, only slightly different, substitutes.

Student workpoint 10.1

Be a thinker—consider and explain

Try to think of an example of a market in your area that is in monopolistic competition. With reference to the assumptions of the model, explain your choice.

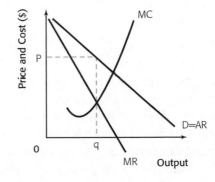

Figure 10.1 The demand curve for a firm in monopolistic competition

The demand curve facing a monopolistically competitive firm is shown in Figure 10.1.

The firm faces a downward sloping demand curve with a marginal revenue curve that is below it and produces so that it is maximising profits where MC = MR. This means that the firm in Figure 10.1 will produce an output of q and sell that output at the price of P.

Possible short-run profit and loss situations in monopolistic competition

Just as in perfect competition, it is possible for firms in monopolistic competition to make abnormal profits in the short run. This is shown in Figure 10.2.

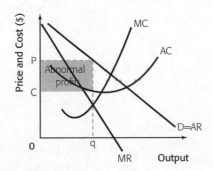

Figure 10.2 Short-run abnormal profits in monopolistic competition

In this case, the firm is maximising profits by producing at the level of output where MC = MR, and the cost per unit (AC) of C is less than the selling price of P. There is an abnormal profit that is shown by the shaded area.

It is also possible that a firm in monopolistic competition may be making losses in the short run and this is shown in Figure 10.3. Once again, the firm is producing where MC = MR, but this time the cost per unit, C, is above the price, P, and the amount of losses is shown by the shaded area.

The long-run equilibrium of the firm in monopolistic competition

Whether firms are making abnormal profits or losses in the short run, because of the freedom of entry and exit in the industry, there will be a long-run equilibrium, where all of the firms in the industry are making normal profits.

If the firms are making short-run abnormal profits, then other firms will be attracted to the industry. Since there are no barriers to entry it is possible for these other firms to join the industry. As they enter, they will take business away from the existing firms, whose demand curves will start to shift to the left. If firms are making short-run losses, then some of the firms in the industry will start to leave. The firms that remain will find that their demand curves start to shift to the right as they pick up trade from the leaving firms.

This analysis explains why it is not uncommon to see similar shops or services spring up in an area. Imagine that a new sushi restaurant opens up in a district. Soon it is so popular that there is a line-up outside the door every evening. Other catering entrepreneurs will be attracted to the possibility of doing so well, and so it is likely that another sushi restaurant will open up in the area. It may not happen immediately, but eventually this is likely to result in a fall in demand for the original sushi restaurant as some of its customers will switch. If demand continues to be strong, then even more restaurants will open. Each restaurant will try to distinguish itself from the others—perhaps by staying open longer, offering a "Happy Hour", special theme nights, or free children's meals to name just a few possibilities. This product differentiation is also known as non-price competition.

Whatever the short-run situation, in the long run the firms will end up in the position shown in Figure 10.4, with all making normal profits. The firms are maximising profits by producing at the level of output where MC = MR and, at that output, the cost per unit, C, is equal to the price per unit, P. Each firm is exactly covering its costs, including its opportunity costs, and so there is no incentive for firms to leave the industry. Firms outside the industry will not enter, since they will be aware that their entrance would lead to losses for everyone.

Table 10.1 summarises the characteristics of monopolistic competition and illustrates how Italian restaurants in a city might be considered to be close to a monopolistic competition market structure.

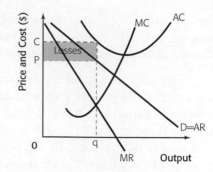

Figure 10.3 Short-run losses in monopolistic competition

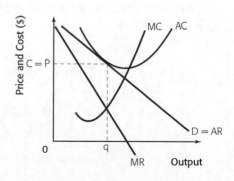

Figure 10.4 Long-run equilibrium in monopolistic competition

Characteristics of monopolistic competition market structure	Italian restaurants
Very large number of firms	✓
Each firm very small relative to the size of the market	✓
Goods are differentiated	✓ (Different menus, emphasis on pasta, emphasis on pizzas)
No barriers to entry or exit	Very low barriers (low capital costs, no special expertise, not likely to be large economies of scale, some brand loyalty)
Perfect information	Fairly open, but not perfect
Abnormal profits possible in short run, but not in long run	More and more Italian restaurants will be set up as long as the existing ones are earning abnormal profits.

Table 10.1 Italian restaurants as an example of a monopolisitic competition market structure

Student workpoint 10.2

Be a thinker—explain and illustrate the following:

1 Why can a firm in monopolistic competition not earn abnormal profits in the long run?

2 Draw a diagram of a firm in monopolistic competition that is in long-run equilibrium. (This is likely to be the most difficult diagram you've done so far, as it is challenging to draw the relationships accurately!)

Productive and allocative efficiency in monopolistic competition

We know that productive efficiency is achieved at the level of output where a firm produces at the lowest possible cost per unit, the point where AC is at a minimum. This is the point where the MC curve cuts the AC curve.

Allocative efficiency is achieved at the level of output where the MC curve cuts the AR curve: the socially optimum level of output.

Figure 10.5 shows the two possible short-run positions in monopolistic competition and abnormal profits and losses. We see that the firm produces at the level of output where profits are maximised, q, as opposed to the productively efficient level of output, q_1, or the allocatively efficient level of output, q_2.

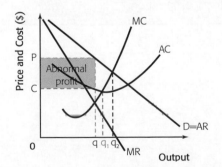
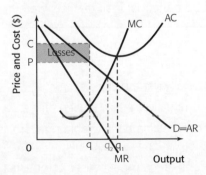

Figure 10.5 Productive and allocative efficiency in the short run in monopolistic competition

In the long run, the situation is the same. This is shown in Figure 10.6. The firm is again producing at the profit-maximising level of output, q, and not at the productively efficient level of output, q_1, or the allocatively efficient level of output q_2.

Monopolistic competition in comparison with perfect competition

Unlike perfect competition, where in the long run the firms are profit-maximisers, productively efficient, and allocatively efficient, firms in the long run in monopolistic competition, although maximising profits, are neither productively nor allocatively efficient.

However, even though the firm in monopolistic competition is not allocatively efficient, because it does not produce where MC = AR, and is not productively efficient, because it does not produce where MC = AC, the inefficiency is *not* due to the firm's ability to restrict output and increase price as in a monopoly. The inefficiency is, in fact, the result of the consumers' desires for variety. Though allocative efficiency does not occur, it is hard to argue that consumers are worse off with monopolistic competition than with perfect competition, since the difference is due entirely to consumer desire to have differentiated products.

Rather than having a perfectly competitive situation, where consumers pay lower prices but are only able to purchase a homogeneous product, monopolistic competition gives consumers the opportunity to make choices. This is why they are prepared to pay slightly higher prices for the products.

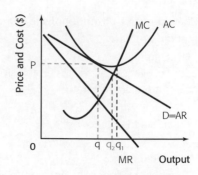

Figure 10.6 Productive and allocative efficiency in the long run in monopolistic competition

Examination questions

Short response questions

1   With the help of a diagram, explain the level of output that a profit-maximising firm will produce at in the long run in monopolistic competition.   *[10 marks]*

2   With the help of a diagram, explain how it is possible for a firm in monopolistic competition to earn abnormal profits in the short run.   *[10 marks]*

3   Explain whether or not a firm in monopolistic competition earning abnormal profits is productively and allocatively efficient.   *[10 marks]*

Essay question

1   a   Explain the differences between the assumptions of perfect competition and monopolistic competition.   *[10 marks]*

    b   Evaluate the view that it would be beneficial if all markets were in perfect competition.   *[15 marks]*

You be the journalist

Headline: Fitness centres springing up all over the city

Economics concept: Monopolistic competition + abnormal profits

Diagram(s): A firm in monopolistic competition earning abnormal profits in the short run and the adjustment to the long-run equilibrium

Hint: Consider each of the assumptions of the monopolistic competition market structure and suggest how each might be relevant here.

11 Oligopoly

By the end of this chapter, you should be able to:

- explain the assumptions of oligopoly
- distinguish between collusive and non-collusive oligopoly
- define a cartel
- explain and illustrate the kinked demand curve
- explain and give examples of non-price competition.

The assumptions of oligopoly

Oligopoly is where a few firms dominate an industry. The industry may have quite a few firms or not very many, but the key thing is that a large proportion of the industry's output is shared by just a small number of firms. What constitutes a small number varies, but a common indicator of concentration in an industry is known as the concentration ratio. Concentration ratios are expressed in the form CR_x where X represents the number of the largest firms. For example, a CR_4 would show the percentage of market share (or output) held by the largest four firms in the industry. The higher the percentage, the more concentrated is the market power of the four largest firms. While other concentration ratios such as a CR_8 are measured, it is the CR_4 that is most commonly used to make a link to a given market structure. While the line between the concentration of market share or sales in different market structures is subject to interpretation, Figure 11.1 offers one view.

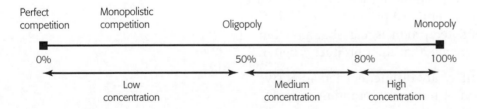

Percentage market share of largest 4 firms (CR_4)

Figure 11.1 CR_4 ratios in different market structures

For example, in the US malt beverages industry, there are 160 firms, and the CR_4 is 90%. Thus the four largest firms produce 90% of the industry's output and it is an industry with a high concentration of market power among the largest four companies. In the frozen fish and seafood industry, there are 600 firms and the CR_4 is 19, suggesting low concentration. We may conclude that the malt industry is an oligopoly and the frozen fish and seafood industry is in monopolistic competition.

● ● ● ● ● ● ● ● ● ● ● ● ● ● ● ● ● ● ●

Student workpoint 11.1

Be a thinker—classify the following

How would you classify each of the following industries in the US?

1 Breakfast cereal manufacturing: 48 firms, $CR_4 = 82.9\%$

2 Textile mills: 3,863 firms, $CR_4 = 13.8\%$

3 Breweries: 494 firms, $CR_4 = 89.7\%$

4 Wineries: 637 firms, $CR_4 = 43.2\%$

● ● ● ● ● ● ● ● ● ● ● ● ● ● ● ● ● ● ●

Student workpoint 11.2

Be an inquirer

The CR_4 tells us how the market share in the industry is concentrated among the four largest firms, but it doesn't necessarily reveal the extent of the competition in the industry. A CR_4 of 80% would suggest high concentration, but if that market share were to be divided up with the largest company having 65% of the market and the other three having 5% each, then this would be very different from each of the four having 20% equal share.

An alternative indicator of concentration in an industry is known as the Herfindahl-Herschmann index.

Research task

What is the Herfindahl-Herschmann index? How might it be a better indicator of concentration than the CR_4? What are the levels of the CR_4 values that distinguish between different categories of competition?

Oligopolistic industries may be very different in nature. Some produce almost identical products, e.g. petrol, where the product is almost exactly the same and only the names of the oil companies are different. Some produce highly differentiated products, e.g. motor cars. Some produce only differentiated products, e.g. shampoo, but spend huge budgets to persuade people that their product is better.

In most examples of oligopoly, there are distinct barriers to entry, usually the large-scale production or the strong branding of the dominant firms, but this is not always the case. In some oligopolies, there may be low barriers to entry. This is explained by contestable market theory (see Chapter 12).

However, the key feature that is common in all oligopolies is that there is interdependence. Whereas in perfect competition and monopolistic competition the firms are all too small relative to the size of the market to be able to influence the market, in oligopoly there is a small number of large firms dominating the industry. As there are just a few firms, each needs to take careful notice of each other's actions. Interdependence tends to make firms want to collude and so avoid surprises and unexpected outcomes. If they can collude and act as a monopoly, then they can maximise industry profits. However, there is also a tendency for firms to want to compete vigorously with each other in order to gain a greater market share.

All in all, however, oligopoly tends to be characterised by price rigidity. Prices in oligopoly tend to change much less than in more competitive markets. Even when there are production-cost changes, oligopolistic firms often leave their prices unchanged.

Collusive and non-collusive oligopoly

Collusive oligopoly exists when the firms in an oligopolistic market collude to charge the same prices for their products, in effect acting as a monopoly, and so divide up any monopoly profits that may be made.

There are two types of collusion. Formal collusion takes place when firms openly agree on the price that they will all charge, although sometimes it may be agreement on market share or on marketing expenditure instead. Such a collusive oligopoly is often called a cartel. Since this results in higher prices and less output for consumers, this is usually deemed to be against the interest of consumers and so collusion is generally banned by governments and is against the law in the majority of countries. If a country's anti-trust authority finds that firms have engaged in anti-competitive behaviour such as price-fixing agreements, then the firms will be penalised with fines or other punishments (see the case study of price-fixing in Australia at the end of this chapter).

Formal collusion between governments may be permitted. The prime example is OPEC (the Organisation for Petroleum Exporting Countries), which sets production quotas and prices for the world oil markets.

Tacit collusion exists when firms in an oligopoly charge the same prices without any formal collusion. This is not as difficult as it sounds. A firm may charge the same price as another by looking at the prices of a dominant firm in the industry, or at the prices of the main competitors. It is not necessary to communicate to be able to charge the same prices.

In both formal and tacit collusion, the process is the same. The firms behave like a monopolist (single producer), charge the monopoly price, make monopoly profits, and share them according to market share. This is shown in Figure 11.2.

Collusive oligopoly offers one explanation of price rigidity in oligopoly. If firms are colluding, either formally or tacitly, and they are making their share of long-run monopoly profits, then they may try to keep prices stable in order that the situation continues.

Non-collusive oligopoly exists when the firms in an oligopoly do not collude and so have to be very aware of the reactions of other firms when making pricing decisions. We say that the behaviour of firms in an oligopoly is strategic behaviour as they must develop strategies that take into account all possible actions of rivals. In order to explain how firms behave in these situations, economists often use "game theory". This is not in the IB Diploma Programme economics course of study, but you may come across it in Theory of Knowledge in the guise of "The prisoner's dilemma".

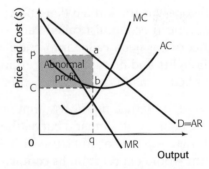

Figure 11.2 Oligopolists acting as a monopolist

Theory of Knowledge

The prisoner's dilemma

The concept of the "prisoner's dilemma" was developed by Flood and Dresher and formalised by Albert Tucker in 1992. The prisoner's dilemma uses the example of two men being arrested by the police. The police require more evidence and so separate the men and offer each of them the following conditions.

1 Testify for the prosecution. If you do, you go free and your partner in crime gets 10 years in prison. Only the first one to confess gets the offer.
2 Say nothing and you get 5 years in prison.

Each prisoner has the choice of cooperating with the other and saying nothing or betraying the other, and so it raises issues of trust, cooperation, and betrayal. Is it human nature to save oneself at the expense of others? Should one sacrifice one's own well-being for the common good?

The principle of the prisoner's dilemma can be applied to real world situations, such as cycling.

Sometimes two riders get away from the main group of riders (known as the peloton). If the two riders cooperate, each taking a share of the lead so that the other can shelter from the wind, they will finish first and second. If they don't cooperate, the peloton will catch them up. What sometimes happens is that one rider (the cooperator) does all the hard work at the front, while the other rider (the betrayer) sits in the slipstream of the first rider (just behind the leader). The betrayer almost always wins.

Theorists have adapted the prisoner's dilemma as part of game theory. Economists apply it to the actions of firms, mainly those in oligopoly.

1 What does it mean to say that firms in an oligopoly are interdependent?
2 Examine some of the price and non-price strategies open to a firm in an oligopoly to improve its position in a market.
3 Do you think it is better for a firm in an oligopoly to cooperate?

One way of attempting to explain the situation in a non-collusive oligopoly is the kinked demand curve, devised in the 1930s by an American economist called Paul Sweezy (1910–2004). Although the theory has been called into question, it does provoke some interesting thoughts and discussion concerning non-collusive oligopoly. The kinked demand curve is shown in Figure 11.3.

We start by making the assumption that, in reality, a firm only knows one point on its demand curve, the one that it holds at present. This is shown as point "a" in Figure 11.3. Now, consider what reactions the firm would expect from its competitors if it were to change its price.

If the firm raises its price then it is unlikely that its competitors would raise theirs and so a lot of demand would be lost to the other firms. This implies that demand would be relatively elastic above the point "a", since a small increase in price would lead to a large fall in quantity demanded.

If the firm were to lower its price then it is likely that competitors would follow. More to the point, it is likely that they would undercut the price of the first firm in order to regain any lost sales. This implies that demand would be less elastic below the point "a", since a decrease in price is unlikely to lead to a noticeable increase in quantity demanded.

Because of these expectations, we see that the demand curve will be kinked around the point "a". It will also possess an MR curve that

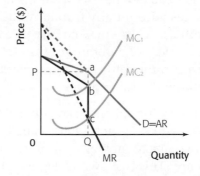

Figure 11.3 The kinked demand curve

has the vertical section bc, since each part of the MR curve will be twice as steeply sloping as the two parts of the demand curve.

The kinked demand curve offers an explanation of why there tends to be price rigidity in non-collusive oligopoly. There are three reasons.

1 Firms are afraid to raise prices above the current market price, because other firms will not follow and so they will lose trade, sales, and probably profit.

2 Firms are afraid to lower their prices below the current market price, because other firms will follow, undercutting them, and so creating a price war that may harm all the firms involved.

3 The shape of the MR curve means that if marginal costs were to rise, then it is possible that MC would still equal MR and so the firms, being profit maximisers, would not change their prices or outputs. This can be seen in Figure 11.3. If we assume that the firm is operating on MC_2, then they are maximising profits by producing Q and selling at P. Marginal costs could rise as high as MC_1 and the firm would still be maximising profits by producing at Q and charging P. Thus the market remains stable, even though there have been significant price changes.

Non-price competition

Because firms in oligopoly tend not to compete in terms of price, the concept of non-price competition becomes important. There are many kinds of non-price competition, such as the use of brand names, packaging, special features, advertising, sales promotion, personal selling, publicity, sponsorship deals, and special distribution features, such as free delivery and after-sales service. Oligopoly is characterised by very large advertising and marketing expenditures as firms try to develop brand loyalty and make demand for their products less elastic. Some may argue that this represents a misuse of scarce resources, but it could also be argued that competition among the large companies results in greater choice for consumers.

Firms undertake all kinds of behaviour to guard and extend their market share. This serves to increase the barriers to entry to new firms. Many rivalries among firms in oligopolies are well known nationally and internationally, for example Coke and Pepsi, or Adidas and Nike. However, many of the branded consumer goods that we purchase are produced in oligopolies and we might have no idea that there are actually just a few companies dominating the market. A walk down a supermarket aisle of washing powders might suggest a vast number of competing companies when, in reality, the majority of the brands are produced by just two companies— Unilever and Procter & Gamble. These two giant multinationals produce a vast number of brands that compete with each other in a number of industries, for example, home care products, personal hygiene, health care, and beauty products.

Student workpoint 11.3

Be an inquirer

1 By referring to the Internet home pages of Unilever and Procter & Gamble, make a list of 20 rival brands produced by each of these giant multinational companies.

2 Find a copy of a consumer magazine of any type (sports, computing, women's interests, men's interest). By looking at the advertisements in the magazine, identify the different ways that firms try to differentiate their products.

Did you know?

Coca-Cola Company is the largest manufacturer, marketer, and distributor of non-alcoholic beverages in the world. Along with Pepsi and Cadbury Schweppes, they make up a non-collusive oligopoly that dominates the world market in beverages.

With the intense pace of globalisation, which makes it easier for multinational companies to operate businesses in foreign countries, Coca-Cola has been able to acquire brands from all around the world. It now has nearly 400 different brand names, selling drinks in around 200 different countries. It produces energy drinks, juices, carbonated soft drinks, sports drinks, iced teas and coffees, and bottled water. Some more famous brand names include the range of colas, Minute Maid, Five-Alive, Powerade, Fanta, Sprite, Nestea, Lemon-Lime Limca in India, Kochakaden Tea in Japan, Inka Cola in Peru, Cepita Nectars in Argentina, and Citra in Zambia.

Coca-Cola competes aggressively with Pepsi, which also sells hundreds of brands around the world, including Pepsi Cola, Mountain Dew, 7-Up, and Tropicana. The intensity and the strategic nature of the competition between these two giants is apparent: they have both hired world-famous celebrities to advertise their products, they have been rivals in getting fast food restaurants to sell their products exclusively, they try to match each other brand for brand in getting new products on the market, and they compete heavily to gain the sponsorship of large national and international events that put their brand names into the limelight.

student workpoint 11.4

Be inquisitive—investigate

Find out the name of the anti-trust authority in your country or another country of your choice and produce a brief report on one case that it has investigated in the last year. Include a summary of who was involved, what the charges were, and what, if any, were the outcomes.

Examination questions

Short response questions

1 Explain why prices tend to be quite stable in a non-collusive oligopoly.   *[10 marks]*

2 Explain why firms in oligopolies engage in non-price competition.   *[10 marks]*

Essay question

1 a Distinguish between a collusive and a non-collusive oligopoly.   *[10 marks]*

   b Evaluate the view that governments should maintain strong policies to control collusive behaviour by oligopolies.   *[15 marks]*

12 Price discrimination and contestable markets

By the end of this chapter, you should be able to:

● define, explain, and illustrate consumer surplus

● define, explain, and illustrate producer surplus

● define and explain price discrimination

● define, illustrate, give examples of, and distinguish between first degree, second degree, and third degree price discrimination

● define and explain contestable market theory.

Consumer and producer surplus

Consider Figure 12.1, illustrating the market for thingies, an imaginary product.

As we can see, the equilibrium price of thingies is $10 and the equilibrium quantity demanded and supplied is ten thingies per week. This is determined by the forces of demand and supply. At the equilibrium point, there are some consumers who would have been prepared to pay a higher price for their thingies.

This is clearly shown by the demand curve. For example, at a price of $15, there would still be five thingies demanded and at a price of $17, there would be demand for three thingies. However, the consumers do not have to pay $15 or $17, they just have to pay the equilibrium price. This means that all of the consumers who purchase the first nine thingies have made a gain. They have paid a price below the one they were prepared to pay.

This illustrates the concept of consumer surplus. This is defined as the extra satisfaction (or utility) gained by consumers from paying a price that is lower than that which they are prepared to pay.

In this case, one consumer was willing to pay as much as $19 for a thingy, but as he only has to pay $10, he is gaining. The total consumer surplus is usually shown by the area under the demand curve and above the equilibrium price. In Figure 12.2, the consumer surplus is shown by the shaded triangle abc.

It should also be clear that at the equilibrium point, some production of thingies would take place at a price lower than $10.

This is clearly shown by the supply curve. For example, at a price of $5, there would still be five thingies supplied and at a price of $3, there would be a supply of three thingies. However, the producer does not have to sell for $5 or $3, she can sell her thingies at the equilibrium price. This means that she will have made a gain on each of the first nine thingies in terms of what she would have accepted for them. She has received a price higher than the one she was prepared to accept.

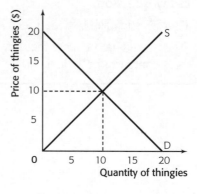

Figure 12.1 The market for thingies

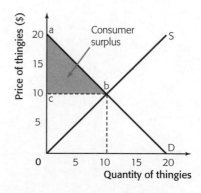

Figure 12.2 Consumer surplus in the market for thingies

This illustrates the concept of producer surplus. This is defined as the excess of actual earnings that a producer makes from a given quantity of output, over and above the amount the producer would be prepared to accept for that output.

In this case, the producer was willing to supply a thingy for as little as $1, but as she receives $10 for each thingy, she is gaining. The total producer surplus is usually shown by the area under the equilibrium price and above the supply curve. In Figure 12.3, the producer surplus is shown by the shaded triangle bcd.

Price discrimination

Price discrimination exists when a producer sells the exact same product to different consumers at different prices. For example, a child's ticket to fly from Vienna to Toronto may cost €500, while his mother's ticket costs €700. The product, a seat on a plane, is exactly the same but the price is different.

In order for a producer to be able to price discriminate, three conditions are necessary.

1 The producer must have some price-setting ability, i.e. the market must be imperfect. The more price-setting ability the producer has, the easier it is for price discrimination to take place, which is why it is most often found in monopoly and oligopoly markets. Price discrimination is not possible in perfect competition.

2 The consumers must have different price elasticities of demand for the product. If they do not, then they would not be prepared to pay different prices for the product. It follows that a consumer with relatively inelastic demand for a product will be prepared to pay a higher price than a consumer with relatively elastic demand, since elasticity tends to signify the importance of a product to consumers.

3 The producer must be able to separate the consumers, so that they are not able to buy the product and then sell it to another consumer. If this were not the case, then the consumers who buy the product at a low price would simply sell to those who were paying the higher price, at a price below that one. This would destroy the ability of the producer to practise price discrimination.

Producers are able to separate markets in a number of different ways. They can do so by:

● *Time:* Consumers are often prepared to pay higher prices at certain times than at others. For example, commuters heading to work in the morning on the train are making a necessary journey and so will be prepared to pay a higher fare than a person who is free all day and would like to go shopping. The commuter's elasticity of demand for travel is more inelastic than that of the shopper. Thus the train company charges higher fares during peak times and lower fares during non-peak times.

● *Age:* Firms may charge different prices to consumers based upon their ages. For example, children are often charged

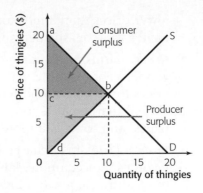

Figure 12.3 Producer surplus in the market for thingies

lower prices than adults for visiting the cinema. The children have a more elastic demand, because their incomes are lower.

● *Gender:* Firms may charge different prices to men than to women. For example, a football club in Sweden charges lower prices for female supporters than for male supporters. It is alleged that female supporters are not as keen on football as males, and so have a more elastic demand.

● *Income:* Firms may charge higher prices to people with high incomes. For example, lawyers will often charge higher fees to wealthy clients and lower fees to clients who do not have high incomes. The wealthy clients will have a relatively inelastic demand for legal services, since they can afford them more easily.

● *Geographical distance:* Firms often sell products in different regions at different prices. This is possible as long as the cost of transferring the product is greater than the difference in the prices. If this is the case, then consumers in the low price region cannot transfer the goods to the high price region, without incurring transport costs that raise their total cost above the price in the high price region. For example, CDs are sold for a lower price in the USA than they are in the EU. This is possible because there are different price elasticities in the two countries and the transportation costs between the countries are greater than the price differential.

● *Types of consumer:* Firms sometimes sell at different prices to different users. For example, electricity companies may charge different rates to industrial users and domestic users. The rates will reflect their different elasticities of demand for power. Museums may charge people who are registered as unemployed a lower price than the standard rate. Market traders may charge foreign tourists a higher price for a product than they charge local consumers.

If the three conditions above do not exist, then price discrimination will not be possible. We need to be careful with price discrimination, since there are often cases that seem to be price discrimination, but are in fact simply examples of sales promotion. For example, students often say that nightclubs letting girls in for free while boys have to pay is an example of price discrimination. However, in reality this is not the case. It is unlikely that there is any difference in the price elasticity of demand for nightclubs between girls and boys. The motivation for the nightclubs is to offer a promotion that will attract girls to the nightclubs, so that lots of boys will then go, attracted by the high number of girls!

There are three degrees/levels of price discrimination to be considered:

1 **First-degree price discrimination** is said to take place when each consumer pays exactly the price that he/she is prepared to pay. This is how it is assumed that traders in a bazaar or market operate when they bargain to try to get the highest price that they can. In Figure 12.4, we see the case of a trader selling World Cup t-shirts to tourists in a market.

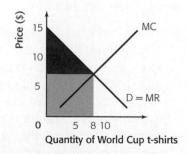

Figure 12.4 First-degree price discrimination

The trader attempts to bargain with the tourists to sell each shirt at the highest price that the tourist is prepared to pay. If the trader is successful, then as we can see, on that day, the trader will sell one shirt at $14, one at $13, one at $12, and so on. If the trader did not price discriminate, then total revenue for the day would be the shaded pale blue rectangle. However, by discriminating, the trader has eliminated the consumer surplus of the tourists and so the trader's total revenue is the shaded pale blue area plus the shaded dark blue triangle. Also since the extra revenue received from each shirt (the marginal revenue) is equal to the price of the shirt, in this case, D = MR.

2 **Second-degree price discrimination** is said to take place when a firm charges different prices to consumers depending upon how much they purchase. This is often how utilities companies (e.g. electricity and gas providers) operate. They may charge a high price for the first number of units, the essential ones, and then a lower price for any extra units consumed. Figure 12.5 shows the situation for the pricing of text messages by a mobile phone company. The first 50 messages per month are charged at a rate of 30¢ each. Any messages sent over this number are charged at the reduced rate of 20¢ per message.

3 **Third-degree price discrimination** is said to take place when consumers are identified in different market segments, and a separate price is charged in each market segment that recognises the different price elasticities in each segment. This is the most common form of price discrimination. Figure 12.6 shows a typical example of price discrimination in a cinema.

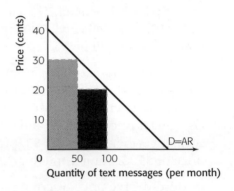

Figure 12.5 Second-degree price discrimination

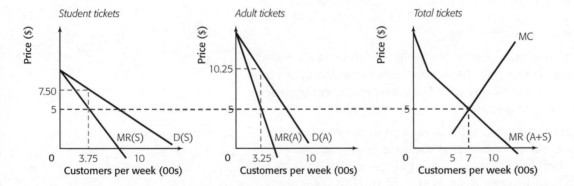

Figure 12.6 Third degree price discrimination

The management of the cinema have identified two distinct market segments in their audience, adults and students. The students have a more elastic demand for going to films because they have lower incomes. Thus the management know that they will have to charge a lower price for students than for adults. They can separate the market segments, because the students need to show some proof of their status before they are allowed into the cinema with a lower price ticket.

2 Microeconomics

Figure 12.6 shows the exact situation for a week at the cinema. The demand curve for students, D(S), is relatively more elastic than the demand curve for adults, D(A). The respective marginal revenue curves are twice as steeply sloping as the demand curves. We assume that the cinema is attempting to maximise profits and so we use the figure for total ticket sales on the right hand side. The marginal cost curve is for the cinema as a whole and the marginal revenue curve is a total of MR(S) and MR(A). This is why it is kinked. The cinema will maximise profits when MC=MR, so it will serve 700 customers per week and the marginal cost will be $5.

When the marginal cost is transferred to each market segment, we can find the profit-maximising position in each. In the student segment, when MC=MR=$5, profits are maximised by charging a price of $7.50 and attracting 375 students. In the adult segment, when MC=MR=$5, profits are maximised by charging a price of $10.25 and attracting 325 adults.

In third-degree price discrimination, a market may be broken up into more than two segments, but the principle will be the same. In cinemas, there are many different prices offered, such as normal adult, student, senior citizen, and under 12, but they all take account of different elasticities and they are all examples of third-degree price discrimination.

Whatever the degree, price discrimination can be both a good thing and a bad thing; it really depends upon the situation and who the stakeholder is.

 There are clear advantages to the firm:

- Price discrimination enables the producer to gain a higher level of revenue from a given amount of sales. This occurs because consumer surplus is eroded.

- Price discrimination may enable the producer to produce more of the product and thus gain from economies of scale. This could benefit everyone, by lowering average costs and lowering prices in all of the market segments.

- Price discrimination may enable a firm to drive competitors out of the more elastic market. If the firm is able to price discriminate, then it may use profits gained in the inelastic market segment to lower prices in the more elastic segment and thus undercut its competitors in that segment. This especially occurs in international trade, where a firm may have inelastic demand in the home market and more elastic demand in foreign markets. Price discrimination may allow the exporting firm to be aggressively competitive in the foreign markets. According to global trading rules set out by the World Trade Organization, firms may not sell in foreign markets at prices below the costs of production. This is known as dumping, and is illegal. However, firms are permitted to sell at lower prices in foreign markets, prices that are below the domestic market prices.

There are also some advantages to the consumer:

● Price discrimination may allow some consumers to purchase a product that they would not have been able to if other consumers were not paying a higher price and thus "subsidising" the poorer consumers. For example, in many countries, lawyers charge high prices to wealthy customers and this enables them to deal with lower-income clients for little or no fee. Doctors often do the same.

● Similarly, price discrimination allows some people to purchase a product at a lower price than they would have had to pay if the producer had not been able to secure higher prices from others. For example, many universities charge foreign students higher tuition fees than for domestic students.

● Price discrimination usually increases total output in a market and so the product is available to more consumers.

● As stated above, price discrimination may lead to economies of scale, lower unit costs, and thus lower prices for consumers in all market segments.

The disadvantages to the consumer are that:

● Any consumer surplus that existed before the price discrimination will be lost.

● Some consumers will pay more than the price that would have been charged in a single, non-discriminated market.

Student workpoint 12.1

Be inquisitive. Investigate the following:

Find three real-world examples of price discrimination. Provide details of the different prices charged to the different groups. Suggest why the elasticities of demand might be different between the market segments, and explain how the producer/seller manages to keep the markets separate (e.g. time, identity card).

Contestable markets

Contestable market theory is an interesting extension of the theory of market forms. It puts its focus not on what the market form is at the moment, but more on the probability of new firms entering the industry in the future.

A firm may have a monopoly at the moment, but what is the likelihood that other firms will be attracted to the industry in the future? If the likelihood is high, then the firm will probably keep prices low and simply make normal profits in order to discourage entry by others. For example, your school may have given the contract for catering to a local firm. That firm has the monopoly of catering in your school. However, the catering firm will be aware that it would be very easy for a new firm to enter the market by offering lower prices to the school. Thus it is likely that the existing firm will keep their prices reasonable and the quality of their food high in order to discourage the possible entry of new firms. The catering firm acts as if it were in a competitive market, even though it is not. If there is little likelihood of new firms entering an industry, because barriers to entry are effective and long-lasting, then we could expect higher prices and, possibly, lower quality products.

Contestable market theorists say that the likelihood of entry by other firms is very much determined by entry costs and exit costs. Entry costs are the costs that a firm must pay if it enters an industry. This could be the costs of building a production plant to generate electricity or, less costly, the costs of renting an office and purchasing office equipment to act as a travel agent. Exit costs are the capital equipment that cannot be sold for other uses if a firm leaves an industry. These are fixed costs and are often known as sunk costs of entry. For example, a travel agent who decides to leave the travel industry would have very low exit costs, since the office can be rented to someone else and even the office equipment can be sold on. However, an electricity generating firms will find it much more difficult to sell their power generating plant and the sunk costs could be considerable.

A market is defined as contestable when barriers to entry are low, firms entering the industry would face similar costs to the firms that are already there, and would be able to get back their entry costs, less depreciation, when they leave the industry.

In simple terms, the lower the sunk costs of entry, the more contestable a market will be. If a market is contestable, the existing firm (if it is a monopoly) or firms (if it is an oligopoly) in the industry are more likely to charge lower prices than the short-run profit-maximising price. They would not want potential rivals to enter the market to try to compete away their profits. Thus it is the potential competition rather than the actual competition in the market which leads to pricing and output decisions.

Case study

The Twin City Liner

The Twin City Liner is a 75-minute boat journey on the Danube, connecting the two capital cities of Vienna and Bratislava. The boat makes three daily journeys from Vienna to Bratislava and three from Bratislava to Vienna.

The prices for the journeys are as follows:

Departing from Vienna		
Time	Weekdays	Saturday, Sunday and holidays
08.30	€23	€25
12.30	€19	€21
16.30	€15	€17
Departing from Bratislava		
10.15	€15	€17
14.15	€19	€21
18.15	€23	€25
Children—50% discount		

We have here an excellent example of price discrimination. People who want to make the journey might want to make a day of it. If they are in Vienna, then this means that they would like to take the first boat of the day at 08.30 and come back on the last boat of the day at 18.15. This will make the price of the round trip €46. Any other combination of journeys will be less expensive than this. Clearly the Twin City Liner company feels that this will be the most desirable trip and they are pricing to take advantage of people's demand. They must also be assuming that more people will want to make the round trip starting from Vienna rather than from Bratislava as all combinations starting from Vienna and returning the same day cost more than their equivalent from Bratislava.

The fact that they are charging a higher price on Saturdays, Sundays, and holidays is also due to differing elasticities of demand. These may be the only days that some people can travel, thus their demand will be less elastic. The company can "take advantage" of this by charging a higher price.

The fact that children are offered a lower price is also an example of price discrimination. They will still occupy a seat, but only pay 50% of the price.

Incidentally, the price for a dog's ticket is only €3. This, however, is not price discrimination as the product being sold isn't identical to a person's ticket. After all, the person will get a seat!

Examination questions

Short response questions

1 Explain the conditions necessary for a seller of a good to be able to price discriminate.   *[10 marks]*

2 Explain what is meant by contestable market theory.   *[10 marks]*

Essay question

1 a Explain the concept of price discrimination.   *[10 marks]*

   b Evaluate the effects of price discrimination on producers and consumers.   *[15 marks]*

Assessment advice: using examples

Always remember to include examples in your written answers. For example, in explaining the concept of price discrimination, you will be able to do so much more effectively if you give examples of situations where price discrimination takes place. To evaluate the effects, you need to be able to consider the effects on the stakeholders in different examples.

You be the journalist

Headline: Government announces plans to raise tuition fees for foreign students

Economics concept: Price discrimination

Diagram: Different elasticities of demand for domestic students and foreign students

Hint: Try to explain why the government might want to do this and consider why the demand for universities from foreign students might be less elastic than the demand from domestic students.

Market failure

By the end of this chapter, you should be able to:

- define community surplus, social efficiency, and Pareto optimality
- define market failure
- explain, illustrate, and give examples of types of market failure
- define and give examples of public goods, merit goods, and demerit goods
- define, distinguish between, illustrate, and give examples of positive and negative externalities of production and consumption
- define and explain tradable emission permits
- evaluate different government methods of intervention to deal with the existence of externalities.

Community surplus

When a market is in equilibrium, with no external influences and with no external effects, it is said to be in a state of Pareto optimality. Pareto optimality exists when it is impossible to make someone better off without making someone else worse off. It does not, however, mean that everyone is equal.

If a market is Pareto optimal, then it is said to be socially efficient. Social efficiency exists when community surplus is maximised. Community surplus is the welfare of society and it is made up of a consumer surplus plus a producer surplus. Standard level students will need to consider the first section in Chapter 12 to understand these concepts. This is shown in Figure 13.1.

In Figure 13.1, we can see that the market is in equilibrium. At the equilibrium price, P, and quantity, Q, community surplus is maximised. Given this supply and demand situation, there is no other combination of price and quantity on the diagram that could give a greater community surplus. Thus the market is Pareto optimal/socially efficient, and there is an optimum allocation of resources. No one could be made better off without making someone else worse off.

As we have seen, the free market, as shown in Figure 13.1, leads to an optimum allocation of resources and maximises community surplus. The supply curve is determined by the marginal costs of production and, since this is the marginal cost to the whole community, we refer to it as marginal social cost. The demand curve is determined by marginal utility (marginal benefit) and, since this is the marginal benefit to the whole community, it is known as marginal social benefit.

Market failure

In the "real world", markets are not perfect. There are a number of things that prevent markets from being perfect and, therefore, from allocating resources in an optimal manner. If this is the case, then

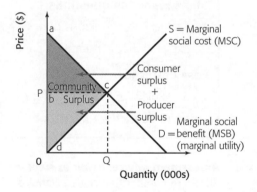

Figure 13.1 Community surplus

community surplus is not maximised and we say that this is a market failure. When markets fail, governments are often expected to intervene in order to attempt to eliminate the market failure and move towards the optimal allocation of resources.

We need to look at the reasons why markets might fail and the possible options that governments might have to try to correct that failure.

Types of market failure

Imperfect competition
Monopolists, and other imperfect markets, restrict output in order to push up prices and maximise profits. Because of this, they are not producing at the socially efficient level of output. Any imperfect market will fail to equate marginal social cost (MSC) and marginal social benefit (MSB). This is shown in Figure 13.2.

Because profits are maximised where MC = MR, Q_1 will be produced at a price of P_1 and the socially efficient level of output, Q^*, is not reached. There is therefore a loss of consumer surplus, shown by the shaded dark blue triangle, and a loss of producer surplus, shown by the shaded pale blue triangle. Thus community surplus is not maximised and we have a situation of market failure. When community surplus falls from the maximum, we say that there has been a welfare loss. This is because the units Q_1–Q^* are not produced, even though the marginal social benefit is greater than the marginal social cost. The welfare loss is shown by the combination of the two triangles.

Governments may try to reduce this market failure by intervening in a number of ways.

● They may use legal measures to make markets more competitive. They may pass laws that do not permit mergers or takeovers that give an individual firm more than a certain percentage of the market, e.g. 25%. In addition, they may pass laws that do not permit mergers or takeovers that enable a specified number of the largest firms in an oligopoly to control more than a certain percentage of the market, e.g. the four largest firms may be restricted to 60%.

● They may set up regulatory bodies to investigate markets where it is felt that monopoly power is being used against the public interest. For example most countries have some sort of "Monopolies Commission" or "monopoly watchdog". These bodies are then empowered to take action of some kind, or to recommend that the government should take action, if it can be shown that the public interest is being harmed.

(Standard level students do not need to understand the details of profit maximisation. They simply need to know that imperfect competition leads to lower output at higher prices and that the socially efficient equilibrium level of price and output is not reached.)

Lack of public goods
Public goods are goods that would not be provided at all in a free market. Since they are goods that are of benefit to society, the lack of

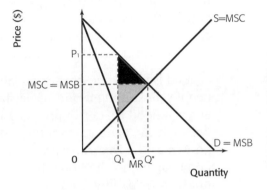

Figure 13.2 Imperfect competition

public goods in a free market is considered to be a market failure. Examples of public goods would be national defence and flood barriers. There is much debate over what is actually a public good and what is not. A number of goods often considered to be public goods could, in theory, be supplied by the free market to some extent, such as street lighting or lighthouses, and because of this, they are sometimes known as quasi public goods.

The reason that public goods will not be provided at all in a free market is that they have two characteristics—they are non-excludable and non-rivalrous—and that makes it pointless for private individuals to provide the goods themselves. If a good does not have both of these characteristics, then it is not a public good. If a good is completely non-excludable and non-rivalrous, such as national defence and flood barriers, then it is called a pure public good.

A good is said to be non-excludable if it is impossible to stop other people consuming it once it has been provided. If a private individual erects a flood barrier to protect a house, the other people in the area will gain the benefit, even though they have paid nothing. This is known as the free-rider problem. Logically, no one will pay for a flood barrier, in the hope that someone else will do it. The good will not be provided by the free market.

A good is said to be non-rivalrous when one person consuming it does not prevent another person from consuming it as well. If a person eats an ice cream, then another person cannot consume that ice cream as well. However, if one person is protected by a flood barrier, it does not stop other people from being protected at the same time. The private benefit from a flood barrier would be very small relative to the cost, although the social benefit to all of the people who were protected by it would be huge and probably greater than the cost. Thus there is no incentive for a private individual to erect a flood barrier.

Governments may try to reduce this market failure by intervening in a number of ways.

● They may provide the public good themselves. This is usually the case with such things as national defence, flood barriers, roads, pavements, street lighting, and lighthouses. The use of taxpayers' money to fund the provision spreads the cost over a large number of people who would not be prepared to pay individually.

● They may subsidise private firms, covering all costs, to provide the good.

Under-supply of merit goods

Merit goods are goods that will be underprovided by the market and, because of this, they will be under-consumed. (We call them merit goods, but they are usually services.) They are goods that the government thinks provide positive benefits for both the people that use them and society as a whole, and therefore they think that such goods should be consumed to a greater degree. All public goods are merit goods. Some examples of merit goods are education, health care, sports facilities, and the opera.

Governments will attempt to increase the supply, and thus the consumption, of merit goods. How they do this will depend upon how important they think the merit good is. In the case of extremely important merit goods, such as education and health care, the government may well provide them directly or subsidise them to the point where they are available at no direct cost to the consumer. Of course, this does not mean that they have no actual cost. The cost is simply shared among taxpayers.

As merit goods become less important in the eyes of the government, then they will be subsidised, but to a lesser extent. Sports facilities are considered to have positive benefits for people and so may well gain subsidies from the government. The opera may be the same, but since the benefits may be considered to be smaller, the subsidy given to the opera may well be smaller.

Theory of Knowledge

Consider the following statements

- All public goods are merit goods.
- Sports facilities are a merit good.
- Therefore, sports facilities are a public good.

Is the conclusion logical? Why or why not?

Over-supply of demerit goods

Demerit goods are goods that will be over-provided by the market and, because of this, they will be over-consumed. They are goods that the government thinks are bad both for people who consume them and for society as a whole, and therefore government would like to see them consumed to a lesser degree, or not at all. Examples of demerit goods are cigarettes, alcohol, hard drugs, and child pornography.

Governments may attempt to reduce the supply and/or the demand for demerit goods. How much they do this will depend upon how harmful they think the demerit good is. In the case of extremely harmful demerit goods, such as hard drugs and child pornography, the government will make them illegal and ban them completely. Of course, this does not mean that they will completely disappear, because in reality illegal black markets appear, attracted by the chance to make profits by fulfilling an existing demand.

 As demerit goods become less harmful in the eyes of the government, then they will be taxed. More harmful goods, such as cigarettes, may be taxed more highly than slightly less harmful goods, such as alcohol.

The existence of externalities

An externality occurs when the production or consumption of a good or service has an effect upon a third party. If the effect is harmful, then we talk about a negative externality. There is an external cost that must be added to the private costs of the producer or consumer to reflect the full cost to society. If the effect is beneficial, then we talk about a positive externality. There has been an external benefit to add to the private benefits of the producer or consumer.

We have already come across marginal social cost (MSC) earlier in this chapter. MSC is equal to marginal private cost (MPC) plus or minus any external cost or benefit of production. If there are no externalities of production, then MSC = MPC. The MPC is essentially the "private" supply curve that is based on the firm's costs of production.

We have also come across marginal social benefit (MSB). MSB is equal to marginal private benefit (MPB) plus or minus any external cost or benefit of consumption. If there are no externalities of consumption, then MSB = MPB. The MPB is essentially the "private" demand curve that is based on the utility or benefits to consumers.

Thus if no externalities exist in a market, then MSC = MSB and we have social efficiency and so maximum community surplus, as in Figure 13.1. If externalities do exist, then MSC does not equal MSB and so we have a market failure and an inefficient allocation of society's resources.

Externalities may be split into four types.

1 Negative externalities of production/external costs
These occur when the production of a good or service creates external costs that are damaging to third parties. These relate mainly, but not exclusively, to environmental problems. For example, if a paint factory emits fumes that are harmful to people in the area, then there is a cost to the community that is greater than the costs of production paid by the firm. The firm has its private costs but then, on top of that, is creating external costs. Thus the marginal social cost of the production is greater than the marginal private cost. The marginal social cost is equal to the marginal private cost plus the external costs. This is shown in Figure 13.3.

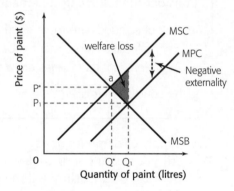

Figure 13.3 A negative externality of production

As we can see, the marginal private costs of the firm are below the marginal social cost, because there is an extra cost to society caused by the pollution that is created, such as respiratory problems for people in the neighbourhood of the polluting firm. The firm will only be concerned with its private costs and will produce at Q_1. It is not producing at the socially efficient output, Q^*, where the marginal social cost is equal to the marginal social benefit and so it is a market failure. There is a misallocation of society's resources; too much paint is being produced at too low a price. There is a welfare loss to society of the extra units from Q_1 to Q^*, because the MSC is greater than the MSB for those units. This is shown by the shaded triangle.

In a free market, this situation would continue because profit-maximising firms will only take into account their private costs of production. Therefore, it is up to the government to rectify the situation. The government has a number of options.

● It could tax the firm in order to increase the firm's private costs and so shift the MPC curve upwards towards the point of social efficiency. If the tax is equal to the external cost of the production, then we say that the government has "internalised the externality". If the tax is not equal to the external cost, then it will reduce the deadweight burden, but not eliminate it. This is shown in Figure 13.4. There is still a welfare loss, but it is less than under the free market with no government intervention.

Although taxes are seen as a way of making the polluter pay, there are some problems with this solution. First, it is often difficult to measure accurately the pollution created and to put a value on it, which can be regained by the tax. Second, it is also difficult to identify which firms are polluting and to what extent each firm is responsible for the pollution. Third, it is often argued that taxes do not actually stop the pollution from taking place.

- The government could legislate and could ban the polluting firms, or restrict their output in some way. It could also pass laws relating to measurable environmental standards in the firm's production units. To meet the standards, the firms would have to spend money, thus increasing their private costs.

One problem with this solution is that a ban or restriction may lead to job losses and the non-consumption of whatever was being produced, which may have been a valuable product. Also, the cost of setting and then policing standards may be greater than the cost of the pollution.

- The government could issue tradable emission permits. These are a market-based solution to negative externalities of production. Tradable emission permits are issued by the government and give firms the licence to create pollution up to a set level. Once they are issued, firms can buy, sell, and trade the permits on the market.

The government decides upon the level of pollution that it will permit each year and then splits the total level of pollution up into a number of tradable emission permits, each allowing a certain level of pollution. The government then allocates these permits to individual firms. Thus each firm now has a quota of emissions that it is allowed to produce.

It is at this point that the market takes over. It is now in the interest of the firms to pollute as little as possible. If a firm pollutes at a higher level than its permit allows, it will need to buy permits from other firms and this will raise its costs. If a firm pollutes less than they are allowed, then they can sell their permit and make money. In the USA, the emission of chlorofluorocarbons (CFCs) is controlled by the use of tradable emission permits.

One problem with this solution is that it does not lead to the reduction of pollution, once the allowable limit has been set. Firms simply pay the cost of polluting, some polluting heavily and others not. Also, the government faces a difficult decision when setting an acceptable level of pollution and it is also difficult to measure a firm's pollution output.

A form of tradable emission permits is being used on an international level to attempt to reduce the emission of greenhouse gases (GHG). The Kyoto Protocol is an agreement made under the United Nations Framework Convention on Climate Change. Its

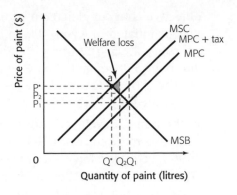

Figure 13.4 Taxing a negative externality of production

objective is to cut global emissions of greenhouse gases. The treaty was negotiated in Kyoto, Japan in 1997, and came into force in February 2005. The treaty covers more than 163 countries globally and over 65% of global GHG emissions. (Two notable exceptions are the USA and Australia, who have signed the treaty but have not ratified it.)

In the treaty, developed countries have agreed that by 2008, they will have reduced their GHG emissions to around 5% below their 1990 levels. Developing countries have no obligations to reduce GHG emissions, but they are in a position where they can be given tradable carbon credits (tradable permits) when they implement domestic GHG projects. Developed economies are allowed to meet their GHG targets by purchasing carbon credits from the developing countries that have earned them.

2 Positive externalities of production/external benefits

These occur when the production of a good or service creates external benefits that are good for third parties. Let us suppose that a large printing firm provides high quality training for its employees. This is a cost to the firm. When employees leave the printing firm and go to other firms, there is a benefit to the other firms who do not have to spend money on training their new workers. This is a positive externality of production to the new firms. Society has gained from the training given by the printing firm, even though the firm itself has not. Thus the marginal private cost of the firm is greater than the marginal social cost. This is shown in Figure 13.5.

As we can see, the printing firm produces at a level of output Q_1 that is below the socially efficient level, Q^*. Between Q_1 and Q^*, there is a potential welfare gain shown by the shaded triangle. If output could be increased to Q^* then welfare would be gained, because for all of the units from Q_1 to Q^*, MSB is greater than MSC.

Once again, in a free market situation, it is up to the government to rectify the situation, if it wishes to do so. The government could:

- Subsidise the firms that offer training. If this were to happen, then the MPC curve would be shifted downwards by the subsidy and, if a full subsidy were given, then MPC would be the same as MSC and the socially efficient point "a" would be reached.

  There are two main problems with this solution. First, it is very difficult for the government to estimate the level of subsidy deserved by every individual firm. Second, the cost of the subsidies would probably imply an opportunity cost and it is likely that the government would have to cut back on spending in other areas, which may be more worthy than this one.

- Provide vocational training through the state, by setting up training centres for workers in certain industries.

  Although this is a possibility, the costs would be high, the trainers may lack the expertise found in the firms, and it may dissuade firms from offering training of their own.

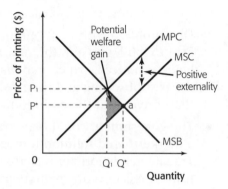

Figure 13.5 A positive externality of production

2 Microeconomics

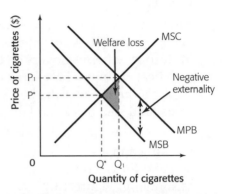

Figure 13.6 A negative externality of consumption

Student workpoint 13.1

Be a thinker

Try to explain why the research and development done by firms may create external benefits of production.

3 Negative externalities of consumption

There are many things that, when they are consumed by individuals, adversely affect third parties. Examples of this would be cigarettes and secondary smoking, cars and air pollution, and loud music and noise pollution. The negative externalities of consumption produced here make the marginal social benefits in each case less than the marginal private benefits. The private utility is diminished by the negative utility suffered by the third party. This is shown in Figure 13.6 with cigarettes as an example.

People who smoke presumably enjoy some private benefits of smoking, but this will create external costs for other people. This is commonly referred to as passive smoking, or second-hand smoking. Other than simple discomfort at the smell of cigarettes, the costs to others are significant. Because there is a free market, consumers will maximise their private utility (benefit) and consume at the level where MSC=MPB. They will ignore the negative externality that they are creating. This means that they will over-consume cigarettes by smoking Q_1 cigarettes at a price of P_1. The socially efficient output is at Q^* and so there is over-consumption of Q_1 to Q^*. Since MSC is greater than MSB for these units, there is a welfare loss to society and a market failure.

The government will act to reduce or eliminate the negative externality and once again, there are a number of options.

- It could simply ban cigarette smoking totally—make it illegal to smoke.

    However, this is not so simple, since this would have a large effect upon the tobacco industry, in terms of shareholders and employment. Governments also make a lot of revenue by taxing cigarettes, which have price inelastic demand, because they are habit-forming. Also, it must not be forgotten that governments need votes and smokers are not likely to vote for a government that bans smoking. Many governments have placed partial bans on smoking. That is, they have made it illegal to smoke in certain places. These are usually highly controversial decisions.

- The government could impose indirect taxes on cigarettes, in order to reduce consumption. This is shown in Figure 13.7.

    If the government imposes an indirect tax, then that will shift the MSC curve upwards to MSC + tax. This will reduce consumption to the socially efficient level of output Q^*, but the price to the consumers will be P_2. The government will gain significant revenue and this may be used to correct some of the negative externalities caused by smoking.

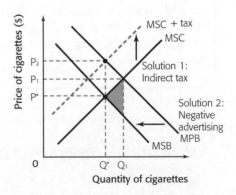

Figure 13.7 Measures to reduce negative externalities of consumption

141

However, the inelastic demand for cigarettes tends to mean that taxes do not manage to reduce quantity demanded very much and so, while government revenue is raised, quantity demanded does not fall to the socially efficient level (which some would say was zero!).

Also, if taxes are raised too much, then experience suggests that people start to look for other sources of supply. This can be seen in Europe, where smokers go to other countries where cigarettes are cheaper to purchase large quantities, for example Austrian smokers can go over the border to Slovakia. Often, this process is illegal and so a black market is formed.

● The government could provide education about the dangers of smoking and also fund negative advertising in order to reduce demand for cigarettes, thus shifting the MPB curve to the left, as shown in Figure 13.7.

However, the costs of this may be high, although if taxes are in place, then the revenue could be used to fund these measures. Also, there is doubt as to the effectiveness of education and advertising in terms of reducing cigarette consumption. Many teenagers, for example, seem prepared to accept the dangers of smoking and are little affected by measures to put them off.

Did you know?

A study published in 2005 by researchers at Georgia State University and the Society of Actuaries revealed that the exposure of non-smokers to second-hand smoke costs the American economy $10 billion per year. This includes $5 billion on the direct medical costs of diseases such as lung cancer, cervical cancer, asthma, ear infections, low birth weight, and coronary heart disease, and another $5 billion on the indirect costs such as lost wages as a result of such illnesses. It should be emphasized that these are the costs of medical problems that are borne by non-smokers, not the smokers themselves.

Student workpoint 13.2

Explain how taking a flight for a holiday abroad may create both negative and positive externalities.

Student workpoint 13.3

Be an inquirer

The incredible pace of economic growth in China is a well-known story. What is also becoming a well-known story are the external costs of this growth on the environment and the people of China. Indeed, as environmental problems cannot be contained within a country's borders, the external costs are fast becoming a global problem. The industrial growth and rising incomes in China have led to ever-mounting problems of acid rain, choking smog, contaminated lakes and rivers, and massive waste management problems. According to the World Bank, 16 of the world's most polluted cities are in China. China's economy is approximately a fifth of the size of the US economy, but China is second only to the US in terms of global emissions of carbon dioxide. According to World Bank estimates,

approximately 300,000 deaths a year are the result of environmental problems. At an environmental conference in the summer of 2005, a Chinese government representative predicted that Chinese pollution would quadruple by 2020 if nothing were to be done. This is clearly a threat to the potential of China to experience sustainable development and the Chinese government is taking action.

Task: Describe two actions that have been taken by the Chinese government to reduce or control the external costs that have accompanied its high rate of economic growth. For each action that you have chosen, explain the source of the problem, state the nature of the external costs, describe how the solution is expected to work, and draw a diagram to illustrate the problem and solution.

4 Positive externalities of consumption

There are certain goods or services which, when consumed (used) will provide external benefits to third parties. When people "consume" health care, for example, they create a positive externality for society. If people are healthier, then they will not pass on illnesses so that other people around them are less likely to become ill, and a healthier workforce means that the economy will be more productive, which may be to the benefit of the whole population. Thus the MSB of consuming health care is greater than the MPB. This is shown in Figure 13.8.

In a free market for health care, people will consume Q_1 at a price of P_1. However, the socially efficient level of consumption would be Q^*, where MSB = MSC. There is a potential welfare gain, shown by the shaded triangle, because for the units from Q_1 to Q^*, MSB is greater than MSC. If the consumption of health care increases from Q_1 to Q^*, then welfare in society will increase.

The other important example of a positive externality of consumption is education, which may also have a marked effect on the welfare of society if its consumption is increased. Less weighty examples might be the use of vaccinations, outdoor music shows, and the use of deodorant.

If a government wishes to increase the consumption of services that create positive externalities of consumption, such as health care, then there are a number of options.

● The government could subsidise the supply of health care. This is shown in Figure 13.9. A subsidy would shift the MSC curve downwards and in this way, the socially efficient level of consumption at Q_1 could be reached, with a price of P_2. Indeed,

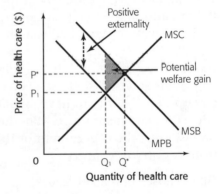

Figure 13.8 A positive externality of consumption

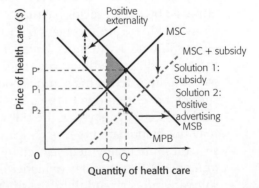

Figure 13.9 Measures to promote positive externalities of consumption

it may be that the government deems the importance of health care to be so great that it will subsidise it to the point where it is free to the consumer, or the state will supply it at no direct cost to the consumer.

 The main problem with such a solution is cost. While this provision is possible in many developed countries, developing countries are not able to fund such schemes and so do not fully benefit from the positive externalities that are to be gained from the consumption of health care.

- The government could use positive advertising to encourage people to consume more health care. This would shift the MPB curve to the right, towards the MSB curve, and would thus increase welfare.

 The problem here is that there may be a high cost to providing the advertising and, although the effect may be beneficial in the long run, it takes a long time to have an effect and so the short-run benefits may be minimal.

- The government could pass laws insisting that citizens have vaccinations against certain diseases, or have regular health checks, but this will only be successful if the government provides this free of charge. Also, people often resent laws of this sort being imposed by the government. They see it as an infringement of their civil liberties.

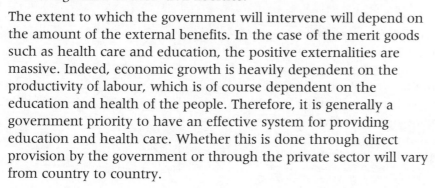

The extent to which the government will intervene will depend on the amount of the external benefits. In the case of the merit goods such as health care and education, the positive externalities are massive. Indeed, economic growth is heavily dependent on the productivity of labour, which is of course dependent on the education and health of the people. Therefore, it is generally a government priority to have an effective system for providing education and health care. Whether this is done through direct provision by the government or through the private sector will vary from country to country.

Other causes of market failure

There are a number of other causes of market failure that might be considered, although they tend not to have the weight of the ones already mentioned.

The immobility of factors of production

In a perfect market, in theory, resources move easily between uses, attracted by higher factor payments. In reality, this does not happen so easily and there are shortages of factors and time lags. Resources do not always find it easy to move between industries quickly. For example, if the coal industry in the north of a country is declining but the computer software industry in the south is booming, then in theory resources should move from one to the other. However, workers may not move easily, since they may lack the skills necessary for the new jobs and also may not be prepared to move their geographical location. Thus we get structural unemployment caused by occupational and geographical immobility. Factor costs are higher than they should be in the computer software industry and there are unemployed resources in the area where the mining jobs have disappeared.

To correct this type of market failure, governments adopt policies that either take work to the workers or take the workers to the work. They will also have to encourage retraining schemes. (See Chapter 20 for more details.)

Problems of information

Theory tells us that in a perfect market, both consumers and producers have perfect knowledge of the market. In reality, of course, this is not the case and so decisions are often being made based upon incomplete information. This makes it very hard for marginal costs and marginal benefits to be equated and this leads to market failure.

Consumers make decisions to purchase goods that they do not often buy, and so have little knowledge of, such as cars and houses. Producers have to estimate demand over a period of time and so often set an average price to cover a range of possibilities.

 Governments may try to improve the flow of information to correct this market failure, but this is expensive and may not be possible for all markets.

The creation of inequality

The free market often leads to the existence of large differences in income and wealth between different groups of people in the economy. Remember that Pareto optimality does not signify equality.

 It may be that society sees the creation of inequality as a failure of the market and may then attempt to use progressive taxation to redistribute income from one group of the population in order to benefit a less fortunate group.

Short-termism

Sometimes, short-term decisions are made that may have severe long-term implications. Let us consider two examples.

First, the private sector is often blamed for pursuing short-term profit-based objectives at the cost of long-term problems. Firms may use up resources in the short term at a rate that means that development in the future will not be able to be sustained at the present rate. This reduces the potential for sustainable development.

The second example concerns the public sector—the government. Governments may intervene in the workings of markets in the short term in order to gain results that will lead to re-election, even though this intervention may go against the long-term best interests of society. They are, in effect, causing a market failure in these markets by their intervention.

Examination questions

Short response questions

1 With the help of a diagram, explain why cigarette smoking is a cause of market failure. *[10 marks]*

2 With the help of a diagram, explain why the provision of health care in an economy is likely to require government intervention. *[10 marks]*

Essay question

1 a Explain the concept of negative externalities of production. *[10 marks]*

b Evaluate **three** policies that may be used by government to reduce external costs of production. *[15 marks]*

You be the journalist

Headline: Government ignites a fire with its announcement of a ban on smoking in bars and restaurants

Economics concept: Negative externality of consumption

Diagram: Negative externality of consumption + solution

Hint: Explain why this would be such a controversial decision—who are the different stakeholders involved?

14 Measuring national income

By the end of this chapter, you should be able to:

- list the five main macroeconomic goals
- illustrate the circular flow of income model of the economy
- distinguish between three equivalent measures of national income
- define and distinguish between gross national product (GNP) and gross domestic product (GDP)
- define and distinguish between gross national product (GNP) and net national product (NNP)
- define and distinguish between nominal GDP and real GDP
- explain the uses of national income statistics
- explain the limitations of using national income statistics.

In Chapters 3 to 13, we looked at microeconomics—the study of individual markets. In Chapters 14 to 22, we will now be looking at macroeconomics—the study of a national economy. Macroeconomics is concerned with the allocation of a nation's resources, and is concerned with five main variables. These variables, and the macroeconomic objectives associated with each variable, are shown in Table 14.1 and form the basis of the macroeconomic analysis for the next eight chapters.

Variable	Macroeconomic objective
Economic growth	A steady rate of increase of national output
Employment	A low level of unemployment
Price stability	A low and stable rate of inflation
External stability	A favourable balance of payments position
Income distribution	An equitable distribution of income

Table 14.1 Macroeconomic objectives

In studying an economy as a whole, a significant concern is the level of the economy's total output. We will see later in this chapter that this is also known as the economy's national income and we will look at the different ways in which this national income can be measured.

Circular flow of income model

To start, we look again at the very simple model of the nation's economy introduced in Chapter 2. In this model, there are two sectors. Households are the people who buy the nation's output of goods and services and the owners of all of the economy's factors of production. They supply these factors of production to the firms and, in turn, they receive payment for their factors. The firms hire the factors of production from households and use these factors to produce the nation's output of goods and services. The factors of production provided and income received are shown in a simplified form in Table 14.2.

Factor of production (provided by households)	Payment to the factor (provided by firms)
Labour	Wages
Land	Rent
Capital	Interest
Entrepreneurship	Profits

Table 14.2 Payment to the factors of production

This is the basis for the circular flow of income two-sector model shown in Figure 14.1. Households provide the factors of production (1) and receive income (2). They buy the goods and services (3) produced by the firms by using the income received (4), and in this way the income circulates throughout the economy.

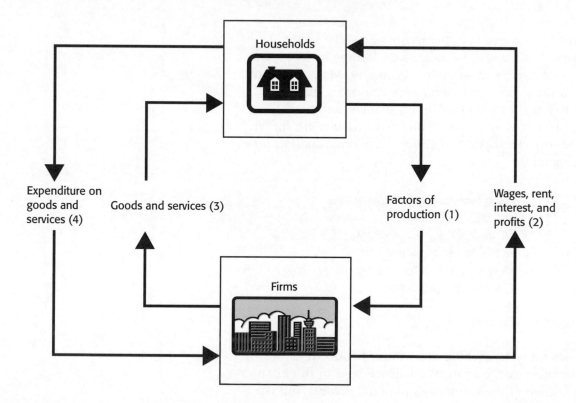

Figure 14.1 Two-sector circular flow of income model

Leakages and injections

The two-sector model described is very much a simplified model of the economy. Common sense is likely to tell you that households do not behave in this very simple way—that is, they do not spend all of the money that they receive in income as suggested by the model. Households can save some of their income. By definition, saving means foregoing current consumption to allow for consumption in the future. People can save by putting money in banks, or other financial institutions. Saving is known as a leakage from the circular flow, as it is income received, but not used to finance expenditure on goods and services. If households do not buy all the output that is produced by the firms, then firms will have unsold stocks of goods and, as a result, they will reduce their output. To reduce output, the firms will use fewer factors of production and thus pay less income. This shows how saving will cause the amount of income circulating in the economy to fall.

However, firms will have access to the savings of households by borrowing money from financial institutions such as banks or pension funds. They can use the money to increase their stock of capital and expand their output. This is known as investment and is an injection into the circular flow of income, as it involves income that does not come straight from the households through their spending on goods and services. Investment allows the amount of income circulating in the economy to rise.

Even though we have made the model slightly more realistic by adding saving and investment into the circular flow, the model is still limited by the fact that there are only two sectors. In reality, of course, there are other sources of income flow in an economy.

If households buy goods and services from other countries, then some of their income flows out of the economy's circular flow. Thus imports are also known as a leakage because they represent expenditure of income not returning to the firms. People in foreign countries buy the country's exports of goods and services. Exports are an injection into the circular flow because they represent a source of income not coming directly from the households. There is no reason to assume that exports will be equal to imports. Countries usually have trade imbalances.

Clearly, households and firms are not the only two sectors acting in an economy. We now introduce the government sector. Some of the income earned by households must be paid to the government in the form of taxes. Thus taxes are a leakage from the circular flow. Governments spend money in the economy on a wide range of things—schools, roads, campaigns to reduce smoking, and hospitals, to name a few examples. Government spending on goods and services represents an injection into the circular flow. There is no reason to assume that government spending will be equal to tax revenues. As you will see in later chapters, governments are able to spend more than they earn in order to deliberately influence the level of leakages and injections in an economy and thereby affect the level of national income.

It is important to point out that there is a category of government spending known as transfer payments that are not included as an injection into the circular flow. Transfer payments are payments to individuals that are not the result of an increase in output. Examples of transfer payments are pensions, unemployment benefits, and child allowance payments. Governments tax the income of some households and transfer this income to others through the payments. As it is a transfer of income, rather than income in exchange for output, this spending does not represent an injection.

Figure 14.2 shows the circular flow of income model with the four sectors—households, firms, the foreign sector, and the government sector—taking into account the leakages and injections.

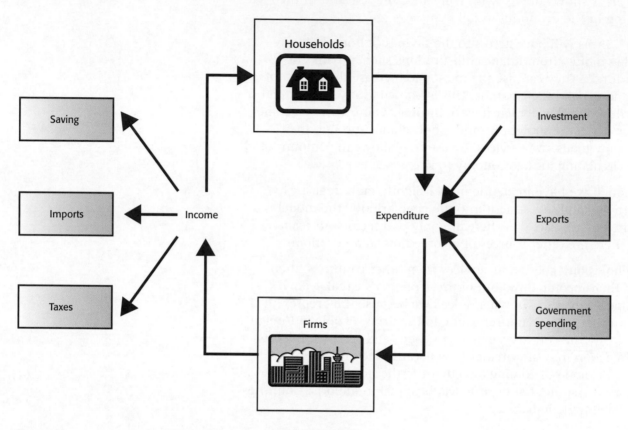

Figure 14.2 Four-sector circular flow with leakages and injections

Even the four-sector model remains a simplification of a complex economy, but it serves to illustrate some important conclusions. The economy is in equilibrium where leakages are equal to injections. If leakages rise, without a corresponding increase in injections, then national output will fall to a new equilibrium, as there will be less income circulating. If injections rise with no corresponding rise in leakages, then the economy will move to a new equilibrium. This will be illustrated graphically in later chapters.

Did you know?

Economics relies on the development of models, and attempts as much as possible to use the scientific method to create models and use the models to make predictions. The goal is to make them replicate the actual workings of an economy as closely as possible. If you go to the New Zealand Institute of Economic Research or the London Science Museum, you can see one of economics' most famous models, but you would probably not recognise it as such! It stands over six feet tall and comprises a number of plastic tanks and tubes through which coloured water flows. Linked to the tanks are gauges, sluices, and pulleys. Valves open and shut the tubes to control the flow of the water. Meters measure the different water levels and record these with the felt tip pins attached to the machine. It is called the Moniac machine and was built in 1949 at the London School of Economics by a New Zealand economist named A.W. Phillips. Its value lies in the way that it dynamically demonstrates the circular flow of income. The water in the model represents a given amount of income and the model is in equilibrium when the outflows (due to saving, taxes, and imports) are equal to the inflows (investment, government spending, and exports). The machine shows how the equilibrium will change as a result of changes to any of the flows. It adjusts to external shocks and shows all the ripple effects of the changes. In fact, after every shock, the model solves nine simultaneous equations to reach a new equilibrium and the movement to the new equilibrium will be visible by the movements of the felt tip pens. When it was first developed it became very popular with economists around the world. Several Moniac machines were built and used in universities in Britain, Australia, and the US. Machines were even bought by the Central Bank of Guatemala and Ford Motor Company. Ultimately, developments in computer technology superseded the model, but it certainly made an impact on the economic theory of its time.

How is national income measured?

The most commonly used measure of a country's national income is gross domestic product (GDP). There are three different methods that are all used to calculate this figure.

1 *The output method:* This measures the actual value of the goods and services produced. This is calculated by summing all of the value added by all the firms in an economy. When we say value added, it means that at each stage of a production process, we deduct the costs of inputs, so as not to "double count" the inputs. The data is usually grouped according to the different production sectors in the economy: agriculture and mining (primary sector), manufacturing (secondary sector), and services (tertiary sector). The output method measures the value of the arrow marked as number (3) in Figure 14.1.

2 *The income method:* This measures the value of all the incomes earned in the economy. This method measures the value of the arrow marked as number (2) in Figure 14.1.

3 *The expenditure method:* This measures the value of all spending on goods and services in the economy. This is calculated by summing up the spending by all the different sectors in the economy. These include:

● spending by households, known as consumption (C)

● spending by firms, known as investment (I)

● spending by governments (G)

● spending by foreigners on exports minus spending on imports. This is known as net exports (X–M).

The expenditure method measures the value of the arrow marked as number (4) in Figure 14.1.

Each approach measures the value of a nation's output differently by looking at different sets of data. Nonetheless, since they are measuring the same thing, their values are necessarily an equal amount. One common and highly acceptable definition of GDP is that it is the total value of all final goods and services produced in an economy in a year. This clearly reflects the output method of calculation. Another widely used definition is that GDP is the total value of all spending in the economy, algebraically expressed as GDP = C + I + G + (X–M). This reflects the expenditure method. Thus regardless of the method chosen, in theory, accounting will result in the same final figure, whether we call it national output, national income, or national expenditure.

In practice, however, the data that are collected to calculate each of the three values come from many different and varied sources, and inevitably there will be inaccuracies in the data, leading to imbalances among the final values. Some of these inaccuracies are the result of the timing of the data gathering; often figures have to be revised at later dates when full information is collected.

Definition

National output = National income = National expenditure

Student workpoint 14.1

Be a thinker—calculate and explain

a   Using the expenditure approach, calculate the GDP of Canada in 2005 using the data below.

	(million CAD$)
Consumer expenditure on goods and services	760,380
Business investment	260,969
Government expenditure	298,506
Exports	519,680
Imports	467,673

Source: Statistics Canada, www40.statcan.ca

b   What percentage of GDP is made up by each of the **four** sectors of the economy?

c   Why don't economists simply ignore the imports figure, instead of actually deducting it, when calculating GDP?

Gross domestic product (GDP) and gross national product (GNP)

Two definitions for gross domestic product (GDP) were given above. A third is useful to be able to make a comparison between GDP and gross national product (GNP). GDP may be defined as the total of all economic activity in a country, regardless of who owns the productive assets. For example, if an Indian multinational company (MNC) is operating in Canada and earning profits, then this income is included in the Canadian GDP and not in the Indian GDP. If the production takes place on Canadian land, then it is recorded on the Canadian GDP.

Gross national product (GNP) is the total income that is earned by a country's factors of production regardless of where the assets are located. In the example above, the profits earned by the Indian MNC would be included in Canada's GDP, but not Canada's GNP because Canada does not own the assets. Similarly, Canada's GDP would not include profits earned by a Canadian MNC operating in Brazil, but its GNP would include such profits. Thus GNP is equal to GDP plus income earned from assets abroad minus income paid to foreign assets operating domestically. The income earned by assets held in foreign countries is known as property income from abroad and the difference between income earned from assets abroad minus income paid to foreign assets operating domestically is known as net property income from abroad.

GNP = GDP + net property income from abroad

Gross national product (GNP) and net national product (NNP)

Throughout the course of a year, a country's capital stock will lose some of its value. This is known as depreciation of capital or capital consumption. This is due to several factors. It may simply be due to wear and tear as machinery is used; there may be damage to capital equipment or technology might make machinery obsolete. In effect, capital gets "used up" and the GDP does not take into account this depreciation of capital. The measure that does take this into account is called net national product (NNP), which is simply gross national product minus depreciation (capital consumption). While NNP gives a more realistic view of the real economic activity of a country, in practice it is very difficult to account for depreciation. Thus gross figures are the more widely used measures.

NNP = GNP − depreciation

Nominal GDP and real GDP

If we were to compare the GDP of a country from one year to another, we would have to take into account the fact that prices in the economy are likely to have risen. If prices of goods and services rise (inflation), then this will overstate the value of GDP. That is, GDP will rise even if there hasn't actually been an increase in economic activity. In order to get a true picture of the change in economic activity, we take the nominal GDP, which is the value at current prices, and adjust it for inflation to get the GDP at constant prices. This is done through the use of a "GDP deflator" and the value is known as real GDP. To compare GDP data over time, it is necessary to use the real value, so that price changes cannot distort the information. (Note: Whenever you see the adjective "real" in front of an economic variable, it means that the variable has been adjusted for inflation. This makes it possible to compare data over time.)

Real GDP = Nominal GDP adjusted for inflation

3 Macroeconomics

GDP per capita

This is the easiest of the national income statistics to measure. It is simply the total GDP divided by the size of the population. While the total economic activity of a country is appropriately measured using the GDP figure, if one is to make any judgment about the progress of a country in comparison with other countries in terms of raising living standards, then the GDP per capita figure is much more appropriate. For example, the GDP of China is US$1,417 billion, significantly higher than that of Canada, with a GDP of US$856.5 billion. This says that the output of China is approximately 65% more than that of Canada. However, when we take the population into account, we find that China's GDP per capita is US $1,100, while the GDP per capita of Canada is US$27,079. Thus the output per person in Canada is almost 26 times that of China's output per person (source: UNDP Human Development Report 2005).

Student workpoint 14.2

Be an inquirer

Pick an OECD country that you can study throughout the macroeconomics part of the course. The student workpoints will allow you to build a good case study of this country. There are several resources that you can use to do the research—the national statistics office for the country and the OECD (www.oecd.org) are two good starting points.

For this first exercise, find the following information and put it into a table. Be sure to note the source.

a   real GDP for the last 10 years

b   real GDP per capita for the last 10 years

c   real GDP growth per year for the last 10 years.

Why are national income statistics gathered?

Definitions of national income are fairly straightforward, but the job of compiling accurate accounts is extremely complicated and necessarily expensive. Every country has an organisation that is responsible for calculating and reporting on the country's national accounts. The United Nations provides guidelines for such work in the System of National Accounts (SNA). The data gathered are used in myriad ways.

● National income statistics can be seen as a "report card" for a country. Economic growth is a stated objective of governments. Economic growth is an increase in a country's national income over time. Therefore, people use the statistics to judge whether or not a government has been successful in achieving its macroeconomic objective of increased growth.

● Governments use the statistics to develop policies.

● Economists use the statistics to develop models of the economy and make forecasts about the future.

● Businesses use statistics to make forecasts about future demand.

- The performance of an economy over time can be analysed (as long as real data are used).

- Because rising national income is often equated with rising living standards, people often use national income accounts as a basis for evaluating the standard of living or quality of life of a country's population. This will be developed further in the next chapter.

- National income statistics are often used as a basis for comparing different countries.

Limitations of the data

Given the importance of national income statistics and their wide use, it is important to be aware of possible limitations of the data, both in terms of the accuracy of the data, in terms of their uses for making comparisons and in terms of their appropriateness in making conclusions about living standards.

- *Inaccuracies:* As noted above, the data that are used to calculate the various measures of national income come from a vastly wide range of sources, including tax claims by households and firms, output data and sales data. Figures tend to become more accurate after a lag time as they are revised when additional data are included. Statisticians in national statistics agencies make every effort to make their data as reliable as possible, and in the more developed countries, they can be assumed to be fairly reliable. The United Nations SNA works with all countries to improve the methods of gathering data. This improves the validity of comparisons.

- *Unrecorded or under-recorded economic activity—informal markets:* It is important to note that national income accounts can only record economic activity that has been officially recorded. They therefore don't include any do-it-yourself work or other work done at home. If you paint your own home, your work will not be included in the country's GDP, but if you pay a house-painting company to do so, the activity will be recorded, and GDP will rise, even though the output is identical. This is perhaps most significant for developing countries, where much of the output does not make it to any recorded market. For example, much of the food consumed in developing countries may be produced by subsistence farmers. These are people who grow their own food. Although estimates of the value of this are made, it is likely that GDP figures are undervalued. Comparisons may be difficult.

   Apart from the do-it-yourself work and subsistence farming, there is another category of economic activity that goes unrecorded or under-recorded. This may be referred to as the hidden economy. This includes activity that is unrecorded because the actual work is illegal, such as drug trafficking. It also includes unrecorded activity that is legal, but the people are doing it illegally. For example, if foreign workers do not have the appropriate work permits to do work such as cleaning, building, or working in restaurants, then their work will go unrecorded. It also includes work that is not recorded because people want to evade paying taxes. For example, when governments impose high taxes on cigarettes, this provides smokers with additional incentive to buy their cigarettes illegally to avoid paying the taxes. High indirect and direct taxes, along with government health and safety regulations, give employers the incentive to avoid the "official" economy and hire workers unofficially. High income taxes give people the incentive to understate their full income. For example, a lawyer will have to declare some official income, but may then pursue work that she does not declare. If she accepts cash for the extra work, then she can avoid officially claiming the income. Statisticians try to estimate the extent of the hidden economy from country to country. Table 14.3 includes some estimates for five OECD countries.

	Hidden economy % of GDP (2002–2003)
Greece	28.2
Italy	25.7
Norway	18.4
Canada	15.2
US	8.4

Source: "The Size of the Shadow Economies of 145 Countries all over the World". Friedrich Schneider University of Linz, Discussion Paper No 1431, December 2004.

Table 14.3 Estimates of size of hidden economy

The official GDP figure of Norway might be underestimated by 18.4% due to the existence of the hidden, or shadow, economy while in the US there is an 8.4% underestimation. It is argued that for the most part, the countries with higher tax burdens have a higher amount of hidden economic activity. The fact that there are different degrees of the hidden economy in different countries, and the fact that they are estimates, means that arriving at accurate measures to compare the values of GDP among countries may be a problem.

● *External costs:* GDP figures do not take into account the costs of resource depletion. Cutting down trees leads to an increase in GDP, but there is no measure to account for the loss of these trees. GDP figures do not make deductions for the negative consequences of air and water pollution and traffic congestion, as these are external costs. Such external costs are almost certain to compromise the quality of life, even as GDP increases.

● *Other quality of life concerns:* GDP may grow because people are working longer hours, or taking fewer holidays. While people may earn higher incomes as a result, they might not actually enjoy higher standards of living. GDP accounting does not include free activities such as volunteer work or people caring for the elderly and children at home. These are all activities that can lead to a better society, but might even be discouraged in the pursuit of economic growth.

● *Composition of output:* It is possible that a large part of a country's output is in goods that do not benefit consumers, such as defence goods or capital goods. If this is the case, then it would be hard to argue that a higher GDP will raise living standards.

3 Macroeconomics

Examination questions

Short response questions

1 Using a diagram of the circular flow of income model, explain the three ways that national income can be measured. [10 marks]

2 Distinguish between GDP, GNP, and NNP. [10 marks]

Essay question

1 a Explain three uses of national income statistics. [10 marks]

b Evaluate the use of GDP figures as a means of comparing countries. [15 marks]

Assessment advice: essay writing

There is a lot of overlap between this chapter and the next chapter, as we take a closer look at how living standards can be measured. The essay question provided here is a typical question about national income accounting, but you may find it easier to answer after the next chapter. In fact, because many of the topics in economics are interlinked, it is likely that you will be increasingly able to bring together concepts from several different sub-topics of the syllabus as you move through the course.

By the end of this chapter, you should be able to:

- distinguish between economic growth and economic development
- appreciate the limitations of using national income statistics in valuing economic welfare and/or measuring economic development
- explain other measures of economic development.

The national income statistics discussed in Chapter 14 provide immensely important information about a country's economic activity. They form the basis for assessing a country's economic growth. Economic growth is very much a one-dimensional concept. It is quite simply, an increase in the real output of an economy over time. Traditional economic theory has tended to make the assumption that increased output of an economy, along with the pattern of industrialisation that accompanies economic growth, is equivalent to economic development. This is no longer a reasonable or correct assumption and the last decades have seen the establishment of a new branch of economics—development economics. At the core of this study is the fact that economic growth is not equivalent to economic development. Economic development is a far more complex and multidimensional concept. While the bulk of the material to do with economic development is addressed in the last section of this book, in this chapter we look at the meaning of economic development and we examine some of the ways that development can be measured.

What is meant by economic development?

In Chapter 1, you were given a very basic definition of development as an improvement in welfare. We now expand on this notion, but must keep in mind the very subjective nature of the concept, and be aware that there is a wide range of possible explanations.

Development economist Amartya Sen (see the biography box) makes a powerful link between development and freedom.

This brief quotation demonstrates the multidimensional nature of development. Development is about increasing people's freedoms. It is about reducing poverty so that people can be adequately fed and sheltered. It is about the public provision of education, health care, and the maintenance of law and order. It is about the guarantee of civil liberties and the opportunity for civic participation.

'Development can be seen, it is argued here, as a process of expanding the real freedoms that people enjoy. Focusing on human freedoms contrasts with narrower views of development, such as identifying development with the growth of gross national product, or with the rise in personal incomes, or with industrialization, or with technological advance, or with social modernization.

Development requires the removal of major sources of unfreedom: poverty as well as tyranny, poor economic opportunities as well as systematic social deprivation, neglect of public facilities as well as intolerance or overactivity of oppressive states. Despite unprecedented increases in overall opulence, the contemporary world denies elementary freedoms to vast numbers—perhaps even the majority of people.

Sometimes the lack of substantive freedom relates directly to economic poverty, which robs people of the freedom to satisfy hunger, or to achieve sufficient nutrition, or to obtain remedies for basic illnesses or the opportunity to be adequately clothed or sheltered, or to enjoy clean water or sanitary facilities. In other cases, the unfreedom links closely to the lack of public facilities and social care, such as the absence of epidemiological programmes, or of organized arrangements for health care or education facilities, or of effective institutions for the maintenance of local peace and order. In still other cases, the violation of freedom results from a denial of political and civil liberties by authoritarian regimes and from imposed restrictions of the freedom to participate in the social, political, and economic life of the community.'

Amartya Sen. 1999. Development as Freedom. Oxford, UK. Oxford University Press. pp 3–4.

Profile Amartya Sen (1933–present)

Amartya Sen was born in West Bengal, India. At the age of 9, he had his first encounter with suffering, meeting victims of the Bengal famine in which three million people died. Later, his work on famine research led to the publication of *Poverty and Famines: An Essay on Entitlement and Deprivation*, addressing the inequalities in access to food.

While at secondary school, Sen was uncertain as to what academic discipline he should study. In his own words, "I seriously flirted, in turn, with Sanskrit, mathematics, and physics, before settling for the eccentric charms of economics."

At the age of 18, Sen left India to study economics at Trinity College, Cambridge, where he earned both his Bachelor of Arts and then his doctorate. He has held several teaching positions, including at the University of Calcutta, Jadavpur University, Delhi, Oxford University, London School of Economics, Harvard, and Cambridge.

While working at Harvard, he teamed up with an old friend Mahbub ul Haq, a reputed Pakistani economist. Together, they contributed to the establishment of the Human Development Index and the Human Development Report, published annually by the United Nations Development Programme (UNDP). Such developments have allowed economic development to be evaluated on a range of measures, rather than on the classical macroeconomic indicators such as GNP or GDP.

Having published an impressive number of books and publications, Sen has also received a number of awards, including the Nobel Prize for Economics in 1998 for his contribution to welfare economics. He has had a powerful influence on the study of development economics as well as on international institutions and national governments.

Student workpoint 15.1

Be knowledgeable

To supplement the brief description of Amartya Sen, prepare an annotated time line of his life, making notes on the key stages in his life along with his major achievements and contributions. See his autobiography written for the Nobel Prize organization as a starting point (http://nobelprize.org).

Did you know?

What is the UNDP?

The United Nations Development Programme (UNDP) is "an organization advocating for change and connecting countries to knowledge, experience and resources to help people build a better life". The UNDP operates in 166 countries, working with them to develop their own solutions to the challenge of development. An important part of this effort involves the development of local capacity. Capacity is defined by the UNDP as "the ability of individuals, organizations and societies to perform functions, solve problems, and set and achieve goals". The ultimate goal is the reduction of poverty, the enhancement of self-reliance, and the improvement of people's lives.

Source: www.undp.org.

3 Macroeconomics

Theory of Knowledge

Three core values

Another economist, Michael Todaro, developed the work of Denis Goulet to present his view of the essential features of development.

At the outset is his observation of "development as the sustained elevation of an entire social system toward a 'better' or 'more humane' life". The use of the words "better" and "more humane" are reminders of the subjective nature of the discussion. However, he identifies three "core values" or fundamental human needs. If life is to be made "better" then there must be progress in meeting these three core values.

1 *Sustenance:* The ability to meet basic life-sustaining needs for food, shelter, health, and protection.
2 *Self-esteem:* The ability of people and communities to develop a sense of self worth, identity, dignity, and respect.
3 *Freedom from servitude and the ability to choose:* This involves expanding the range of choices for people and societies and granting them freedom from oppression from external factors.

Does the subjective nature of the topic make it impossible to accept that these are "universal truths"?

Human development index

Given the multidimensional nature of economic development, it is hardly surprising that it is difficult to measure. The United Nations Development Programme (UNDP) provides the human development index (HDI) as one measure. The HDI is a composite index that brings together three variables. There are three basic goals of development that can be "measured". These are: a long and healthy life, improved education, and a decent standard of living. A long and healthy life is measured by life expectancy at birth on the assumption that people who live longer have benefited from good health. Education is measured by the adult literacy rate combined with a measure of primary, secondary, and tertiary school enrolment. The standard of living, or the ability to meet basic needs, is measured by the GDP per capita, converted at PPP US$ (see box). The three indicators are combined to give an index value between 0 and 1, with higher values representing a higher level of development. The UNDP classifies countries into three categories according to their HDI. These categories are shown in Table 15.1.

Category	HDI value
High human development	0.800 and above
Medium human development	0.500–0.799
Low human development	Less than 0.500

Table 15.1 HDI country classifications

3 Macroeconomics

HL

Did you know?

What are purchasing power parity exchange rates?

The national income of Nigeria is calculated in Nigerian naira, the national income of Thailand in Thai baht and the national income in China in yuan renminbi. If we want to understand the value of the GDP in other countries, or if we want to make comparisons between countries, then we clearly need to be able to convert those national values into a common currency. Typically, the US dollar is chosen as the international currency for comparison. However, this poses some problems.

As you will learn in more detail later, currencies change in value. If the Chinese yuan renminbi were to increase in value against the US dollar, then the value of China's national output converted in US dollars would also rise, even if there were actually no increase in output. Countries can maintain the value of their currencies at a given level. If they maintain the value at a high level, then this will overstate the true value of their output. This can make the GDP figures converted at official rates unreliable for measuring the level of national output.

A second problem is that goods and services simply don't cost the same amount in different countries. That means that the purchasing power of a person's income will be different in different countries. For example, a loaf of bread will cost less in Nigeria than it will in Vienna. In fact, the price of most things will be less in Nigeria than in Vienna. When we convert

the Nigerian GDP per capita into US dollars, we get US$428 (2003 figure). However, that $428 actually has much higher purchasing power in Nigeria than it would in Vienna because things cost less in Nigeria.

To avoid this problem, economists calculate what is called the purchasing power parity (PPP) exchange rate. This exchange rate attempts to equate the purchasing power of currencies in different countries. It is calculated by comparing the prices of identical goods and services in different countries. The PPP that is most widely used is the one calculated by the World Bank. *The Economist* magazine also calculates a PPP rate based on the price of Big Macs in different countries. They call it the Big Mac index, and refer to the study as Burgernomics!

While there are, of course, limitations to the reliability of the data, when we convert GDP figures into US dollars at the PPP rates we get a more valid figure for making judgments about the ability of people to meet their basic needs. The Nigerian GDP per capita converted at the PPP rate into US dollars is $1,050. While this is still a small figure, and represents a very low income indeed, it is more realistic than the $428 converted at official exchange rates. Typically, the difference between the GDP converted into the US dollar at official rates is considerably lower than the GDP converted at PPP rates for lower income countries.

How can the HDI information be used?

Prior to the establishment of the HDI in 1990, GDP per capita had been the yardstick for measuring development, under the assumption that higher national income translated directly into a higher level of development. If we compare a country's ranking in terms of its HDI with its ranking in terms of its GDP per capita, we may make some useful conclusions about the country's success in translating the benefits of national income into achieving economic development. Consider the data in Table 15.2. Norway has the highest HDI value, but it is ranked third in terms of GDP per capita. The United States is ranked 4th in terms of its GDP per capita, but 10th in terms of its HDI. Had we simply used GDP per capita figures to make conclusions about development concerns, the data would have been misleading. There are even more extreme discrepancies. Consider Saudi Arabia, ranked 44th for its GDP per capita, but 77th for its HDI. It has a GDP per capita that is slightly higher than that of Argentina, but its HDI is considerably lower, with Argentina classified as a high human development country. Using this information it may be possible to make hypotheses about the emphasis of government policies with respect to development.

The UNDP observes that one of the uses of the HDI is to "re-emphasize that people and their capabilities should be the ultimate criteria for assessing the development of a country, not economic growth" (http://hdr.undp.org).

High human development (57 countries)	HDI value	HDI rank	GDP per capita (PPP US$)	GDP per capita (PPP US$) rank	GDP per capita (PPP US$) rank minus HDI rank*
Norway	0.963	1	37,670	3	2
Sweden	0.949	6	26,750	20	14
United States	0.944	10	37,562	4	−6
Italy	0.934	18	27,119	19	1
Argentina	0.863	34	12,106	46	12
Kuwait	0.844	44	18,047	33	−11
Bahamas	0.832	50	17,159	37	−13
Tonga	0.810	54	6,992	71	17
Bulgaria	0.808	55	7,731	65	10
Medium human development (88 countries)					
Macedonia	0.797	59	6,794	75	16
Mauritius	0.791	65	11,287	49	−16
Dominica	0.783	70	5,448	91	21
Saudi Arabia	0.772	77	13,226	44	−33
Ecuador	0.759	82	3,641	112	30
Turkey	0.750	94	6,772	76	−18
Georgia	0.732	100	2,588	121	21
Guyana	0.720	107	4,230	105	−2
Honduras	0.667	116	2,665	119	3
South Africa	0.658	120	10,346	52	−68
Tajikistan	0.652	122	1,106	158	36
Bangladesh	0.520	139	1,770	140	−1
Togo	0.512	143	1,698	146	3
Zimbabwe	0.505	145	2,443	125	−20
Low human development (32 countries)					
Madagascar	0.499	146	809	170	24
Cameroon	0.497	148	2,118	129	−19
Haiti	0.475	153	1,742	144	−9
Nigeria	0.453	158	1,050	160	2
Tanzania	0.418	164	621	175	11
Central African Republic	0.355	171	1,089	159	−12
Niger	0.281	177	835	169	−8

* A positive figure indicates that the HDI rank is higher than the GDP per capita (PPP US$) rank, a negative the opposite.

Source: Adapted from Table 1 of UNDP Human Development Report, 2005, (Column 5—OUP 2007)

Table 15.2 GDP per capita and HDI for selected countries

Student workpoint 15.2

Be a thinker

Use the data provided in Table 15.2 to draw conclusions about how the following pairs of countries differ in terms of their GDP per capita ranking and their

HDI ranking. What might this say about the countries' national policies on health and education?

a   Cameroon and Togo

b   South Africa and Tonga

Other indicators of development

Is the HDI sufficient as the only guide to a country's development?

Certainly not, but it is more effective than the simple GDP figure. The fact remains that there are many different aspects to development other than the three included in the HDI. It should also be noted that the country's HDI is still an average figure that can mask inequalities within the country. Inequalities that are likely to occur are between rural and urban citizens, between men and women, and between different ethnic groups. There are several other composite indicators and a vast number of single indicators, i.e. indicators that measure one thing, that attempt to measure the different dimensions of development.

The gender-related development index

Along with the country's national HDI, the UNDP attempts to break down the figures to present HDI values for different groups. For example, there is the gender-related development index (GDI) that looks at the same indicators as the HDI but takes into account the inequalities in these indicators for men and women. Inequality between men and women will result in a GDI figure that is lower than its HDI. We could say that the GDI is essentially the HDI adjusted for inequality between men and women. Table 15.3 provides some data for just a few countries.

Country	HDI	GDI	Difference
France (high HDI)	0.938	0.935	.003
United Kingdom (high HDI)	0.939	0.937	.002
Brazil (medium HDI)	0.792	0.786	.006
Turkey (medium HDI)	0.750	0.742	.008
Eritrea (low HDI)	0.444	0.431	.013
Chad (low HDI)	0.341	0.322	.019

Source: Adapted from Tables 1 & 25 of UNDP Human Development Report 2005, (Column 3—OUP 2007)

Table 15.3 HDI and GDI for selected countries

3 Macroeconomics

Theory of Knowledge

Often when you are asked a question, you are fooled into answering in a given way. For example, consider the following question about the data in Table 15.3.

"Explain, with reference to the data, the link between the value of a country's HDI and its GDI." You might be tempted to conclude that countries which have a higher level of development according to the HDI exhibit less gender inequality than low HDI countries as the disparity between the two values rises as the HDI values fall. This is certainly what this set of data implies. However, the problem with this is that there is not enough data to make this conclusion. Consider the following additional information.

Country	HDI (1)	GDI (2)	Difference (1) – (2)
France (high HDI)	0.938	0.935	.003
Argentina (high HDI)	0.863	0.854	.009
Saudi Arabia (medium HDI)	0.772	0.749	.023
Guatemala (medium HDI)	0.663	0.649	.014
Rwanda	0.450	0.447	.003
Kenya	0.474	0.472	.002

Source: Adapted from Tables 1 & 25 of UNDP, Human Development Report, 2005 (Column 3—OUP 2007)

Is the conclusion still valid? Why or why not?

This is not to say that one should not try to make conclusions. But you should always recognize the possible limitations of such conclusions. Where statistics are concerned, be sure to take into account the sample size as a possible limitation.

The gender empowerment measure

Given that one aspect of development involves developing self-esteem and creating opportunities and freedom for all people, it is valuable to measure whether development in a country is helping to create such freedoms and opportunities for women. To this end, the UNDP calculates the gender empowerment measure (GEM), which measures the extent to which women are able to actively participate in economic and political life. The GEM looks at the number and percentage of women in leadership, managerial, and parliamentary positions and in technical and professional jobs. It examines their participation in the labour force and their share of national income. A high value (index values range from 0 to 1) indicates a higher level of empowerment for women. If a country has a low GEM value in relation to its GDI value, this would imply that the access to basic needs, education, and health is not necessarily being translated into greater opportunities and participation for women.

'Women's empowerment helps raise economic productivity and reduce infant mortality. It contributes to improved health and nutrition. It increases the chances of education for the next generation.'
UNDP 2006 Annual Report

The human poverty index (HPI)

The UNDP attempts to measure the level of deprivation and poverty experienced in a country. While the HDI measures the achievements of a country in three variables, the HPI looks at the proportion of people who are deprived of the opportunity to reach a basic level in each area. It is also a composite index and looks at indicators that are comparable with the indicators in the HDI. The indicators are shown in Table 15.4.

Development goal	HDI measure	HPI measure illustrating deprivation in meeting the development goal
A long and healthy life	Life expectancy	% of people who do not reach the age of 40
Education	Literacy + school enrolment	% of adults who are illiterate
Ability to meet basic needs	GDP per capita (PPP$US)	% of population without access to safe water + % of children who are underweight for their age

Table 15.4 Human poverty index

Where the HDI represents development achievements for an average citizen, the HPI is useful for observing how evenly the benefits of development are spread within a country. The HPI value is expressed as a percentage, with a higher percentage indicating a greater level of deprivation and thus a higher level of poverty. Two countries might have similar HDI values, but very different HPI values. For example, Bangladesh has a slightly higher HDI than Congo, but in Bangladesh the HPI is 44.1% and in Congo it is 30.1%. This would suggest that the benefits of development are being shared less equally in Bangladesh, even though the HDI suggests a slightly higher level of development.

Lorenz curve and Gini index

HL

Income inequality in an economy can be measured. The most common representation of inequality comes in the form of a Lorenz curve. This takes data about household income gathered in national surveys and presents them graphically. Consider the following data.

Country	Survey year	Lowest 20%	2nd 20%	3rd 20%	4th 20%	Highest 20%	Gini index
Australia	1994	5.9	12.0	17.2	23.6	41.3	35.2
Brazil	2001	2.4	5.9	10.4	18.1	63.2	59.3
Croatia	2001	8.3	12.8	16.8	22.6	39.6	29
Hungary	2002	9.5	13.9	17.6	22.4	36.5	26.9
Sierra Leone	1989	1.1	2.0	9.8	23.7	63.4	62.9

Table 15.5 Income distribution for selected countries

Households are ranked in ascending order of income levels, and the share of total income going to groups of households is calculated. For example, if we look at Brazil, we see that the poorest 20% of households receive only 2.4% of total household income while the richest 20% of the population receives 63.2%. This contrasts with Hungary, where the data suggest more equality in distribution, with the poorest 20% receiving 9.5% of total household income, and the richest 20% receiving 36.5%.

The information can be graphed using Lorenz curves shown in Figure 15.1. The x-axis shows the cumulative percentage of the total population divided up in the quintiles shown in Table 15.3. The y-axis shows the cumulative percentage of total income earned by the quintiles. The line of absolute equality indicates a perfectly equal distribution of income where, for example, 10% of the population earns 10% of the income, and 90% of the population earns 90% of the income. Each country has its own Lorenz curve based on the income data. The farther away a country's curve is from the line of absolute equality, the more unequal is the distribution of income. In our example, the curve drawn for Brazil is farther away than that of Hungary. We can quickly observe from the diagram that income is less equally distributed in Brazil than it is in Hungary.

An indicator that neatly summarises the information presented in the table and on the Lorenz curve is the Gini index. The Gini index is derived from the Lorenz curve and is a ratio of the area between the line of equality and a country's Lorenz curve (a) to the total area under the line of equality (a) + (b). The higher the Gini index, the more unequal is the distribution of income. Gini index values are given in Table 15.5.

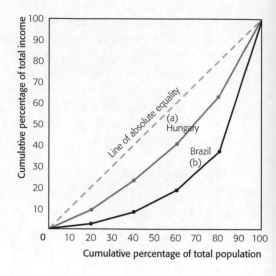

Figure 15.1 Lorenz curves for Hungary and Brazil

Student workpoint 15.3

Using graph paper and the data from Table 15.5, draw Lorenz curves for Croatia, Australia, and Sierra Leone. Remember that the points are drawn by adding up the cumulative values of total share of income and the total share of population. How does the shape of the curves confirm the relationship between a country's Lorenz curve and its Gini index?

Although a reduction in income inequality may be an important objective of development, one must be very careful in using Gini index numbers as a basis for evaluating a county's development progress. While low-income countries tend to have higher levels of inequality than high-income countries, there is no hard and fast correlation between the level of development of a country measured by its HDI and its Gini index. There are countries with a high level of human development such as the US that have a relatively high Gini index (40.8) and countries with a low level of human development, such as the Central African Republic, with a much lower Gini value (30.0).

Moreover, it would not be correct to assume that it is necessary to have more equality in order to raise living standards. Assume that the poorest 20% of the population earns 2.4% of the national income as in Brazil. If the national income rises and the income distribution pattern remains the same, then the poorest will receive a larger amount, even if their share remains the same. They get the same proportion of a larger amount!

Other indicators of development

While the UNDP calculates the composite HDI based on three key indicators, there are a huge number of other single indicators that measure different dimensions of development. These include:

- indicators to measure the ability to lead a long and healthy life:
  - infant mortality rate
  - under-five mortality rate
  - maternal mortality ratio
  - children underweight for age
  - population with sustainable access to an improved water source
  - population with sustainable access to improved sanitation
  - population undernourished
  - number of one-year-olds fully immunised against tuberculosis
- indicators to measure the ability to acquire knowledge:
  - enrolment in each level of education
  - literacy
  - Internet users per 1000 people
  - telephone mainlines per 1000 people.

Student workpoint 15.4

Be an inquirer

In 2000, the United Nations established eight Millennium Development Goals (MDGs), along with 18 targets for reaching these goals.

a What are the eight MDGs?

b What are the corresponding targets?

c Pick one country that is in the low human development category and one country that is in the medium development category. Using development indicators, assess the progress made by each of these countries in reaching the first seven targets.

The genuine progress indicator: postscript to Chapter 14

In Chapter 14, we looked at some of the reasons why GDP statistics are not a good indicator of living standards. In this chapter, we have furthered that discussion but with an emphasis on measuring development in developing countries. It is now important to consider one alternative measure of welfare that has been established in the more developed countries. This is known as the genuine progress indicator (GPI). This indicator attempts to measure whether a country's growth, which is simply an increase in the output of goods and services, has actually led to an improvement in the welfare of the people. To the GDP figures, it adds a measure of non-monetary benefits such as the benefits of household work, parenting, and volunteer work. Given that economic growth generates many costs, an indicator of genuine progress needs to deduct such costs, rather than add them to GDP. These include estimates of:

- environmental costs such as: air, water, and noise pollution; loss of farmland, wetlands, and forests; resource depletion; ozone depletion; pollution abatement
- social costs such as family breakdown, crime, personal security (e.g. home security systems), loss of leisure time

'The GDP measures everything except that which makes life worthwhile'
Robert Kennedy

3 Macroeconomics

- commuting costs
- costs of automobile accidents.

While such variables are, of course, difficult to measure, the realization that rising GDP does not equate with rising welfare means that welfare economists and environmental economists are constantly looking for ways to measure the consequences of growth so that developed and developing countries can aim for growth that is equitable and sustainable.

Examination questions

Short response questions

1 Distinguish between economic growth and economic development.   *[10 marks]*

2 Explain why PPP exchange rates are used when comparing national income among countries.   *[10 marks]*

HL

3 What is the relationship between a country's Lorenz curve and its Gini index?   *[10 marks]*

Essay question

1 a Explain the concept of economic development.   *[10 marks]*

b Evaluate the view that economic development is best measured using the human development index.   *[15 marks]*

By the end of this chapter, you should be able to:

- define aggregate demand (AD)
- define the components of AD
- explain the determinants of the components of AD
- explain how governments can use monetary and fiscal policy to alter the level of AD in an economy
- illustrate AD and shifts in AD.

'*Developing countries like India must make sure that their integration in the global economy helps lead to an increase in jobs, a more equitable distribution of income, and decreased poverty. The most important way of doing this is for the government to maintain as high a rate of aggregate demand as possible.*'
webIndia123.com, January 8, 2006

Aggregate demand (AD)

If you are confident in your understanding of the microeconomic concepts of demand and supply, then you have the necessary groundwork to understand the macroeconomic concepts of aggregate demand and aggregate supply.

In this chapter, we begin our macroeconomic analysis by examining the concept of aggregate demand. By definition, aggregate demand is defined as the total spending on goods and services in a period of time at a given price level. On a diagram, it looks very much like the demand curve in the sense that it is downward-sloping as shown in Figure 16.1.

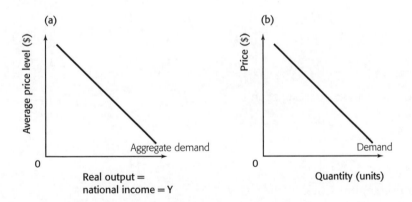

Figure 16.1 **(a)** Macroeconomic aggregate demand curve; **(b)** microeconomic demand curve

However, the demand curve shows the relationship between the price of one good, e.g. soccer balls, and the demand for that one good. The fact that it is a demand curve for one market makes it a microeconomic concept. Macroeconomics considers the working of the whole economy, including all the goods and services demanded. Where the microeconomic demand curve has the "price" of the one good on the y-axis, the macroeconomic aggregate demand curve has a measure of the average price level of all goods and services. Where the microeconomic demand curve has the "quantity" of the one good on the x-axis, the macroeconomic aggregate demand curve has the total quantity of all goods and services, which is national output. Given what you learned in Chapter 14, you will also realise that national output is equivalent to national income and national expenditure. In macroeconomic analysis, the x-axis is commonly labelled "real output" (the value of national output adjusted for inflation) or national income (Y). Thus the aggregate demand curve shows the relationship between the *average price level* and *real output*. The two different diagrams are shown to help you see and learn the difference between the microeconomic concept of demand and the macroeconomic concept of aggregate demand.

The AD diagram illustrates the inverse relationship between the average price level and the total real output demanded; at a lower average price level, a higher quantity is demanded. Essentially, this is the Law of Demand on an aggregate level. The word "aggregate" means "total". Therefore, in constructing an aggregate demand curve, we look at the demand from all possible sectors within the economy. This gives us the components of aggregate demand described in the next section.

Consumption

Consumption (C) is the total spending by consumers on domestic goods and services. In looking at consumer demand for goods, we look at two categories of goods—durable goods and non-durable goods. Durable goods are goods such as cars, computers, mobile phones, and bicycles that are used by consumers over a period of time (usually more than one year). Non-durable goods are goods such as rice, toilet paper, and newspapers that are used up immediately or over a relatively short period of time.

Student workpoint 16.1

Be reflective

Make a list of five durable goods and five non-durable goods used in your household.

Investment

Investment (I) is defined as the addition of capital stock to the economy. Investment is carried out by firms. Firms have two types of investment.

● Replacement investment occurs when firms spend on capital in order to maintain the productivity of their existing capital.

● Induced investment occurs when firms spend on capital to increase their output to respond to higher demand in the economy.

The economy's capital stock includes all goods that are made by people and are used to produce other goods or services such as factories, machines, offices, or computers. Investment is not to be confused with buying shares, or putting money in a bank. We tend to call this investment in "everyday" English, but it is, in fact, "saving" as it is a leakage from the circular flow.

Government spending

Governments at a variety of levels (federal, state/provincial, municipal/city) spend on a wide variety of goods and services. These include health, education, law and order, transport, social security, housing, and defence. The amount of government spending (G) depends on its policies and objectives.

Net exports (X–M)

Exports are domestic goods and services that are bought by foreigners. When the firms in a country sell exports to foreigners, it results in an inflow of export revenues to the country. Imports are goods and services that are bought from foreign producers. When imports are bought, it results in an outflow of import expenditure. The net trade component of AD is actually export *revenues* minus import *expenditure*, but it is simplified by noting it as exports minus imports (X−M). The figure can be either positive, whereby export revenues exceed import expenditure, or negative, whereby import expenditure exceeds export revenues. If the net figure is positive, it will add to AD; if the net figure is negative, it will reduce AD.

Aggregate demand can be presented as a formula **C + I + G + (X − M)** and as a diagram, as shown in Figure 16.2.

When the average price level in the economy falls from PL_1 to PL_2, the level of output demanded by consumers (C) plus firms (I) plus governments (G) and the net foreign sector (X–M) increases from Y_1 to Y_2.

Note: You will find that different books use different labels for the x-axis. You may find any of national income (Y), national expenditure, national output or real output. Whichever one you choose, be sure that it is distinct from simply quantity or Q, which would indicate a single market in a microeconomic analysis.

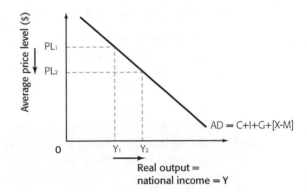

Figure 16.2 The aggregate demand curve

Changes in AD

A change in the price level will result in a movement along the AD curve, from one level of real output to another. A change in any of the components of aggregate demand will cause a shift in the demand curve as shown in Figure 16.3.

An increase in any of the components of aggregate demand will result in an increase in aggregate demand and a shift of the AD curve to the right from AD_1 to AD_2. A decrease in any of the components of aggregate demand will result in a fall in aggregate demand and a shift of the AD curve to the left from AD_1 to AD_3.

Changes in the components of aggregate demand

What causes changes in consumption?

Changes in income

The most significant determinant of consumption is income. As incomes rise, people have more money to spend on goods and services, so consumption increases. In a growing economy where national income is rising, there will be an increase in consumption, and therefore an increase in aggregate demand.

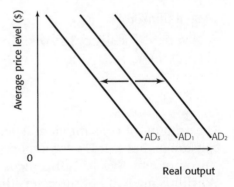

Figure 16.3 Shifts in aggregate demand

Changes in interest rates

Spending on non-durable goods is carried out with the day-to-day money that people earn (their income). But some of the money that is used to buy durable goods comes from money which people borrow from the bank. When people borrow money, they must pay for the borrowed money by paying interest to the bank. If there is an increase in interest rates, which is essentially the price of borrowed money, then there is likely to be less borrowing (because it is more expensive to borrow). Therefore consumption will fall, resulting in a fall in AD.

For example, borrowed money is usually used to buy houses. To buy a house, most consumers get a loan for housing called a mortgage. If interest rates increase, then this loan becomes more expensive on a month-to-month basis. This means that people will have less money to spend on other goods and services, so consumption will fall. Also, a rise in the interest rate makes saving more attractive; people would prefer to put their extra income in the bank to earn money rather than spend it on goods and services. This is another reason why changes in interest rates affect consumption.

Overall, an increase in interest rates leads to a fall in consumption. On the other hand, a fall in interest rates will lead to an increase in consumption, *ceteris paribus*, as it becomes more attractive to borrow money to spend on durable goods and services. In addition, if interest rates fall, then mortgage repayments may fall, leaving more money to spend on goods and services and it becomes less appealing to save money in the bank when the return on the savings (the interest earned) is relatively low.

Student workpoint 16.2

Be a thinker

Identify five goods or services that people might need a bank loan to purchase.

Changes in wealth

The amount of consumption depends on the amount of wealth that consumers have. It is very important not to confuse the concepts of "income" and "wealth". Income is the money that people earn. Wealth is made up of the assets that people own. This includes physical assets, such as houses, art, antiques, or jewellery, and monetary/financial assets, such as shares in companies, government bonds, or bank savings. There are two main factors that can change the level of wealth in the economy.

- *A change in house prices:* When house prices increase across the economy, consumers feel more wealthy and are likely to feel confident enough to increase their consumption by saving less or borrowing more.

- *A change in the value of stocks and shares:* Many consumers hold shares in companies. If the value of those shares increases, then people feel more wealthy. This might encourage them to spend more. Alternatively, they might sell those shares and then use the earnings to increase consumption.

Changes in expectations/Consumer confidence

If people are optimistic about their economic future then they are likely to spend more now. For example, if they think that they are likely to get a promotion in the future due to a booming economy and strong sales then they will feel more confident about taking a loan or using up savings. Thus high consumer confidence is likely to lead to increased consumption. However, if people expect economic conditions to worsen, then they are likely to reduce their consumption today in order to save for the future. Economists regularly measure consumer confidence and put the information together in the form of a "consumer confidence index" or "consumer sentiment index". An increase in the index indicates that confidence is rising; if this is the case, then consumer spending is likely to rise as well. This is illustrated in the accompanying excerpt from *The Australian*.

● ●

Student workpoint 16.3

Be a thinker

Read the short text below and answer the questions that follow.
Use the data from the text to support your answers.

CONSUMER CONFIDENCE ON THE RISE

CONSUMER CONFIDENCE has risen to a seven-month high, adding to recent evidence from retail sales and personal borrowing that households are shaking off their conservatism. The Melbourne Institute Consumer Index is now 5 per cent higher than in the second half of last year, with improved news on the housing market and people less anxious about the economic outlook.

Slow consumer spending dragged the economy to an annual growth rate of just 1.5 per cent over the second half of last year, despite generous tax cuts in last year's budget. However, the 1.3 per cent rise in the consumer sentiment index in March is the third in three months.

"Confidence is steadily improving from the lows of the second half of 2005, when sharp rises in petrol prices and interest rates uncertainty hampered consumers," Westpac chief economist Bill Evans said yesterday. Mr. Evans said the best news consumers had received over the past month was the 2 per cent rise in housing prices.

The Australian, March 16, 2006

1 With the help of a diagram, explain how the change in confidence among Australian consumers would affect Australian AD.

2 Suggest reasons for the change in consumer confidence.

Student workpoint 16.4

Be an inquirer

Consumption makes up most of the aggregate demand in most countries. Consider the national income data in workpoint 14.1 and note the percentage of aggregate demand that comes from consumption in Canada. You will find that this is rather typical of the developed countries.

Investigate the distribution of AD for the country that you chose in workpoint 14.2.

'*The entire world economy rests on the consumer; if he ever stops spending money he doesn't have on things he doesn't need – we're done for.*'
Bill Bonner

What causes changes in investment?

Interest rates

In order to invest, firms need money. The money that firms use for investment comes from several sources. For example, they can use their "retained profits" or they can borrow the money. Both of these are affected by the interest rate. If the money is to be borrowed, then an increase in the cost of borrowing may lead to a fall in investment. If interest rates are high, then firms may prefer to put their retained profits in the bank to earn higher returns as savings, rather than use them to invest. Therefore there is an inverse relationship between interest rates and the level of investment, as shown in Figure 16.4.

A decrease in the interest rate, from 7% to 4%, will decrease the incentive to save and decrease the cost of borrowing, so is likely to lead to an increase in borrowing that is likely to result in an increase in the level of investment from I_1 to I_2. An increase in the interest rate will have the opposite effect.

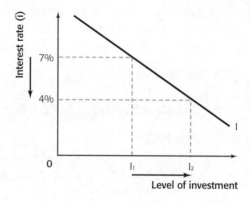

Figure 16.4 The relationship between investment and the interest rate

Changes in the level of national income

As national income rises, this leads to an increase in consumption, as discussed above. If national income and consumption are rising rapidly, there will be pressure on the existing capacity of firms. This is likely to encourage firms to invest in new plant and equipment to meet the increase in demand. This is what we referred to as induced investment. We say that investment accelerates when national income rises. Higher level students will come back to the concept of the accelerator effect in Chapter 18.

Technological change

In any dynamic economy, there is likely to be a quick pace of technological change. In order to keep up with advances in technology and to remain competitive, firms will need to invest.

Expectations/business confidence

Businesses make decisions about the amount of investment they should make based to a large extent on their expectations for the future, and their confidence in the economic climate. There would be little point in investing to increase the potential output of a firm if consumer demand is likely to fall in the future. If businesses are very confident about the future of the economy and expect consumer demand to rise, then they will want to be ready to meet the increases in consumer demand, by investing to increase potential output and productivity. Economists regularly measure the confidence of businesses and publish data in the form of a business confidence index.

What causes changes in government spending?

The amount and nature of government spending depends on a vast range of factors and the goals of the government. For example, we looked at government subsidies in Chapter 6. If the government has made a commitment to financially support a given industry, then government spending will rise. If governments are obliged to spend to correct market failure, then government spending will rise. A new education or health policy might require increased public spending on schools or hospitals. We look at government policies to affect AD shortly.

What causes changes in net exports?

Exports

Exports are goods or services that are bought by foreigners. If foreign incomes rise, then their consumption of imported goods and services will rise. For example, as the Chinese national income rises, Chinese people are more willing and able to buy imported goods and services from Europe. Thus European exports rise as the Chinese economy grows. Similarly, as China grows, investment in China expands. This is likely to involve some measure of imported capital. Thus as China grows, German exports of capital equipment may also rise.

Imports

It has already been established that when a country's national income is growing, there is likely to be an increase in consumption. As people consume more goods and services, it will necessarily be the case that some of these goods and services will be imported. Similarly, as national income rises, there is likely to be greater investment. Part of the capital goods that are purchased will be imported capital goods and/or components. Thus as national income rises, so does spending on imports. If national income falls, there will be reduced spending on imports.

Thus net exports (the difference between export revenues and import expenditure) depends both on domestic national income and foreign national incomes.

Government policies affecting aggregate demand

Governments have two broad categories of policies available to affect the level of aggregate demand in the economy. These are known as fiscal policy and monetary policy.

Fiscal policy

Fiscal policy is defined as the set of a government's policies relating to its spending and taxation rates. Direct taxes (taxes on income) and indirect taxes (taxes on goods and services) can be raised or lowered to alter the amount of disposable income consumers have. Governments use expansionary fiscal policy to increase aggregate

3 Macroeconomics

demand and contractionary, or deflationary, fiscal policy to reduce aggregate demand.

Expansionary fiscal policy

- If a government would like to encourage greater consumption, then it can lower income taxes to increase disposable income. This is likely to increase AD.

- If a government would like to encourage greater investment, then it can lower corporate taxes so that firms enjoy higher after-tax profits that can be used for investment. This is likely to increase AD.

- Governments have major investment projects themselves and may increase their spending in order to improve or increase public services. This directly impacts upon AD.

⬤⬤⬤⬤⬤⬤⬤⬤⬤⬤⬤⬤⬤⬤⬤⬤⬤⬤

Student workpoint 16.5

Be a thinker

Explain the elements that would be included in a contractionary fiscal policy. Illustrate the effects of a contractionary fiscal policy on AD.

Monetary policy

Monetary policy is defined as the set of official policies governing the supply of money in the economy and the level of interest rates in an economy. The level of money supply in an economy is an advanced topic that is not dealt with in the IB Diploma Programme syllabus. However, you must be aware of how changes in interest rates can affect the level of AD in an economy.

In any economy, there is a vast array of different interest rates. Advertisements offering low mortgage rates or "competitive financing" are examples of the interest rates offered by private profit-making businesses such as commercial banks. Although banks are regulated by the government, they are mainly free to set these rates themselves. When we talk about interest rates as a tool of monetary policy, we are talking about the *base rate* (or *discount rate* or *prime rate*) that is set by a country's central bank. The central bank is not a private profit-making bank, but is essentially the government's bank, and the ultimate authority in control of the money supply in an economy. In some countries, the government controls the central bank, but in most industrialised countries these days, the central bank is an independent body with the primary responsibility of maintaining a low and stable rate of inflation in the economy. Changes in the central bank's base rate ultimately impact upon all borrowing and lending in the economy and are an important signal of a country's monetary policy. Even though the central bank may be largely independent, we usually consider its activities as part of government monetary policy.

Changes in the central bank's base rate can affect the level of AD in the economy. To increase aggregate demand, the central bank might lower the base rate. This ultimately reduces the cost of borrowing and can lead to increases in both consumption and investment. This would be known as expansionary or "loose" monetary policy. To operate a contractionary or "tight" monetary policy to reduce aggregate demand, the central bank would increase the base rate.

● ● ● ● ● ● ● ● ● ● ● ● ● ● ● ● ● ● ● ●

Student workpoint 16.6

Be a thinker

Draw an aggregate demand diagram to illustrate an increase in AD, and one that shows a decrease in AD. Be sure to label the axes accurately. Decide whether each of the following factors would lead to an increase or a decrease in AD and write out the point beneath the appropriate diagram. In each explanation, explain which component(s) of AD is likely to be affected and why.

Example: A fall in income tax is likely to lead to an increase in AD because consumers' disposable incomes will rise, leading to an increase in consumption, *ceteris paribus*.

a   a fall in house prices

b   a rise in consumer confidence

c   an increase in foreign incomes

d   a fall in the consumer confidence index

e   a decrease in interest rates.

3 Macroeconomics

Examination questions

Short response questions

1   Using a diagram, explain the differences between an increase in demand and an increase in aggregate demand.   *[10 marks]*

2   Explain three factors that could cause an increase in the level of consumption in an economy.   *[10 marks]*

3   Using a diagram, explain how the government can use fiscal policy to alter the level of AD in the economy.   *[10 marks]*

4   Using a diagram, explain how a change in interest rates is likely to affect the level of investment in an economy.   *[10 marks]*

Assessment advice:
analysis and evaluation

We will save questions that involve more analysis and evaluation until we have taken the vital step of looking at the interaction between aggregate demand and aggregate supply.

3 Macroeconomics

Data response exercise

Read the following article and answer the questions that follow.

Public investment aids growth as rising taxes hit consumers

BRITAIN'S economy relied heavily on a large rise in public (government) investment to support growth in the third quarter as rising taxes cut consumers' spending power and businesses continued to show reluctance to invest. In detailed national accounts breaking down **aggregate demand** and third-quarter performance, growth was left unrevised at a modest 0.4%, upsetting the Bank of England hopes of an improvement.

The crucial services sector did expand a little more vigorously than previously reported, with its third-quarter growth revised up to 0.7%, from 0.6%.

Despite services' more positive performance, economists gave warning of the driving forces behind recent growth, highlighting reliance on taxpayer-funded investment while private sector activity stayed sluggish.

The national accounts showed that government investment spending surged 16.5% in the third quarter, boosting overall growth in investment spending in the quarter to 2.2%, from an initial estimate of 1.0%.

While household wages and salaries climbed by 0.8% in the third quarter, a 3.9% rise in taxes on income and a 2.5% rise in national insurance and pension contributions meant that **disposable incomes** rose by only 0.2%. The **durable goods** sector was negatively affected by the small growth in incomes. The figures also raised doubts over hopes that higher exports and business **investment** will boost growth next year. A revised 0.4% drop in third-quarter exports meant that net exports subtracted a hefty 0.7 percentage points from quarterly growth.

Business investment rose by a tiny 0.3% in the quarter. Business profits were low and companies opted to increase dividends rather than invest.

The Times, December 23, 2005

1 Define the following terms used in the text:

   a aggregate demand

   b disposable incomes

   c durable goods

   d investment.

2 Using the information from the text, try to explain changes to any of the components of AD.

17 Aggregate supply

By the end of this chapter, you should be able to:

- define short-run aggregate supply (SRAS)
- illustrate SRAS
- explain the causes of a shift in SRAS
- distinguish between short-run aggregate supply (SRAS) and long-run aggregate supply (LRAS)
- distinguish between a "Keynesian" LRAS and a neo-classical LRAS
- explain the source of increases in the LRAS.

Aggregate supply

In this chapter, we continue our macroeconomic analysis by introducing the concept of aggregate supply. The concept of the "supply side" of the economy is extremely important in the study of the overall productive capacity of the economy. By definition, aggregate supply is the total amount of goods and services that all industries in the economy will produce at every given price level. It is essentially the sum of the supply curves of all the industries in the economy. In contrast to the theory of aggregate demand, however, we distinguish between the short run and the long run in looking at aggregate supply.

Short-run aggregate supply

Graphically, the short-run aggregate supply curve (SRAS) looks very much like a microeconomic supply curve in that it is upward-sloping. There is a positive relationship between the price level and the amount of output that a country's industries will supply. This relationship is shown in Figure 17.1

At any given price level, industries will supply a certain level of output. Let us look at what happens in the short run if the country's industries want to increase the level of output. It is necessary to understand what is meant by the short run. In our macroeconomic analysis, the short run is defined as the period of time when the prices of the factors of production do not change. Most importantly, the price of labour, the wage rate, is fixed.

If a larger level of output is to be produced, firms are likely to face higher average costs of production. For example, in order to produce more, firms will have to provide incentives to workers to produce a larger amount. Most commonly, this is done by paying "overtime" wages. These might be one and a half times the normal wage and so costs rise. Higher level students should recall that the law of diminishing returns means that marginal and average costs will rise as output increases in the short run. In the short run then, an increase in output will be accompanied by an increase in average costs. Industries will pass on an increase in costs in the form of a higher price level.

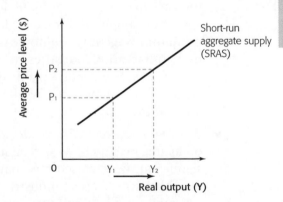

Figure 17.1 The SRAS curve

This explains why the SRAS curve is upward sloping. In Figure 17.1, an increase in the level of output from Y_1 to Y_2 will be accompanied by an increase in the price level from P_1 to P_2.

Shifts in SRAS

We have shown that the SRAS curve shows the relationship between the average price level and the level of national output under the *ceteris paribus* assumption. That is, we assume that factor costs remain constant. A change in the price level results in a change in the level of output and is shown as a movement along the SRAS curve as shown in Figure 17.1. This is similar to the microeconomic supply curve, where an increase in the price leads to an increase in the quantity supplied, and is shown as a movement along the supply curve. But just as with the microeconomic supply curve, a change in anything *other* than the price will lead to a shift in the whole curve. Thus a change in any of the factors *other than the price level* will result in a shift in the SRAS curve. These may be referred to as "supply-side shocks".

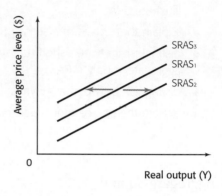

Figure 17.2 Shifts in the SRAS curve

Figure 17.2 shows an increase in the short-run aggregate supply ($SRAS_1 \longrightarrow SRAS_2$) and a decrease in the SRAS ($SRAS_1 \longrightarrow SRAS_3$).

The most straightforward explanation of supply-side shocks is that they are factors that cause changes in the costs of production. Similar to our microeconomic analysis, a decrease in costs results in an increase in aggregate supply, while an increase in costs results in an decrease in aggregate supply.

Typical examples of changes in the costs of production include the following.

- *A change in wage rates:* An increase in wages will result in an increase in the costs of production to firms, and therefore a fall in aggregate supply. If, for example, the government raised the legal minimum wage it would increase labour costs. If labour unions in manufacturing industries, whose priority is usually to ensure good wages and conditions for workers, were to negotiate higher wages for manufacturing workers, then this would also result in a fall in the SRAS.

- *A change in the costs of raw materials:* For a change to have an effect on aggregate supply, we are assuming an increase in the price of significant, widely used raw materials. An increase in the price of rubber would affect industries that use rubber as a factor, but this might not be significant enough to affect aggregate supply noticeably. However, a change in the price of oil would have an impact on all industries, as oil is widely used in most production processes.

- *A change in the price of imports:* This point is linked to the previous point. If the capital or raw materials used by a country's industries are imported, then a rise in import prices will increase the costs of production. This can occur due to changes in the exchange rate of a country's currency. For example, if the value of the euro falls, then this makes the import price of the raw materials and capital used by European producers relatively more expensive, raising their costs of production.

Student workpoint 17.1

Be a thinker

Draw a SRAS curve and label it SRAS$_1$. Be sure to label the axes accurately. Now show a new SRAS curve demonstrating an increase in SRAS. Label this SRAS$_2$. Explain two possible reasons for this increase in SRAS.

Combining AD and AS in the short run

The economy will operate where aggregate demand is equal to aggregate supply. This is shown in Figure 17.3.

At the average price level (PL), all the output produced by the country's producers is consumed. There is no incentive for producers to either increase output or raise prices. The concept of macroeconomic equilibrium will be discussed in more detail in the next chapter.

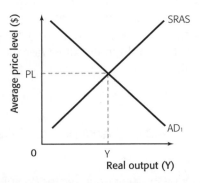

Figure 17.3 Short-run macroeconomic equilibrium

Long-run aggregate supply

There is considerable debate among economists regarding the long-run aggregate supply curve (LRAS). There are two main "schools of thought" concerning the shape of the LRAS. The first one discussed is the one developed by the followers of the famous economist John Maynard Keynes (see box in Chapter 18). We will then look at the LRAS of the economists known as neo-classical economists. The different-shaped LRAS curves lie at the basis of controversies about appropriate policies to be followed by governments.

Keynesian LRAS

The shape of the curve that is known as the Keynesian LRAS shows three possible phases. These are shown in Figure 17.4 as regions (1), (2), and (3).

1 In this view, the aggregate supply curve will be perfectly elastic at low levels of economic activity. Producers in the economy can raise their levels of output without incurring higher average costs because of the existence of "spare capacity" in the economy. That is, there are high levels of unused factors such as unemployed labour and under-utilised capital. Should there be a need for greater output, these can be used to their fullest capacity at constant average costs. This corresponds to the region (1) in Figure 17.4.

2 As the economy approaches its potential output (Y$_f$), and the spare capacity is "used up", the economy's available factors of production become increasingly scarce. As producers continue to try to increase output, they will have to bid for the increasingly scarce factors. Higher prices for the factors of production mean higher costs for the producers, and the price level will rise to compensate for the higher costs. This corresponds to region (2) with an upward-sloping LRAS.

3 When the economy reaches its full capacity (Y$_f$), it is impossible to increase output any further because all factors of production

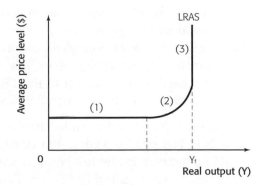

Figure 17.4 Keynesian LRAS curve

are fully employed. This suggests that LRAS is perfectly inelastic, and is shown as region (3).

At this point, it is sufficient to understand that the full capacity of the economy is shown by the output level Y_f. This is really a simplification. This level of output is known as the "full employment level of output". We will go into it in greater depth in Chapter 18, but at this stage it is useful to introduce the term. One point that is necessary to clarify is that full employment does not mean that there is no unemployment at all.

Student workpoint 17.2

Be a thinker

Draw the Keynesian aggregate supply curve and add notes to your diagram to describe each of the phases.

Neo-classical LRAS

Neo-classical economists, also known as free market economists, believe that the LRAS curve is perfectly inelastic at the full employment level of output. They believe that the potential output of the economy is dependent on the quantity and quality (productivity) of the factors of production, not on the price level. Thus the LRAS curve is independent of the price level. This is shown in Figure 17.5. The price level may rise from P_1 to P_2 but the level of output does not change.

Shifts in the LRAS

As a country's factors of production are constantly changing, we would expect to see steady increases in its LRAS. This is effectively an illustration of potential economic growth. An outward shift of a country's LRAS curve means that its productive potential has increased. In fact, a shift in the LRAS can be likened to an outward shift of the production possibilities curve (PPC).

A shift in the LRAS can be shown from either a Keynesian perspective as in Figure 17.6(a) or a neo-classical perspective as in Figure 17.6 (b). The increase in the full employment level of output is equivalent to the outward shift of the PPC in Figure 17.7.

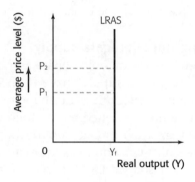

Figure 17.5 Neo-classical LRAS curve

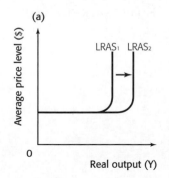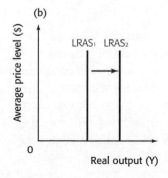

Figure 17.6 A shift in the LRAS curve **(a)** from the Keynesian perspective and **(b)** from the neo-classical perspective

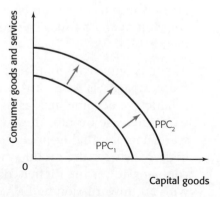

Figure 17.7 An increase in productive potential equivalent to an increase in the LRAS

The LRAS curve will shift to the right if there is an improvement in the quality of the factors of production or an increase in the quantity of the factors of production. For example, technological advances might make capital more productive, thus shifting out the LRAS curve. Improvements in education might make existing labour more productive. Discoveries of new sources of raw materials will increase the quantity of goods that may be produced. Increasing the quantity of the labour force will also shift out the LRAS. Government policies that are put in place to increase the long-run aggregate supply of the economy are known as supply-side policies.

Supply-side policies

The overarching goal of supply-side policies is to increase the potential output of the economy by increasing the quantity of the factors of production and/or improving the quality of the factors of production. We can divide these policies into two categories: market-oriented policies and interventionist policies.

Market-oriented supply-side policies

These policies focus on allowing markets to operate freely, with minimal government intervention. The word "incentives" is often used in describing these policies, as they are designed to increase the incentives for labour to work harder and more productively, and to increase the incentives for firms to increase productivity.

- *Reduction in income taxes:* If people work harder and make more money, it is possible that they will have to pay higher taxes on the higher levels of income.

  This may act as a disincentive to work. If taxes are reduced, it is hoped that there will be a greater incentive for labour to work harder and to become more productive, thus increasing the potential output of the economy.

- *Reductions in corporation taxes:* If businesses are able to keep more of their profits, then they will have more money available for investment. As investment is the addition of capital stock to the economy, this will increase the potential output of the economy. Moreover, if businesses know that they are going to be able to keep a larger share of their profits, rather than give it to the government in taxes, then they will have more incentive to produce efficiently.

- *Reduction in trade union power:* It is often perceived that trade unions push wages up too high and increase the costs of production to firms. Following this, it can be argued that a reduction in trade union power will reduce the ability of unions to negotiate high wages and therefore lower the costs of production to firms, thus increasing their potential output.

  However, one of the main goals of unions is to protect the rights of workers, and reduced union power may result in the exploitation of workers.

- *Reduction or elimination of minimum wages:* By the same token, it can be argued that because a government-set minimum wage will keep the price of labour at a level above its free market level, if the minimum wage were to be abolished, then this would also decrease the costs of production and increase aggregate supply.

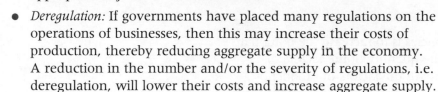

While this might provide some benefit in terms of the overall growth of the economy, it will reduce living standards for those workers who were working for minimum wages.

● *Reduction in unemployment benefits:* If unemployed people are given generous unemployment benefits from the government, it may be argued that they have less incentive to find jobs. Market-oriented supply-side economists would recommend that unemployment benefits be reduced to encourage unemployed people to take the available jobs in the economy. Of course, this policy is only appropriate if jobs are in fact available.

● *Deregulation:* If governments have placed many regulations on the operations of businesses, then this may increase their costs of production, thereby reducing aggregate supply in the economy. A reduction in the number and/or the severity of regulations, i.e. deregulation, will lower their costs and increase aggregate supply.

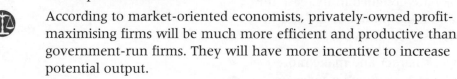

Unfortunately, this might include reduced regulations on safety or environmental standards, and this can have severe negative consequences for workers and the environment.

● *Privatisation:* This is the sale of public, government-owned firms, to the private sector.

According to market-oriented economists, privately-owned profit-maximising firms will be much more efficient and productive than government-run firms. They will have more incentive to increase potential output.

All of the policies mentioned above emphasize the reduced role of the government in the economy and the importance of allowing all markets, especially labour markets, to operate freely.

Interventionist supply-side policies

As the name suggests, these policies are based on the idea that the government has a fundamental role to play in actively encouraging growth.

● *Education and training:* In order to constantly increase the quality of labour, it is the responsibility of the government to ensure that education and training facilities are geared to providing the necessary skills and knowledge for a dynamic economy. This is related to both the skills and knowledge that young people need to help them enter the labour force and also to the retraining of workers to help them adjust to changing economic circumstances. Such training can take place in schools, universities, training institutions and apprenticeship programmes.

● *Research and development (R&D):* It is important that an economy's firms are able to stay up-to-date with modern developments, to develop new production techniques and to constantly seek improved methods of production. All of these may increase the economy's potential output, but all involve extensive spending on research and development. Governments can actively encourage research and development by firms by offering tax incentives. For example, they could allow firms not to pay taxes on the retained profits used for R&D. This is known as a tax credit. Firms may be reluctant to spend on R&D if they think that they will not be able to reap the full benefits of their spending. Governments can thus encourage R&D by guaranteeing intellectual property rights such as patents and copyrights. Alternatively, governments themselves could finance R&D in public research facilities and universities.

● *Provision of infrastructure:* The productive potential of an economy will be enhanced by improved infrastructure, such as better transportation linkages and telecommunications.

● *Improved information:* Governments can finance trade fairs to facilitate the sharing of expertise and information among a country's firms.

 All the interventionist policies above have significant costing implications and governments must weigh up the opportunity costs of such spending. The benefits of such spending are likely to be more evident in the long term than in the short term.

Student workpoint 17.3

Be an inquirer

In reality, all governments employ a mixture of market-oriented and interventionist supply-side policies. Investigate the policies on the points listed above for your chosen OECD country.

Examination questions

Short response questions

1   With the help of a diagram, explain three possible causes of a decrease in the SRAS curve.   *[10 marks]*

2   With the help of diagrams, explain the difference between the Keynesian LRAC and the neo-classical LRAC.   *[10 marks]*

3   How might a reduction in taxes be considered as both a demand-side policy and a supply-side policy?   *[10 marks]*

Essay question

1   a   Using a diagram, explain the concept of potential economic growth.   *[10 marks]*

   b   Evaluate three policies that might be used to increase LRAS.   *[15 marks]*

You be the journalist

Headline: Government strikes fear in the hearts of workers and trade unions with its new package of supply-side policies designed to encourage economic growth

Economics concept: Supply-side policies

Diagram: Long-run aggregate supply curve from the neo-classical view

Hints: The reason that a neo-classical LRAS curve is appropriate here is because it is likely to be the market-oriented supply-side policies that will worry workers.

By the end of this chapter, you should be able to:

- identify the equilibrium level of national income/output
- explain and illustrate that the difference between the equilibrium level of national income and the full employment level of national income will result in an inflationary or deflationary gap
- discuss the difference between Keynesian (interventionist) and neo-classical (free market) economists in their view of macroeconomic equilibrium
- explain and illustrate the effects of changes in aggregate demand and aggregate supply
- explain and illustrate the business cycle (trade cycle)

HL
- explain the multiplier effect of injections on national income
- calculate the value of the multiplier
- explain the accelerator effect of investment on national income.

Remember that national income is equivalent to the level of output that a country produces and is a key sign of the economic health of an economy. The actual level of output, and its corresponding price level, are determined by the interaction between aggregate demand and aggregate supply. Our next important concept is that of the equilibrium level of national income (or output). Simply put, the equilibrium level of national income is where aggregate demand is equal to aggregate supply. But, as shown in the previous chapter, economists distinguish between a short-run and a long-run aggregate supply curve; therefore we have a short-run and a long-run macroeconomic equilibrium.

Although we don't get into a detailed look at unemployment and inflation until Chapters 19, 20 and 21, there are constant references to these two major macroeconomic topics in this chapter. Joblessness and rapidly rising prices are a significant problem in any economy.

Short-run equilibrium output

The economy is in short-run equilibrium where aggregate demand equals short-run aggregate supply (SRAS). Graphically, it looks very much like the short-run equilibrium for a particular market, but of course the labels on the axes are different, as shown in Figure 18.1.

The economy is in short-run equilibrium where aggregate demand equals short-run aggregate supply, producing an output level of Y at the price level of P. The output produced by the economy is exactly equal to the total demand in the economy and so there is

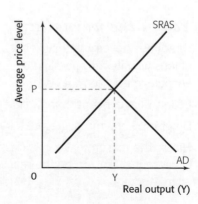

Figure 18.1 Short-run equilibrium output

3 Macroeconomics

no reason for producers to change their levels of output. Because aggregate demand is equal to aggregate supply, there is no upward or downward pressure on the price level. In other words, there is no inflationary or deflationary pressure. As long as nothing changes to influence AD or AS, the economy rests at this equilibrium.

Long-run equilibrium output

The long-run equilibrium is where aggregate demand is equal to long-run aggregate supply. Given that there is disagreement among economists as to the shape of the long-run aggregate supply curve, we distinguish between the Keynesian long-run equilibrium output and the neo-classical long-run equilibrium output.

Keynesian perspective

In each case, the equilibrium level of output is where aggregate demand is equal to long-run aggregate supply. According to the Keynesian economists, however, this equilibrium level of output may occur at different levels. Significantly, they believe that the economy may be in long-run equilibrium at a level of output below the full employment level of national income (Y_f). This will be the case if the economy is operating at a level where there is spare capacity. In this view, the equilibrium level of output depends mainly on the level of aggregate demand in the economy. Figure 18.2 illustrates this important view of the Keynesian perspective.

If aggregate demand is at the level shown in Figure 18.2, then equilibrium will occur at a real output level of Y, with a price level of P. As noted in the previous chapter, aggregate supply can be perfectly elastic because of the existence of spare capacity, with high levels of unused factors of production such as unemployed workers and/or underutilised capital. It is important to observe that in this case, the equilibrium level of output is below the full employment level of output. We say that there is a *deflationary gap* whereby the level of aggregate demand in the economy is not sufficient to buy up the potential output that could be produced by the economy at the full employment level of output. This may also be referred to as an *output gap* and, though not easily measurable, could be shown as the distance from a point inside a country's hypothetical production possibility curve to a point on the curve, as shown in Figure 18.3.

In the Keynesian view, aggregate demand can increase such that there is an increase in the level of real output, without any consequent increase in the price level. This is shown in Figure 18.4.

If there is an increase in aggregate demand from AD_1 to AD_2, then there will be an increase in real output from Y_1 to Y_2, but no change in the price level. This is due to the existence of spare capacity in the economy. Producers can employ the unused factors of production to increase output with no increase in costs. Thus there is no inflationary pressure.

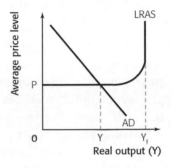

Figure 18.2 The Keynesian perspective of long-run equilibrium output below the full employment level of output

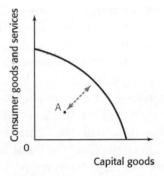

Figure 18.3 Output gap illustrating the difference between an economy's actual output and its potential output

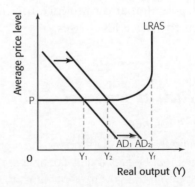

Figure 18.4 The Keynesian perspective of the impact of an increase in AD when the economy is operating below full employment

If aggregate demand increases further, to AD_3 in Figure 18.5, then the economy starts to experience inflationary pressure, as available factors of production become scarcer and their prices are bid up. The price level rises from P_1 to P_2 to compensate producers for their higher costs.

If the economy is operating at full employment, and there is an increase in aggregate demand, then the outcome will be "purely inflationary". That is, there is no increase in output, and the only change is an increase in the price level. This is because it is impossible for the economy to produce any further increase in output in the long run, given the existing factors of production. This is illustrated in Figure 18.6.

An increase in aggregate demand from AD_1 to AD_2 results in no change in output as the economy cannot produce output beyond the full employment level of output. The only impact is an increase in the price level from P_1 to P_2. We say that there is an *inflationary gap* whereby the level of aggregate demand cannot be satisfied given the existing resources. As a result, the price level rises to allocate the scarce resources among the competing components of aggregate demand, i.e. consumers, producers, the government, and the foreign sector.

Demand-side policies

The diagrams and explanations illustrate the Keynesian perspective of different possible long-run positions of the economy. What is important is the conclusion that the long-run equilibrium level of output is not necessarily equal to the full employment level of income, and that the economy can rest in equilibrium at a level of output that is below full employment. This has significant implications for the role of the government in the economy. Governments seeking to intervene to steer the economy towards full employment will use demand-side or demand management policies. These involve the fiscal and monetary policies introduced in Chapter 16. Expansionary policies are used to increase aggregate demand to increase the equilibrium level of output as in Figure 18.4. Increasing the level of output implies an increase in the demand for labour and so such policies are designed to reduce unemployment. Contractionary policies are used to decrease aggregate demand to reduce the inflationary pressure that is caused when the price level rises.

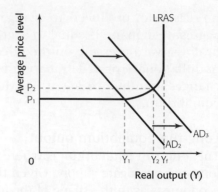

Figure 18.5 The Keynesian perspective of the impact of an increase in AD when the economy is close to full employment

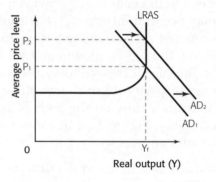

Figure 18.6 The Keynesian perspective of the impact of an increase in AD when the economy is at full employment

Student workpoint 18.1

Be a thinker

Using the Keynesian model, draw an AD/AS diagram, with AD at a level that creates a deflationary gap. Show and explain what can happen if the government wants to reduce unemployment and does so by using expansionary fiscal policy.

Profile **John Maynard Keynes** (1883–1946) ●●●●●●●●●●●●●●●●●●●●●●●●●

Keynes (pronounced Canes) was one of most influential economists of the twentieth century. He was born in Cambridge, England into a highly intellectual family and was educated in the elite academic British institutions of Eton and Cambridge. Although highly intelligent, Keynes did not dwell exclusively on academics, but found ample time for literary pursuits and political activities. He was well-known for his connection with the progressive literary Bloomsbury Group in London, which included many intellectuals such as Bertrand Russell and Virginia Woolf. He joined the British civil service in 1906. In order to enter the civil service, he had to write entrance examinations and ironically, he was not as successful in his economics exam as one might expect—but as he explained later, "I evidently knew more about economics than my examiners."

Following a short period with the civil service, he went back to study at Cambridge and then went to work at the British Treasury. He was the principal representative of the British Treasury at the Paris Peace Conference in Versailles in 1919, but he was very much against the conclusions of the conference in which Germany was expected to make massive payments to the Allied countries as reparations for World War One. As a result, he resigned from the Treasury and wrote *The Economic Consequences of the Peace*. His argument was that it

would be impossible for Germany to pay the amounts demanded of it. He predicted that the consequences would be very damaging, and he turned out to be quite right.

The views for which Keynes is most well-known were published in 1936 in *The General Theory of Employment, Interest and Money*. It was based on his study of the increasingly poor British economy in the 1920s. Prior to his time, the governing economic orthodoxy was that of the classical economists, who believed in *laissez faire* and minimal government intervention. Keynes, however, observed that the persistent levels of high unemployment of the 1920s were not going to disappear if left to market forces. He explained the problem in terms of a shortage of aggregate demand in the economy, and promoted the idea that the government should intervene in the economy to fill the gap. The theories established by Keynes were adapted to create the Keynesian long-run aggregate supply curve that we use in this chapter. According to Keynes, the government should run a budget deficit during a period of low economic activity, spending more than it earned in tax revenues. Such demand management policies are the core of Keynesian economics. They became the new economic paradigm and remained so until the late 1960s and early 1970s, when they came under increasing challenge from the neo-classical school of thought. Nonetheless, they continue to hold great value to governments committed to achieving the economic goals of low unemployment and stable inflation.

●●●

Neo-classical perspective

According to neo-classical economists, the economy will always move towards its long-run equilibrium at the full employment level of output. Thus the long-run equilibrium is where the aggregate demand curve meets the vertical long-run aggregate supply curve as shown in Figure 18.7.

The impact of any changes in aggregate demand will be on the price level only. This is illustrated in Figure 18.8, where an increase in aggregate demand from AD_1 to AD_2 results in an increase in the price level from P_1 to P_2 without any increase in the level of real output.

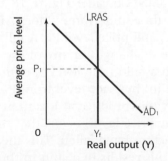

Figure 18.7 The neo-classical perspective of long-run equilibrium

It is valuable to look at the adjustment from the short run to the long run in order to understand the neo-classical perspective. The Keynesians and neo-classical economists agree on the shape of the short-run aggregate supply curve, but as stated above, the neo-classical economists argue that the economy will always move automatically to its long-run equilibrium. The word "automatically" in the last sentence means "without any government intervention" and illustrates the significance that the neo-classical economists place on free markets. In their view, there may be a short-run increase in output if there is an increase in aggregate demand, but the economy will always return to its long-run equilibrium.

The neo-classical perspective showing a combination of the short run and the long run is illustrated in Figure 18.9. Initially, the economy is at its long-run equilibrium at Y_f. If there is an increase in aggregate demand, AD_1 to AD_2, due to changes in any of the components of aggregate demand, then in the short run, there will be an increase in output from Y_f to Y_1. According to the neo-classical economists, this is *only* possible in the short run. It is possible for output to increase along the short-run aggregate supply curve by paying existing workers overtime wages as a short-term solution. But as the economy is originally at the full employment level of output, there are no unemployed resources. In their effort to increase their output, the firms in the economy are competing for increasingly scarce labour and capital and as the diagram shows, the increase in aggregate demand results in an increase in the price level from P_1 to P_2. The increase in the average price level means that on average, *all* prices in the economy have risen as the firms bid up the prices of the factors of production in order to increase their output. The rise in the price level means an increase in costs to firms as the prices of the factors of production (e.g. the prices of labour, raw materials, and capital) have risen. At this point, you must remember what happens to short-run aggregate supply when the costs of production rise. The result is a shift in the short-run aggregate supply from $SRAS_1$ to $SRAS_2$. Although firms were willing to supply a higher level of output due to the higher prices they were receiving in the short run, their higher costs of production result in no **real** gain, so they reduce output back to Y_f. The final result is that output returns to its full employment level, but at a higher price level.

We can use similar analysis to see what happens if aggregate demand falls. Consider Figure 18.10. Originally, the economy is at its long-run equilibrium, where AD_1 intersects with $SRAS_1$, at output Y_f and price level P_1. A fall in aggregate demand from AD_1 to AD_2, due to changes in any of the components of aggregate demand, results in a fall in the level of national output from Y_f to Y_1 and a decrease in the price level from P_1 to P_2. In the short run, the economy will produce at less than full employment output, but the fall in the price level means that the prices of the economy's factors of production have fallen. This means that firms' costs of production fall and this results in a shift in the short run aggregate supply from $SRAS_1$ to $SRAS_2$. As the diagram shows, the economy returns to its long-run equilibrium at the full employment level of output, at a lower price level.

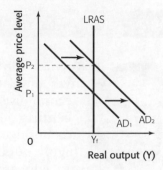

Figure 18.8 The neo-classical perspective of the impact of an increase in AD in the long run

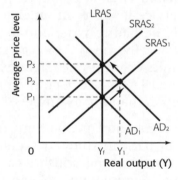

Figure 18.9 The neo-classical perspective of the impact of an increase in AD in the short run and in the long run

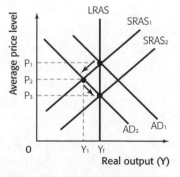

Figure 18.10 The neo-classical perspective of the impact of a decrease in AD in the short run and in the long run

The diagrams and explanations illustrate the neo-classical perspective of the long-run equilibrium in the economy. What is important is the conclusion that the long-run equilibrium level of output is equal to the full employment level of income, and that the economy will move towards this equilibrium without any government intervention as a result of free market forces. According to this model, an increase in aggregate demand will be purely inflationary in the long run, and thus there is no role for the government to play in trying to deliberately steer the economy towards full employment. Although there may be deviations from full employment in the short run, neo-classical economists would not see a role for the government in filling these gaps. They would recommend leaving the economy to market forces, rather than using demand management.

Student workpoint 18.2

Be a thinker

Using the neo-classical model, draw an AD/AS diagram with the economy in short-run equilibrium at the full employment level of income. Show and explain what can happen in the short run and the long run if rising consumer confidence results in an increase in consumption.

Changes in long-run aggregate supply

Remember from Chapter 17 that a country's long-run aggregate supply is based on the quantity and quality of its factors of production and that these change. Therefore, the full employment level of output also changes. As economic growth occurs, the LRAS curve shifts to the right. As noted earlier, this represents an increase in the potential output of the economy. A country seeking to increase the rate of economic growth and the full employment level of real output will use supply-side policies to increase the quantity or improve the quality of its factors of production. The impact of such policies depends to a large extent on the view of the economy that one takes.

For Keynesian economists, the impact of an increase in the LRAS depends on the initial equilibrium position of the economy. If the economy is operating below the full employment level of output, then the increase in the long-run aggregate supply will have no effect on the equilibrium output, as shown in Figure 18.11.

The economy is initially in equilibrium at Y below full employment. An increase in the long-run aggregate supply increases the potential of the economy to produce a higher level of output, but the aggregate demand is not sufficient to buy up this potential. The equilibrium will remain at Y. While Keynesian economists certainly do not underestimate the importance of supply-side policies in achieving economic growth, this emphasizes their view that the government must intervene if the economy is operating below full employment.

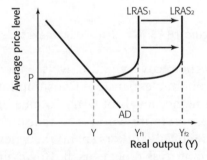

Figure 18.11 The Keynesian perspective of the impact of an increase in the LRAS when the economy is operating below full employment.

An increase in the long-run aggregate supply from a neo-classical viewpoint will have an entirely favourable impact as shown in Figure 18.12. There will be an increase in the full employment level of income from Y_{f1} to Y_{f2} and a fall in the price level from P_1 to P_2. This is why such economists are sometimes referred to as "supply-side economists". According to this view, supply-side policies are the most effective way of achieving a country's macroeconomic goals.

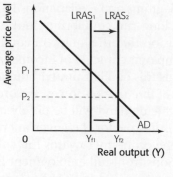

Figure 18.12 The neo-classical perspective of the impact of an increase in the LRAS

The business cycle

In developed country economies, we can generally see a pattern where there are periods of rising growth, followed by periods of slowing growth, and even falling growth. This is known as the business cycle, or trade cycle. The business cycle is the periodic fluctuations in economic activity measured by changes in real GDP. The phases of the business cycle are known as boom, recession, trough, and recovery. While the fluctuations are in practice highly irregular, the most common illustration of the business cycle shows a standard periodic cycle. This is illustrated in Figure 18.13.

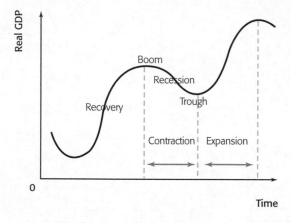

Figure 18.13 The standard business cycle

In the recovery phase, we see increased aggregate demand and an economic expansion. Consumption and investment rise, resulting in higher levels of GDP. To meet increased aggregate demand, firms take on more workers so that unemployment falls. The newly employed workers spend their new incomes on durable goods and the process repeats itself. However, capacity constraints in the economy are likely to slow down the increases in GDP and lead to inflationary pressure. GDP will reach its highest level at the peak of the cycle, the boom. However, demand for money for investment is likely to increase interest rates. The combination of higher inflation and higher interest rates will ultimately lead to a fall in consumption and investment. This is the beginning of the recession phase of the cycle.

A recession is defined as two consecutive quarters of negative GDP growth, that is, falling GDP. During a recession, consumption and investment fall. Falling aggregate demand will lead firms to lay off workers, so unemployment rises. If more people are unemployed, there will be even less consumption. Low levels of demand result in lower rates of inflation, or even deflation.

At some point the contraction will come to an end. This is known as the trough. Output cannot continue to fall for ever as there will always be some people with jobs to maintain a given level of consumption, foreigners will demand exports, governments will continue to spend by running budget deficits, and people will be able to use savings to finance consumption. Additionally, the low demand for money for investment will result in lower interest rates. Thus aggregate demand will pick up, the economy will enter the recovery phase, and the cycle will repeat itself.

As the diagram shows, the second recovery is at a higher level of real GDP than the first and each boom is higher than the last. This illustrates the important point that economies tend to go through periodic fluctuations in real GDP around their long-term growth trend, or long-term potential output. This is shown in Figure 18.14.

The periodic fluctuations in growth are shown as the actual output line, while the economy's long-term potential is shown as a steady increase in output. This represents the growth rate that the economy can sustain over time (but is *not* to be confused with sustainable development!). The difference between actual output and potential output is known as the output gap. At point A, there is a negative output gap. The economy is producing below its potential output and unemployment is likely to be a problem. At point B, there is a positive output gap. The economy is producing above its potential, i.e. beyond capacity, and inflation is likely to be a problem. This illustrates an interesting feature of economics. In the short run, it is quite possible that economies will face a "trade-off" between inflation and unemployment. When operating below potential, unemployment will be a problem, while operating above potential will result in inflationary pressure (rising rate of inflation). This will be addressed in greater detail later.

Economists have long studied the causes of business cycles, and have often hypothesised about the length and magnitude of a "typical" cycle. However, there are no straight answers to these questions. One theory (of many) is that a country's business cycle may be linked to its electoral cycle. That is, a government will stimulate an economy with expansionary policies to create a boom and lower unemployment just before an election, and then put into place less popular contractionary policies after it has been elected. A criticism of such policies is that they can widen the magnitude of the cycle, with higher levels of unemployment and inflation than there would be if the economy were left on its own.

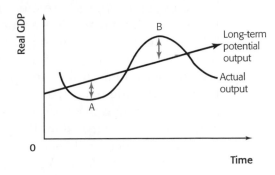

Figure 18.14 Long-term potential output and output gaps

3 Macroeconomics

Did you know?

Since the second world war, most business cycles have lasted three to five years from peak to peak. The average duration of an expansion is 44.8 months and the average duration of a recession is 11 months. As a comparison, the Great Depression—which saw a decline in economic activity from 1929 to 1933—lasted 43 months from peak to trough (source: Investopedia).

A link to international economics

During an expansionary phase, when national income is rising, an economy tends to purchase more imports of goods and services. Remember that income is a major determinant of consumption. As income rises, so does consumption, and much of what consumers buy is likely to be imported. Even if the final products consumed are produced domestically, it is quite possible that they will be made up of some imported components. Thus, as incomes rise, import spending is likely to rise. Also, as inflationary pressure builds during an expansion, the prices of the country's exported goods and services will also rise. This will make its exports less competitive on world markets and may lead to lower export revenues. Therefore we can observe that in an economic expansion, import expenditure rises and export revenues may fall, thus worsening the country's balance of trade in goods and services. This is known as its current account balance, and will be dealt with in Chapter 27.

During a contractionary phase, the opposite happens. Import spending may fall as people can afford fewer imported goods and services. Export prices may become more competitive internationally and this may result in greater export revenues. Thus the current account balance may improve.

As you should remember from Chapter 14, governments have five main macroeconomic goals, and we can link the first four to the business cycle. In Table 18.1 you will see that it is difficult to achieve all four goals at the same time. We call this the conflict among policy objectives.

Goal	Expansion	Contraction
Economic growth	Achieved—GDP rises	Not achieved—GDP falls
Low unemployment	Achieved—more workers are needed to produce the growing output	Not achieved—as workers are laid off when less output is demanded
Low and stable rate of inflation	Not achieved—inflationary pressure builds	Achieved—inflation falls
Favourable balance of payments position	Not achieved—as the current account worsens	Achieved—the current account improves

Table 18.1 The conflict among macroeconomic objectives

Student workpoint 18.3

Be a thinker

Make an annotated copy of the business cycle diagram, noting:

- the different phases through which an economy is likely to pass
- the positive and negative features of such phases
- the long-run potential growth line
- positive and negative output gaps.

· ·

Student workpoint 18.4

Be an inquirer

Make four graphs to illustrate the following information about your OECD country for the last five years:

1 growth rate (you have the data from workpoint 14.2)

2 unemployment rate

3 inflation rate

4 current account balance.

Luxembourg

GDP
% change on a year earlier

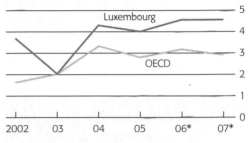

Source: *The Economist*, 15–21 July 2006, p. 84

Assessment advice: interpreting data

A common error is for students to interpret a fall in the growth of GDP as a fall in GDP, and therefore a recession. Consider the data for Luxembourg: From 2002 to 2003, the rate of growth of GDP fell from 3.5% to 2%. You must not think that this means that the actual output of GDP was less in 2003 than it was in 2002. It means that GDP grew, but at a slower rate than it had the previous year. From 2003 to 2004, the rate of growth increased sharply to about 4.2% and then slowed slightly in the next year to 4%. In all years, the GDP of Luxembourg was rising.

HL

The multiplier

If a government decides to fill a deflationary gap by increasing its own spending, the final increase in aggregate demand will actually be greater than the amount of spending. In fact, any increase in aggregate demand will result in a proportionately larger increase in national income. This is explained by the *multiplier effect*. In order to understand this concept, it is necessary to remember the concepts of injections and withdrawals introduced in Chapter 14.

Government spending and business investment are injections into the circular flow of income and any injections are multiplied through the economy as people receive a share of the income and then spend a part of what they receive.

For example, a government spends $100 million on a school building project. This $100m goes to a vast number of people for the factors of production that they provide. The money goes as income for the labour provided by people such architects, engineers, builders, electricians, plumbers, designers. The providers of the capital and raw materials such as concrete, steel, minerals, water, electricity also receive a share of this spending. So $100m ends up as income in the pockets of people who provide the factors of production for the building project. What do the people do with this income? Some of it goes back to the government as taxes, some of it is saved, some of it is spent on foreign goods and services, and the rest is spent on domestically produced goods and services. You should recognize the first three options as withdrawals from the circular flow of income. The money that is spent goes as income to a new set of recipients, who then behave in the same way—they pay some in taxes, some is saved, some is spent on imports, and the rest is spent on domestic goods and services. During each "round", some income is withdrawn from the circular flow and some stays to be re-spent.

Consider this simplified numerical example. The government spends $100 million in an economy. In the economy, the average behaviour is observed as follows: 20% of all additional income goes to taxes, 10% is saved, and 10% is used to buy imports of goods and services.

This means that the remaining income, which represents 60% of all additional income, is spent on domestic goods and services. This is known as the *marginal propensity to consume (MPC)* and is expressed as a decimal. In this particular economy, the MPC is 0.6. When the government spends its $100m, it goes to the people such as architects, plumbers, engineers, electricians, providers of raw materials, etc. They pay $20m in taxes, $10m leaks from the circular flow as saving, and $10m is spent on imports. The rest, $60 million, is spent. They spend on a wide range of things such as food, clothing, entertainment, books, and car repairs, and the recipients of this $60 million behave in the same way, with 40% leaving the circular flow and 60% remaining to be re-spent as other people's income.

Table 18.2 illustrates the rounds of spending and re-spending.

Initial spending by government in $millions	100.00
2nd round of spending = 60% of 100	60.00
3rd round of spending = 60% of 60	36.00
4th round of spending = 60% of 36	21.60
5th round of spending	12.96
6th round of spending	7.78
7th round	4.67
8th round	2.80
9th	1.68
10th	1.01
11th	0.60
12th	0.36
13th	0.22
14th	0.13
18th	0.08
16th	0.05
18th	0.03
18th	0.02
19th	0.01
20th	0.01
Total spending, including initial spending by government	249.99

Table 18.2 The multiplier effect

The final addition to national income, when all the money has been spent and re-spent, amounts to $250 million, i.e. 2.5 times the original government spending of $100 million. In this example, the multiplier is equivalent to the value 2.5. Any injection into the circular flow of this economy would contribute 2.5 times its amount to national income.

Rather than complete a rather complicated table to find the value of the calculator, there are formulas that can be used. The value of the multiplier can be calculated by using either the marginal propensity to consume (mpc) or the value of the marginal propensity to withdraw (mpw). The mpw is the value of the marginal propensity to save (mps) plus the marginal rate of taxation (mrt) plus the marginal propensity to import (mpm).

Formulas:

$$\text{The multiplier} = \frac{1}{1-mpc} \quad \textbf{OR} \quad \frac{1}{mps + mpm + mrt} = \frac{1}{mpw}$$

From the example above, where the mpc = 0.6, the multiplier is:

$$\frac{1}{1-0.6} = \frac{1}{0.4} = 2.5$$

or

the mps = 0.1, mrt = 0.2, and the mpm = 0.1, the multiplier is:

$$\frac{1}{0.1 + 0.2 + 0.1} = \frac{1}{0.4} = 2.5$$

Example

a   Calculate the multiplier for an economy where the marginal propensity to consume is 0.75
b   By how much will national income increase in total if there is an investment of $50,000?

a   The multiplier $= \dfrac{1}{1-0.75}$

$$= \frac{1}{0.25}$$

$$= 4$$

b   An investment of $50,000 will result in a final increase in national income of $200,000 (4 x $50,000)

Any change in any of the withdrawals from the circular flow will result in a change in the economy's multiplier. If the taxation rate increases, for example, then the value of the multiplier will fall. If the marginal propensity to import falls, then there will be an increase in the multiplier.

If a government is planning to intervene to try to fill a deflationary gap, it must have some idea of two things. First, it must try to estimate the gap between equilibrium output and full employment output. Second, it must have some estimate of the value of the multiplier so as to be able to judge the suitable increase in aggregate demand that is necessary to inject into the economy in order to fill the gap. The difficulties in estimating both of these values illustrate one of the limitations of government fiscal policy aimed at managing aggregate demand in the economy.

3 Macroeconomics

Student workpoint 18.5

Be a thinker

For each of the following, show your workings.

1 An economy has a marginal propensity to consume of 0.8. Calculate:

   a its marginal propensity to withdraw

   b its multiplier

   c the amount of injections that would be needed if national income is to rise by $10,000,000.

2 In a country, the marginal propensity to save is 0.1, the marginal rate of taxation is 0.3 and the marginal propensity to import is 0.1. How will the value of the multiplier change if the government lowers taxes, such that the marginal rate of taxation drops to 0.2?

The accelerator theory

Firms must always engage in replacement investment to replace the equipment that is wearing out. When capital equipment loses its value over time, it is known as *depreciation*. Let us assume that firms are working at their full capacity and are spending a constant amount on investment in order to maintain the level of their existing capital. Now consider what will happen if national income rises. You know that income is a determinant of consumption and if national income rises, then demand from consumers will rise. If firms are already working at capacity, yet want to increase their output to meet the rising demand, then they will have to increase the level of their investment to increase their capacity. They will have the incentive to invest in *new* plant and equipment to meet the increase in demand. We call this type of investment induced investment because the firms are induced to buy new equipment to increase their capacity.

For example, consider the firm Rooney's that manufactures luxury retro toasters. It has an annual demand of 200,000 toasters and operates 20 machines in order to meet this demand. Each machine costs $20,000 and each year, the firm must replace one-tenth of its machines due to depreciation. Now assume that national income rises such that demand for Rooney's toasters rises by 5% to 210,000 toasters. The firm's existing machinery is not able to produce the extra amount of toasters, so if Rooney's wants to meet this demand, it will have to invest in new machinery. In order to maintain its original capital–output ratio (of 10:1), Rooney's will need 21 machines. Usually, the firm spends $40,000 on investment in order to replace the two machines that have worn out. But as a result of the increased demand, Rooney's is induced to invest in one extra machine so that it has 21 machines. Thus investment will be $60,000—a 50% increase from Rooney's regular annual investment. This shows how a reasonably small increase in demand of 5% can lead to a large increase in investment of 50%. We can say that investment *accelerates* when demand rises.

The accelerator theory suggests that the level of induced investment will be determined by the rate of change of national income. When national income is rising rapidly, then firms will want to meet increasing demand by expanding their capacity. But as the rate of growth of GNP falls, businesses will no longer need to add to

3 Macroeconomics

capacity, so investment levels will fall back to the original level necessary to maintain/replace the capital that has worn out.

It is valuable to make a link to the previous section on the multiplier. The induced investment discussed above is subject to the multiplier effect, increasing national income even further. This is known as the combined multiplier/accelerator effect and can explain the upward momentum in the recovery phase of the business cycle.

Theory of Knowledge

Paradigm shift

In Theory of Knowledge, you might come across the concept of a "paradigm shift". In 1962, Thomas Kuhn introduced this concept in the natural sciences to explain that advances in science do not come about in a gradual, evolutionary manner, but occur in a revolutionary way as scientists actually change the complete way that they look at the world. According to Kuhn, all scientists work within a given paradigm. This is essentially a framework that explains and justifies the theories of their discipline. There are different paradigms in different fields; for example, the theoretical paradigm on which all chemists base their work is that matter is composed of atoms made up of negatively-charged electrons surrounding a positively-charged nucleus. Within a given discipline, the vast majority of the theorists accept the paradigm. It forms the basis of all the thinking and it accurately explains and justifies all the knowledge within that discipline.

According to the theories of Kuhn, paradigms are strikingly resistant to change. If anomalies occur that cannot be explained within the paradigm, they tend to be disregarded. However, it is possible for paradigms to shift. If a significant number of anomalies arise, it may come to the point where the existing framework of theories can no longer reliably account for the discrepancies. There may be some time when the scientists cling to their old framework, believing that the discrepancies are the exception, rather than the rule, but ultimately, the old paradigm is discarded as it cannot account for mounting evidence against it. Thus a scientific revolution occurs.

The clearest example of this in the natural sciences involves the scientific revolution in which the dominant world view that the sun, planets, and the moon revolved around the earth as established by Ptolemy in the first century was eventually replaced. For about 2000 years, this paradigm was widely accepted in spite of the number of anomalies that occurred. In the 1530s, Copernicus presented a radical challenge to the Ptolemaic paradigm in presenting the heliocentric system whereby the earth revolves around the sun. For at least a century, this view was so unacceptable to astronomers and the church that one of the followers of his ideas was actually burned at the stake in 1600. It was considered to be heretical to challenge the view that the Earth was at its God-given position at the centre of the universe. Ultimately, the work of many scientists, including Isaac Newton, was instrumental in establishing the heliocentric system as the new paradigm of astronomers. This is known as a paradigm shift.

Kuhn's work illustrates a common feature of humankind. All disciplines have certain ways of looking at things that tend to be fairly entrenched. When new ideas come along that challenge the paradigms that guide theorists in a given field, it is very difficult to accept them. In slang terms, we could say that it is "hard to think outside the box."

We can apply this principle to economic theories. Before the time of John Maynard Keynes, the main economic theories were based on the work of the classical economists, whose paradigm rested on a belief in the power of the free market to achieve the most efficient allocation of resources and a conviction that there should be minimal government intervention in the economy. This was essentially the paradigm among most economists, and their views were widely accepted among Western governments. The massive unemployment of the 1930s presented an anomaly; according to the theories of the paradigm, such unemployment should not persist. Thus governments were not encouraged to intervene to help solve the problem. Keynes' proposition that it was actually government's responsibility to intervene to pump aggregate demand into a sluggish economy took a very long time to be accepted, as it was such a challenge to the guiding paradigm. Ultimately it was accepted as government after government realized that demand management could be used to fine-tune the economy. For approximately 30 years, Keynesian demand theory became the new paradigm that guided economic policy.

It should be noted, however, that a paradigm in the social sciences will be less rigid than a paradigm in the natural sciences and may not satisfy all theorists within the field. For example, while Keynesian economics dominated much public policy, there was always some opposition to the theories derived from the tenets of the paradigm. There were still classical economists opposing Keynesian economic policies, and by the 1970s, economic circumstances had changed so considerably that Keynesian policies were no longer widely acceptable.

Examination questions

Short response questions

1 With the help of a diagram, explain the difference between the equilibrium level of output and the full employment level of output. *[10 marks]*

2 With the help of a diagram, explain the effects of an increase in long-run aggregate supply on national income and the price level. *[10 marks]*

3 With the help of a diagram illustrating the neo-classical perspective, explain how an increase in aggregate demand will affect an economy in the short run and the long run. *[10 marks]*

4 Explain two factors that would cause the value of a country's multiplier to increase. *[10 marks]*

5 What is the role of induced investment in explaining the accelerator effect? *[10 marks]*

Essay question

1 a Explain the components of aggregate demand. *[10 marks]*

   b Evaluate the extent to which an increase in aggregate demand is beneficial for an economy. *[15 marks]*

Inflation and deflation

By the end of this chapter, you should be able to:
- explain the concepts of inflation and deflation
- discuss the costs of inflation and deflation
- explain the causes of inflation and deflation
- explain the measures that may be taken to reduce inflation

HL
- explain how inflation is measured
- discuss the problems in measuring inflation.

Inflation

In Chapter 14, you learned that one of a government's macroeconomic goals is price stability. Another way to express this is to say that governments desire a low and stable rate of inflation. Inflation is defined as a persistent increase in the average price level in the economy, usually measured through the calculation of a consumer price index (CPI). The word "persistent" is of great importance in your understanding of the concept. A single increase in prices is not called inflation. When inflation occurs, there is a sustained increase in the price level. It is also very important not to confuse inflation with an increase in the price of a particular good or service.

Costs of inflation

The reason that governments wish to have a low rate of inflation is because there are a significant number of negative consequences associated with high levels of inflation.

- *Loss of purchasing power:* If the rate of inflation is 2%, then this means that the average price of all goods and services in the economy has risen by 2%. If your income remains constant, then you will not be able to buy as many goods and services as you could before the increase in the average price level. We say that there is a fall in real income, which means that there is a decrease in the purchasing power of income. If your income is linked to the inflation rate, so that you automatically get a 2% "cost-of-living" increase, then you will not face a fall in your real income. This is the case for many jobs, particularly where there are strong unions. However, many people have jobs that don't offer the security of inflation-linked incomes. This may be because they are on fixed incomes or because they have weak bargaining power or because they are self-employed. Thus inflation reduces the purchasing power of their incomes, and will reduce their living standards. It is important to realise that expectations about inflation are important. Even when people's incomes are linked to inflation, they can be negatively affected if the actual rate of inflation turns out to be higher than the expected rate. For example, if the expected rate of inflation is 1.5% and wages are therefore increased by 1.5%, then workers will lose purchasing power if inflation turns out to be 2.5%.

● *Effect on saving:* If you save $1,000 in the bank at 4% annual interest, then in one year's time you will have $1,040. If the inflation rate is 6%, then the real rate of interest (the interest rate adjusted for inflation) will be negative, and your savings will not be able to buy as much as they could have in the previous year. You would have been better off spending the money rather than saving it, because it will have lost some of its purchasing power. Therefore, we say that inflation discourages saving. If people do want to save money, rather than spend on consumption, then they may choose to buy fixed assets, such as houses or art. This means that there are fewer savings available in the economy for investment purposes, and this has negative implications for economic growth.

● *Effect on interest rates:* Commercial banks make their money from charging interest to people who borrow money from them. If there is a high rate of inflation, then banks raise their *nominal* interest rates in order to keep the real rate that they earn positive.

● *Effect on international competitiveness:* If a country has a higher rate of inflation than that of its trading partners, then this will make its exports less competitive, and will make imports from lower-inflation trading partners more attractive. This may lead to fewer export revenues and greater expenditure on imports, thus worsening the trade balance. It might lead to unemployment in export industries and in industries that compete with imports.

● *Uncertainty:* Not only might there be reduced investment due to a fall in the availability of savings, and higher nominal interest rates, but firms may be discouraged from investing due to the uncertainty associated with inflation. Again, this has negative implications for economic growth.

● *Labour unrest:* This may occur if workers do not feel that their wages and salaries are keeping up with inflation. It may lead to disputes between unions and management.

Did you know?

The most famous case of inflation in the twentieth century was the hyperinflation in Germany in 1923. The following list of the price of a single loaf of bread gives you an idea of how quickly prices rose.

Date	Price of a loaf of bread in Marks
June 1922	3.50
May 1923	1200
July 1923	100,000
September 1923	2 million
October 1923	670 million
1 November 1923	3 billion
15 November 1923	80 billion

In May 1923, it became necessary for people for use suitcases (or even wheelbarrows!) rather than wallets for their money. This is not surprising given the fact that it cost 50 billion Marks to buy a glass of beer!

Source: www.joelscoins.com

Deflation

Deflation is defined as a persistent fall in the average level of prices in the economy. There are two broad explanations for a fall in the price level, and economists have used these to categorise "good deflation" and "bad deflation".

The first type of deflation, "good" deflation, comes about from improvements in the supply side of the economy and/or increased productivity. A simple aggregate demand/aggregate supply diagram will illustrate that an increase in the long-run aggregate supply curve can result in an increase in real output and a fall in the price level. If the level of real output increases, then we can assume that there is a lower level of unemployment as more workers will be needed to produce the higher level of output.

The second type of deflation, "bad" deflation, finds its source in the demand side of the economy. Another simple aggregate demand/aggregate supply diagram will illustrate that a fall in aggregate demand will result in a decrease in the price level and a decrease in real output. If real output decreases, then it is assumed that the level of unemployment will rise, as firms will need fewer workers if there is less demand.

Both causes of deflation result in a fall in the price level, but we might say that the first is positive because it results in an increase in real output and a fall in unemployment, while the second is negative because it results in a fall in real output and a rise in unemployment.

Student workpoint 19.1

Be a thinker

Draw and accurately label two aggregate demand/aggregate supply diagrams, one to illustrate "good" deflation and one to illustrate "bad" inflation.

It is very important that you do not confuse deflation with a falling rate of inflation, which might be referred to as disinflation. Consider Figure 19.1, which shows the inflation rate for a country for the years 1999 to 2005. From 1999 to 2000, the inflation rate rose from 1.2% to 1.6%. From 2000 to 2001, the inflation rate fell from 1.6% to 1.3%. This means that the average level of prices rose, but at a lower rate than in the previous year. This may be referred to as disinflation. In the next two years, the inflation rate continued to fall. Prices were still rising, but by a smaller and smaller amount. Moving into 2004, the country experienced deflation, where the average level of prices actually fell by 0.5%. From 2004 to 2005, the country was still in a period of deflation, where average prices fell by 0.3%.

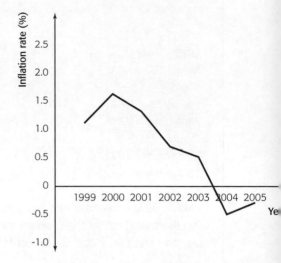

Figure 19.1 Changing rates of inflation and deflation

Student workpoint 19.2

Be a thinker. Explain the following:

Consider the data for Luxembourg and the average of the OECD countries in the accompanying graph and answer the questions that follow. Note that 2006 and 2007 are predictions.

1 From 2002 to 2005, Luxembourg experienced a persistent increase in the percentage change in consumer prices. This means that the inflation rate was rising throughout the period. What is the difference between the rate of change of prices from 2002 to 2003 and from 2003 to 2005?

2 What is forecast to happen to prices in 2006 and 2007? (Be careful here!)

Consumer prices
% change on a year earlier

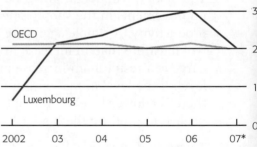

Source: *The Economist*, 15–21 July 2006, p. 84

Costs of deflation

Although as consumers we might be pleased to face falling prices, a significant number of problems can be associated with a fall in the price level. In fact, economists might argue that the costs of deflation are greater than the costs of inflation.

● *Unemployment:* The biggest problem associated with deflation is unemployment. If aggregate demand is low, then businesses are likely to lay off workers. This may then lead to a deflationary spiral. If prices are falling, consumers will put off the purchase of any durable goods as they will want to wait until the prices drop even further. This may be referred to as deferred consumption. This will further reduce aggregate demand. If households become pessimistic about the economic future, then consumer confidence will fall. Low consumer confidence is likely to further depress aggregate demand. Thus a deflationary spiral may occur.

- *Effect on investment:* When there is deflation, businesses make less profit, or make losses. This may lead them to lay off workers. Furthermore, business confidence is likely to be low, and this is likely to result in reduced investment. This has negative implications for future economic growth.

- *Costs to debtors:* Anyone who has taken a loan (this includes all homeowners who have taken a mortgage to buy their home) suffers as a result of deflation because the value of their debt rises as a result of deflation. If profits are low, this may make it too difficult for businesses to pay back their loans and there may be many bankruptcies. This will further worsen business confidence.

Student workpoint 19.3

Be knowledgeable

Read the following article written about the Japanese economy in 2001. Note the problems associated with deflation.

THE JAPANESE CLIMATE REMAINS OVERCAST

As Japan enters the new millennium in a state of deflation, the mood could hardly be more different from the euphoric confidence of a decade ago when the economy was booming.

The evidence of the country's difficulties can hardly be in doubt. Banks continue to collapse, unemployment remains stubbornly high and consumers refuse to spend to help rekindle growth. Confidence is at an all-time low. On top of all of this is a huge government debt, as governments have desperately tried to kick-start the economy to fight deflation by increasing their own spending.

Prospects for economic recovery are rather dim. If consumers are convinced that Japan faces more protracted problems, the economy will be caught firmly in a self-fulfilling downward spiral.

International Herald Tribune, 2 January 2001.

Causes of inflation

We can divide the causes of inflation into three main types: demand-pull inflation, cost-push inflation and inflation due to excess monetary growth.

Demand-pull inflation

As the name suggests, demand-pull inflation occurs as a result of increasing aggregate demand in the economy. This can occur when the economy is approaching full employment as in Figure 19.2(a) or when the economy is at the full employment level of income as in Figure 19.2(b).

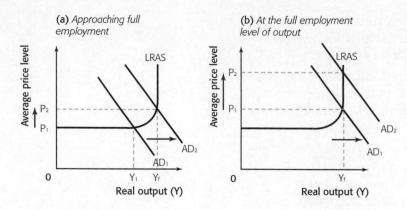

Figure 19.2 Demand-pull inflation

In Figure 19.2(a), the economy is near the full employment level of income, with a small amount of spare capacity in the economy. An increase in aggregate demand will result in an increase in the average price level along with an increase in real output. In Figure 19.2(b), there is a similar increase in aggregate demand, but in this case, the economy is at the full employment level of income and cannot expand output to meet the increased demand. In this case, the result is purely inflationary. In each case, the increase in aggregate demand "pulls up" the average price level. The reasons for the increase in aggregate demand in either example could be due to changes in any of the components of aggregate demand. For example, there could be a high level of consumer confidence, causing consumers to increase consumption. There could be a high level of demand for a country's exports due to rising foreign incomes. The increase might be due to an increase in government spending.

Cost-push inflation

Cost-push inflation occurs as a result of an increase in the costs of production. As you know, an increase in costs results in a fall in short-run aggregate supply from $SRAS_1$ to $SRAS_2$. This results in an increase in the average price level and a fall in the level of real output. Cost-push inflation is illustrated in Figure 19.3

The causes of increases in costs are discussed in Chapter 17. Increases in the price level due to increases in the costs of labour may be referred to as wage-push inflation. Changes in the costs of domestic raw materials will increase firms' costs of production, creating cost-push pressures. Increases in the costs of imported capital, components, or raw materials also increase costs of production to firms, causing import-push inflation. It is worth noting that a fall in the value of a country's currency can cause import-push inflation. This is because a lower exchange rate makes imported capital, components, and raw materials more expensive, thereby increasing the costs of production to the country's firms.

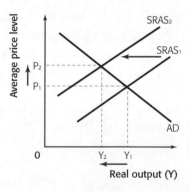

Figure 19.3 Cost-push inflation

Demand-pull and cost-push inflation together

Regardless of the source of the increase in the average price level, one of the problems associated with inflation is its tendency to perpetuate itself. For example, consider what happens if there is an increase in aggregate demand due to increased wealth in the economy (perhaps due to rising house prices). Let's look at the effects in the short run as shown in Figure 19.4.

If we assume that the economy is near full employment, then the increase in aggregate demand results in an increase in demand-pull inflation as the price level rises from P_1 to P_2, as shown in movement (1) in Figure 19.5. The diagram shows what may happen next. The higher price level means that costs of production rise. Also, because the price level increases, workers will negotiate for higher wages and this further increases the costs of production. Thus there will be a shift in the short-run aggregate supply curve from $SRAS_1$ to $SRAS_2$ as a result of cost-push pressures. This is the movement (2) in the diagram. The cycle will not necessarily stop there. Higher wages may give households the illusion that they have more spending power and this might encourage further increases in consumption, shown as another increase in aggregate demand to AD_3 and the movement (3) in the diagram. This may be referred to as an inflationary spiral.

Inflation due to excess monetary growth

A group of economists known as monetarists identified a third cause of inflation. This view gained popularity in the 1970s. One proponent of this view was Milton Friedman whose famous quotation is: "Inflation is always and everywhere a monetary phenomenon." Monetarists argue that excessive increases in the money supply by government are the cause of inflation. As noted in Chapter 16, the level of money supply in the economy is an advanced topic not covered in the IB Diploma Programme syllabus. However, you can rely on your common sense to recognize that if there is more money in the economy, then there will be more spending, thus higher aggregate demand. Monetarism is a "branch" of neo-classical economics and so we use the neo-classical long-run aggregate supply curve to show this type of inflation. This is shown in Figure 19.6.

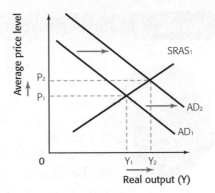

Figure 19.4 Demand-pull inflation

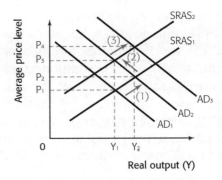

Figure 19.5 An inflationary spiral

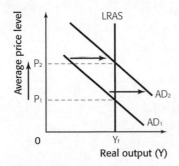

Figure 19.6 Inflation due to excess monetary growth

Monetarists say that increases in the money supply result in higher aggregate demand from AD_1 to AD_2. Because the economy rests at the full employment level of output in the long run, such increases in aggregate demand due to increases in the money supply are purely inflationary, with the price level rising from P_1 to P_2.

3 Macroeconomics

Profile Milton Friedman (1912–2006) ●●●●●●●●●●●●●●●●

Milton Friedman was born in New York City. His parents were working class immigrants from what is now Ukraine. He studied at Rutgers University, achieving his Bachelor's degree when he was twenty years old. He then went on to earn a Masters degree at the University of Chicago in 1933 and a PhD from Columbia University in 1946. He won a prestigious award honouring economists under the age of forty in 1952, and in 1976 he was awarded the Nobel Prize for Economics for "his achievements in the fields of consumption analysis, monetary history and theory, and for his demonstration of the complexity of stabilization policy" (http://nobelprize.org). He published a vast number of books and articles, including a number of publications with his wife, Rose Friedman.

Friedman was a passionate supporter of the free market, and in this sense, might be referred to as a *neo-classical* economist. Yet he is most well-known for his work as a monetarist economist. Challenging the Keynesian paradigm in the 1950s, Friedman presented a modern application of an old economic equation called the quantity theory of money to justify his claim that the price level in an economy is dependent on the money supply. Although Keynesian economic theories maintained their prominence through much of the sixties, the work of Friedman and his fellow monetarists became increasingly more attractive towards the end of the sixties and the seventies. During this time, the combined economic problems of high rates of inflation and high levels of unemployment (known as stagflation) could not be solved through the application of Keynesian demand management policies. One famous quotation of Friedman is, "inflation is always and everywhere a monetary phenomenon", meaning essentially that inflation is always caused by increases in the money supply. The monetarist argument made famous by Friedman rests on a conviction that strict control of the money supply is necessary to control inflation. In his commitment to the value of free markets, he was also a strong advocate of the importance of a limited role of the government in the economy.

●●

Reducing inflation

The appropriate policies to reduce inflation depend on the type of inflation. Given that demand-pull inflation is due to excess aggregate demand, then an appropriate policy would be to reduce aggregate demand. Thus the government could use deflationary fiscal policy (increase taxes and lower government spending) and/or deflationary monetary policy (raise interest rates and reduce the money supply).

However, there are problems associated with such policies. First of all, from a political standpoint, such policies are highly unpopular. A voting population is unlikely to be happy to accept higher taxes as it reduces disposable income and the level of consumption. A reduction in government spending will inevitably impact upon a variety of groups in the economy, and this may result in less support for the government. Higher interest rates will also harm some people in the economy, most obviously anybody who has taken a loan or mortgage. Higher interest rates mean higher loan and mortgage repayments and will therefore be unpopular. A government that is concerned about being re-elected will be reluctant to use these methods to fight inflation.

However, as noted in Chapter 16, monetary policy is carried out by central banks, and in most industrialised countries the central bank is an independent body whose main goal is the maintenance of a low and stable rate of inflation. In some countries, including Poland, South Korea, Canada, England, Australia, and New Zealand, the central bank sets an explicit target rate of inflation. The quotation in Did you know? stating the policy of the National Bank of Poland (NBP), shows that this central bank uses changes in interest rates to keep the inflation rate within the targeted range of 2.5% plus or minus 1%. Other central banks, such as the Federal Reserve in the US and the European Central Bank, have an implicit target rate of inflation. That means that there is an informal target rate that these central banks choose, rather than an officially stated one.

Did you know?

Case study: the policy of the central bank of Poland

"Since 1999 the direct inflation target strategy has been utilised in the implementation of monetary policy. Within the framework of this strategy, the Monetary Policy Council defines the inflation target and then adjusts the NBP basic interest rates in order to maximise the probability of achieving the target. Since the beginning of 2004, the National Bank of Poland has pursued a continuous inflation target at the level of 2.5% with a permissible fluctuation band of +/− 1 percentage point. The NBP maintains interest rates at a level consistent with the adopted inflation target by influencing the level of nominal short-term interest rates on the money market. Money market rates affect loan and deposit rates at commercial banks and thus the size of loans, the demand within the economy and the inflation rate."

Source: www.nbp.pl

The movement towards independence for central banks started in many countries in the 1980s and was partially due to the tendency of governments to use monetary policy to pursue short-term political objectives. Such tendencies often resulted in unacceptably high levels of inflation as governments, keen to be popular, were reluctant to adopt any policies such as higher interest rates in order to fight inflation. As a result of the greater independence for central banks and inflation targeting, many countries have successfully prevented high inflation from occurring.

Targeting inflation, whether explicitly or implicitly, is said to be beneficial as it results in a reduction in inflationary expectations. That is, as long as people have faith in the central bank's ability to contain inflation, then they will not expect higher rates of inflation. If they do not expect higher inflation, then they will not make demands for increases in wages any higher than the expected rate of inflation, and this will keep the costs of labour from rising excessively. This suppresses cost-push inflationary pressure.

3 Macroeconomics

It is fair to say that the more independent the central bank, the more likely that price stability will be maintained. If inflation is rising or inflationary pressures are building up, then a way to bring these down would be to raise interest rates. Central banks keep very close watch on signs of inflation and are ready to raise interest rates to reduce inflationary pressure. While a government would be reluctant to do this, the central bank can make the politically unpopular decision because it does not have to worry about being re-elected!

Student workpoint 19.4

Be an inquirer—conduct an investigation

Investigate the role of the central bank and inflation in your OECD country. Write a brief report to include an explanation of its recent inflation history along with a discussion of the way in which its central bank attempts to maintain price stability. Does this central bank target a specific rate of inflation?

 Nowadays, monetary policy is considered to be the most effective way of managing aggregate demand in the economy and changes in interest rates are considered the best weapon in the fight against inflation. Fiscal policy is not seen to be as effective as monetary policy in battling inflation. It would be very difficult for governments to reduce their spending because of their commitments to the public. Moreover, even if governments could reduce their spending, it would take a long time for the cuts to have any effect on the price level.

If inflation is of a cost-push nature, then deflationary demand-side policies may bring down the price level, but they will result in lower national output and are likely to cause unemployment to rise. Thus demand-side policies are ineffective and supply-side policies such as the policies described in Chapter 17 are the appropriate policies to deal with cost-push inflation. However, as you might predict, when inflation does occur, it is difficult to distinguish the demand-pull from the cost-push factors, and so policy-makers are likely to use a mix of solutions.

For monetarists who believe that inflation is caused by excessive growth of the money supply, then the solution is plain. The money supply should only increase by the same amount as the real increase in national output. That is, if national output is growing by 3%, then the money supply should also grow by 3%. If money supply increases by more than 3%, then the economy will face a situation where "there is too much money chasing too few goods" and so prices will rise to ration the output. Practically speaking, it is very difficult for governments and/or central banks to control the money supply in the economy, and it is not within our syllabus to discuss how they try to do so.

student workpoint 19.5

Be a thinker

Read the text below and answer the questions that follow.

FED CHIEF EXPECTING INFLATION TO RETREAT

The US Federal Reserve expects inflation to retreat from recent highs but could still raise interest rates, Ben Bernanke, chairman, told Congress yesterday. His testimony came as the Fed chairman released forecasts suggesting that it is prepared to bring inflation down gradually to minimize the damage to the economy.

The forecasts to Congress show that Fed policymakers are willing to tolerate an inflation rate, on its core measure, of 2% or slightly above this year and next, providing it is heading in the right direction. Officials think that this will allow the economy to grow at close to its trend rate of 3% to 3.5% over this year and next.

The Fed chair told senators that the forecasts are based on the assumption that a slowdown from above-trend growth is already under way and that this would reduce inflationary pressure over time. This is primarily due to weaker consumer demand as a result of higher energy costs and a softening housing market with fewer house sales and a fall in the growth of house prices. However, he did add that there are still some inflation risks. The combination of high energy prices and high levels of capacity utilization may sustain inflationary pressure.

Financial Times, 19 July 2006

1 Using a diagram, explain which phase of the business cycle the US economy seems to be in.

2 Explain **two** reasons why inflation can cause "damage to the economy".

3 Use a diagram to explain how the Fed could attempt to "bring inflation down".

HL
How is inflation measured?

It is necessary to have some kind of an accurate measure of the increase in the price level. The most widely used statistic to measure inflation is known as the consumer price index (CPI). In some countries, this is referred to as the retail price index (RPI).

Not all prices change by the same amount over a given period of time; for example, the price of chocolate might increase by 5% in a year, while the price of petrol might increase by 10%. Neither of these is an appropriate measure of the change in the average price level. Statisticians in different countries around the world have slightly different ways of measuring the rate of inflation, but the central idea is the same. Simply put, they choose what is known as a representative "basket" of consumer goods and services and measure how the price of this basket changes over time. When the price of the basket increases, then this means that the average price level has risen.

3 Macroeconomics

What is meant by a "representative basket of consumer goods and services"? It would be impossible to devise a measure of inflation that includes all goods and services bought by consumers. In each country, the agency in charge of the compilation of economic data creates a list of the typical goods and services consumed by the average household. These items are grouped into a number of different categories. The prices of these items are measured each month to calculate the change in the price of the "basket". The change in the price of the basket is reflected in the measure called the consumer price index. It is important to point out that some of the goods and services consumed are far more important than others, because they take up a larger share of consumers' income. Thus the categories are given a weight in the index to reflect their importance in the average consumer's income. The weights for the different categories for the United States CPI along with some examples of the items that are included are shown in Table 19.1.

Category	CPI weight (%)
Housing (rent of main residence, owners' equivalent rent, heating, bedroom furniture)	40.1
Transportation (new vehicles, airline fares, gasoline/petrol, motor vehicle insurance)	19.7
Food and beverages (breakfast cereal, coffee, chicken, wine, service meals)	16.5
Recreation (televisions, pets and pet products, sports equipment, admission prices)	5.1
Medical care (prescription drugs and medical supplies, doctors' services, eyeglasses)	5.1
Education and communication (university tuition, postage, computer software and accessories, telephone services)	5.6
Apparel (women's dresses, men's shirts, jewellery)	4.1
Other (haircuts and other personal services, funeral expenses, cigarettes)	3.6

Source: United States Bureau of Labor Statistics. www.bls.gov

Table 19.1 US CPI: categories and their weights

From the data, we can conclude that spending on food and beverages makes up 16.5% of the spending of the "typical" or average household. Thus changes in the prices of the food and beverage products in the basket will be given a weight of 16.5% in the calculation of the index. The components and the weighting of the basket are determined by surveys of household spending habits, and will change according to changes in consumption habits (see Table 19.2 for some examples of recent changes to the UK "basket"). The price of the basket is measured regularly by collecting prices from shopping outlets throughout the country, and a national average price is determined. This is the measure of the national consumer price index and changes in the index represent the "headline" inflation rate. This is the rate of inflation most commonly used and the one that we are most familiar with for judging the overall state of the country's economy.

Changes to the UK CPI basket made in 2005

Note that the categories are not exactly the same as the categories shown in the data for the US CPI.

This illustrates the fact that the statistics are calculated differently in different countries.

CPI category (sub-grouping)	Change	Comment
Recreation and culture (household goods)	Added—Small pet, e.g. hamster	This improves the coverage of spending on pets and accessories
Miscellaneous goods and services (personal goods and services)	Added—Razor cartridge blades	This replaces disposable razors
Furniture, household equipment and maintenance (household goods)	Added—Wooden patio set	This replaces plastic patio sets
Food and non-alcoholic beverages (food)	Added—500 ml fizzy bottled drink	Previously, only canned fizzy drinks and fizzy drinks in large bottles were included
Clothing and footwear (clothing and footwear)	Removed—Children's shorts	Removed due to some difficulty in collecting prices.
Food and non-alcoholic beverages (food)	Removed—French stick/baguette and tinned corned beef	
Recreation and culture (leisure goods)	Removed—Analogue camcorder	It has been difficult to collect prices due to the growth of the digital camcorder market. The Office of National Statistics is researching methods of quality adjustment of digital camcorder prices before these are introduced to the basket.

Source: Consumer Prices Index and Retail Prices Index: The 2005 Basket of Goods and Services. David Roe, Office for National Statistics

Table 19.2 Changes to the CPI basket of goods in the UK in 2005

Problems involved in the measurement of inflation

● Measuring inflation using the consumer price index has one main limitation. The basket used in any country represents the purchasing habits of a "typical" household, but this will not be applicable to all people. The purchasing habits of different people will clearly vary greatly. For example, the "basket" of a family with children will be very different from that of an elderly couple or a single person with no children. There may be variations in regional rates of inflation within a country. Although regional figures are published, the national figure is the more widely-used measure, and this may not be an accurate reflection for a particular area. If the national average is used as the basis for wage negotiations or pension changes, then these might not accurately reflect the price changes for a particular group. This will be harmful if the group has a higher cost of living than suggested by the national average, and beneficial for those whose spending costs are less than the average.

● There may be errors in the collection of data that limit the accuracy of the final results. Because it would be utterly impossible to collect the prices of all items bought by all households in all possible locations, it is necessary to take sample items in a sample of selected cities and a sample of selected outlets. The layers of sampling are likely to lead to some degree of inaccuracy. The larger the sample, the more accurate will be the results, but this is time-consuming and very costly.

● As Table 19.2 showed, statisticians try to take into account changes in consumption habits by making changes to the basket. Items are removed or added to be more representative of the typical household's demand. However, this takes a good deal of time. Moreover, if the items in the basket are changed, then this limits the ability of analysts to make comparisons from one time period to another. This is complicated by the fact that the quality of goods changes over time. For example, when a computer company upgrades a computer to include more built-in memory, then the quality of the product improves. The price of the computer may rise to reflect the improvement. If the computer is in the typical basket, then this will feed into a higher rate of inflation, yet the product isn't really the same product.

● Countries measure their rate of inflation in different ways, and include different components. This can make it problematic to make international comparisons.

● Prices may change for a variety of reasons that are not sustained. For example, seasonal variations in the prices of food and volatile oil prices may lead to unusual movements in the inflation rate and can be misleading. Statisticians make some effort to reduce such distorting effects by identifying a "core" rate of inflation that uses the information of the consumer price index but excludes food and energy prices.

● The CPI only measures changes in consumer prices, yet clearly other price changes are important in judging the economic health and prospects of a country. For this reason economists also measure changes in producer prices and commodity prices. These give economists a good idea of possible cost-push pressures.

Examination questions

Short response questions

1 With the help of a diagram, explain the concept of demand-pull inflation.   *[10 marks]*

2 With the help of a diagram, explain the concept of cost-push inflation.   *[10 marks]*

3 With the help of a diagram, explain the monetarist explanation of inflation.   *[10 marks]*

4 Explain three consequences of inflation.   *[10 marks]*

5 Explain three consequences of deflation.   *[10 marks]*

HL   6 Explain three problems involved in the measurement of inflation.   *[10 marks]*

Essay questions

1 a Explain the main consequences of inflation.   *[10 marks]*

   b Evaluate the methods that might be used to reduce inflation.   *[15 marks]*

2 a Explain the main causes of inflation.   *[10 marks]*

   b Evaluate the extent to which demand-side policies are effective in reducing inflation.   *[15 marks]*

20 Unemployment

By the end of this chapter, you should be able to:

- explain what is meant by unemployment
- define the different measures of unemployment and explain the limitations to their validity
- discuss the costs of unemployment
- distinguish between the different causes of unemployment
- evaluate the measures that may be taken to reduce unemployment.

As we know, a low level of unemployment is one of the main macroeconomic goals of every government. Unemployment is a highly publicised topic; a low and/or falling unemployment rate is widely interpreted as a sign of improved health of an economy. The following article introduces a few of the key issues surrounding the topic of unemployment. It is useful to have a quick look at these before developing the theory.

CANADIAN UNEMPLOYMENT RATE EDGES UP TO 6.4%

Canadian Unemployment Rate Edges Up to 6.4% Canada's jobless rate increased slightly to 6.4 per cent in April as job growth slowed, Statistics Canada said Friday. The rate rose a tenth of a percentage point from March, but still remained near 30-year lows.

Statistics Canada said 22,000 new jobs – all full time – were added to the nation's payrolls last month, significantly more than the 15,000 that economists had expected.

That brings the number of jobs created since the start of the year to 124,000. Employment in the first four months is growing by twice the rate off the same period last year.

Ontario led the country in job creation for the second straight month as the province added 23,800 jobs, mostly among adult women. Ontario has added 108,000 new jobs over the past 12 months as growth in service sector positions has outweighed losses in manufacturing.

Employment in Quebec fell by about 24,000 in April for the province's first significant decline this year. It was the only province to record a new job loss last month.

Job creation in Alberta and British Columbia was relatively flat last month after outpacing the rest of the country for the past 12 months. Those two provinces still have the lowest jobless rates in the country.

For once, manufacturing jobs actually rose. Stats Can said 24,500 factory jobs were added in April. That still leaves the country's manufacturers with 165,000 fewer jobs than in 2002 when the Canadian dollar began its relentless rise towards the current level of 90 cents US.

Statistics Canada said that strong full-time employment growth over the last year and an unemployment rate perched around its record low continue to push wages up. The average hourly wage in April was up 3.1 per from April 2005. (257 words)

CBC News, May 5, 2006.

Some of the points raised in the article are as follows.

- Unemployment essentially means just what it says—"jobless".

- A change in the unemployment rate of even a tenth of a percentage point is considered to be "news".

- The unemployment rate is affected by how many jobs are created in the economy.

- The number of jobs created will vary in different industries (e.g. manufacturing or services) and may be different for different groups of people (e.g. men or women).

- While a country will publicise a national unemployment rate (Canada = 6.4%), the rates in different regions will differ from this national average.

- Many things will affect the unemployment rate, e.g. exchange rates, costs of raw materials, and international economic conditions.

- The unemployment rate will have an effect on wage rates.

What is unemployment and how is it measured?

According to the International Labour Organization (ILO), unemployment is defined as "people of working age who are without work, available for work and actively seeking employment" (www.ilo.org).

By definition, the unemployment rate is the number of people who are unemployed expressed as a percentage of the total labour force (not the whole population). The labour force, otherwise known as the work force, is essentially the "economically active population". Although it varies from country to country, there is a specified age at which people are eligible to start work and to retire. Anybody outside this age is not part of the work force. Students attending school are not part of the work force, as they are not looking for work. Similarly, parents who stay at home to look after children are not considered to be part of the labour force. People who are not considered to be part of the labour force would include children, students, stay-at-home parents, retired people, and others who are choosing not to (or are not able to) work. Even though they do not have jobs, such groups are not considered to be unemployed. Because they are not actively seeking employment, they are not part of the labour force.

It may be surprising to realize that it is actually quite difficult to measure the size of the labour force and the number of people that are unemployed. Each country has its own national system for measuring the number of people that are unemployed. Information is gathered from national censuses and surveys of the population, along with administrative records such as unemployment insurance records and social security information. It is worth noting that there may be inaccuracies in such data and there may also be inconsistency in the definitions across different countries.

The following gives an example of possible differences in measurement. Unemployment data may be based on the people who are registered as unemployed, as in Austria or Switzerland. Alternatively, it may be calculated as the number of people who are claiming unemployment benefits, as in Britain and Belgium. However, even within these two approaches, there may be problems measuring the true number of people unemployed. For example, the incentive to register as unemployed is likely to depend on the availability of unemployment benefits. A person who is not entitled to any benefits is not likely to register as unemployed. There is a category of workers known as "discouraged workers". These people are long-term unemployed who have given up the search for work and are no longer eligible for benefits. As soon as they give up the search, they are no longer part of the unemployed.

Student workpoint 20.1

Be an inquirer

You have already gathered the data for the unemployment rate in your chosen OECD country. Now find out exactly how the government defines and calculates the unemployment rate.

Did you know?

What does the International Labour Organization do?

The International Labour Organization is the UN specialized agency which seeks promotion of social justice and internationally recognized human and labour rights. It was founded in 1920 and is the only surviving major creation of the Treaty of Versailles which brought the League of Nations into being; it became the first specialized agency of the UN in 1946.

The ILO formulates international labour standards in the form of Conventions and Recommendations setting minimum standards of basic labour rights: freedom of association, the right to organize, collective bargaining, abolition of forced labour, equality of opportunity and treatment, and other standards regulating conditions across the entire spectrum of work-related issues. It provides technical assistance primarily in the fields of:

- vocational training and vocational rehabilitation
- employment policy
- labour administration
- labour law and industrial relations
- working conditions
- management development
- cooperatives
- social security
- labour statistics and occupational safety and health.

It promotes the development of independent employers' and workers' organizations and provides training and advisory services to those organizations. Within the UN system, the ILO has a unique tripartite structure, with workers and employers participating as equal partners with governments in the work of its governing organs.

Source: www.ilo.org

Student workpoint 20.2

Be knowledgeable

a Read through the description of the mandate of the ILO in the Did you know? box.

b Have a look at the homepage of the ILO (www.ilo.org) to develop an awareness of the type of work carried out by this international organisation. At the time of writing, some of the issues being discussed are:

- labour market flexibility and security in the robust economies of the West Balkans

- new measures on occupational safety and health (given that the ILO estimates that some 6000 workers die each day as a result of work-related accidents or illness)

- an investigation into "Trafficking for Labour and Sexual Exploitation" during the football World Cup

- Better Factories Cambodia, a programme of the ILO for improvement of working conditions in the garment industry

- the promotion of the World Day against Child Labour (12 June 2006).

Make your own list of four contemporary issues being addressed at the ILO.

Distribution of unemployment

Along with differences in methods of measurement, it is worth pointing out another limitation of the unemployment rate. As with many other indicators, a national unemployment rate establishes an average for a whole country, and this is very likely to mask inequalities among different groups within an economy. One should be careful in using the national rate as a basis for making conclusions about different groups of people. These are some of the typical disparities that exist among different groups of people within a country:

- *Geographical disparities:* Unemployment is likely to vary quite markedly among regions in a country, as most countries do have some regions that are more prosperous than others. Inner city unemployment might be quite a bit higher than suburban or rural unemployment.

- *Age disparities:* Unemployment rates in the under-25 age group are higher than the national averages in many countries.

- *Ethnic differences:* Ethnic minorities often suffer from higher unemployment rates than the national average. This may be the result of differences in educational opportunities or possibly due to attitudes and/or prejudices of employers.

- *Gender disparities:* Unemployment rates among women have tended to be much higher than rates for men in many industrialised countries. There may be all kinds of reasons for this: differences in education, discrimination by employers, or other social factors.

Student workpoint 20.3

Be an inquirer

Investigate the distribution of unemployment in your chosen OECD country by looking at the unemployment rates for:

● different regions

● different age groups
● different ethnic groups
● men and women.

Present the information in the form of tables or graphs. Other than the national statistics office or the OECD, the ILO might be a useful resource.

Costs of unemployment

The reason that governments place such importance on reducing the level of unemployment is because unemployment poses great costs on an economy. These costs can be grouped into different categories.

● *Costs of unemployment to the unemployed people themselves:* People who are unemployed face several costs. First of all, unemployed people will receive less income that they would do if they were employed. This is assuming that they receive some unemployment benefits. Clearly if there are no unemployment benefits, then the situation is much worse. A reduction in income implies a lower standard of living for those that are unemployed and perhaps their families as well. The costs worsen the longer the people are unemployed. It is quite likely that a person who remains unemployed for a long period of time could become increasingly dejected and this could contribute to high levels of stress and the problems associated with stress such as anxiety and depression. Erosion of mental health can lead to relationship break-downs and, in the extreme, higher levels of suicide.

● *Costs of unemployment to society:* The social costs of unemployment can most clearly be seen in areas where there are high levels of unemployment in the form of poverty, higher rates of crime and vandalism, increased gang activities and so on. While it would be a simplification to blame these problems entirely on unemployment, they are not unconnected.

● *Costs of unemployment to the economy as a whole:* A production possibility curve can be used to illustrate the key problem facing an economy with unemployment—if actual output is less than potential output due to the unemployment of the factor of production, labour, then the economy is foregoing possible output and would be operating at a point within its production possibility curve. This loss of output, and income to the unemployed, has other implications for the economy as a whole. For instance, there is the opportunity cost of the government's spending on unemployment benefits. If unemployed people who have lower incomes pay less direct tax and spend less money, so the government earns less in indirect taxes as well. The government may have to spend more money to solve the social problems created by unemployment.

It should be pointed out that the costs of unemployment increase the longer that people are unemployed. The costs listed above are really those costs associated with long-term unemployment.

Student workpoint 20.4

Be a thinker. Illustrate the following.

Using a production possibility curve, explain the costs of unemployment to an economy.

Student workpoint 20.5

Be an inquirer

Try to assess some of the problems associated with unemployment in your chosen country.

'*You take my life when you do take the means whereby I live.*'
William Shakespeare,
The Merchant of Venice

What are the main factors affecting the level of unemployment?

At any given point in time, there will be a number of people that are unemployed. This may be referred to as the "pool" of unemployment. But this "pool" will be in a constant state of change. At any given time, people are becoming unemployed, while others are gaining employment. The level of unemployment depends on the relationship between these two. If more people are becoming unemployed than gaining jobs, then the level of unemployment will rise. If more jobs are being created so that more people are gaining jobs than losing jobs, then the level of unemployment will fall. These can be referred to as the inflows and outflows into the "pool" of unemployment and are illustrated in Figure 20.1.

These factors cause the level of unemployment to rise

Inflows (those becoming unemployed)
- People who have lost their jobs
- People who have resigned
- People who have left school, but have not yet found work
- People who are trying to return to work after having left it (e.g. stay-at-home parents returning to the workforce)
- People who have immigrated into the country but have not yet found work

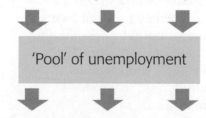

'Pool' of unemployment

These factors cause the level of unemployment to fall

Outflows (those no longer considered to be unemployed)
- People who find jobs
- People who retire
- People who go (back) into education
- People who choose to stay at home to look after children
- People who emigrate to other countries
- People who give up the search for jobs

Note that other than the first point, the rest of the people are no longer considered to be unemployed because they have left the labour force—they are no longer 'people of working age who are without work, available for work and actively seeking employment'.

Figure 20.1 Inflows and outflows from the "pool" of unemployment

The movements in and out of the pool of unemployment affect the supply of labour in an economy at any given time. This, along with the demand for labour, will determine the level of employment and unemployment in an economy.

Causes of unemployment

There are two main categories of unemployment. Although these terms are not specifically mentioned on the IB Diploma Programme syllabus, they help to understand the causes of unemployment. The categories are: equilibrium unemployment and disequilibrium unemployment. Before looking at each type, it is necessary to introduce the concepts and diagrams explaining an economy's labour market.

The labour market
The labour market is illustrated in Figure 20.2.

The diagram shows the macroeconomic labour market. The y-axis on the diagram represents the price of labour, as measured by the average real wage rate. This shows the average level of wages, adjusted for inflation. The labour market represents the demand and supply for *all* labour in the economy. Thus the demand for labour is more accurately called the aggregate demand for labour (AD_L) as it includes the demand not just for one type of worker but for all the labour that is involved in producing an economy's goods and services. For example, it includes the demand for teachers, assembly line workers, sales people, pizza deliverers, motorcycle mechanics, and bankers to name a few. The aggregate demand curve shows the total demand for labour at every given average wage rate. The aggregate demand curve slopes downwards, because at a lower real wage level, producers are more willing to take on more labour—i.e. producers' demand for workers increases. As the wage level increases, firms attempt to reduce the amount of labour that they use, perhaps by using more capital-intensive production methods.

The aggregate supply of labour curve (AS_L) illustrates the total number of an economy's workers that are willing and able to work in the economy at every given average wage rate. As the average wage rate increases, more people are willing to work and so the ASL curve slopes upwards.

The labour market is in equilibrium where the aggregate demand for labour is equal to the aggregate supply of labour. Although it resembles any microeconomic demand and supply diagram, it is actually a macroeconomic model, as it describes aggregates in the economy. The equilibrium wage for the economy is established by this interaction of ADL and ASL and is shown on the diagram as W_e.

Disequilibrium unemployment

Disequilibrium unemployment occurs when there are any conditions that prevent the labour market from "clearing", that is, reaching the labour market equilibrium. There are two types of disequilibrium unemployment.

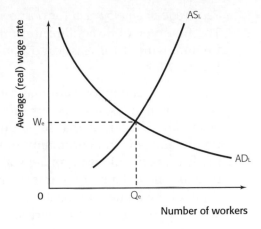

Figure 20.2 Equilibrium in the labour market

Real-wage unemployment (or classical unemployment)
The first type of disequilibrium unemployment, real-wage unemployment (or classical unemployment), is illustrated in Figure 20.3.

This type of unemployment may be referred to as classical unemployment as it represents the view of classical (and neo-classical) economists that argue that some unemployment is caused by trade unions and government minimum wages interfering with the labour market. Trade unions negotiate wages that are higher than the equilibrium and a minimum wage is set above the equilibrium. As a result of the higher enforced wage (W_1), the aggregate supply of labour is greater than the aggregate demand for labour, and unemployment of a-b is created. (You should be able to see that this "surplus" of labour represents the same outcome as discussed in Chapter 4 on minimum prices.) In this situation, the trade unions and/or the government are preventing the market from clearing.

Solutions to real-wage unemployment
The solutions to this type of unemployment are clear. If the trade unions are preventing the labour market from clearing, then the government should reduce the ability of unions to negotiate higher wages. Similarly, if the minimum wage prevents the market from clearing, then the minimum wage should be reduced, or even abolished.

There are obvious consequences to such policies. First of all, it might be quite difficult to reduce union power. Second, and perhaps more importantly, the effects of such policies will harm poorest workers the most. High-income workers are not the ones who receive minimum wages; a reduction in the minimum wage will reduce the income and living standards of those workers who are already earning low wages. Thus such a policy can lead to a worsening distribution of income within an economy—greater inequity.

Demand-deficient unemployment or cyclical unemployment
This type of disequilibrium unemployment is associated with the cyclical downturns in the economy. As an economy moves into a period of slower growth (or negative growth in the case of a recession), aggregate demand tends to fall as consumers spend less on goods and services (see Figure 20.4(a)). This is likely to lead to a fall in the demand for labour, as firms cut back on production. This is illustrated in Figure 20.4(b).

Assume that the economy is initially operating at a high level of economic activity at Y_1 in Figure 20.4(a). There is aggregate demand for labour at AD_L in 20.4(b) so the equilibrium wage will be W_1, for Q_e workers. The labour market is in equilibrium.

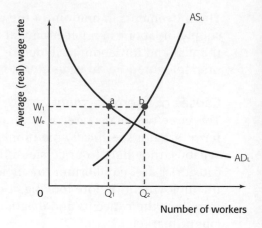

Figure 20.3 Real-wage unemployment

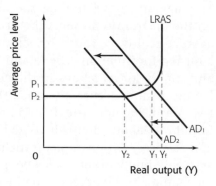

Figure 20.4 (a) A decrease in AD

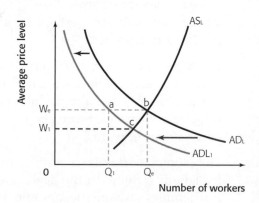

Figure 20.4 (b) Demand-deficient unemployment

3 Macroeconomics

If the economy slows down, aggregate demand is likely to fall as shown in Figure 20.4(a). To reduce their output, firms will reduce their demand for labour from AD_L to AD_{L1} as shown in Figure 20.4(b). If labour markets functioned perfectly, then the average real wage would fall to W_1. However, this is not the case, and we say that wages are "sticky downwards". This means that while workers' wages can easily increase, it is less likely that real wages will fall. There are several reasons for this wage "stickiness". First of all, firms realise that paying lower real wages is likely to lead to discontent and reduced motivation among workers. This may result in lower worker productivity and is undesirable. Secondly, firms may not be able to reduce wages due to labour contracts and trade union power. Since wages are likely to remain "stuck" up at W_e, the aggregate supply of labour will be greater that the aggregate demand for labour, and unemployment of a–b will be created.

This type of unemployment has a third name—Keynesian unemployment. As discussed in Chapter 18, Keynes observed that it was quite possible for the economy to operate well below full employment, and this was likely to result in high levels of unemployment.

Solution to demand deficient unemployment:
Given that the problem is due to the low level of aggregate demand, the solution to this type of unemployment should also be clear—the government can intervene to bring about an increase in aggregate demand through the use of fiscal or monetary policies. That is, the government can use Keynesian demand management policies. These policies will be evaluated later.

Equilibrium unemployment (natural unemployment)

Theoretically, the labour market may be in equilibrium, with no demand deficient or real-wage unemployment, but there might still be unemployed people. This is because there are other types of unemployment that occur even when the labour market is in equilibrium. When the labour market is in equilibrium, the number of job vacancies in the economy is the same as the number of people looking for work. This is full employment where there is no disequilibrium unemployment. Jobs exist, but people are either unwilling or unable to take the jobs that are available. This is best understood through the use of Figure 20.5.

This diagram introduces a new curve—a measure of the total labour force (LF). Why is the number of workers in the labour force greater than the aggregate supply of labour? Recall that the aggregate supply of labour shows the number of people *willing and able to work at every given wage rate*. But at any given wage rate, there will be more people looking for jobs than those who are actually willing and/or able to take the jobs. Thus, at W_e, Q_e people are willing and able to take jobs, yet a–b unemployment exists.

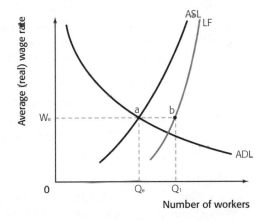

Figure 20.5 Equilibrium unemployment

Although it is difficult to observe on the diagram, the fact that there is no disequilibrium in the labour market means that there *are* jobs available but a–b people are either not willing or not able to take the jobs. For example, perhaps there are job vacancies in the financial services industry, but the unemployed assembly line workers are not able to take the jobs because they lack the appropriate education and skills. Or perhaps there are job vacancies in the domestic services industry, but the unemployed mechanical engineers are unwilling to take them. Or perhaps there are jobs available for computer programmers, but the unemployed computer programmers are not aware that these jobs are available. In each of these three examples, the unemployed workers are either unable (the assembly line workers and the computer programmers) or unwilling (the mechanical engineers) to take the jobs that are available.

Notice that the gap between the aggregate supply of labour curve and the labour force curve becomes smaller at higher wages. This is common sense. At low wage rates, there are fewer workers that are *willing* to work; people would rather be unemployed than take the jobs that are available. But as the real wage rate rises, more people are willing to take the jobs, thus the gap between the two decreases.

There are three main types of equilibrium unemployment—frictional, seasonal, and structural unemployment. Together they make up what is known as the natural unemployment in the economy. An economy is at full employment when the unemployment that exists in the economy is only the natural employment.

In the next section, the three types of natural unemployment are explained. In simplified terms, there is one common feature—jobs exist but the people are either unwilling or unable to take these jobs. Thus the solutions for each type of unemployment share the characteristic that they are designed to make people more *able* to take the vacant jobs, or encourage them to be more *willing* to take the available jobs. As a result, in each case the aggregate supply of labour will shift to the right. Solutions to these types of unemployment are types of supply-side policies, as they are designed to increase the quantity and improve the quality of labour. These are generally the same as explained in Chapter 17, but these policies are focused specifically on the labour market. Remember that we tend to group supply-side policies into two categories— interventionist and market-oriented policies. True to their name, the interventionist policies rely on government involvement in the labour market, while the market-oriented policies emphasize the importance of allowing the labour market to function freely without government intervention.

Frictional unemployment

This is the short-term unemployment that occurs when people are in between jobs, or they have left education and are waiting to take up their first job. This type of unemployment is easily recognisable as *natural* unemployment as it is natural for people to leave jobs in the hopes of finding better ones. Moreover, it is not generally perceived to be a negative outcome in any dynamic economy. If people leave one job, the assumption is that they will move on to a job where they can be more productive. As soon as such members of the labour force get a job, they will be able to contribute more to the economy.

Solutions to frictional unemployment
Even though frictional unemployment is not seen as a serious problem in an economy due to its short-term nature, there are ways that governments can reduce this level of unemployment if it is believed that people are remaining unemployed for too long a time. Some would argue that people will have little incentive to find a job if the unemployment benefits available to them in their country are generous and allow them to take their time in looking. Thus economists who prefer to allow markets to operate freely would say that governments should lower unemployment benefits to encourage unemployed workers to take the jobs that are available rather than allow them the chance to wait for a better one to come along. If unemployment benefits were reduced, then the unemployed workers might become more willing to work, thus shifting the aggregate supply of labour to the right.

Sometimes people who are frictionally unemployed remain without work because they are not aware of appropriate vacancies that exist. In such a case, frictional unemployment can be reduced by improving the flow of information from potential employers to people looking for jobs. This can be through such things as Internet job sites, newspapers, job centres, and employment counsellors. This would reflect a more interventionist approach.

Seasonal unemployment

It is natural in many economies for some workers to be employed on a seasonal basis. That is, the demand for certain workers falls at certain times of the year. For example, in temperate climates where there is a cold winter, there may be unemployed construction workers or farmers. The tourism industry tends to work in seasons—for example, there is not much call for a ski instructor in Austria in July.

Solutions to seasonal unemployment:
Such unemployment can be reduced by encouraging people to take different jobs in their "off season". The methods mentioned above, reduced unemployment benefits and greater flow of information, are appropriate here as well.

Structural unemployment

This is by far the worst type of equilibrium unemployment and occurs as a result of the changing structure of an economy. Structural unemployment occurs when there is a *permanent* fall in demand for a particular type of labour. This is natural in a growing economy, as while there will always be new types of jobs being created (e.g. software engineers), other jobs in a country may disappear (e.g. coal mining), making people unemployed. One reason that it is so harmful is that it tends to result in long-term unemployment as people who lose their jobs in one area lack the necessary skills to take on the newly-created jobs. We say that they lack the occupational mobility to change jobs. It may be that jobs are created in one part of the country, while the unemployed are living in another part of the country. Here, we say that they lack the geographic mobility.

There are different causes of structural unemployment.

- It is possible that new technologies can make certain types of labour unnecessary. By its very nature, automation reduces the need for labour. For example, automated teller machines (ATMs) have reduced the demand for human bank tellers. This can be referred to as technological unemployment.

- Demand for a particular type of labour might fall due to lower-cost labour in foreign countries. For example, there is less demand for furniture makers in Italy as a result of competition with Chinese furniture makers whose costs are lower. This is resulting in higher unemployment among Italian furniture makers.

- Changes in consumer taste may lead to a fall in demand for a particular type of labour. For example, people in some areas are increasingly concerned about the negative externalities associated with the production and consumption of coal. This has led to a search for alternatives, and a fall in the demand for coal in some countries. As a result, coal miners have become structurally unemployed.

Solutions to structural unemployment: interventionist policies
A key here is to try to enhance the occupational mobility of people, so that they become more able to take available jobs.

- A long-term solution involves an education system that trains people to be more occupationally flexible. Evidence suggests that people in more developed economies will have to change jobs several times in their career. Thus it is clear that an education system must make people able to learn the skills to adapt to rapidly changing economic conditions.

- Another strategy to improve occupational mobility involves spending on adult retraining programmes to help people acquire the necessary skills to match available jobs.

- Another possibility is for the government to give subsidies to firms that provide training for their workers.

- If jobs exist in other parts of a country, a government might provide subsidies or tax breaks to encourage people to move to those areas. This enhances their geographic mobility.

- Governments can also support apprenticeship programmes, such as those available in Germany and Austria, so that potential workers can acquire the skills needed in the labour force.

There are two main disadvantages to such policies. The first is that they are likely to involve a high opportunity cost as governments will have to forego spending in other areas in order to be able to afford the strategies. The second is that these policies are really only effective in the longer term.

Solutions to structural unemployment: market-oriented/free market policies

- One strategy is similar to the suggestion to reduce frictional unemployment. Governments should reduce unemployment benefits to give unemployed people the incentive to take the jobs that are available.

- Market-oriented economists feel that government intervention and labour market regulations reduce "labour market flexibility" and discourage businesses from hiring workers. They would argue that regulations about hiring and firing, for example, make businesses less willing to take on new workers, so they would argue in favour of deregulation of labour markets. This would involve reducing or removing the legislation that businesses must follow in their hiring, firing, and employment practices.

 The burden of such policies falls on two groups of people. First, people who lose their unemployment benefits will have lower living standards, and so such a policy can be said to increase inequity in an economy. Second, it can be assumed that labour market regulations are in place to protect workers from unfair treatment, such as being fired without due cause. Labour market regulations also guarantee certain conditions of work such as working time, holidays, and safety at work. If there is labour market deregulation, it would not be surprising to find worse working conditions for labour. So although unemployment might fall, and the economy's output might rise, there might be a high cost for the workers themselves. Again, this can contribute to inequity in the economy where the benefits of higher economic growth are not shared by all.

Student workpoint 20.6

Be an inquirer

Research the labour market policies of the government in your chosen country. Consider the following questions:

a   How extensive are the labour market regulations (e.g. minimum wage, hiring and firing rules (job security), safety standards, length of work day, paid holidays)?

b   What does the government do to reduce the level of unemployment? Try to identify the policies that are interventionist and the policies that are market-oriented.

Are demand-side policies or supply-side policies more effective in reducing unemployment?

It should be clear that the solutions to unemployment depend very much on the type of unemployment. If an economy is experiencing a downturn in economic activity, then it is likely that demand-deficient unemployment will rise, making demand management policies suitable.

 There are of course concerns associated with such policies. In order to use expansionary fiscal policy, a government may have to run a budget deficit and spend more than it takes in revenues. While not necessarily a problem, particularly in the short run, this may lead to fiscal problems in the longer run. If governments reduce taxes, there is no guarantee that people will spend their extra disposable income; if consumer confidence is low, then people might prefer to save and aggregate demand might remain depressed. If governments reduce interest rates to encourage spending, there is no guarantee that it will have the desired effect of increasing consumption and/or investment. Once again, if consumer or business confidence is low, then there is unlikely to be an increase in borrowing to finance consumption and investment. Even when successful, there is likely to be a lag before they come into effect. It is possible that aggregate demand will increase, but by the time that it does, the economy may have already recovered, and the extra impetus can then be inflationary.

Another problem that occurs is due to the fact that even when the economy is at full employment, there will be some unemployment. We now know that this type of unemployment is natural unemployment and the solutions to these types are best found in supply-side policies. Using demand management policies to cure this type of unemployment will be unsuccessful. At full employment, the economy is producing near full capacity. Increases in aggregate demand at this point would result in inflationary pressure.

The problem facing policy makers is that in practice it might be very difficult to distinguish between the different types of unemployment. Moreover, an economy may be suffering from several different types of unemployment. At any rate, it would be most common to see governments using a mix of demand- and supply-side policies. Demand-side policies, particularly the manipulation of interest rates, are commonly used to narrow possible business cycle fluctuations and reduce output gaps. Supply-side policies are vital to ensure that labour is suitably skilled and flexible to adapt to changing economic conditions so that the LRAS is always shifting to the right.

HL

Crowding out

When governments run budget deficits in order to stimulate an economy and reduce unemployment, there is a potential problem known as "crowding out". To run a budget deficit, the government has to borrow money. Governments do this by selling government bonds such as treasury bills or treasury bonds to financial institutions who then sell them on to people who want to save their money. What they are essentially doing is increasing demand for the savings, or loanable funds, that are in the economy. We illustrate the consequences of this increase in demand in Figure 20.6.

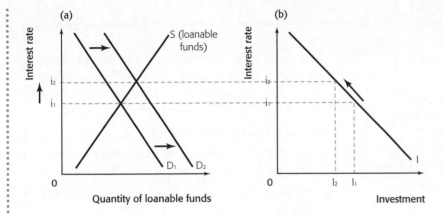

Figure 20.6 Crowding out

There is a given amount of savings in the economy, and this is represented by the supply of loanable funds curve. The price of these loanable funds is the interest rate. The increased demand from D_1 to D_2 in Figure 20.6(a) for savings in order to finance a deficit results in an increase in the interest rate from i_1 to i_2. The higher interest rate may reduce the incentive for businesses to invest, so it is possible that investment will fall from I_1 to I_2, as shown in Figure 20.6(b). So we have a situation where the government wished to increase aggregate demand by increasing government spending, but the higher interest rate causes interest-sensitive private investment to fall, thus reducing aggregate demand.

Whether or not crowding out does occur and the extent to which it might occur is a subject of much debate in economics. To simplify the argument, Keynesian economists say that it will not occur if the economy is producing at less than full employment. The neo-classical economists, who are opposed to the use of demand management policies, argue that crowding out is a significant problem of increased government spending.

It has been suggested that there are two other forms of crowding out.

- *Physical crowding out:* This occurs if the economy is close to its productive capacity. Increased spending on government projects could see resources, such as labour, being directed away from the private sector towards the public sector.

- *Psychological crowding out:* This occurs if the private sector worries about what it perceives to be too much intervention by the government in the economy. In this case, the private sector may delay or cancel investment projects.

3 Macroeconomics

Did you know?

The OECD urges more dynamic government policies on employment and incomes

OECD countries urgently need to get more people into paid employment if they want to boost living standards and keep welfare systems functioning. They can do this by moving away from policies that discourage people from working and companies from hiring and by doing more to raise workers' skills.

At present, the OECD says, many people on welfare find little financial advantage in taking a job. What's more, even those who do seek work often find their chances of getting a job hampered by poorly designed regulations, lack of job-search support or their own lack of skills. The result is to hold down economic growth and put a brake on increased prosperity.

The OECD makes it clear that there is no single set of economic policies that can solve a given country's employment problems. Some countries achieve good employment results by maintaining relatively low welfare benefits and implementing light regulations, but at the expense of relatively wide inequality in earnings. Others obtain similar success with generous welfare benefits and strong activation of job seekers, but at a high cost in terms of public spending on labour market policies.

But a number of basic conditions are needed. Countries that have succeeded in boosting employment share an emphasis on macroeconomic stability and strong product market competition, the OECD says. In addition, most of them provide strong job-search support combined with strict requirements on the unemployed to accept job offers.

Some countries have introduced reforms that boost employment without cutting welfare benefits, for example by accompanying welfare benefits with measures to ensure that recipients look for work and have a financial incentive to take a job. Family-friendly policies such as support for childcare can also help in boosting employment, especially among mothers.

The OECD urges governments to:

- set macroeconomic policies which aim to achieve price stability and sustainable public finances
- ensure that recessions do not lead to permanent falls in employment
- make it more attractive for people to work than to stay on welfare benefits
- make sure that benefit recipients receive high-quality services, particularly in relation to their quest for jobs, and that this is monitored closely, backed up by the threat of benefit sanctions
- adapt regulations and tax policies so as to encourage companies to take on staff rather than to avoid new hires
- strengthen competition in product markets
- ensure that legislation to protect job security does not undermine the dynamism of the labour market or lead to discrimination in hiring and firing
- provide people of working age with the education and training opportunities that they need to get jobs and raise their incomes.

The OECD acknowledges that among the toughest tasks facing governments are likely to be winning public support for some necessary changes and implementing them effectively. Countries that fail to reform, the OECD asserts, face the prospect of continued weak employment performance, which in turn will hamper improvements in living standards. But the successes achieved by some countries over the past decade show what can be achieved if there is the political will to reform.

Adapted from www.oecd.org, 13 June 2006

3 Macroeconomics

Student workpoint 20.7

Be a thinker. Explain the following.

The data on the ILO on page 217 highlights many of the points raised by the economic theory. This should remind you that economic theory really can be applied to the real world!

Read the text and make notes to answer the following questions.

1 What are the possible barriers to job creation by firms?

2 What are the possible reasons that people don't take available jobs?

3 What is a possible consequence of low welfare benefits combined with light regulations?

4 What are the problems associated with generous welfare benefits and government support for job seekers?

5 How can it be said that the OECD is promoting a blend of interventionist and market-oriented policies?

6 What might prevent countries from pursuing the recommended policies?

Student workpoint 20.8

Be a thinker

You have come across many types of unemployment in this chapter. Create a table that will show all of the different types of unemployment under the headings of equilibrium unemployment and disequilibrium unemployment.

3 Macroeconomics

Examination questions

Short response questions

1 With the help of a diagram, explain the cause of demand-deficient unemployment.   *[10 marks]*

2 With the help of a diagram, explain two possible causes of structural unemployment.   *[10 marks]*

HL   3 Explain the concept of crowding out.   *[10 marks]*

Essay questions

1 a Explain the costs associated with unemployment.   *[10 marks]*

 b Evaluate the policies available to a government that wishes to reduce its country's unemployment rate.   *[15 marks]*

2 a Distinguish between equilibrium and disequilibrium unemployment.   *[10 marks]*

 b Evaluate the view that the only effective way to reduce unemployment is through government intervention.   *[15 marks]*

Assessment advice: using diagrams and real-world examples

Sadly, students do not always read the instructions at the beginning of examinations. Therefore you are warned that the following words appear on the front cover of *all* of your economics exams: "Use fully labelled diagrams and real-world examples wherever possible." Here is the opportunity for you to make use of the information that you gathered about your chosen country. Put the information into your answer to support the economic theory.

All that work should pay off!

You be the journalist

Headline: Recession moves into its fourth quarter and takes its toll on the unemployed

Economic concept: Demand-deficient unemployment

Diagram: Disequilibrium unemployment

Hints: Explain why unemployment is likely to rise and consider the negative effects this might create. You could bring in ideas about what actions the government might be considering

The inflation–unemployment trade-off debate

HL

By the end of this chapter, you should be able to:

- explain and illustrate the short-run Phillips curve
- explain and illustrate the long-run Phillips curve
- explain the concept of the natural rate of unemployment (NRU)
- evaluate the extent to which there might be a trade-off between inflation and unemployment.

Two main goals of any government are to have a low and stable rate of inflation and a low level of unemployment. But what is the relationship between these two economic problems? Once again, there is much debate!

The Phillips curve

In 1958, Alban Williams Phillips (the New Zealand-born economist working at the London School of Economics who created the Moniac machine mentioned in Chapter 14) published a significant work in which he presented his argument that there was an inverse relationship between the rate of change of money wages (i.e. wages *not* adjusted for inflation) in the economy and the rate of unemployment as shown on Figure 21.1. His observation was based on his study of UK data from 1861 to 1913.

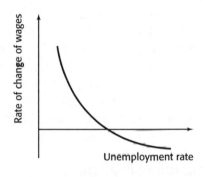

Figure 21.1 The original Phillips curve

The explanation for this was that if there was a low level of unemployment, firms would have to pay higher wages to attract labour. If unemployment was high, then unemployed workers would be competing with each other to obtain available jobs, so that wages offered could be relatively low. During an economic expansion, when more output is demanded and more workers are needed, wages rise more quickly than they would if there was a contraction in activity and lower levels of demand. The rate of change of money wages could actually become negative, i.e. wages could fall at high levels of unemployment because workers would be willing to accept the lower wages rather than remain unemployed.

Other economists adapted the relationship established by Phillips and applied it to data from other countries to establish the pattern that we now refer to as the Phillips curve. This shows the inverse relationship between the inflation rate (rather than the change in money wages) and the unemployment rate of an economy as shown in Figure 21.2. This is due to the fact that since wages make up a large proportion of firms' costs, changes in wages feed directly through to changes in the price level.

Another way to express this relationship is to say that there is a "trade-off" between inflation and unemployment. For example, as shown in Figure 21.2, an unemployment rate of 5% might be

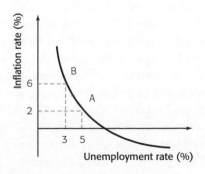

Figure 21.2 The Phillips curve, as it is usually drawn

3 Microeconomics

accompanied by an inflation rate of 2%. If unemployment were to fall to 3%, then inflation would rise to 6%. As one variable decreases, the other increases. The implication of this trade-off for government objectives is clear. If the main objective of a government is to reduce the rate of unemployment, this can be done, but at the expense of a higher rate of inflation. Similarly, if inflation is perceived to be too high, then it can be lowered by allowing the unemployment rate to increase. The trade-off can also be explained using aggregate demand/aggregate supply analysis, as shown in Figure 21.3.

The economy is initially in equilibrium at Y_1, at a price level of P_1. If the government feels there is too much unemployment at this point, then it might use Keynesian demand management techniques to bring about an increase in AD, from AD_1 to AD_2. This will result in an increase in output, which is produced by hiring more workers, so unemployment is assumed to fall. However, there is also a higher price level, that is, higher inflation. In agreement with the Phillips curve, a decrease in unemployment occurs at a cost of higher inflation. This would be like the movement from A to B in Figure 21.2.

This existence of a trade-off between inflation and unemployment was supported by data up to the 1970s. From this time on, however, evidence about inflation and unemployment began to suggest that the relationship shown by the Phillips curve was no longer valid, as both inflation and unemployment rose in many economies. The combination of high inflation and high levels of unemployment is known as stagflation. According to the Phillips curve, the two problems should not worsen simultaneously and so the model came under attack.

Long-run Phillips curve

It was the monetarist economists led by Milton Friedman who were the biggest critics of the original Phillips curve. According to their analysis, there is no trade-off between inflation and unemployment. This is consistent with the explanation of the neo-classical long-run aggregate supply provided in Chapter 17. Recall that according to the neo-classical economists, the economy will automatically tend towards its long-run equilibrium at the full employment level of output.

Figure 21.4 can be used to explain this adaptation of the Phillips curve model.

Assume that the economy is in long-run equilibrium at point A on $SRPC_1$. The labour market is also in equilibrium so that the only unemployment that exists is the natural unemployment of 6%. The inflation rate is 2%. People *expect* inflation to be 2% and negotiate any pay increases based on this expected rate. Now, consider what would happen if the government decided that they wanted to reduce unemployment and so adopted an expansionary demand-side policy, for example increasing government expenditure. Aggregate demand would increase and this, in turn, would lead to an increase in the demand for labour and so an increase in wage levels. However, at the same time, there would be an increase in the inflation rate, in this case to 6%.

In the short run, there would be a fall in unemployment as workers who had not been prepared to take jobs at existing wage levels

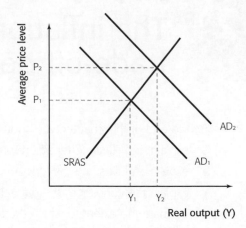

Figure 21.3 Phillips curve relationship through AD/AS analysis

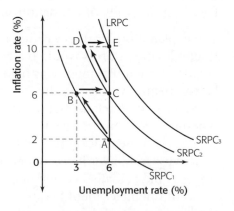

Figure 21.4 The long-run Phillips curve

before are now attracted by what they think are higher wages and the economy moves from A to B on the diagram. However, these are higher *nominal* wages and *real* wages have not risen. In this case, we would say that the workers have suffered from money illusion. When the workers realize that their real wages have not risen, they then leave the jobs and unemployment goes back to the natural rate, but now at an inflation rate of 6%.

The economy does not return to point A. Now that inflation is running at 6%, people will expect prices to continue to rise at 6% and negotiate an equivalent increase in wages, so the economy will be at point C on the diagram, on a new short-run Phillips curve, $SRPC_2$. Unemployment has returned to its natural rate at a higher rate of inflation. Any attempt to use demand management again to reduce the unemployment below this natural rate will only result in higher inflation (C to D to E) and a move to another short-run Phillips curve, $SRPC_3$.

The natural rate of unemployment is the unemployment rate that is consistent with a stable rate of inflation. It is for this reason that the natural rate of unemployment has also been given the complicated name of the non-accelerating inflation rate of unemployment (NAIRU). As long as governments do not use expansionary policies, inflation will not accelerate at the natural rate of unemployment. However, if expansionary policies are used, then inflation will accelerate.

The long-run Phillips curve is vertical at the natural rate of unemployment (NRU). At any given point in time, there may be a short run trade-off between inflation and unemployment, but the economy will always return to unemployment at the natural rate. Governments cannot reduce this rate by using demand management policies. The natural rate of unemployment is the unemployment that occurs when the economy is at full employment and the labour market is in equilibrium.

Of course this is not to say that the long-run unemployment rate cannot be reduced at all! The key point here is that supply-side policies, not demand management policies, are the solution for reducing the natural rate of unemployment. Supply-side policies will reduce the natural rate of unemployment and shift the long-run Phillips curve to the left from $LRPC_1$ to $LRPC_2$ as shown in Figure 21.5. This would be the equivalent of a rightward shift in the long-run aggregate supply curve or an outwards shift in a country's production possibilities curve.

This confirms conclusions drawn about unemployment at the end of Chapter 20. Demand-side policies may be appropriate for reducing cyclical demand-deficient unemployment, but not for reducing the frictional, seasonal and structural unemployment that make up the natural unemployment.

The OECD itself admits that the natural rate of unemployment "can only be estimated with uncertainty". Nonetheless, estimates of the NRU are made. What is evident is that it varies considerably over time and between countries. Table 21.1 provides OECD estimates for several countries.

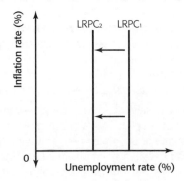

Figure 21.5 Supply-side policies can reduce the NRU

Country	NRU 1995	NRU 1999
Australia	7.1%	6.8%
Belgium	8.0%	8.2%
Canada	8.8%	7.7%
France	10.3%	9.5%
Japan	2.9%	4.0%
Switzerland	3.3%	2.4%
US	5.3%	5.2%

Source: OECD

Table 21.1 Natural rate of unemployment estimates

Differences between countries are due to a number of things including the availability of unemployment benefits, trade union power, the extent of labour market regulations, and wage-setting practices by firms. Countries with more benefits and considerable regulation of labour markets tend to have a higher NRU. When organizations like the OECD recommend that countries make labour market reforms to reduce unemployment, they are usually referring to measures that will reduce the natural rate.

Examination questions

Short response questions

1 Using an appropriate diagram, explain why there might be a trade-off between unemployment and inflation in the short run. *[10 marks]*

2 Explain two policies that might be used to reduce the natural rate of unemployment. *[10 marks]*

Essay questions

1 a Explain the concept of the natural rate of unemployment. *[10 marks]*

b Evaluate the methods available to a government that wishes to reduce the level of unemployment in an economy. *[15 marks]*

Assessment advice: essay writing

When the question asks you to use an "appropriate" diagram, then it is likely that there are at least two possibilities. In the first short response question given here, you could use an AD/AS diagram or a short-run Phillips curve diagram. The Phillips curve approach is a bit more sophisticated and may be more appropriate in a higher level exam.

You may observe that the essay question given here is similar to the one at the end of the last chapter. This is because we have extended the theory. The concepts of the natural rate of unemployment and the long-run Phillips curve where there is no trade-off between unemployment and inflation are a more theoretical explanation of the reasons why demand-side policies are not likely to reduce the natural rate of unemployment. The question can be answered without this extra theory, but the use of these concepts will result in a more sophisticated approach.

Don't forget to include information from your case study!

Data response exercise

Consider the following data and answer the questions.

Japan	2000	2001	2002	2003	2004	2005
Consumer price index (% change from previous year)	−0.8	−0.8	−0.9	−0.3	0.0	−0.3
Unemployment rate (% of labour force)	4.7	5.0	5.4	5.3	4.7	4.4

Mexico	2000	2001	2002	2003	2004	2005
Consumer price index (% change from previous year)	9.5	6.4	5.0	4.5	4.7	4.0
Unemployment rate (% of labour force)	2.2	2.1	2.4	2.5	3.0	3.5

United States*	2000	2001	2002	2003	2004	2005
Consumer price index (% change from previous year)	3.4	2.8	1.6	2.3	2.7	3.4
Unemployment rate (% of labour force)	4.0	4.8	5.8	6.0	5.5	5.1

Note: Labour market data are subject to differences in definitions across countries.

* The methodology for calculating the Consumer Price Index has changed considerably over the past years, lowering measured inflation substantially.

Source: OECD, Economic Outlook 79 database

1 Define the following terms indicated in bold:

   a consumer price index   *[2 Marks]*

   b unemployment rate.   *[2 Marks]*

2 With reference to the data, explain why we can say that Japan experienced deflation in the period shown.   *[4 Marks]*

3 With reference to the data, explain the trends in inflation and unemployment in Mexico and the United States.   *[4 Marks]*

4 Using evidence from the text and your knowledge of economics, evaluate the validity of the Phillips curve relationship.   *[8 Marks]*

Assessment advice: evaluation

In terms of the different ways that you can evaluate, the best thing here would be to look at the time frame involved. You have enough data to make a possible conclusion for a short-run period, but is there enough information for the long run?

3 Macroeconomics

By the end of this chapter, you should be able to:

- define direct taxes and indirect taxes
- explain how government can alter the distribution of income through the use of tax policies
- explain the difference between progressive, regressive, and proportional taxation systems
- explain how government can alter the distribution of income through the use of taxes
- explain how government can alter the distribution of income through the use of transfer payments
- evaluate the use of government policies to redistribute income

HL
- use the Laffer Curve to illustrate and explain the link between tax rates and government tax revenues.

One of the characteristics associated with free market economies is an unequal distribution of income. For example, the principal of a school is likely to earn a greater income than a cafeteria worker. Inequality occurs to different extents in different countries. The reasons for difference in income and the consequences of inequality are many and complex. They can form the basis of massive debate among economists, politicians, sociologists, colleagues, parents and children, friends, and even classmates in an economics class!

There is one argument that suggests that huge inequalities in income are *unfair*. People with low incomes will experience relatively low living standards, and fewer opportunities than people with high incomes. They may live in a state of absolute poverty whereby they do not have access to the basic necessities needed to sustain life. Or they may live in relative poverty whereby their living standards are well below an observed "average" in an economy. Their incomes may be low because they themselves were born into a household where incomes were low and they experienced little opportunity to break out from the conditions associated with poverty such as poor education, malnutrition, and perhaps the necessity to find work before completing an education. Incomes may be low because human capital keeps some people in low-paying jobs. Income may be low due to unemployment. These are some of the issues that result in fierce debate.

Even if it is perceived that an unequal distribution of income is unfair, economic reasoning will show that higher incomes act as an incentive for people to work harder. If people did not believe that their hard work in school or at work would allow them to raise their human capital and provide them with the opportunity to earn higher incomes, then this would have huge implications for the supply side of an economy, resulting in a lower overall level of economic activity.

Purely economic analysis will not lead to an answer as to exactly how much inequality is acceptable or appropriate. This is very much a normative issue. What can be agreed upon is the fact that market economies do result in inequality of income. In this chapter, we will look at the ways in which governments use their policies on taxation and government spending to affect the distribution of income in an economy.

Student workpoint 22.1

Be communicative. Discuss the following.

To what extent do you feel that it is a government's obligation to reduce inequality?

Taxation

Governments at all levels (municipal, provincial, national) impose a huge array of different taxes for a range of reasons. Taxes may be used to reduce the consumption of goods that create negative externalities. Taxes on imported goods (tariffs) may be imposed to reduce the consumption of imported goods. Taxes may be raised or lowered to manage the level of aggregate demand in the economy. In this section, we are looking only at the way in which taxation is used to change the distribution of income.

Direct taxes

Direct taxes are taxes imposed on peoples' income or wealth, and on firms' profits. The income from households comes in various forms such as employment income and interest on savings and dividends from the ownership of shares. Some of the income is taxed directly by employers, while some is charged based on the annual "tax return" form that people are usually obliged to fill out. Theoretically, such taxes are unavoidable, because households and firms are obliged to declare their full income to governments and pay taxes on it accordingly.

Indirect taxes

Indirect taxes are also known as expenditure taxes, or consumption-based taxes, and have different names in different countries. Canada and Australia have a "goods and services tax (GST)"; the UK has a "value-added tax (VAT)" and so does Austria (*Mehrwertsteuer*). In this case, consumers who buy the goods pay the tax to the seller, or producer, who then pays the tax to the government. In a sense these taxes are avoidable, as consumers have the choice as to whether to buy the good or not, and in what quantities. Governments vary the rate of indirect tax that they charge on different goods and services, with necessity and valued goods such as food at the supermarket, being charged a lower tax rate than luxuries, such as food in restaurants.

Student workpoint 22.2

Be an inquirer

Researching the same country as in previous chapters, try to find out the following.

1 What is the name of the indirect tax in the country?

2 What are the different rates of taxes and what are the different categories on which they are charged? Give examples.

There are three different categories into which we can place these two different types of taxes, and these differ in the effect that they have in terms of changing people's incomes.

Progressive taxes

Many countries use a progressive tax as the main way to redistribute income from higher income earners to low income earners, as a progressive tax means that as incomes rise, people pay a higher proportion of this income in taxes. Usually, there is a certain amount of income that is non-taxed, so a person earning a low income might pay no taxes at all, However, when the income moves beyond this minimum, then a certain percentage of the income will have to be paid to the government. Then, as income rises further, a progressive tax would take larger percentages at higher incomes. Consider a simple hypothetical example where there are four tax "brackets" as shown in Table 22.1.

"Taxable" income ($)	% to be paid as tax
0–10,000	0
10,001–25,000	30%
25,001–50,000	40%
50,001 and higher	50%

Table 22.1 Tax rates for different income levels (hypothetical)

If a person were to earn $15,000, then they would pay no taxes on the first $10,000 and 30% on the next $5,000 so they would pay $1500 in taxes. This represents an average tax of 10%.

A person earning double this income, $30,000, would pay nothing on the first 10,000, 30% on the next 15,000 ($4,500) and then 40% on the remaining 5,000 ($2,000) for a total of $6,500. This represents an average tax of approximately 22%. As we can see, the average tax rises as income rises, making it a progressive tax.

Student workpoint 22.3

Be a thinker. Calculate the following.

Using the tax structure given in Table 22.1, calculate the total tax paid and the average tax paid for a person earning each of the following incomes.

Put your answers in the form of a table.

a $7,000

b $14,000

c $28,000

d $56,000

It is important to observe that the example given in Table 22.1 represents a vastly simplified tax structure. In reality most countries' tax structures are infinitely more complicated. The biggest complication comes in the form of "tax deductions" and the calculation of "taxable" income. Tax deductions allow people to reduce their "taxable income" as a result of spending on certain things. For example, if a worker must travel a long distance to work, and this costs $1,000 a month, the government might allow the person to deduct this spending from her taxable income, thus reducing the amount of tax that she pays. The government might do this because it feels that this will encourage people to find work and lower unemployment. What is considered to be a tax deduction is different from country to country.

Student workpoint 22.4

Be an inquirer

Find four examples of tax deductions that households can make in the country that you are investigating. (If you cannot access such information, then research your home country.) Suggest reason(s) why governments might allow each to be a tax deduction.

A progressive tax means that higher income people pay higher taxes, and can lead to a redistribution of income to the less well-off. There will be an evaluation of progressive taxes later in this chapter.

Regressive taxes

A tax is known as a regressive tax if the proportion of income paid in tax (the average rate of tax) falls as income rises. Indirect taxes are regressive taxes. Consider an example of a $1.00 tax on a litre of petrol and assume that people end up spending $50 per month in petrol taxes. For a person earning $500 per month, the tax will take 10% of income. For a person earning $2500 per month, the tax will represent 2% of their income. The tax is regressive because a higher proportion of income is paid at lower levels of income.

 Regressive taxes may be a good source of government revenue and they might discourage the consumption of demerit goods, but they can worsen income inequality.

Proportional taxes

A tax is a proportional tax if the proportion of income paid in tax is constant for all income levels. Many countries are now promoting the idea of proportional direct taxes, or flat taxes, whereby the same percentage of tax is paid at all levels of income. There are several reasons for this.

 The first relates to the huge complexity of most tax systems. A glance at the tax guide for most countries will confirm that taxation is an incredibly complicated process, with ample room for error and manipulation. This may result in governments earning less revenue

'*In this world, nothing can be said to be certain, except death and taxes.*'
Benjamin Franklin

than expected as people find ways to avoid paying taxes. The second relates to the possible disincentive effects of taxes on working. It might be argued that high rates of taxes discourage people from working harder, moving into higher paid jobs and taking risks, as they will be reluctant to lose their own gains to higher taxes. If taxes were to be constant, then this could be viewed as a supply-side policy to encourage greater incentives to work and therefore raise labour supply.

Transfer payments

Governments can use tax revenues to redistribute income and provide different types of assistance to groups in the economy to improve their living standards. These are known as transfer payments. While transfer payments are not included as income in national income accounting because they do not represent payment for the production of a good or a service, they are payments made to increase the income of particular groups within the economy. Examples of transfer payments include child support assistance, pensions, unemployment benefits, payments to disabled people, and subsidies to producers.

Other government policies to affect distribution of income

A minimum wage policy is a policy that ensures that workers are paid what is determined to be a "fair" wage. Governments may also legislate that firms pay social security benefits such as a designated minimum amount to cover medical insurance and/or pensions for their workers. Both of these policies serve to redistribute income from firms to workers. It could also be said that government-sponsored training schemes are a way of helping workers find gainful employment and thus raise their living standards.

Evaluation of redistribution of income policies

At the outset, it was pointed out that the question of income redistribution is a highly charged one. While many would agree that it is a government's obligation to ensure that its citizens enjoy a "reasonable" standard of living, this is a problematic issue for many reasons, not the least of which is the question of what constitutes a reasonable standard!

As might already be perceived, economists who support a neo-classical point of view tend to argue against the active role of government in redistributing income for the simple reason that it interferes with market forces and results in inefficiencies. As we know, this view argues that the optimal allocation of resources occurs in free markets and so government taxation must be kept to a minimum. They might argue that:

- if firms have to pay insurance and social security costs for workers, then this will encourage firms to hire fewer workers, thus contributing to unemployment

- high taxes in a country might discourage entrepreneurial activity and even encourage entrepreneurs to leave a country in search of more "favourable" tax climates

3 Macroeconomics

● high taxes have negative effects on overall growth in the economy due to the disincentive effect mentioned earlier; lower taxes will encourage economic activity leading to an overall increase in output that will be to the benefit of all people.

This is not to say that there is no role for government in an economy, and no reason for taxes to be collected. However, economists promoting a free market view might argue that taxes should be used to finance the obligations of the government to ensure property rights, reduce the effects of market failure, provide an effective security and judicial system, and promote competition, but taxation should not be used to redistribute income.

HL

The Laffer curve

The view that higher direct taxes create a disincentive effect and ultimately a negative effect on government revenues became popular in the 1970s as a result of the work of the American economist, Arthur Laffer, who was associated with the free market supply-side economists. He developed what is now known as the Laffer curve to illustrate the relationship between direct tax rates and government revenues. This is shown in Figure 22.1.

Two points about the relationship and the curve are immediately apparent. If the direct tax rate is 0%, then the government would earn no money in tax revenues. If the direct tax rate is 100%, then there would be no incentive to work and thus there would be no income for the government to tax.

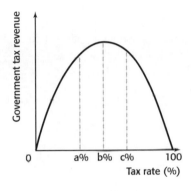

Figure 22.1 The Laffer curve

The points in between reflect the view that ultimately, higher direct taxes will cause people to work less hard, thus earning less income and paying less in taxes. According to this theory, an increase in the direct tax rate from a% to b% will result in higher tax revenues, but a further increase from b% to c% would lead to a fall in tax revenue. It follows that if direct tax rates are above b%, at c% for example, the government could increase tax revenue by reducing the direct tax rate, thus giving people an incentive to work harder, since they can keep a larger share of their earned income. This model would suggest that there is an optimal direct tax rate at which government revenue is maximized. Clearly this optimum tax level will vary from country to country, and would not necessarily be at the 50% implied by this diagram.

3 Macroeconomics

Examination questions

Short response questions

HL

1 Distinguish between a progressive tax system and a regressive tax system. *[10 marks]*

2 Using a diagram, explain the concept of the Laffer curve. *[10 marks]*

Essay question

1 **a** Explain two ways that a government might redistribute income in an economy from the more well-off to the less well-off. *[10 marks]*

   b Evaluate the consequences of income redistribution policies on an economy. *[15 marks]*

Assessment advice: internal assessment

It is recommended that one of your commentaries be about macroeconomics, and you should be able to see that there are a large number of possible topic areas here. Your country investigation might be useful here as it is possible that you used contemporary articles in gathering your information. Perhaps one of these will be suitable for a commentary. Just remember that the article has to have been written no earlier than six months before you started this IB Diploma Programme course.

Having finished macroeconomics, you are likely to be able to bring together many topics that are interwoven and this will give you an opportunity to evaluate. For example, you may find an article about a central bank's efforts to control inflationary pressures through interest rate increases. Evaluation in such a case may involve an assessment of the likely effects of this on the stakeholders and a consideration of the potential conflict among policy objectives.

Please remember that all four of the articles that you use to write your commentaries must come from different sources. This not only gives you the opportunity to read articles that may come from different perspectives, but ideally, it should allow you to learn about economics in different parts of the world.

3 Macroeconomics

23 Why do countries trade?

By the end of this chapter, you should be able to:

- define international trade
- identify and explain the gains from trade
- define and give examples of specialization and the division of labour
- define, explain, illustrate, and give examples of absolute advantage

HL:
- define, explain, illustrate, and give examples of comparative advantage
- explain the limitations of comparative advantage theory.

The gains from international trade

International trade is the exchange of goods and services between countries. There are a number of gains to be made from international trade and we should consider them at this point.

1 *Lower prices:* The main gain from trade is the ability to buy goods and services at a lower price than the domestic one. Consumers are able to buy less expensive products and producers are able to purchase less expensive raw materials and semi-manufactured goods. This is the main reason for trade.

   Prices may be lower in some countries than others because of access to natural resources, differences in the quality of the labour forces, or differences in the quality of capital and the levels of technology. The cause of these lower prices is mainly determined by the concept of comparative advantage, which is a higher level topic, and is dealt with in the next section.

2 *Greater choice:* International trade enables consumers to have a greater choice of products. They now have access not just to domestically produced products, but also to products that come from a number of different countries.

3 *Differences in resources:* Different countries possess different resources. There are some resources that a country may need, but quite simply does not have. For example, many countries do not possess copper, diamonds, or oil naturally. However, they may need them in order to produce other products and so have no option but to import the commodities they lack. To do this, they will need to export goods or services, in order to earn foreign currency and so buy the required resources.

   Some countries, such as Singapore, have very few natural resources and so are dependent on trade for their survival, economic growth, and well-being. Singapore has to import almost every natural resource, even water! However, Singapore is

4 International Economics

245

able to export high levels of goods and services in order to fund their exports.

4 *Economies of scale:* When producing for an international market, as well as for a domestic one, the size of the market, and thus demand, will increase. This means that the level of production and the size of production units will also increase.

As we know from Chapter 7, the increased levels of production should provide scope for economies of scale to be achieved and production should become more efficient. Also, larger production units will enable the amount of specialization to increase. When firms are large, individuals may specialize in specific, narrower tasks, such as accounting manager or marketing manager, and they should become more knowledgeable and so more efficient. Larger production units will also lead to greater scope for the division of labour. This is where a production process is broken down into a number of simple and basic tasks. Workers may then concentrate on a small, repetitive task and achieve a high degree of efficiency.

In addition, if countries specialize in the production of certain commodities, such as chemicals, there will be cost benefits to be gained from acquiring experience and expertise. This is known as moving down the "learning curve" (the long-run average cost curve).

International trade, and with it larger markets and production units, should enable production in a country's export industries to become more efficient in the long run. It should also make the producers more competitive. It should lead to a reduction in long-run average costs.

5 *Increased competition:* International trade may lead to increased competition, as domestic firms compete with foreign firms. This should lead to greater efficiency and may mean that consumers gain by being offered less expensive goods and services. It is also likely that the quality and variety of goods available to consumers will increase, with increased competition.

Putting together the five points above, it is clear that there are huge gains to be achieved from trade. As a concluding comment, it is fair to say that for all the reasons listed above, international trade can make a major contribution to a country's economic growth. We now look at a more theoretical approach to international trade theory for higher level students.

Student workpoint 23.1

Be a thinker

Make a list of goods that you commonly use that are imported. This can include food, clothing, electronics, etc. If possible, identify the source of the good.

HL

Comparative advantage theory

We have already said that there are many advantages to international trade. But which goods should a country produce for export and which goods should it import? The answer to this question lies in the concept of comparative advantage.

Absolute advantage

Let us start by looking at the concept of absolute advantage. A country is said to have an absolute advantage in the production of a good if it can produce it using fewer resources than another country.

Table 23.1 shows the production outcomes where two countries, Australia and China, are using the same quantities of resources to produce lamb and cloth.

Country	Kilos of lamb	Metres of cloth
Australia	6	1
China	4	3
Total without trade	10	5

Table 23.1 Absolute advantage

It is clear from the table that Australia has an absolute advantage in producing lamb and that China has an absolute advantage in the production of cloth.

In this situation, the answer to our previous question, "Which goods should a country produce for export and which goods should it import?" is simple. Australia should specialize in the production of lamb and China should specialize in the production of cloth. The output of both products will be maximised when the countries specialize and, after trading, both countries will gain.

Australia would produce lamb and, if it doubled its resources, then assuming constant returns to scale, total output from the resources would be 12 kilos, an increase of 2 kilos. In the same way, China, with twice as many resources and constant returns to scale, would have a total output from its resources of 6 metres of cloth, an increase of 2 metres. Thus total output of both goods has risen, following specialization.

The situation above, where each country has an absolute advantage in the production of one product, is known as reciprocal absolute advantage.

Comparative advantage

The whole concept of absolute advantage seems obvious, but what happens if there is not a situation of reciprocal absolute advantage as shown in the above example? In the early nineteenth century, David Ricardo was the first economist to prove mathematically that trade could still be beneficial to both countries when one of the countries had an absolute advantage in producing all goods. Ricardo considered the opportunity cost of production and used this to explain the concept of comparative advantage.

A country is said to have a comparative advantage in the production of a good if it can produce the good at a lower opportunity cost than another country. In other words, country A has to give up fewer units of other goods to produce the good in question than does country B.

This is best shown by an example. Table 23.2 shows the production outcomes where two countries, France and Poland, are using the same quantities of resources to produce wine and cheese.

Country	Litres of wine	Opportunity cost of 1 litre of wine	Kilos of cheese	Opportunity cost of 1 kilo of cheese
France	3	⅘ kilos of cheese	4	¾ litre of wine
Poland	1	3 kilos of cheese	3	⅓ litre of wine

Table 23.2 Comparative advantage

This shows that France has an absolute advantage in the production of both goods. However, in terms of comparative advantage, France has a comparative advantage in the production of wine and Poland has a comparative advantage in the production of cheese.

This is because France only has to give up 4/3 kilos of cheese to produce a litre of wine, whereas Poland has to give up 3 kilos, but Poland only has to give up 1/3 litre of wine to produce a kilo of cheese, whereas France has to give up 3/4 litre of wine.

The theory of comparative advantage tells us that France should specialize in the production of wine and Poland should specialize in the production of cheese. France will then consume the wine that they wish and use any extra wine to exchange for cheese. In the same way, Poland will consume the cheese that it wants and use any extra cheese to exchange for wine.

The situation can also be shown on a simple diagram as in Figure 23.1, using simplified production possibility curves.

Figure 23.1 shows the same information as Table 23.2. However, even without the information in Table 23.2, it is possible to use Figure 23.1 to show comparative advantage.

In simple terms, when a country has an absolute advantage in producing both goods, as France has here, and the scale of the axes is the same, the comparative advantage for the better producer is in the good where the distance between the production possibilities is greatest, shown by (a) in the diagram, and the comparative advantage for the less efficient producer is in the good where the distance between the production possibilities is least, shown by (b) in the diagram. Thus, as we know, France has the comparative advantage in producing wine and Poland has the comparative advantage in producing cheese.

This is not a mathematical justification, but simply a useful trick to employ when using diagrams such as this. The real reason relates to the relative slopes of the lines, since it is the slope of the lines that shows the opportunity costs, which in this model is always shown as constant opportunity cost.

One point to bear in mind is that the theory of comparative advantage works so long as the opportunity costs faced by the two countries are different. If the two countries face the same

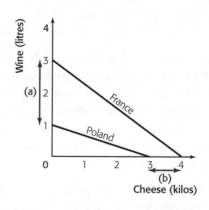

Figure 23.1 Production possibility curves to show comparative advantage

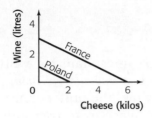

Figure 23.2 Identical opportunity costs

opportunity costs, then there would be no point in trade taking place. This situation is shown in Table 23.3 and Figure 23.2.

Country	Litres of wine	Opportunity cost of 1 litre of wine	Kilos of cheese	Opportunity cost of 1 kilo of cheese
France	3	2 kilos of cheese	6	½ litre of wine
Poland	1	2 kilos of cheese	2	½ litre of wine

Table 23.3 Identical opportunity costs

As we can see in Figure 23.2, if the slopes of the two production possibility curves are the same, then opportunity costs for each country will be identical, and there will be no gains to be made by trading.

What gives a country a comparative advantage?

To a large extent, comparative advantage is based on a country's factor endowments. A country that is "endowed" with a large amount of arable land may develop a comparative advantage in agricultural products. A country with abundant unskilled labour can develop its comparative advantage in the production of labour-intensive, low-skilled, manufactured goods. A country with abundant well-educated labour may have a comparative advantage in the output of financial services. A country with beautiful beaches and a favourable climate may develop its comparative advantage in the output of tourist services, illustrating that "climate" can actually be a factor of production! The abundance of a particular factor will make the price of this factor relatively lower than the price of other factors, thereby allowing the opportunity cost of the goods or services using that factor to be lower than it would be in other countries.

4 International Economics

Student workpoint 23.2

Be a thinker. Consider the following diagram.

1 Should trade take place between Japan and Malaysia? Why?

2 In which product should each country specialize?

3 Can you suggest why each country might have the comparative advantage suggested by the diagram?

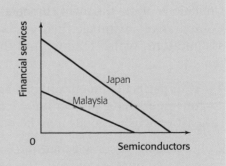

Profile **David Ricardo** (1772–1823) •••••••••••••••••••••••••••••••••••

David Ricardo was born in London into a Dutch-Jewish family in April, 1772. At a young age and without a great deal of formal education, he joined his father working at the London Stock Exchange. When he married a Quaker woman, his orthodox Jewish family disinherited him and broke off all contact.

At the age of 27, Ricardo read Adam Smith's famous work, *The Wealth of Nations*, and this encouraged him to further study political economy. It was 10 years before he was first published in 1809, when he contributed to *The Monthly Chronicle* on the issue of inflation in England and the "bullion controversy". His views represent early monetarist thought that the inflation was caused by the willingness of the Bank of England to issue excessive amounts of bank notes.

Ricardo was very successful at the stock exchange and made a fortune as a stockbroker and loan broker. He purchased a country estate in Gloucestershire and moved there on his retirement from business in 1814. In 1815, Ricardo's publication, *Essay on the Influence of the Low Price of Corn on the Profits of Stock*, presented the theory now known as the law of diminishing returns. His study of the relationship between labour, capital, and land in agriculture led him to the conclusion, now well-known, that as increasing amounts of labour and machinery are used on a fixed area of land, additions to total output will eventually diminish.

Ricardo's most famous work was *Principles of Political Economy and Taxation*, published in 1817. At the time, the protectionist British Corn Laws were in place to restrict imports of wheat into Britain. In examining comparative costs between different producers, Ricardo arrived at the conclusions that are known today as the theory of comparative advantage. His famous case study, now presented widely to economics students, looked at the production of wine and cloth in England and Portugal. Although Portugal might be better at producing both wine and cloth, Ricardo showed that both countries would benefit if each specialized and they traded freely. He was thus an early advocate of free trade.

In the same publication, Ricardo made another of his important contributions to economic thought, his explanation of the theory of rents. In studying the production of food and the need to feed increasing populations by using less productive areas of land, Ricardo was able to show that it would be landowners who would benefit from population growth the most, as they would be able to extract high levels of rent.

Throughout his career, Ricardo was influenced by his friendships with James Mill, Jeremy Bentham, and Thomas Malthus, important names in nineteenth-century economic, political, and philosophical thought. Ricardo died in 1823, at the age of 51. In a relatively short career of 14 years as a "professional" economist, he made several lasting contributions to the economic theory that we study today.

•••

Limitations of the theory of comparative advantage

Comparative advantage theory is based upon a number of assumptions, which tend to limit the application of the theory in real life.

1 As in perfect competition, it is assumed that the producers and consumers have perfect knowledge and are aware of where the least expensive goods may be purchased.

2 It is usually assumed that there are no transport costs. However, in reality, this is not true. The existence of transport costs may erode a country's comparative advantage and not make international trading worthwhile, since it may eliminate its competitiveness.

3 Basic theories assume that there are only two economies producing two goods. However, this is not such a problem. The theory may be applied to more countries and more products and it is still possible to discern where the comparative advantages lie. The use of computer simulations has made the multi-country/multi-product analysis much easier to conduct.

4 It is usually assumed that costs do not change and that the returns to scale are constant, i.e. there are no economies or diseconomies of scale. However, the existence of economies of scale would, in all probability, increase a country's comparative advantage, as relative costs of production fell even more.

5 It is usually assumed that the goods being traded are identical, such as barley, cotton, or bananas. However, problems arise with goods such as consumer durables. A Toshiba television will be different from a Phillips television and so it is much harder to prove that Japan has the comparative advantage in producing televisions.

6 It is usually assumed that factors of production remain in the country. However, it may be the factors of production, rather than the goods, that move from country to country. For example, developed countries, rather than exporting finished goods to LDCs, may invest capital in LDCs to enable goods to be produced there. Labour may migrate from low-wage to high-wage countries.

7 It is usually assumed that there is perfectly free trade among countries, but of course, in reality, there are likely to be government-imposed trade barriers in many industries.

In spite of its limitations, comparative advantage theory is at the core of international trade theory and goes a long way to explaining patterns of trade. Countries that specialize in producing goods in which they have a lower opportunity cost than other countries can capture the gains from trade listed at the beginning of this chapter.

student workpoint 23.3

Be reflective—think ahead

In the next chapter, we will be looking at some of the barriers that countries put in place to effectively reduce international trade.

Given that there are so many benefits to be gained from trade, try to think of reasons why governments would want to prevent trade in any way.

Examination questions

Short response questions

1 Explain the benefits that can be gained as a result of international trade.   *[10 marks]*

2 Using a diagram, explain the concept of comparative advantage.   *[10 marks]*

By the end of this chapter, you should be able to:

- define free trade
- explain, give examples of, and evaluate the arguments for protectionism
- explain the arguments against protectionism
- explain and illustrate free trade
- define, explain, illustrate, and give examples of types of protectionism
- define and explain the aims of the World Trade Organization
- explain the benefits and weaknesses of the World Trade Organization
- understand some of the problems that developing countries face in world trade.

Free trade is said to take place between countries when there are no barriers to trade put in place by governments or international organizations. Goods and services are allowed to move freely between countries.

Arguments for protectionism

If international trade is so good for all the countries concerned, why is it that countries do not trade freely? Why do they often protect their economies from imports? A number of reasons have been put forward for this, although the arguments are not always valid. Let us look at some of the arguments.

Protecting domestic employment

At any given time in an economy, there will be some industries that are in decline (sunset industries) because they cannot compete with foreign competition. If the industries are relatively large, this will lead to high levels of structural unemployment, and governments often attempt to protect the industries in order to avoid the unemployment.

However, this argument is not very strong, since it is likely that the industry will continue to decline and that protection will simply prolong the process. Although there will be short-run social costs, it could be better to let the resources employed in the industry move into other, expanding areas of the economy. But, in some cases, the negative externalities of a rapidly declining major industry may be so great that the government feels obligated to intervene and protect the market.

Protecting the economy from low-cost labour

It is often argued that the main reason for declining domestic industries is the low cost of labour in exporting countries and that the economy should be protected from imports that are produced in countries where the cost of labour is very low. For example, there have been demands in the US to protect the domestic clothing industry against cheap imports from Asia, where wages are much lower. While trade may create many benefits for an economy as a whole, these gains may be spread widely, while the cost in terms of job losses may be concentrated in particular industries. There is much greater job insecurity among manufacturing workers throughout the more developed countries as workers fear that they will lose their jobs to workers in emerging markets such as China and India. Workers and their trade unions may lobby vigorously for protection against imported goods.

An example is the shipbuilding industry. In 1998, the hourly wage for shipbuilding in the US was $19.19, but in South Korea, it was $9.27. Not surprisingly, South Korea is now the largest shipbuilder in the world. In 2004, South Korea produced 14,768 large commercial ships, whereas the US produced only 289.

However, this argument goes against the whole concept of comparative advantage. It would mean that domestic consumers would pay higher prices than they should and that production in the protected economy would take place at an inefficient level. The country wishing to export would lose trade and their economy would suffer.

It should be realised that comparative advantage changes over time, and that a country that has a comparative advantage in the production of a good at present may not have it in the future. For instance, it is quite likely that the US did have a comparative advantage in shipbuilding at one time. As relative factor costs change in different countries, it is important that resources should move as freely as possible from industries where comparative advantage is waning, into industries where it is growing. Supply-side policies that focus on labour markets emphasize the importance of making labour flexible enough to adapt to changing economic circumstances. This puts some responsibility on governments to help those workers who have lost their jobs due to increased competition from countries that have developed their comparative advantage in the production of labour-intensive goods.

Protecting an infant (sunrise) industry

Many governments argue that an industry that is just developing may not have the economies of scale advantages that larger industries in other countries may enjoy. The domestic industry will not be competitive against foreign imports until it can gain the cost advantages of economies of scale. Because of this, it is argued that the industry needs to be protected against imports, until it achieves a size where it is able to compete on an equal footing.

However, there are possible flaws in this argument. Most developed countries have highly efficient capital markets, which allow them access to large amounts of financial capital, even more so since the advent of globalisation. Because of this, it can be argued that there is no basis for the idea that industries in developed countries will set up in a relatively small way and thus not benefit from economies of scale. With access to highly developed capital markets, it is hard to imagine that a new industry would not set up at the most efficient size. For example, the Saudi Arabian government has been diversifying into petrochemical production in recent years. It has undertaken a number of projects in partnership with large multinationals, such as Chevron, BP, and Exxon Mobil. The plants constructed have been among some of the largest in the world, gaining almost immediately from economies of scale.

It is likely that developing countries, without access to sophisticated capital markets, can use the infant industry argument to justify protectionist policies. However, whether they have the international political power to be able to impose protectionist policies, without complaints and action from developed countries, is debatable.

To avoid the risks of over-specialization

Governments may want to limit over-specialization, if it means that the country could become over-dependent on the export sales of one or two products. Any change in the world markets for these products might have serious consequences for the country's economy. For example, changes in technology could severely reduce the demand for a commodity, as the development of quartz crystal watches did for the Swiss wristwatch industry, harming the economy. The introduction of new products, or changes in the patterns of demand and supply, can have serious effects on the economies of developing countries, which tend to over-specialize in the production of primary products, without choice. For example, the invention of synthetic rubber had a large negative effect on the rubber industry in Malaysia, and the over-supply of coffee on the world market, causing falling prices, did the same for Ethiopia.

There are no real arguments against this view. It does not promote protectionism, it simply points out the problems that countries may face if they specialize to a great extent.

Strategic reasons

It is sometimes argued that certain industries need to be protected in case they are needed at times of war, for example, agriculture, steel, and power generation. Steel, for example, is needed for many defence items such as planes and tanks, and a steel industry would argue that it must be protected in order to stay competitive.

To a certain extent, this argument may be a valid one, although it is often overstated. In many cases, it is unlikely that countries will go to war or, if they do, that they will be completely cut off from all supplies. It is likely that the argument is being used as an excuse for protectionism.

To prevent dumping

Dumping is the selling by a country of large quantities of a commodity, at a price lower than its production cost, in another country. For example, the EU may have a surplus of butter and sell this at a very low cost to a small developing economy. This may ruin the domestic producers in the developing country. Where countries can prove that their industries have been severely damaged by dumping, their governments are allowed under international trade rules to impose anti-dumping measures to reduce the damage.

However, it is very difficult to prove whether or not a foreign industry has actually been guilty of dumping. In addition, a government that subsidizes a domestic industry may actually support dumping. For example, developing countries argue that when the EU exports subsidized sugar, it is actually a case of dumping because the price doesn't reflect the actual costs of the EU sugar producers. So, if dumping does occur, it is more likely that there will be a need for talks between governments, rather than any form of protectionism. There is always a danger that protectionism will invite retaliatory actions by foreign governments and this reduces the benefits that can be gained by all consumers and producers in all countries.

Student workpoint 24.1

Be a thinker. Read the article and answer the questions that follow.

EU IMPOSES LONG-TERM TARIFFS ON ASIAN SHOES

Faced with the overwhelming flow of low-cost Asian shoes into Europe, EU nations agreed on Wednesday to impose long-term tariffs on leather footwear from China and Vietnam. But the deal bitterly divided the European Union, which will now look into changing the way that it imposes such duties.

Both the shoe dispute and the review of EU duties arrive at a time of profoundly mixed feelings in Europe about the rise of Asian economies. On the one hand, the EU is eager to get a bigger bite of the vast and growing Far Eastern markets for its products and services. On the other hand, many businesses, especially in manufacturing, fear the legion of lower-paid Asian workers who can produce products at a fraction of the cost in Europe.

The shoe issue opened a rift in the EU between north and south, with countries like Germany, Britain, and the Nordic members opposing the tariffs, with backing from shoe sellers hungry for low-cost products. Italy along with France, Spain, and Portugal lobbied hard for them. The Italians argued that their shoemakers – small-scale and often family-run businesses with high labour costs – were being unfairly smothered by their huge-scale Asian counterparts.

An EU study this year said that China and Vietnam were dumping shoes in Europe by unfairly helping their leather-shoe manufacturers with favourable financing deals and low rents that distorted the value of their products, harming European competitors. The commission had imposed temporary tariffs, but those expire on Friday. The new tariffs, of 16.5 percent against China and 10 percent against Vietnam, go into effect on Saturday on most categories of leather shoe imports.

From 2001 to 2005, Chinese leather shoe exports to the EU increased tenfold. The Vietnamese increased theirs by 95 percent over the period. On average, the unit price from the two countries fell 28 percent. Meanwhile, the commission says, the production of footwear in the bloc decreased about 30 percent, while 40,000 European jobs in the sector were lost.

International Herald Tribune, 5 October 2006

> **1** Define dumping.
> **2** Outline the arguments for and against the European imposition of tariffs on the Chinese and Vietnamese shoes.

To protect product standards

A country might wish to impose safety, health, or environmental standards on goods being imported into its domestic market, in order to ensure that the imports match the standards of domestic products. For example, the EU has banned the importing of American beef, because it has been treated with hormones.

 This is a valid argument, as long as the concerns themselves are valid. However, many of the reasons given for bans when standards are not reached are considered to be simply subtle means of protectionism. Certainly, there is a strong feeling among US cattle farmers that this is the case with beef. They say that EU medical authorities have no hard evidence to back up their claims that hormone-treated beef is bad for consumers and that the ban is simply an excuse for protectionism. Where there is a dispute over product standards, a response by the exporting country might be to use retaliatory protectionist policies. In the EU–US beef dispute, the US retaliated against the EU in May 1999 by imposing trade sanctions on $117 million worth of imports from Europe.

To raise government revenue

In many developing countries, it is difficult to collect taxes and so governments impose import taxes (tariffs) on products in order to raise revenue. The International Monetary Fund estimated that, on average, import duties accounted for approximately 15% of total government revenue for the developing countries listed in its Government Financial Statistics Yearbook in 2002.

 This is not so much an argument for protectionism, but more a means of raising government revenue. In effect, the import duties are actually a tax on the consumers in the country who are buying the imports.

To correct a balance of payments deficit

Governments sometimes impose protectionist measures to attempt to reduce import expenditure and thus improve a current account deficit whereby the country is spending more on its imports of goods and services than it is earning for its exports of goods and services.

However, this will only work in the short run. It does not address the actual problem, because it does not rectify the actual causes of the deficit. Also, if countries do this, then it is likely that other countries will retaliate with protectionist measures of their own.

Arguments against protectionism

The arguments against protectionism are really related to the reasons why countries trade, which were discussed in Chapter 23. In brief, the arguments against protectionism include the following.

- Protectionism may raise prices to consumers and producers of the imports that they buy.

- Protectionism would lead to less choice for consumers.

- Competition would diminish if foreign firms are kept out of a country, and so domestic firms may become inefficient without the incentive to minimize costs. Innovation may also be reduced for the same reason.

- Protectionism distorts comparative advantage, leading to the inefficient use of the world's resources. Specialization is reduced and this would reduce the potential level of the world's output.

- For the reasons listed above, protectionism may hinder economic growth.

Types of protectionism

There are a number of different methods used to protect economies from imports. In order to look at them, it is best to first consider what the situation would be if a country had free trade in a given commodity, for example, wheat. We will then consider how different protectionist measures might alter the free trade situation.

Figure 24.1 shows the situation where free trade is taking place in a country, where wheat is both produced domestically and imported.

If there was no foreign trade, then domestic farmers would produce $0Q_e$ tons of wheat at a price of P_e per ton. If we now assume that the market is open and that foreign trade does take place, then the situation changes. Consumers find that they can import wheat at the world price and that, if they are prepared to pay the world price, they can import as much wheat as they like. This means that the supply curve faced by the importers, S (World), is perfectly elastic. S (World) must be below P_e or there would be no point in trading.

With free trade, the price of wheat in the country will be S (World). At this price, domestic farmers will only be prepared to supply $0Q_1$ tons of wheat. However, the demand for wheat will be $0Q_2$ and so the excess demand is satisfied by imported wheat. Foreign producers will supply Q_1Q_2 tons of wheat. Thus domestic consumers get to consume Q_eQ_2 more wheat at a lower price.

Now that we know what happens in a free trade situation, let us look at the different types of protectionism that may be employed.

Tariffs

A tariff is a tax that is charged on imported goods. As we know from Chapter 6, any tax placed upon a good shifts the supply curve upwards by the amount of the tax. In the case of a tariff, it will shift the world supply curve upwards, since it is placed on the foreign producers of the good and not the domestic producers. The effect of a tariff on imported wheat is shown in Figure 24.2.

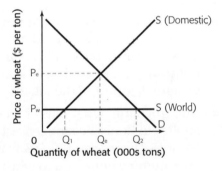

Figure 24.1 Free trade in wheat

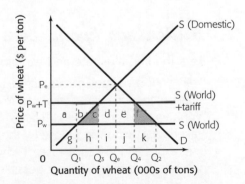

Figure 24.2 A tariff on wheat imports

Before the tariff, $0Q_2$ tons of wheat were being consumed at a price of P_w. Domestic production was $0Q_1$ and imports were Q_1Q_2. When the tariff is imposed, S (World) shifts up by the amount of the tariff to S (World)+tariff and so the market price rises to P_w+T. Total quantity demanded falls from $0Q_2$ to $0Q_4$, because the price has risen.

Domestic producers increase production to $0Q_3$ and so their revenue increases from g to g+a+b+c+h. Foreign producers supply the rest, which is now Q_3Q_4. They receive P_w+T, but have to pay the tariff to the government. Thus their revenue falls from h+i+j+k to only i+j. The government now receives tariff revenue of d+e.

The importers must pay a higher price for the imported good. In the case of wheat, the higher price will be passed on to millers and eventually to the cereal companies or bakeries that buy the refined wheat. As another example, if a government introduced a tariff on automobile component parts, then this would raise the costs to car-makers and eventually lead consumers to have to pay higher prices for their cars. If the car-maker is an exporter, then the higher cost of imported components could reduce its international competitiveness.

Tariffs are the most common type of anti-dumping measure. If a country has been able to prove that dumping has taken place, then it can place a tariff on the imported goods to raise their prices and eliminate the cost advantage of the dumped imports.

There are two further outcomes.

● Q_4Q_2 tons of wheat are not now demanded. Consumers keep the amount k that they would have spent on the wheat, but there is a loss of consumer surplus equivalent to f, because the wheat is not now purchased. This is known as a dead-weight loss of welfare, because of the loss of consumer surplus.

● After the tariff, Q_1Q_3 tons of wheat are now produced by relatively inefficient domestic farmers, as opposed to more efficient foreign farmers. The foreign farmers would produce this quantity for a minimum revenue of h, whereas the domestic producers need a minimum revenue of h+c. Thus c represents the inefficiency of the domestic producers and a loss of world efficiency, since more of the world's resources are being used to produce the wheat than are necessary. This is another dead-weight loss of welfare.

● ● ● ● ● ● ● ● ● ● ● ● ● ● ● ● ● ● ●

Student workpoint 24.2

Be a thinker. Illustrate and explain the following.

Draw your own copy of the tariff diagram, with semi-conductors in Japan as the example. Make a table with two columns, one headed "Winners" and one headed "Losers". In each column, make a list of the stakeholders who win or lose by the imposition of the tariff and give a brief explanation in each case of why the stakeholder is either a winner or loser. Be sure to consider possible international implications. Use the letters in the diagram to specifically identify the costs and benefits.

Subsidies

As we saw in Chapter 6, a subsidy is an amount of money paid by the government to a firm, per unit of output. In this case, the government is giving a subsidy to domestic producers to make them more competitive and so the effect will be to shift the domestic supply curve downwards by the amount of the subsidy. If we continue with our wheat example, then the effect of a subsidy granted to domestic wheat producers is shown in Figure 24.3.

Before the subsidy, $0Q_2$ tons of wheat were being consumed at a price of P_w. Domestic production was $0Q_1$ and imports were Q_1Q_2. When the subsidy is granted, S (Domestic) shifts downwards by the amount of the subsidy to S (Domestic)+subsidy. The market price stays at P_w and so demand remains at $0Q_2$.

However, domestic producers increase production to $0Q_3$, because they are now receiving P_w+subsidy per unit that they produce. This means that their revenue increases from a to a+b+e+f+g. Foreign producers supply the rest, which is now Q_3Q_2. Thus their revenue falls from b+c+d to only c+d. The government pays the subsidy, which is shown by the area e+f+g in total.

As with a tariff, Q_1Q_3 tons of wheat are now produced by relatively inefficient domestic farmers, as opposed to more efficient foreign farmers. The foreign farmers would produce this quantity for a minimum revenue of b, whereas the domestic producers need minimum revenue of b+g. Thus g represents the inefficiency of the domestic producers and a misallocation of the world's resources, since more of the world's resources are being used to produce the wheat than are necessary. This is another dead-weight loss of welfare.

There is no loss of consumer surplus, because the price of the wheat does not change. However, consumers are indirectly affected as governments will use tax revenues to fund the subsidies. This may mean higher tax payments and also involves an opportunity cost in terms of reduced government spending on other things.

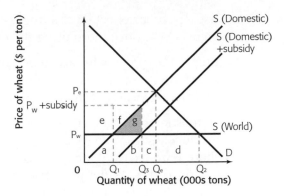

Figure 24.3 A subsidy on domestic wheat production

4 International Economics

● ●

Student workpoint 24.3

Be a thinker. Illustrate and explain the following.

Draw your own copy of the subsidy diagram, with cotton in the USA as the example. Make a table with two columns, one headed "Winners" and one headed "Losers". In each column, make a list of the stakeholders who win or lose by the granting of a subsidy and give a brief explanation in each case of why the stakeholder is either a winner or loser. Be sure to consider possible international implications. Use the letters in the diagram to specifically identify the costs and benefits.

Quotas

A quota is a physical limit on the numbers or value of goods that can be imported into a country. For example, the EU imposes import quotas on Chinese garlic and mushrooms. The imposition of a quota has a peculiar effect on the free trade diagram and this is shown in Figure 24.4, once more using the example of the wheat market.

Before the quota is imposed, $0Q_2$ of wheat is purchased at a price of P_w. Domestic supply is $0Q_1$ and imports are Q_1Q_2. Let us now assume that the government imposes a quota of Q_1–Q_3 tons of wheat.

Domestic producers supply $0Q_1$ at a price of P_w and the importers produce their quota of Q_1–Q_3. However, once this has happened, there is an excess demand of Q_3–Q_2 at the price P_w and so price begins to rise. As the price rises, importers are not allowed to supply more wheat, because they have filled their quota, and domestic producers begin to enter the market, attracted by the higher price of wheat. The domestic supply curve has, in effect, shifted to the right, above P_w. Eventually, the price settles at P_{Quota}, where demand now equals supply again and the total quantity of wheat demanded falls to Q_4.

Domestic producers now supply $0Q_1$ and Q_3–Q_4 tons of wheat at a price of P_{Quota}. Their revenue rises from a to a+c+d+f+i+j. Foreign producers now supply their quota of Q_1Q_3 tons of wheat and also receive a price of P_{Quota}. Thus their income changes from b+c+d+e to b+g+h. This is usually a fall in income but, in theory, it does not have to be.

Once again, as in tariffs, there are two areas of dead-weight loss of welfare that are caused by the imposition of the quota.

- Q_4Q_2 tons of wheat are not now demanded. Consumers keep the amount e that they would have spent on the wheat, but there is a loss of consumer surplus equivalent to k, because the wheat is not now purchased. This is a dead-weight loss of welfare, because of the loss of consumer surplus.

- After the quota, Q_3Q_4 tons of wheat is now produced by relatively inefficient domestic farmers, as opposed to more efficient foreign farmers. The foreign farmers would produce this quantity for a minimum revenue of c+d, whereas the domestic producers need a minimum revenue of c+d+j. Thus j represents the inefficiency of the domestic producers and a loss of world efficiency, since more of the world's resources are being used to produce the wheat than are necessary. This is another dead-weight loss of welfare.

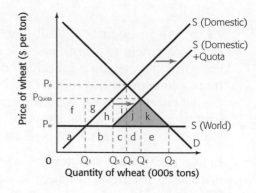

Figure 24.4 A quota on wheat imports

Student workpoint 24.4

Be a thinker. Illustrate and explain the following.

Draw your own copy of the quota diagram, with textiles in Europe as the example. Make a table with two columns, one headed "Winners" and one headed "Losers". In each column, make a list of the stakeholders who win or lose by the imposition of the quota and give a brief explanation in each case of why the stakeholder is either a winner or loser. Be sure to consider possible international implications. Use the letters in the diagram to specifically identify the costs and benefits.

Voluntary export restraints (VERs)

Voluntary export restraints are agreements between exporting and importing countries in which the exporting country agrees to limit the quantity of exports of a specific good below a certain level. This is usually to avoid the imposition of legal restrictions by the importing country. The agreement may be reached at either industry or government level. For example, China has agreed to limit its export of textiles to South Africa.

Student workpoint 24.5

Be an inquirer

Find a current example of a country agreeing to a voluntary export restraint. Note the countries that are involved and explain why the exporting country has agreed to the limitation.

Administrative barriers

When goods are being imported, there are usually administrative processes that have to be undertaken. This may be known as "red tape". If these processes are lengthy and complicated, then they can act as a restriction to imports. For example, making importers go through complicated paperwork, before they can get their goods into a country, will slow down imports. In addition, if the paperwork requires a large amount of legal work, then it will slow the process down even more and raise the cost to the importer. Sometimes, countries may designate certain ports of entry that are difficult to reach and also more expensive. This may cause border delays and again raise costs.

Health and safety standards and environmental standards

This is where various restrictions are placed upon the types of goods that can be sold in the domestic market, or on the methods used in the manufacture of certain goods. These regulations will apply to imports and may restrict their entry. As mentioned earlier, while it is important that countries are able to guarantee the health and safety of their population by preventing the import of unhealthy or unsafe goods, it is extremely important that governments are legitimately keeping out imports rather than simply protecting their own country's workers.

Moreover, while the maintenance of product standards is extremely important, developing country exporters face a particular difficulty in this regard as they may find it difficult or prohibitively expensive to carry out the necessary certification to prove that they meet the international standards. The costs involved in certification may make it difficult for such countries to successfully exploit their comparative advantage.

Embargoes

In effect, an embargo is an extreme quota. It is a complete ban on imports and is usually put in place as a form of political punishment. For example, the US has a trade embargo on all products from Cuba. Complete embargoes are rare. More commonly, countries put in place a set of economic sanctions against an offending country. These limit the exports or imports of one or a few key products and are also used as a form of political punishment, or to achieve a desired political objective.

Student workpoint 24.6

Be an inquirer

Find an example of a situation where a country, or set of countries, has imposed economic sanctions on another country. Note the countries that were involved and explain why the sanctions were imposed. Also try to conclude whether the imposing country/countries achieved their objectives.

Nationalistic campaigns

Governments will sometimes run marketing campaigns to encourage people to buy domestic goods instead of foreign ones in order to generate more demand for domestic goods and preserve domestic jobs. Such campaigns have happened in countries such as the UK, Australia, and the US. This may be described as "moral suasion", where the government links consumption of imported goods to the creation of unemployment.

The World Trade Organization (WTO)

The WTO is an international organization that sets the rules for global trading and resolves disputes between its member countries. The WTO was established on 1 January 1995 and now has 149 members. It replaced the General Agreement on Tariffs and Trade (GATT), which had been set up after the second world war. The WTO, along with its predecessor the GATT, is largely credited with the fact that since 1947, average world tariffs for manufactured goods have declined from approximately 40% to 4%.

All WTO members are required to grant "most favoured nation" status to one another, which means that, usually, trade concessions granted by a WTO country to another country must be granted to all WTO members.

Aims of the WTO

The WTO aims to increase international trade by lowering trade barriers and providing a forum for negotiation.

The functions of the WTO are:

● to administer WTO trade agreements

● to be a forum for trade negotiations

● to handle trade disputes among member countries

● to monitor national trade policies

● to provide technical assistance and training for developing countries

● to cooperate with other international organizations.

The WTO operates through a system of trade negotiations, or rounds. The first ones, held under GATT, dealt mainly with the reduction of tariffs, but later negotiations included other areas such as anti-dumping legislation and non-tariff issues.

The current round of negotiations is called the *Doha round*, after the site of the meeting where negotiations were started in November 2001. The programme, called the Doha Development Agenda, covers many areas, including agricultural tariffs, non-agricultural tariffs, trade and environment, anti-dumping, subsidies, competition policy, transparency in government procurement, and intellectual property.

The negotiations have been very contentious and no agreement has yet been reached, even though there were ministerial conferences in Cancun in 2003 and in Hong Kong in 2005. In July 2006, Doha round negotiations broke down and were ultimately suspended as a result of an inability to come to agreement on fundamental issues. There were two key concerns. First, the EU and the US are being urged to reduce their agricultural subsidies to improve market access for developing country exports. Second, the more developed countries want the larger developing countries such as Brazil and India to lower their barriers to imports of manufactured goods. Despite a widespread view that such measures will increase growth in all countries, there has so far been no success in reaching a compromise.

Is the WTO a success or failure?

This is a very difficult, if not impossible, question to answer. There are many different views on the subject. Perhaps it is best to state the claims of the WTO and the arguments of their critics.

The WTO claims that there are a number of benefits to be gained from its work.

- The system helps to promote peace in the world. The more that countries trade freely, the less likely that they are to be in conflict.
- Disputes are now handled constructively and there is a forum for this to take place.
- Rules make life easier for everyone. Small countries have an equal say and gain from "collective bargaining" with the larger countries.
- Freer trade cuts the cost of living for the majority of consumers.
- Freer trade provides more choice of products and better quality products.
- Trade raises incomes and stimulates economic growth.
- The system encourages good government.

However, critics of the WTO raise a number of important points to consider.

- The WTO supposedly operates on a consensus basis, with equal decision-making power for all. In reality, many important decisions get made in informal negotiations between small groups of the wealthier nations. Thus many of the WTO's developing country members are often excluded from decision-making negotiations.

- Many developing countries cannot afford to participate in all negotiations or even to have a permanent representative at the WTO. This means that their interests are not represented.

- The WTO's General Agreement on Trade and Services includes a long list of services that should be privatised. These include childcare, care for the aged, sewage, garbage disposal, park maintenance, and postal services. It is argued that those least able to pay for vital services, low-paid workers and poor communities, will suffer from this.

- It is argued that free trade does not make life better for ordinary people, but only leads to rich people and nations becoming better off.

- It is argued that WTO treaties are unfairly biased towards the interests of multinational corporations and the rich nations. Examples cited are:

  - rich countries being allowed to maintain high import duties and quotas in certain products, such as textiles, stopping imports from developing countries

  - the existence of highly protected agriculture in developed countries, while developing countries are being pressured to open up their markets

  - intellectual property rights, banning developing countries from incorporating technology that originates in developed countries into their systems (this especially applies to pharmaceuticals)

  - the increasing number of non-tariff barriers, like anti-dumping legislation, that are allowed to be used against developing countries.

- It is claimed that in the quest for free trade, issues of health, safety at work, and environmental protection are too often ignored to the great detriment of health, safety, and the environment. Animal rights lobbyists also argue that in its attempt to liberalize trade, the WTO rules contribute to abuses of animal rights (as in the case of the trade of furs of animals that have been trapped in steel-jaw leghold traps) or even towards the extinction of endangered species (as in the case of dolphins killed in the process of tuna fishing).

Student workpoint 24.7

Be reflective

Now that you have been given some of the main claims and doubts about the workings of the WTO, conduct some research of your own, and then answer the following essay question:

"Evaluate the extent to which the WTO has been successful in improving the economic situation in developing countries."

Examination questions

Short response questions

1 Using a diagram, explain the likely effects of a tariff on imported bicycles.   *[10 marks]*

2 Using a diagram, explain the likely effects of a quota on imported shoes.   *[10 marks]*

Essay question

1 a Explain the benefits of international free trade.   *[10 marks]*

   b Evaluate the arguments used by governments when they erect barriers to free trade.   *[15 marks]*

Data response exercise

Read the following text and answer the questions that follow.

"Let's Stick With the Steel Tariffs"

Based on a letter by Leo Gerard, International President, United Steel Workers of America

Eighteen months ago the US steel industry was reeling. Years of unfair foreign trade and **dumping** had devastated our domestic market, and the results were grim: more than 30 companies bankrupted, 17 companies sold out, more than 50,000 jobs destroyed, and the health-care benefits of more than 200,000 retirees wiped out.

President Bush recognized this grave danger and put in place a three-year programme of tariffs on targeted steel products. His goal was to protect American manufacturing jobs, help the steel industry get back on its feet to regain its **comparative advantage**, and stand up for the core principle that free trade must be fair trade.

Across our industry, companies are benefiting. Labour and management have forged agreements that increase worker productivity and reduce unnecessary levels of management. Productivity is up. And billions have been invested in new technologies and improved facilities. None of this would have been possible without the breathing room provided by the three-year steel programme.

Just as important, the gloomy predictions of opponents of the programme have not come to pass. Steel prices in America are among the lowest in the world. Steel supplies are readily available. Above all, the industries that are the biggest consumers of steel are in better competitive shape today than they were before the programme was introduced.

We have made great strides, but significant work remains.

Rebuilding an industry isn't an event; it's a process. And we are very much in the middle of that process.

The president's steel programme envisioned three years of gradually declining tariffs. Despite the critics the challenge now is to stay the course so that the sweeping changes made possible by the tariffs can be fully realized and turned into a foundation for long-term strength. We are confident that the president will continue to be true to his word so that this vital industry can continue its recovery. And manufacturing jobs will remain secure in America.

Adapted from original articles that appeared in *The Washington Post*, Letter to the Editor, 3 October 2003

Data response exercise

1 Define the following terms indicated in bold in the text:

    a dumping   *[2 marks]*

    b comparative advantage.   *[2 marks]*

2 Use a supply and demand diagram to show the effects of the US tariff on imported steel.   *[4 marks]*

3 Using a diagram explain one other type of protectionist policy that the American government might have considered in order to support the steel industry.   *[4 marks]*

4 Using your knowledge of economics and the information in the article, evaluate the arguments for and against the protectionism in the steel industry.   *[8 marks]*

N05 economics HL P3, q5

Assessment advice: internal assessment

At any given time, you can find information about a multitude of international trade disputes. There are a number of concepts and theories that can be used in a commentary on international trade and carrying out a search on any of the key words (tariff, quota, Voluntary Export Restraint, subsidies) should yield results. Keep in mind that the case studies that you investigate in your portfolio can provide you with useful examples to use during exams. The top mark bands in essay mark schemes all call for the use of examples; the writing of commentaries allows you to expand your awareness of real-world examples and enhance your international-mindedness.

Assessment advice: reading data

Always consider who the author of the text is, in order to determine a potential bias in the writing. In this case, it was the president of the Steel Workers' Union writing a letter. His bias should be mentioned in the evaluation.

By the end of this chapter, you should be able to:

- define and explain globalization
- define, and give an example of, a multinational corporation
- define foreign direct investment
- define, explain, and give examples of different types of trading blocs

HL :
- explain and give examples of obstacles to economic integration
- define, explain, illustrate, and give examples of trade creation
- define, explain, illustrate, and give examples of trade diversion.

Economic integration describes a process whereby countries coordinate and link their economic policies. As the degree of economic integration increases, the trade barriers between countries decrease and their fiscal and monetary policies are more closely harmonized.

Globalization

From the 1980s to the present day, there has been an increasingly rapid globalization of the world economy. Globalization may be defined as the increased integration of national economies into global, rather than national markets, prompted by liberalized capital flows, liberalized trade flows, significant advances in information technology, and marked decreases in the costs of international transport.

Multinational corporations (MNCs) have played a significant role in the process of globalization. They are defined as companies that produce in more than one country. MNCs are creating global factories, where production takes place in a number of countries, taking advantage of the cost differences in those countries. A product may have component parts made in several countries and then final construction may take place in yet another. This is known as integrated international production. For example, a Toyota car may be designed in Japan, the leather upholstery may be produced in Argentina, the engine might be constructed in Mexico, the car may be assembled in Brazil, and it may then be transported to the US for sale.

MNCs are associated with foreign direct investment (FDI). FDI is long-term overseas investment by MNCs. The contribution of MNCs to the process of globalization and global economic growth cannot be over-estimated. In Chapter 32, we will examine the possible effects of FDI on developing countries.

Did you know?

- The total production of MNCs amounts to almost 25% of world output.
- Fifty-one of the world's largest economies are MNCs, not countries.
- There are now approximately 63,000 MNCs.
- In 1997, MNCs controlled $12 trillion in foreign assets, employed 30 million people, and earned $9.5 trillion in revenues—more than the annual GDP of the US or the EU.

Source: UNCTAD World Investment Report 2000

Trading blocs

A trading bloc is defined as a group of countries that join together in some form of agreement in order to increase trade between themselves and/or to gain economic benefits from cooperation on some level. This coming together is economic integration. The Hungarian economist Béla Balassa identified six stages of economic integration and we will look at them now.

1 *Preferential trading areas:* A preferential trading area (PTA) is a trading bloc that gives preferential access to certain products from certain countries. This is usually carried out by reducing, but not eliminating, tariffs.

   An example of a PTA is the one between the EU and the ACP (Africa, the Caribbean, and the Pacific) countries. This is an agreement between the EU and 71 countries in the ACP. Many of the countries were former colonies of EU members. It enables the EU to guarantee regular supplies of raw materials and the ACP countries gain tariff preferences and access to special funds that are used to try to achieve price stability in agricultural and mining markets.

2 *Free trade areas:* A free trade area is an agreement made between countries, where the countries agree to trade freely among themselves, but are able to trade with countries outside of the free trade area in whatever way they wish. This situation is shown in Figure 25.1.

   In this hypothetical case, countries A, B, and C have signed a free trade agreement and are now trading freely among themselves. However, under the agreement, each country may trade with any other country in any way it sees fit. Thus country A has political grievances with country D and so has placed a complete embargo on foreign trade. Country B protects its economy from country D by placing tariffs on a number of its imports. Country C has good relationships with country D and trades freely with it.

   An example of a free trade area would be the North American Free Trade Area (NAFTA), which comprises the US, Canada,

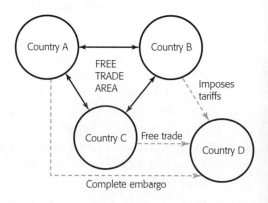

Figure 25.1 A free trade area

4 International Economics

and Mexico. NAFTA was established in January 1994 and, following a final tariff reduction between Canada and Mexico in January 2003, virtually all trade in the NAFTA region is now tariff-free. Over 50% of Canada's manufacturing production now goes to the US, and Mexico's share of the US import market has grown from approximately 7% in pre-NAFTA times to approximately 12% today.

Other examples of free trade agreements are the European Free Trade Association (Iceland, Norway, Switzerland, and Liechtenstein), and the South Asia Free Trade Agreement (India, Pakistan, Nepal, Sri Lanka, Bangladesh, Bhutan, and the Maldives).

3 *Customs unions:* A customs union is an agreement made between countries, where the countries agree to trade freely among themselves, and they also agree to adopt common external barriers against any country attempting to import into the customs union. This situation is shown in Figure 25.2.

Countries A, B, and C have joined in a customs union and are trading freely with each other. If country D wishes to export goods to the customs union, the goods will be treated in the same way, no matter which country the goods enter. If the customs union has agreed to place tariffs on the products of country D, then those tariffs will be imposed, no matter what the point of entry to the customs union.

All common markets and economic and monetary unions are also customs unions, thus the EU has a customs union. Other examples would be the Switzerland–Liechtenstein customs union; the East African Community, which is a customs union comprising Kenya, Uganda, and Tanzania; and Mercosur, which is a customs union between Brazil, Argentina, Uruguay, Paraguay, and Venezuela.

4 *Common markets:* A common market is a customs union with common policies on product regulation, and free movement of goods, services, capital, and labour.

The best-known example of a common market is the EU. The CARICOM Single Market and Economy (CSME) is another example, which is expected to be fully implemented by 2008 with harmonisation of economic policy and, possibly, a single currency. The current members are Barbados, Belize, Guyana, Jamaica, Suriname, Trinidad and Tobago, Antigua and Barbuda, Dominica, Grenada, St Kitts and Nevis, St Lucia, and St Vincent and the Grenadines. Montserrat is also expected to join.

5 *Economic and monetary union:* An economic and monetary union is a common market with a common currency. The best example of an economic and monetary union is the Eurozone, which includes the member countries of the EU that have adopted the Euro as their currency.

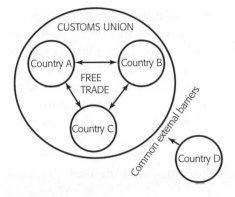

Figure 25.2 A customs union

6 *Complete economic integration:* This would be the final stage of economic integration, at which point the individual countries involved would have no control of economic policy, full monetary union, and complete harmonisation of fiscal policy. This is what the Eurozone is moving towards.

An evaluation of trading blocs

The extent of the advantages and disadvantages of trading blocs clearly depends to a large extent on the degree of integration. In purely economics terms, the benefits of being a member of a trading bloc are similar to those of free trade. These include a greater size of market with the potential for larger export markets, increased competition leading to greater efficiency, more choice, and lower prices for consumers. The consequences may not be even, as some domestic producers are likely to gain from the larger market while others may find themselves unable to compete.

There may be a further stimulus for investment due to the larger market size, and foreign investment might be attracted from outside the bloc as a way of getting a foot in the door of the larger market.

There is also an argument that along with the economic gains, a trading bloc will foster greater political stability and cooperation. It is also possible that trade negotiations may be easier in a world made up of a number of large trading blocs, rather than among 149 sovereign states.

However, by their very nature, trading blocs favour increased trade among members, but enact discriminatory policies against non-members and this can be damaging to the achievements of the multilateral trading negotiations of the WTO. There is concern that the breakdown in WTO talks in Geneva in July 2006 will lead to an increase in the number of individual trade negotiations. These may undermine the international trade rules and limit the potential gains to trade achievable with more liberalized world trade. This may not be as much of a problem for large economies as it might be for small or poor economies that have little bargaining power.

● ● ● ● ● ● ● ● ● ● ● ● ● ● ● ● ● ● ●

Student workpoint 25.1

Be knowledgeable

Make a table to summarize the information about trading blocs. Include the name of each of the six types of economic integration, a definition, and examples. The table should illustrate how economic integration increases at each stage.

Did you know?

Brazil, Argentina, Uruguay, and Paraguay were the original members of Mercosur, otherwise known as the Common Market of the South. In 2006, Venezuela joined the customs union. Mercosur covers a land area of 12 million square kilometres, which is more than four times the size of Europe. It represents a potential market of 250 million people and has a joint GDP of US$1.1 trillion, making it the world's fourth largest economy after NAFTA, the EU, and Japan.

While the Mercosur countries have often been united on issues such as their opposition to subsidies that high-income countries may give their farmers, there has been criticism of the inability of the union to move forwards in integrating the union's economies. This has been delayed by trade disagreements among members, particularly between Brazil and Argentina.

Mercosur is not the only trading bloc where disputes exist among members. For example, there has been a long-standing dispute between Canada and the US over timber and lumber trade between the two NAFTA members. Fierce debates, intensive lobbying, tariffs, and retaliatory tariffs are some of the signs of the discord.

Thus membership in a trading bloc is a signal that members wish to liberalize trade, but is no guarantee that free trade will take place.

Student workpoint 25.2

Be an inquirer

1 Choose one trading bloc to research. Make an annotated time line to show the steps involved in its establishment and evolution. Be sure to note any significant achievements and/or setbacks.

2 Pick one country in the bloc and evaluate how it has been affected by membership of the zone.

HL

Obstacles to economic integration

When economic integration takes place, there are bound to be some people who are not in favour for various reasons. The two most common reasons stated against economic integration are these:

1 Economic integration takes away a country's political sovereignty. If integration reaches the stage of a customs union, then political decisions start to be made by a central body and this reduces the power of the domestic government in the country. This may not be popular with domestic politicians and also with those members of the population who are especially patriotic. An example of this would be the European Parliament making decisions for EU countries.

2 Economic integration takes away economic sovereignty. Again, if integration reaches the stage of a customs union, then economic decisions also start to be made by a central body. Governments and

4 International Economics

271

citizens in any given country may be reluctant to give up the right to make decisions about economic matters. An example of this would be the European Central Bank making decisions relating to interest rates. Integration into a common market may "force" a country to change its economic policies. For example, if there are greater tax benefits in one country and factors of production are free to move from one to the other, then the government in the country with higher taxes may have to lower them in order to discourage such movement.

The greater the level of economic integration, the more member countries will lose control over political and economic affairs.

Trade creation and trade diversion

When a country joins a customs union, there are advantages and disadvantages. Two possible outcomes need to be considered here.

Trade creation

Trade creation occurs when the entry of a country into a customs union leads to the production of a good or service transferring from a high-cost producer to a low-cost producer. This is an advantage of greater economic integration. The concept is best explained by an example.

Let us assume that when the UK joined the EU in 1973, it had a comparative advantage over France, a member of the EU at that time, in the production of lawnmowers. However, as a non-member of the EU, the EU had placed a tariff on UK lawnmowers. The situation is shown in Figure 25.3.

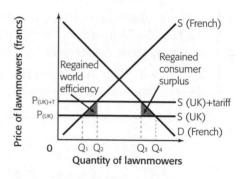

Figure 25.3 Trade creation

With the tariff on UK lawnmowers in place, the French would produce $0Q_2$ lawnmowers themselves and would import Q_2Q_3 lawnmowers from the UK. On entering the EU, the tariff on UK lawnmowers is relaxed and the UK can now make full use of its comparative advantage. With the tariff gone, French production falls to $0Q_1$ and imports rise to Q_1Q_4. There are Q_3Q_4 more lawnmowers bought and thus trade has been created. In addition, the extra demand means that there is an increase in consumer surplus, shown by the shaded triangle.

There is also a movement from high-cost to low-cost producers, since Q_1Q_2 lawnmowers, which were being made by relatively inefficient French producers, are now being made by more efficient UK producers. Although the French lawnmower producers may have lost out, there has been a world welfare gain, because fewer resources are being used to produce these lawnmowers.

It should be remembered that this ought to be a two-way process. It is highly likely that, with free trade, there will also be French products that the UK will now buy more of because the French have the comparative advantage, for example wine.

Trade diversion

Trade diversion occurs when the entry of a country into a customs union leads to the production of a good or service transferring from a low-cost producer to a high-cost producer. This is a disadvantage of greater economic integration. Once again, the concept is best explained by an example.

Let us assume that when the UK joined the EU in 1973, it had been producing textiles itself and importing textiles from Thailand, which had a comparative advantage in the product. However, once the UK joined the EU, it had to place a tariff on Thai textiles, because the EU already had one in place. The situation is shown in Figure 25.4.

Before the entry into the EU, the UK would produce $0Q_1$ metres of textiles domestically and would import Q_1Q_4 metres of textiles from Thailand. On entering the EU, the UK is forced to impose the same tariff on Thai textiles as the other EU countries. With the tariff in place, Thai textiles become more expensive than textiles produced in the EU. Because of this, the UK will now produce $0Q_2$ metres of textiles itself and will import Q_2Q_3 metres of textiles from the EU. There will be an overall fall in the quantity demanded of textiles of Q_3Q_4 metres and so a loss of consumer surplus shown by the shaded triangle.

There is also a movement from low-cost to high-cost producers, since Q_1Q_2 metres of textiles that were being produced by relatively efficient Thai producers, are now being produced by less efficient UK producers. Although the UK producers may have gained, there has been a world welfare loss, because more resources are being used to produce these textiles.

To make matters worse, the production of Q_2Q_3 metres of textiles has transferred from efficient Thai producers to relatively inefficient EU producers, so the trade diversion is even greater, as is the loss of world welfare. This represents a misallocation of the world's resources and represents a disadvantage of economic integration.

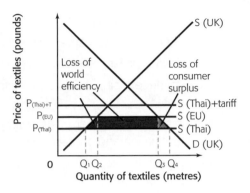

Figure 25.4 Trade diversion

Examination questions

Short response question

1 Using a diagram, explain the difference between a free trade area and a customs union. *[10 marks]*

Essay question

1 a What do economists mean when they refer to trading blocs? *[10 marks]*

  b Evaluate the likely effects of membership in a trading bloc. *[15 marks]*

Tip Remember to include examples. Your case study may help.

4 International Economics

You be the journalist

Headline: Polls show that a small majority favours the government's decision to join the regional customs union

Economic concept: Economic integration

Diagram(s): Higher level students—trade creation

Hints: You could pick any country with which you are familiar and explain why certain groups within the country would favour membership of a customs union. If space allows, consider why some groups (probably some producers) would be against it.

By the end of this chapter, you should be able to:

- define, explain, and give examples of an exchange rate
- define, explain, and give examples of different exchange rate systems
- distinguish between devaluation and depreciation and between revaluation and appreciation
- explain the advantages and disadvantages of high and low exchange rates
- explain government measures to intervene in the foreign exchange market

HL
- explain the advantages and disadvantages of fixed and floating exchange rates
- explain the advantages and disadvantages of a single currency/monetary union
- define and explain the theory of purchasing power parity (PPP).

Student workpoint 26.1

Be a thinker

Make a list of 20 different international currencies and their countries. Put together an information poster, for overseas travellers, which includes this list and illustrates some of the world's currencies.

Exchange rates

An exchange rate is the value of one currency expressed in terms of another currency, for example, €1 = US$1.28. This means that one euro may be exchanged for 1.28 US dollars. Currencies are exchanged (traded) on the foreign exchange market, the largest market in the world in terms of cash movements. The market includes the trading of foreign currencies between governments, central banks, private commercial banks, MNCs, and other financial institutions.

Did you know?

The international foreign exchange market is known as the Forex market. There are five main centres of Forex trading and these are based in London, New York, Zurich, Frankfurt, and Tokyo. On any given day, the total trading in the Forex market can exceed US$1.5 trillion!

When individuals, such as travellers or importing companies, wish to buy foreign currencies, they do not buy from the Forex market. They buy from the commercial banks that charge a higher price (their commission) than is found on the Forex market. This is one of the ways that commercial banks make their profits. Charging different rates of commission is how banks can compete with each other.

Exchange rates are usually expressed as a comparison of the values of two single currencies, for example, Australian dollars for Japanese yen. However, it is possible to express one currency against a collection (basket) of other currencies, and when this is done, the outcome is known as an exchange rate index. The exchange rate index is a weighted average index, like the consumer price index. In this case, it shows the exchange rate of one currency, expressed as an index, relative to the weighted exchange rates of a selection of other currencies. The currencies chosen are usually the country's major trading partners and the weighting is usually based upon the relative value of trade with each country.

Student workpoint 26.2

Be an inquirer

Australia uses a "trade weighted index" (TWI). Find out the following.

1 Why is it called the trade weighted index?

2 What are its current weightings?

3 What are the current values compared to a year ago?

4 Which currencies have contributed most to the change?

Use the website: www.rba.gov.au

Exchange rate systems

There are a number of different exchange rate systems operating in the world. The way that a country manages its exchange rate is known as its exchange rate regime. There are three main types, which are a fixed exchange rate, a floating exchange rate, and a managed exchange rate, and we will now look at each in turn.

Fixed exchange rates

A fixed exchange rate is an exchange rate regime where the value of a currency is fixed, or pegged, to the value of another currency, or to the average value of a selection of currencies, or to the value of some other commodity, such as gold. As the value of the variable that the currency is pegged to changes, then so does the value of the currency.

Deciding upon, and then maintaining, the fixed value of the currency is usually carried out by the government or the central bank. If the value of the currency, in a fixed exchange rate regime, is raised, then we say that this is a revaluation of the currency. If the value is lowered, then we say that this is a devaluation of the currency. These terms are very specific and must be used in the appropriate circumstances, i.e. when referring to changes in fixed exchange rates.

Floating exchange rates

A floating exchange rate is an exchange rate regime where the value of a currency is allowed to be determined solely by the demand for, and supply of, the currency on the foreign exchange market. There is no government intervention to influence the value of the currency.

The market for a currency is shown in Figure 26.1. In this case, it is the market for US dollars in terms of euros. As we can see, the demand curve is downward sloping and represents the demand for dollars by people in the EU, or at least people who hold euros. The supply curve is also normal and represents the supply of dollars, which of course comes from the US. The equilibrium price, the exchange rate, is US$1 = €0.80. Correct labelling, as is the case with all diagrams in economics, is crucial.

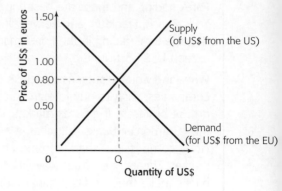

Figure 26.1 A floating currency

If the value of the currency in a floating exchange rate regime rises, then we say that this is an appreciation of the value of the currency. If the value falls, then we say that there has been a depreciation of the value of the currency. These terms must be used with floating exchange rates and must not be confused with the terms revaluation and devaluation, which relate to changes in currency values in a fixed exchange rate regime.

Consider a change in the value of the US$ from a first exchange rate of US$1 = €0.80 to a second exchange rate of US$1 = €0.85.

What does this mean?
This shows that the dollar has appreciated against the euro. In the first instance US$1 could buy €0.80 and in the second it has increased in value to be able to buy €0.85. For example, if a bottle of French wine costs €10, then under the first exchange rate, this would be equal to US$12.50 [$1 = €0.8]. Under the second rate of exchange, the price of the bottle of wine falls to US$11.77 [$1 = €0.85]. This shows that the purchasing power of the dollar has risen. It means that a given amount of US$ will buy more European goods.

Let's consider the euro value of dollars given the same exchange rates. If US$1 = €0.80, then €1 = US$1.25. When the exchange rate changes to US$1 = €0.85, then €1 = US$1.18. This shows that the euro has depreciated; in the first instance, it is worth US$1.25, in the second it has fallen to US$1.18. This means that a given amount of euros will buy fewer American goods.

Notice that the appreciation of the US dollar against the euro occurs at the same time as the depreciation of the euro against the US dollar. Essentially, they are two sides of the same coin. This relationship is further illustrated in Figure 26.2, which shows the value of the Canadian dollar in euros and the value of the euro in Canadian dollars for the period of time from 10 July to 6 August 2006.

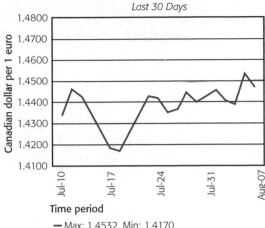

student workpoint 26.3

Be a thinker

Using the data in Figure 26.2, explain how the value of the Canadian dollar has changed in terms of euros and how the euro has changed in terms of Canadian dollars for the time period shown. Look carefully at the labels on the axes.

What can you say about the relationship between the two graphs?

What causes a change in the value of a country's currency in terms of another currency?
We now need to consider what factors will shift the demand and supply curves for a currency. First let us look at the demand curve, using the example of the demand for US dollars by people in the EU. People in the EU will have to buy US dollars in the foreign exchange market in order to:

● buy US exports of goods and services and to travel in America

● invest in US firms (FDI or portfolio investment)

● save their money in US banks or other financial institutions

● make money by speculating on the US dollar.

Thus the demand for the US dollar will rise if:

● there is an increase in the demand for US goods and services. This could be caused by:

– US inflation rates being lower than EU inflation rates, making US goods and services relatively less expensive than EU goods and services

– an increase in incomes in the EU, so people in the EU increase their demand for all things, including imports from the US

– a change in tastes in the EU in favour of US products

● US investment prospects improve

● US interest rates increase, making it more attractive to save there than in EU financial institutions

● speculators in the EU think the value of the US dollar will rise in the future, so they buy it now. If they are correct, then they will be able to sell those US dollars in the future, when they are worth more, and make a financial gain.

An increase in the demand for the US dollar is shown in Figure 26.3.

As we can see, an increase in the demand for the US dollar from the EU will shift the demand curve for the US dollar to the right to D_1. When this happens, the value of the dollar will appreciate and it will now be worth 0.90 euros. Each US dollar may be exchanged for a larger amount of euros.

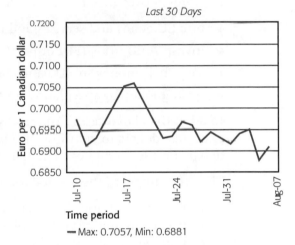

Figure 26.2 Changing values of the Canadian dollar and the euro

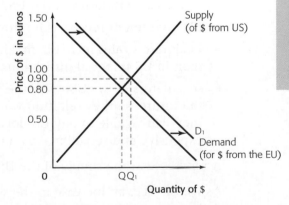

Figure 26.3 An increase in the demand for the US dollar

4 International Economics

277

Student workpoint 26.4

Be a thinker

1 List and explain the factors that might lead to a fall in the demand for the US dollar in terms of the euro.

2 Draw a diagram to illustrate the fall in the demand for the US dollar and its effect upon the exchange rate of the US dollar in terms of the euro. Be sure to label the axes fully and accurately.

Now let us look at the supply curve, and consider the supply of US dollars, using the same example. The US dollar will be supplied on the foreign exchange market when Americans wish to:

● buy EU goods and services and to travel in Europe

● invest in EU firms (FDI or portfolio investment)

● save their money in EU banks or other financial institutions

● make money by speculating on the euro.

In all of the above cases, Americans will need euros and will have to exchange dollars to get those euros. This will increase the supply of dollars on the foreign exchange market.

Thus the supply of the US dollar will rise if:

● Americans increase their demand for EU goods and services, thus exchanging more US dollars for euros. This could be caused by:

 – US inflation rates being higher than EU inflation rates, and thus US goods and services becoming relatively more expensive than EU goods and services

 – an increase in incomes in the USA, so people in the USA increase their demand for all things, including imports from the EU

 – a change in tastes in the USA in favour of EU products

● EU investment prospects improve

● EU interest rates increase, making it more attractive to save there than in US financial institutions

● speculators in the US think the value of the US dollar will fall in the future, so they sell it now and buy euros. If they are correct, they will be able to buy US dollars back again when they are less expensive and so will make a financial gain.

An increase in the supply of the US dollar is shown in Figure 26.4.

As we can see, an increase in the supply of the US dollar on the US dollar/euro market will shift the supply curve of the US dollar to the right to S_1. When this happens, the value of the dollar will depreciate and it will now be worth €0.70. Each US dollar may be exchanged for a smaller amount of euros.

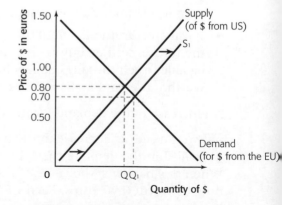

Figure 26.4 An increase in the supply of the US dollar

● ● ● ● ● ● ● ● ● ● ● ● ● ● ● ● ● ● ●

Student workpoint 26.5

Be a thinker

1 List and explain the factors that might lead to a fall in the supply of the US dollar in the US dollar/euro market.

2 Draw a diagram to illustrate the fall in the supply of the US dollar and its effect upon the exchange rate of the US dollar in terms of the euro.

Managed exchange rates

In reality, there is no currency in the world that is allowed to be completely freely floating. Even where governments try to be as non-interventionist as possible, there will come times when the currency is subject to extreme fluctuations and the government, or central bank, will feel that they must intervene. In the same way, frequent changes in the exchange rate, if it is completely freely floating, may cause uncertainty for businesses, which is not good for trade, and so governments will be forced to intervene in order to stabilize the exchange rate.

Because of the above, most exchange rate regimes in the world are managed exchange rates. These are exchange rate regimes where the currency is allowed to float, but with some element of interference from the government.

The most common systems are where a central bank will set an upper and lower exchange rate value and then allow the currency to float freely, so long as it does not move out of that band. If the exchange rate starts to get close to the upper or lower level, then the central bank will intervene in the foreign exchange market for its currency. Central banks do not make the upper and lower level values public, for fear of speculation, but they do exist.

The possible advantages and disadvantages of high and low exchange rates

The actual level of the exchange rate will have marked economic effects upon a country and we need to look at these now to understand fully why governments intervene to influence the value of the exchange rate. Subsequently, we look at how governments intervene.

Let us look in turn at the possible advantages and disadvantages of high and low exchange rates.

Possible advantages of a high exchange rate

● *Downward pressure on inflation:* If the value of the exchange rate is high, then the price of finished imported goods will be relatively low. In addition, the price of imported raw materials and components will reduce the costs of production for firms, which could lead to lower prices for consumers. The lower price of imported goods also puts pressure on domestic producers to be competitive by keeping prices low.

● *More imports can be bought:* If the value of the exchange rate is high, then each unit of the currency will buy more foreign currencies, and so more foreign goods and services. This would include both visible imports, such as technology, and invisible imports, such as foreign travel.

● *A high value of a currency forces domestic producers to improve their efficiency:* The high exchange rate will threaten their international competitiveness so they will forced to lower costs and become more efficient in order to maintain competitiveness. While this might result in the laying off of workers (see next point), there are other means of increasing efficiency that will result in greater economic productivity for the country.

Possible disadvantages of a high exchange rate

● *Damage to export industries:* If the value of the exchange rate is high, then export industries may find it difficult to sell their goods and services abroad, because of their relatively high prices. This could lead to unemployment in these industries.

● *Damage to domestic industries:* With greater levels of imports being purchased, because imports are now relatively less expensive, domestic producers may find that the increased competition causes a fall in the demand for their goods and services. This may lead to a further increase in the level of unemployment as firms cut back.

Possible advantages of a low exchange rate

● *Greater employment in export industries:* If the value of the exchange rate is low, then exports from the country will be relatively less expensive and so more competitive. This in turn may lead to more employment in the export industries.

● *Greater employment in domestic industries:* The low exchange rate will make imports more expensive than they were. This may encourage domestic consumers to buy domestically produced goods, instead of imports, and this may also raise employment.

Possible disadvantages of a low exchange rate

● *Inflation:* A low value of the currency will make imported final goods and services, imported raw materials and imported components, more expensive. The raw materials, and components are needed by firms and are costs of production that will rise, possibly leading to higher prices in the economy. The final goods and services will have higher prices. Thus there is a serious likelihood of inflation.

Important summary

A high value of a currency may be good to fight inflation, but may create unemployment problems, whereas a low value of a currency may be good for solving unemployment problems, but may create inflationary pressure.

● ● ● ● ● ● ● ● ● ● ● ● ● ● ● ● ●

Student workpoint 26.6

Be a thinker

1 With the help of a diagram, explain why a high value of a currency may worsen unemployment in a country.

2 With the help of a diagram, explain why a low value of a currency may create inflationary pressure in a country.

Government measures to intervene in the foreign exchange market

There are a number of reasons why governments may intervene in the foreign exchange market to influence the value of their currency. They may wish to:

● lower the exchange rate in order to increase employment

● raise the exchange rate in order to fight inflation

● maintain a fixed exchange rate

● avoid large fluctuations in a floating exchange rate

● achieve relative exchange rate stability in order to improve business confidence

● improve a current account deficit, which is where spending on imported goods and services is greater than the revenue received from exported goods and services (see Chapter 27).

Government intervention in the foreign exchange market

Whatever the reason for the intervention, we should now consider how governments attempt to manipulate the exchange rate. There are two main methods.

1 *Using their reserves of foreign currencies to buy, or sell, foreign currencies:* If the government wishes to increase the value of the currency, then it can use its reserves of foreign currencies to buy its own currency on the foreign exchange market. This will increase the demand for its currency and so force up the exchange rate.

In the same way, if the government wishes to lower the value of its currency, then it simply buys foreign currencies on the foreign exchange market, increasing its foreign currency reserves. To buy the foreign currencies, the government uses its own currency and this increases the supply of the currency on the foreign exchange market and so lowers its exchange rate.

2 *By changing interest rates:* If the government wishes to increase the value of the currency, then they may raise the level of interest rates in the country. This will make the domestic interest rates relatively higher than those abroad and should attract financial investment from abroad. In order to put money into the country, the investors will have to buy the country's currency, thus increasing the demand for it and so its exchange rate.

In the same way, if the government wishes to lower the value of the currency, then they may lower the level of interest rates in the country. This will make the domestic interest rates relatively lower than those abroad and should make financial investment abroad more attractive. In order to invest abroad, the investors will have to buy foreign currencies, thus exchanging their own currency and increasing the supply of it on the financial exchange market. This should lower its exchange rate.

Student workpoint 26.7

Be a thinker

Read the text and answer the questions that follow.

Two American senators are proposing legislation to impose steep tariffs on Chinese goods unless Beijing significantly raises the value of its currency by the end of September (2006). It is felt by American politicians and manufacturers that the yen is undervalued by as much as 40% against the dollar, giving Chinese exporters an unfair trading advantage.

On 21 July 2005, China allowed a 2.1% **revaluation** of its currency and agreed to

further increases in its value over time. It is now only 3.5% higher than its original fixed level. (This is less than some currencies fluctuate in a single day.) The almost imperceptible increase in the value of the yuan renmimbi convinces Americans that China is deliberately manipulating its currency in an unacceptable manner and they are proposing the tariffs as a response.

1 Define the term **revaluation** as used in the text.
2 With the help of a diagram, explain one way that the Chinese government can keep the yuan undervalued.
3 Explain how an undervalued yuan might give "Chinese exporters an unfair trading advantage".
4 With the help of a diagram, explain why the American politicians are "proposing a tariff as a response".

The advantages and disadvantages of fixed and floating exchange rates

Whichever exchange rate regime a country chooses to operate, there are bound to be advantages and disadvantages and we now look at these in turn.

Advantages of a fixed exchange rate

1 A fixed exchange rate should reduce uncertainty for all economic agents in the country. Businesses will be able to plan ahead in the knowledge that their predicted costs and prices for international trading agreements will not change.

2 If exchange rates are fixed, then inflation may have a very harmful effect on the demand for exports and imports. Because of this, the government is forced to take measures to ensure that

inflation is as low as possible, in order to keep businesses competitive on foreign markets. Thus fixed exchange rates ensure sensible government policies on inflation.

3 In theory, the existence of a fixed exchange rate should reduce speculation in the foreign exchange markets. (However, in reality, this has not always been the case and there are often attempts to destabilize fixed exchange rate systems in order to make speculative gains.)

Disadvantages of a fixed exchange rate

1 The government is compelled to keep the exchange rate fixed. The main way of doing this is through the manipulation of interest rates. However, if the exchange rate is in danger of falling, then the government will have to raise the interest rate in order to increase demand for the currency, but this will have a deflationary effect on the economy, lowering demand and increasing unemployment. This means that a domestic macroeconomic goal (low unemployment) may have to be sacrificed.

2 In order to keep the exchange rate fixed and to instil confidence on the foreign exchange markets, a country with a fixed exchange rate has to maintain high levels of foreign reserves in order to make it clear that it is able to defend its currency by the buying and selling of foreign currencies.

3 Setting the level of the fixed exchange rate is not simple. There are many possible variables to take into account and, also, these variables will change with time. If the rate is set at the wrong level, then export firms may find that they are not competitive in foreign markets. If this is the case, then the exchange rate will have to be devalued, but again, finding the exact right level is very difficult.

4 A country that fixes its exchange rate at an artificially low level may create international disagreement. This is because a low exchange rate will make that country's exports more competitive on world markets and may be seen as an unfair trade advantage. This may lead to economic disputes or to retaliation.

Advantages of a floating exchange rate

1 Because the exchange rate does not have to be kept at a certain level, interest rates are free to be employed as domestic monetary tools and can be used for demand management policies, such as controlling inflation.

2 In theory, the floating exchange rate should adjust itself, in order to keep the current account balanced. For example, if there is a current account deficit, then the demand for the currency is low, since export sales are relatively low, and the supply of the currency is high, since the demand for imports is relatively high. This should mean that the market will adjust and that the exchange rate should fall. Following this, export prices become relatively more attractive, import prices relatively less so, and so the current account balance should right itself. (This will depend upon the Marshall-Lerner condition being satisfied—see Chapter 27.)

3 Because reserves are not used to control the value of the currency, it is not necessary to keep high levels of reserves of foreign currencies and gold.

Disadvantages of a floating exchange rate

1 Floating exchange rates tend to create uncertainty on international markets. Businesses trying to plan for the future find it difficult to make accurate predictions about what their likely costs and revenues will be. Investment is more difficult to assess and there is no doubt that volatile exchange rates will reduce the levels of international investment, because it is difficult to assess the exact level of return and risk.

2 In reality, floating exchange rates are affected by more factors than simply demand and supply, such as government intervention, world events like 9/11, and speculation. Because of this, they do not necessarily self-adjust in order to eliminate current account deficits.

3 A floating exchange rate regime may worsen existing levels of inflation. If a country has high inflation relative to other countries, then this will make its exports less competitive and its imports more expensive. The exchange rate will then fall, in order to rectify the situation. However, this could lead to even higher import prices of finished goods, components, and raw materials, and thus cost-push inflation, which may further fuel the overall inflation rate.

The advantages and disadvantages of a single currency/monetary union

On 1 January 1999, the European single currency, known as the euro, came into existence as an accounting currency. On 1 January 2002, it was introduced as a physical currency. The euro (€) is the official currency in 12 EU member states: Austria, Belgium, Finland, France, Germany, Greece, Ireland, Italy, Luxembourg, the Netherlands, Portugal, and Spain. Together, these countries are known as the Eurozone, and it is a monetary union. All existing members of the EU who are not using the euro are eligible to join the Eurozone—if they meet certain economic and monetary requirements. For new members to the EU, eventually adopting the euro is a mandatory obligation. Slovenia will begin to use the euro on 1 January 2007. The European Central Bank (ECB) manages the euro. Let us look at the advantages and disadvantages to be gained from participating in a monetary union.

Advantages of a single currency system

1 A single currency reduces the level of transaction costs. The countries in the Eurozone do not have to keep changing currencies in order to trade and so do not have to pay commission on currency exchange.

2 When trading between Eurozone countries, businesses no longer have to worry about possible exchange rate fluctuations and thus changes in their relative costs and prices. This reduces risk and increases business confidence in the countries that are members of the monetary union.

3 When countries employ a single currency, it is easier to make price comparisons between the countries. Comparing prices between Spanish products and Italian products was not that simple when they were expressed in pesetas and lira, but now that both countries have the euro, it is very easy indeed.

4 It is likely that greater FDI will be attracted to the monetary union because of the reduced transactions costs, reduced uncertainty, and the large size of the single currency market.

Disadvantages of a single currency system

1 With a single currency like the euro, a central body sets the interest rates for the whole area—in this case, the ECB sets the rates for the Eurozone. This means that individual countries lose the ability to set their own interest rate levels and so lose the ability to adopt an independent monetary policy.

2 In a single currency system, it is not possible for one country to depreciate or devalue its currency to ease a balance of trade problem. All countries have to operate with the same exchange rate against non-member countries.

3 There is a cost of transition from national currencies to a single currency; not only for governments in physically changing the currencies, but also for firms, who will have to do such things as reprogramme computers, and produce new price lists, at first in both old and new prices. However, this is a one-off cost.

The Big Mac index

The Economist introduced the Big Mac index in 1986, as an informal and amusing way of attempting to measure the PPP between different currencies and the US dollar. The "basket of goods" is simply a McDonald's Big Mac hamburger.

The Big Mac PPP exchange rate between the US and other countries is calculated by dividing the cost of a Big Mac in one country, in its domestic currency, by the cost of a Big Mac in the US, in US dollars. When this has been done, a PPP exchange rate is gained which may then be compared with the actual exchange rate on the foreign exchange markets.

The table below shows a selection of Big Mac index figures, for 10 countries, from the 20th birthday index, which was published in *The Economist* in May 2006.

Country	Big Mac prices		Implied PPP of 1 (US$)	Actual US$ exchange rate (22 May 2006)	Under (–)/Over (+) valuation against the $ (%)
	In local currency	In US$			
US	$3.10	3.10	-	-	-
Argentina	Peso 7	2.29	2.26	3.06	−26
China	Yuan 10.5	1.31	3.39	8.03	−58
Euro area	€2.94	3.77	1.05	1.28	+22
Indonesia	R 14,600	1.57	4,710	9,325	−49
New Zealand	NZ$4.45	2.75	1.44	1.62	−11
Pakistan	Rupee 130	2.16	41.9	60.1	−30
South Africa	Rand 13.95	2.11	4.50	6.60	−32
Switzerland	SFr6.30	5.21	2.03	1.21	+68
Turkey	Lire 4.20	2.72	1.35	1.54	−12

Source: *The Economist*, May 2006

Table 26.1 The Big Mac index

Consider Argentina. Remember that the Big Mac PPP is the exchange rate that would mean that a burger cost the same in the US as anywhere else. The cost of a Big Mac in Argentina is 7 pesos, compared with an average US price of $3.10. To make the two prices the same would require an exchange rate of US$1 = 2.26 pesos. However, the actual foreign exchange market rate is 3.06. This means that the peso is 26% undervalued against the dollar. This is why, when converted into dollars, using the actual exchange rate, the Argentinean burger is less expensive than the American one.

As we can see from the table, the cheapest burger, and thus the most undervalued currency, is the Chinese one. Meanwhile, the most overvalued currency would appear to be the Swiss franc.

The index was never intended to be an exact predictor of currency movements, more a general indicator of whether a currency is near its PPP long-run level. The index actually has a good record in predicting exchange rate movements: currencies that show up as undervalued often tend to strengthen over time, and vice versa. But you must always remember that the index has limitations. Big Macs are not traded between countries and prices are distorted by differences in local taxes and property costs.

Student workpoint 26.8

Be an inquirer

Write a 500-word report summarizing the specific reasons why the UK is refusing to adopt the euro, despite being a member of the EU.

Purchasing power parity theory (PPP)

You have already met the theory of purchasing power parity in Chapter 15, but now we will consider it in a little more detail.

Purchasing power parity theory argues that, in the long run, exchange rates should move towards levels that would equalize the prices of an identical basket of goods and services bought in either of the two countries whose exchange rates are being compared. It equates the long-run exchange rate with the relative inflation rates in each country.

PPP suggests that exchange rates will be in long-run equilibrium when the rate enables people in different countries to buy the same basket of goods with an equal amount of money. For example, if the exchange rate between the UK pound and the US dollar is £1 = US$1.80, and the same basket of goods may be bought for £100 in the UK and US$180 in the US, then the actual exchange rate is the same as the PPP exchange rate.

Let us now assume that because of inflation, prices rise by 10% in the UK and by only 2% in the US over the next year. Now, to buy the same basket of goods, one would need £110 and US$183.6. Thus the PPP exchange rate, the rate that would allow the same baskets of goods to be bought, would now be £1 = US$1.67.

PPP theory suggests that the actual exchange rate should move towards the PPP exchange rate over time, since UK goods and services have become relatively more expensive. There should be an increased demand for US imports in the UK, and so the supply of pounds on the foreign exchange market will have increased. In the same way, there should be a fall in demand for UK goods and services in the US and so the demand for the pound will fall. Thus the value of the pound relative to the US dollar should start to depreciate towards the PPP exchange rate.

In simpler words, if inflation rises by 3% in a nation, *ceteris paribus*, the value of the currency should fall by 3%. As noted in Chapter 15, *The Economist* magazine has developed its own version of a measure of purchasing power parity exchange rates, as described in "The Big Mac index".

Although PPP theory is very useful in making comparisons between countries, it is a little simplistic. As we know, exchange rates are not only affected by demand and supply for goods and services, and thus for currencies. In reality, speculation, government interest rate manipulation, business confidence, and world events, may mean that the long run is never achieved, because of so many short-run fluctuations, and so the actual exchange rate is unlikely to reach the optimum level of the PPP exchange rate. As economist Abba Lerner said, "In the long run, there's just another short run."

Student workpoint 26.9

1 According to the information in Table 26.1, state whether the Indonesian rupee is over-valued or under-valued against the dollar. Explain how this is determined. Given this information, what would you expect to see happen to the Indonesian rupee over time? Why?

2 *The Economist* updates its Big Mac index frequently. Make a table in which you compare the current over- or under-valuations with the ones shown in Table 26.1. Note which currencies are moving towards their purchasing power parity value according to the Big Mac index.

Examination questions

Short response questions

1 With the help of a diagram, explain **three** factors that would cause a currency to appreciate in value. *[10 marks]*

2 With the help of a diagram, explain the likely effects of a high rate of inflation on a country's currency. *[10 marks]*

Essay question

1 a Explain **three** factors that could cause a country's currency to depreciate. *[10 marks]*

  b Evaluate the likely effects of such a depreciation on the country's economy. *[15 marks]*

Higher level essay question

2 a Explain how currency values are determined in a floating exchange rate system. *[10 marks]*

  b Evaluate the relative advantages and disadvantages of a floating exchange rate system in contrast with a fixed exchange rate system. *[15 marks]*

You be the journalist

Headline: Government tells complaining manufacturers to face reality—it will take no action to bring down the currency

Economic concept: Exchange rates

Diagram: Exchange rate diagram to show what the government could do

Hints: Choose a country to set the article in and explain why the manufacturers in that country might be "complaining". Show what they would like the government to do. Suggest what the government might expect the manufacturers to do.

By the end of this chapter, you should be able to:

- define and explain the balance of payments account
- define and explain the current account
- define and explain the elements that make up the current account
- define and explain the capital account
- define and explain the elements that make up the capital account
- explain the consequences of current account and capital account imbalances
- define, explain, and give examples of expenditure-switching policies
- define, explain, and give examples of expenditure-reducing policies

HL
- define and explain the Marshall-Lerner condition
- define, explain, and illustrate the J-curve effect.

The balance of payments account

The balance of payments account is a record of the value of all the transactions between the residents of one country with the residents of all other countries in the world over a given period of time. This is usually one year, although monthly balance of payments accounts are also produced. There are two main parts to the balance of payments account: the current account and the capital account.

Note that there are many different names used to identify the various parts of the balance of payments account. The headings change from country to country and even from time to time within the same country. Where possible, alternative names will be given.

The current account

The current account is a measure of the flow of funds from trade in goods and services, plus other income flows. It is usually sub-divided into three parts.

1 The balance of trade in goods

The balance of trade in goods is also variously known as the visible trade balance, the merchandise account balance, or simply the balance of trade. It is a measure of the revenue received from the exports of tangible (physical) goods minus the expenditure on the imports of tangible goods over a given period of time. It includes trade in all tangible goods, from airplanes to chickens.

Exports occur when an international transaction relating to goods or services leads to an inflow of money into the country. Imports occur when an international transaction relating to goods or services leads to an outflow of money from the country.

When export revenue is greater than import expenditure, then we say that there is a surplus on the balance of trade in goods. When import expenditure is greater than export revenue, then we say that there is a deficit on the balance of trade in goods.

2 The balance of trade in services

The balance of trade in services is also known as the invisible balance, the services balance, or net services. It is a measure of the revenue received from the exports of services minus the expenditure on the imports of services over a given period of time. It includes the import and export of all services such as banking, insurance, and tourism. For example, an Italian tourist on holiday in Vienna would be spending money that represents an invisible export to the Austrian economy (money coming in) and so an invisible import to the Italian economy (money going out).

Student workpoint 27.1

Be a thinker

Identify whether each of the following elements represents an invisible import, a visible import, an invisible export, or a visible export on the UK current account.

1 UK computer manufacturers buy semi-conductors from Malaysia.
2 Lloyds of London sells insurance to Chinese shipping companies.
3 Canadian football fans buy tickets to a Manchester United game.
4 British football fans attending the World Cup 2006 stay in hotels in Berlin.
5 France buys North Sea natural gas from UK companies.

---

3 Net income flows

This is usually split into two sections.

● *Net investment incomes (net factor income from abroad):* This is a measure of the net monetary movement of profit, interest, and dividends moving into and out of the country over a given period of time as a result of financial investment abroad.

Domestic firms may have set up branches in other countries and any profits being repatriated will count as a positive item in this account. In the same way, profits sent out of the country by foreign firms set up within the country will count as a negative item.

Residents and institutions in the country may have invested in banks and other financial institutions in other countries and any interest received from these financial investments will count as a positive item. In the same way, any payment of interest to foreign investors that leaves the country will count as a negative item.

Residents and institutions may have purchased shares in foreign companies and any dividends received from those companies will count as a positive item. In the same way, any dividends paid by domestic firms to foreign shareholders will count as a negative item.

● *Net transfers of money (current transfers or net unilateral transfers from abroad):* These are payments made between countries when no goods or services change hands. At a government level, it includes things such as foreign aid and grants. At an individual level, it includes foreign workers sending money back to their families in their home country (remittances) or private gifts sent from a person in one country to a person in another.

Did you know?

"Remittances, funds received from migrants working abroad to developing countries, have grown dramatically in recent years from US$18 billion in 1980 to over US$126 billion in 2004. They have become the second largest source of external finance for developing countries after foreign direct investment (FDI), both in absolute terms and as a proportion of GDP. Furthermore, unlike other capital flows, remittances tend to be stable even during periods of economic downturns and crises."

The World Bank—Finance Research

Current account balance = Balance of trade in goods + Balance of trade in services + Net income flows

Note that any of these accounts might be in surplus or deficit at any given time—there could be a deficit on the trade in goods, a surplus on the trade in services, a surplus on net income flows, and an overall surplus on the current account. The current account balance is an overall balance and may be in deficit or in surplus.

The capital account

The capital account is a measure of the buying and selling of assets between countries. **Assets** in this case include anything that can be owned and that has value, such as land, real estate, companies, bank deposits, stocks and shares, treasury bills, government bonds, foreign currency, and all other types of financial instruments.

In a number of countries the capital account is now called the financial account, and in some there is both a capital account and a financial account. For simplicity we shall just deal with the buying and selling of all assets under the heading of the capital account.

The capital account measures the net change in foreign ownership of domestic assets. If foreign ownership of domestic assets increases more quickly than domestic ownership of foreign assets then there is more money coming into the country than going out and so there is a capital account surplus. In the same way, if domestic ownership of foreign assets increases more quickly than foreign ownership of domestic assets then there is more money going out of the country than coming in and so there is a capital account deficit.

There are a number of different ways of classifying assets. Perhaps the simplest is to separate assets that represent ownership and assets that represent lending.

● Assets that represent ownership include buying property, purchasing a business, or purchasing stocks or shares in a business. In all cases the asset is expected to have a positive return in the future by making profits or by increasing in value over time. The investment does not have to be paid back and there is no guarantee that it will provide a positive return. The buyer of the asset is taking a risk.

● Assets that represent lending include treasury bills, government bonds, and savings account deposits. In these cases the investor is lending the money in order to purchase the asset in the expectation that interest will be paid upon the investment and that the money will be repaid at a given point in time. These assets are simply borrowing and lending on the international market.

Sometimes assets may be classified in other ways, such as foreign direct investment (FDI; investment by multinational corporations in another country), portfolio investment (investment in stocks and shares) and other investment (currency transactions and bank and savings account deposits).

Included in the capital account, or financial account, are changes in the official reserve account. All countries hold reserves of gold and foreign currencies, which are itemised in the official reserve account, and it is movements into and out of this account that ensure that the balance of payments will always balance to zero. If there is a surplus on all of the other accounts combined, then the official reserve account total will increase, if there is a deficit on all of the other accounts combined, then the official reserve account total will decrease. It is net changes in the official reserve account over the period of time being considered that balance the accounts.

However, in reality, the accounts will not balance, because there are simply too many individual transactions taking place for the measurement to be exact. There will always be some transactions that have not yet been recorded when the figures are being put together. A balancing item (sometimes known as net errors and omissions or statistical discrepancy) is therefore put into the accounts to ensure that they do balance. As trading accounts are revised over the years more data come to light and the balancing item invariably gets smaller.

A selection of the balance of payments figures for the US, from 2003 to 2005, is shown in Table 27.1. They illustrate the way that balance of payments accounts are created.

We can see that in all three years there was a large deficit on the current account balance (line 12). Although the balance of trade in services (line 6) was positive in every year, the balance of trade in goods (line 3) and the net income flows (line 11) were both negative.

In the US, there is a capital account and a financial account. However, if all changes in asset ownership are totalled and allowance is made for the balancing item (in the US case it is called statistical discrepancy) then the total capital account balance should be the opposite of the current account balance and the balance of payments should sum to zero. In the US, net changes in the official reserve account are included in the financial account and so the accounts balance.

Line	US balance of payments figures (millions of dollars)			
	(Credits +; debits −)	*2003*	*2004*	*2005*
	Current account			
1	Exports of goods	713,415	807,516	894,631
2	Imports of goods	−1,260,717	−1,472,926	−1,677,371
3	**Balance of trade in goods (lines 1 + 2)**	−547,302	−665,410	−782,740
4	Exports of services	302,681	344,426	380,614
5	Imports of services	−250,276	−290,312	−314,604
6	**Balance of trade in services (lines 4 + 5)**	52,405	54,114	66,010
7	Income receipts *(investment income)*	303,062	374,913	474,647
8	Income payments *(investment income)*	−266,469	−347,321	−463,353
9	**Net income receipts (lines 7 + 8)** *(net investment income)*	36,593	27,592	11,294
10	**Unilateral current transfers, net**	−69,210	−81,582	−86,072
11	**Net income flows (lines 9 + 10)**	−32,617	−53,990	−74,778
12	**Current account balance (lines 3 + 6 + 11)**	−527,514	−665,286	−791,508
13	**Capital account**			
14	Capital account transactions, net	−3,321	−2,261	−4,351
15	**Financial account**			
16	US-owned assets abroad, net (financial outflow)	−326,424	−867,802	−426,801
17	Foreign-owned assets in the US, net (financial inflow)	864,769	1,450,221	1,212,250
18	Statistical discrepancy	−7,510	85,128	10,410
19	**Capital and financial account balance (lines 14 + 15 + 17 + 18)**	527,514	665,286	791,508

Source: Bureau of Economic Analysis (BEA), US Department of Commerce

Table 27.1 US balance of payments statistics 2003–2005

Table 27.1 also shows that the US is experiencing persistent current account deficits (line 12). The US has growing deficits on the trade in goods balance (line 3) that are not balanced by the surpluses on the trade in services balance (line 6). The current account deficit is largely financed by the foreign-owned assets in the US (line 17). You can see that the current account balance (line 12) is equal to the capital and financial account balance (line 19) for all three years.

The US economy has been experiencing strong levels of economic growth. One result is that there has been increasing demand for imports of goods and services. This illustrates the link between growth in the economy and a worsening of the current account. It implies that the US economy is borrowing heavily from abroad in order to finance its current international expenditure. There has been some debate among economists as to how long this situation can continue.

Student workpoint 27.2

Be a thinker

Using the correct terminology and actual numbers, describe the US balance of payments position in 2005, as shown in Table 27.1. Consider each of the components of the balance of payments, using real numbers to explain whether each is in surplus or deficit. Explain how the balance of payments as a whole is balanced.

The consequences of current account and capital account imbalances

The existence of a deficit or surplus in either the current or capital accounts is bound to have economic consequences that will affect the economy and we can consider some of these effects.

Consequences of a current account deficit

We know that if the current account is in deficit then the capital account will have to be in surplus in order to balance out the current account deficit. This means one of three things.

1 Foreign exchange reserves may be used to increase the capital account and so to regain balance with a deficit in the current account. If reserves are taken from the official reserve account then they are a positive entry into the capital account. However, no country, no matter how rich and powerful, is able to fund long-term current account deficits from its reserves. Eventually, the reserves would run out.

2 It may be that a high level of buying of assets for ownership is financing the current account deficit. Foreign investors may be purchasing such things as property, businesses, or stocks or shares in businesses. In this case this inflow into the capital account is funding the current account deficit, but as it must be based upon foreign confidence in the domestic economy it is not considered to

be harmful. However, there are sometimes fears that if foreign ownership of domestic assets were to become too great then this may be a threat to economic sovereignty. Moreover, if there is a drop in confidence then foreign investors might prefer to shift their assets to other countries. Selling the assets would result in an increase in the supply of the currency and a fall in its value.

3 It may be that it is financed by high levels of lending from abroad. If this is the case then high rates of interest will have to be paid, which will be a short-term drain on the economy and will further increase the current account deficit in years to come. There is also always the danger that the governments or people lending the money may, at some time, withdraw their money and place it elsewhere. This would lead to massive selling of the currency and a very sharp fall in the exchange rate.

Consequences of current and capital account surpluses

If the current account is in surplus, there may be other consequences.

1 A current account surplus allows a country to have a deficit on its capital account by building up its official reserve account or by purchasing assets abroad. However, one country's surplus is another country's deficit and it may lead to protectionism by other countries in order to attempt to reduce their own deficits.

2 A current account surplus usually leads to an appreciation of the currency on the foreign exchange markets as it implies an increase in demand for the currency. This will make imports cheaper so reducing inflationary pressures, but will also make exports more expensive, which harms exporters.

Note that a capital account surplus, based upon the purchasing of assets for ownership, is mainly a positive thing for the country and allows a current account deficit. However, a capital account surplus based upon high levels of borrowing from abroad is the opposite and is normally a response to a current account deficit. This results in the concerns raised in point 3.

How big is a "big" current account deficit or surplus?

There are two ways to interpret the size of a country's current account deficit or surplus. One is to consider the value of the total—for example, the current account surplus in Germany is US$108.1 billion while the current account deficit in the US is US$808.5 billion. However it is easier to understand the magnitude of the deficit if it is placed in the context of the country's GDP. This would be similar to understanding how much a person is in debt. A billionaire who owes US$1000 to a credit card company is in a very different situation to an unemployed student who owes US$1000. The burden of a deficit depends on the ability to pay. This is not so much a concern when a country has a current account surplus, although there are possible problems arising from the appreciation of the currency, but it is a problem when current account deficits reach a certain percentage of GDP. In the case of the US the current account deficit is currently approximately 6.8% of its GDP and for Germany it is approximately 3.6%.

The Bank of Italy shifts from dollars

Italy's central bank, the Bank of Italy, has switched almost a quarter of its foreign currency reserves into Great Britain's pound sterling (GBP), selling billions of dollars worth of US Treasury Bonds.

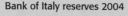

Bank of Italy reserves 2004

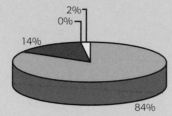

2%
0%
14%
84%

US dollar ■ Japanese yen □ GB pound □ Swiss franc

Bank of Italy reserves 2005

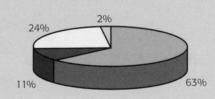

2%
24%
11%
63%

US dollar ■ Japanese yen □ GB pound □ Swiss franc

A year ago the Bank of Italy held no reserves in pounds. The proportion of GBP reserves is now up to 24%, with a significant fall in the holdings of

US dollars and a small fall in its yen reserves. The move is partially in response to the expectation that US interest rates have reached their peak. If interest rates don't rise this makes holdings of US bonds less profitable. There is also concern about the sustainability of the US's massive current account deficit.

There has been a movement away from US dollars in other central banks. The Riksbank in Sweden has reduced its holdings in US dollars from 37% to 20%, and the United Arab Emirates and Qatar have both indicated that they might move their reserves into euros. Russia has cut its US reserves from approximately 65% to 40%.

The countries that hold the biggest US dollar reserves are China and Japan. Indeed, it is argued that the buying of US government bonds by Asian governments is what has allowed the US to finance its current account deficit. For these countries it is very difficult to move away from US dollars as it would be widely interpreted as a fall in confidence. This would be likely to lead to widespread selling of US dollars and therefore a sharp fall in the value of the US dollar, leaving those central banks holding US dollars with a big drop in the value of their US assets.

In spite of the view that there will not be a collapse of the US dollar, there is still international concern about possible consequences of the massive American current account deficit, particularly in terms of its effect on the US dollar.

The Daily Telegraph, 3 August 2006

Student workpoint 27.3

Be a thinker. Illustrate and explain the following.

Read the data in the Bank of Italy article and, using a diagram, explain what could happen to the US dollar if central banks decided to move away from holding US dollars as foreign reserves.

Methods of correcting a persistent current account deficit
When attempting to correct a persistent current account deficit governments are able to adopt two types of policy.

Expenditure-switching policies
Expenditure-switching policies are any policies implemented by the government that attempt to switch the expenditure of domestic consumers away from imports towards domestically produced goods

and services. If successful, then expenditure on imports will fall and so the current account deficit should improve.

Examples of this type of policy are the following.

- *Government policies to depreciate or devalue the value of the currency:* If the government adopts policies that will reduce the level of the exchange rate then exports should become less expensive and imports should become more expensive. Depending upon how responsive domestic consumers and foreign consumers are to these price changes, this should see an improvement in the current account as export revenue rises and import expenditure falls.

(Higher level students should see the next section on the Marshall-Lerner condition.)

- *Protectionist measures:* The government may attempt to restrict the imports of products either by reducing their availability using embargoes, quotas, voluntary export restraints, and administrative, health and safety, and environmental barriers, or by increasing their prices using tariffs. If this happens, then domestic consumers will switch their expenditure from imports to domestic products.

However, governments are often reluctant or unable to use such measures because they tend to lead to retaliation and are often against WTO agreements. Also, protecting domestic industries reduces competition, which may encourage them to be inefficient. Therefore it is not a long-run solution.

Expenditure-reducing policies

Expenditure-reducing policies are any policies implemented by the government that attempt to reduce overall expenditure in the economy, so shifting AD to the left. If this occurs, then expenditure on all goods and services should fall and, since this would include expenditure on imports, the current account deficit should improve. The size of the fall in imports will depend upon the level of the marginal propensity to import.

However, there is a conflict here between external and internal objectives. Deflating the economy may reduce the current account deficit but the policy is likely to lead to a fall in domestic employment and a fall in the rate of economic growth. This makes it a difficult decision for a government to make.

Examples of this type of policy are the following.

- *Deflationary fiscal policies:* Increasing direct tax rates and/or reducing government expenditure. Clearly, these would be politically unpopular and a government might be reluctant to use such a policy.

- *Deflationary monetary policies:* Increasing the rate of interest and/or reducing the money supply. Interestingly, the higher interest rates should also increase capital flows from abroad, as foreigners put money into financial institutions attracted by the higher rates. This would lead to a surplus on the capital account, which helps to offset the current account deficit. This type of policy would also be politically unpopular as higher interest rates will increase people's mortgage, loan, and credit card payments.

4 International Economics

Moreover, the higher costs of borrowing as a result of higher rates of interest may act as a disincentive to domestic investment and limit potential growth.

The economic costs of reducing a large current account deficit suggest why it is important to prevent it from occurring. To avoid these costs many governments are actively pursuing export promotion policies, which may include government-run trade missions, hoping to develop new markets, and government-sponsored advertising campaigns.

The Marshall-Lerner condition

Theoretically if a country's currency depreciates or is devalued then this will lead to an increase in exports (they become less expensive in foreign markets) and a decrease in imports (they become more expensive domestically). This should result in an improvement in a country's current account, but this is not necessarily the case. We know that the effect of a price change on spending or revenues depends on price elasticity of demand. The price of exports might fall because of depreciation of the currency and, according to the law of demand, the quantity demanded will increase, but whether or not this leads to an increase in export revenues depends on foreigners' price elasticity of demand for exports. Similarly the price of imported goods will rise if a currency falls in value and, according to the law of demand, the quantity demanded will fall, but whether or not this leads to a fall in expenditure on imports depends on the price elasticity of demand for imports.

The Marshall-Lerner condition is a rule that tells us how successful a depreciation or devaluation of a currency's exchange rate will be as a means to improve a current account deficit in the balance of payments. The condition states that reducing the value of the exchange rate will only be successful if the total value of the price elasticity of demand for exports and the price elasticity of demand for imports is greater than one. It may be written as an equation, stating that a fall in exchange rate will reduce a current account deficit if

$$PED_{exports} + PED_{imports} > 1$$

This is a fairly straightforward application of the concept of elasticity of demand. If the demand for exports was price inelastic and price fell as a result of a fall in the exchange rate, then the proportionate increase in the quantity of exports demanded would be less than the proportionate decrease in the price of exports and export revenue would fall. In the same way, if the demand for imports was price-inelastic and price rose following a fall in the exchange rate, then the proportionate fall in the demand for imports would be less than the proportionate increase in the price of imports and import expenditure would actually increase. The current account deficit would become worse.

student workpoint 27.4

Be a thinker

1 Draw revenue boxes (as shown in Chapter 5) to illustrate the following:

   a the effect of a depreciation or devaluation of a currency on export revenues when the demand for exports is inelastic

   b the effect of a depreciation or devaluation of a currency on export revenues when the demand for exports is elastic

   c the effect of a depreciation or devaluation of a currency on import expenditure when the demand for imports is inelastic

   d the effect of a depreciation or devaluation of a currency on import expenditure when the demand for imports is elastic.

2 Under which of the conditions above will a current account deficit improve, i.e. become smaller?

We know that one of the determinants of elasticity of demand is the time period under consideration. Remember that demand becomes more elastic over a longer period of time. This applies to the elasticity of demand for exports and imports.

A study of trade elasticities in 2000[1] produced estimates of short-run and long-run price elasticities of demand for exports and imports for a number of countries. These are shown in Table 27.2.

Country	Short-run PED$_{exports}$	Short-run PED$_{imports}$	Total short-run PED	Long-run PED$_{exports}$	Long-run PED$_{imports}$	Total long-run PED
Canada	0.5	0.1	0.6	0.9	0.9	1.8
France	0.1	0.1	0.2	0.2	0.4	0.6
Germany	0.1	0.2	0.3	0.3	0.6	0.9
Italy	0.3	0.0	0.3	0.9	0.4	1.3
Japan	0.5	0.1	0.6	1.0	0.3	1.3
UK	0.2	0.0	0.2	1.6	0.6	2.2
US	0.5	0.6	1.1	1.5	0.3	1.8

Table 27.2 Short-run and long-run PED values in G-7 countries

The figures show the following.

1 In almost all cases the short-run elasticity values are lower than the long-run values. This is exactly what we would expect to find from the theory stated in Chapter 5, which tells us that price elasticity values increase over time.

2 Only the US would meet the Marshall-Lerner condition in the short run, but all countries, other than France and Germany, meet the condition in the long run.

[1] *Trade elasticities for the G-7 countries*, Hooper, Johnson & Marquez, Princeton Studies in International Economics, No.87, August 2000

The J-curve

If a government is facing a current account deficit, it may reduce the exchange rate of its currency in order to make exports relatively less expensive and imports relatively more expensive. If this happens and the Marshall-Lerner condition is satisfied, i.e.

$$PED_{exports} + PED_{imports} > 1$$

then we would expect an improvement in the current account deficit.

However in the short run this is not the case and the current account deficit actually gets worse before it gets better. This is known as the J-curve effect. The J-curve shows what happens to a current account deficit over time when the exchange rate is devalued or depreciated. It is shown in Figure 27.1.

Let us assume that a country's current account deficit is at X and the government lowers the exchange rate.

The price of exports will fall, but communication is not perfect and it will take time for other countries to realize that the prices in this country have fallen. Also, other countries will have entered into contracts for goods and services that cannot be broken quickly, so they cannot change their suppliers immediately. This means that, in the short run, the PED for exports will be inelastic and export revenue will fall as prices have fallen by proportionately more than demand will have risen. This will increase the current account deficit and start moving from X to Y on the J-curve.

In the same way the price of imports will rise but purchasers of imports will take time to find new suppliers. Also, they may be tied into contracts and will have to wait for them to expire before they can move to other suppliers. This means that, in the short run, the PED for imports will also be inelastic and import expenditure will increase, as prices have risen by proportionately more than demand will have fallen. This will further increase the current account deficit and add to the movement from X to Y on the J-curve.

As we saw in Table 27.2, the value of PED for exports and imports increases with time. By the time that the current account deficit reaches the point Y, the values of PED for exports and imports have increased to the point where, when added together, they are greater than one so the Marshall-Lerner condition is satisfied. From this point onwards the less expensive exports and more expensive imports should lead to increased export revenue and decreased import expenditure and therefore an improvement in the current account balance, as shown by the movement from Y towards Z on the J-curve.

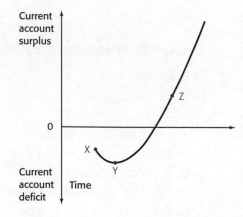

Figure 27.1 The J-curve

Student workpoint 27.5

Be a thinker

Use the data in Table 27.2 to answer this question.

If Japan was experiencing a current account deficit and brought about a fall in the value of the yen, what would you expect to happen to the deficit:

1 in the short run? Why?

2 in the long run? Why?

Student workpoint 27.6

Be an inquirer

Research the balance of payments position of the country that you studied earlier. Consider the following questions.

● Does it have a current account surplus or deficit?

● How is the balance distributed between the visible balance and invisible balance?

● Can you explain why there is a surplus or deficit? (If there is a deficit, you may be able to link this to the business cycle. If there is a surplus, it may be due to the type of goods that it exports.)

● Is this surplus or deficit of a worrying level? Why or why not?

● If there is a deficit, how is it being financed?

Examination questions

Short response questions

1 Explain the components of a country's balance of payments.   *[10 marks]*

2 Using a diagram, explain why a current account deficit might result in a depreciation of a country's currency.   *[10 marks]*

3 With the help of a diagram, explain the link between the Marshall-Lerner condition and the J-curve.   *[10 marks]*

Essay question

1 **a** Explain the disadvantages associated with a current account deficit.   *[10 marks]*

   b Evaluate the methods available to a government wishing to reduce its current account deficit.   *[15 marks]*

HL

Data response exercise

Read the following article and answer the questions that follow.

DOLLAR FALLS TO ALL-TIME LOW AGAINST EURO

The dollar fell sharply everywhere yesterday, hitting an all-time low against the euro. The euro traded as high as $1.2018—above $1.20 for the first time—as the dollar fell to new lows against the UK pound and the Canadian dollar, and a six-month low against the Swiss franc.

Yesterday's fall added to the massive selling of the US dollar, which has dropped by 14 per cent against the euro so far this year. The financial markets are growing increasingly concerned that the US will not be able to attract enough investment to finance its exploding current account deficit, which is at record levels.

Lehman Brothers was the latest Wall Street bank to take a pessimistic view, warning its

clients that the dollar remained "unattractive", because the Federal Reserve (the Fed) has been keeping interest rates so low. "By insisting that rates remain at historic lows, the central bank has only added to the doubts about the US recovery. If on the other hand, the Fed begins hinting that rates will head higher than we think, it could prove an important turning point for market confidence in the US—maybe not enough to turn the **exchange rate** trend, but certainly enough to slow it down."

Yesterday the UK pound rose to a fresh five-year high of $1.7238, its strongest since October 1989. The pound has risen 1.6 per cent against the dollar since the Bank of England raised interest rates. Most of the burden of the

dollar's **depreciation** has fallen on the euro as the major Asian economies have defended their currencies against any appreciation. China's renminbi is pegged to the dollar and the Chinese administration has rejected suggestions from the White House that the Chinese allow the currency to rise.

Japan, which is struggling with a decade-long downturn, has repeatedly intervened to prevent the yen from rising. Their fear is that a high-valued yen will further depress the Japanese economy. It has spent a record ¥17.8 trillion (£95.9 billion) so far this year on keeping the yen down.

Adapted from original articles that appeared in *The Independent*, November 2003

1 Define the following terms indicated in bold in the text:
   a exchange rate [2 marks]
   b depreciation. [2 marks]
2 With the help of an appropriate diagram, explain **one** reason for the fall in the value of the US dollar. [4 marks]
3 With the help of an AD/AS diagram, explain why Japan fears a "high-valued yen". [4 marks]
4 Evaluate two methods that the US government might use to correct its "exploding current account deficit". [8 marks]

N05 economics SL P2, q5

By the end of this chapter, you should be able to:

- define, explain, calculate, and give examples of the terms of trade
- distinguish between an improvement and a deterioration in the terms of trade

HL

- explain the causes of changes in the terms of trade
- define and explain the price elasticity of demand for exports
- define and explain the price elasticity of demand for imports
- explain the possible effects of an improvement in the terms of trade on the current account balance
- explain the significance of deteriorating terms of trade for developing countries.

In the previous chapter, we looked at the concept of the balance of trade, specifically referring to the balance of trade in visible goods. We now introduce a new concept called the terms of trade. It is very important to note that students often confuse these two terms, but they are very different concepts. The significant issue in discussing the terms of trade is that it is one of the big problems facing many developing countries. This does not simply mean that they face obstacles in the international trading system; it has a very specific meaning in context.

Mathematically, the terms of trade is an index that shows the value of a country's average export prices relative to their average import prices. It is calculated with a simple equation:

$$\text{terms of trade (TOT)} = \frac{\text{Weighted index of average export prices}}{\text{Weighted index of average import prices}} \times 100$$

The indices of export and import prices are weighted to reflect the relative importance of different goods and services to the country's export revenue and import expenditure. Table 28.1 shows some possible different situations over five years.

We use the values in Table 28.1 to explain what the TOT index actually represents. Year 1 is the base year so the value is set at 100. In year 2, export prices rise and import prices stay where they are and so the value of the TOT rises to 102. We say that this is an improvement in the TOT. This means that, on average, the country's exports will now buy 2% more imports than they did in the previous year. In Year 3, although export prices rise again the increase in import prices is relatively more great and so the TOT value falls a little to 101.92. We say that there has been a deterioration in the TOT, which means that a given amount of

Year	Index of average export prices	Index of average import prices	Calculation	Terms of trade
Year 1	100	100	$\frac{100}{100}$ X 100	100
Year 2	102	100	$\frac{102}{100}$ X 100	102
Year 3	106	104	$\frac{106}{104}$ X 100	101.92
Year 4	110	110	$\frac{110}{110}$ X 100	100
Year 5	108	106	$\frac{108}{106}$ X 100	101.89
Year 6	106	108	?	?

Table 28.1 Terms of trade figures

exports can buy fewer imports than in year 2. However, the TOT in year 3 are still better than in year 1. In year 4, import prices rise by relatively more than export prices and so the value of the TOT falls again, back to 100. So in year 4 a given amount of exports will buy the same amount of imports as in year 1. In year 5 export prices fall but import prices fall by more, which this leads to an improvement in the TOT and the value rises to 101.89.

We can see from the example that if export prices rise relative to import prices, or if they fall by relatively less than import prices fall, then the TOT will improve. In the same way, if import prices rise by more than export prices, or if they fall by relatively less than export prices fall, then the TOT will deteriorate.

The key thing to realise is that if the TOT improve, then a given quantity of exports will buy a larger quantity of imports than before. We often talk about a "basket" of exports, in the same way as measuring inflation. If the price of a basket of exports falls, then a country will need to sell more exports in order to keep imports at the same level.

Student workpoint 28.1

Be a thinker

1 Using the data in Table 28.1, calculate the TOT for year 6.
2 Describe the changes in the TOT from year 5. What does this mean about the "buying power" of the country's exports?
3 How does the buying power of the country's exports in year 6 compare with year 1?

Theory of Knowledge

Language may be misleading. It should be noted that the expressions "improvement in the TOT" and "deterioration of the TOT" do not **necessarily** mean what they mean in everyday language. A deterioration of the TOT may not necessarily be a bad thing and an improvement does not necessarily result in a good thing. We will look at the consequences of changes in the TOT in future material.

While language is used to access knowledge it can sometimes be used to confuse or even exclude. Can you think of other examples of economic language that would make it difficult for non-economists to know what economists are talking about?

HL: Causes of changes in a country's terms of trade in the short run and the long run

Short-run causes

Short-run changes in the TOT may be caused by the following.

- Changes in the conditions of demand and supply—if the demand for exports changes, i.e. if the demand curve shifts, then there will be a change in the price of exports. Prices of competitive goods in other countries may change, affecting the competitiveness of the exports, incomes in importing countries may change, affecting the demand for imports, and consumer tastes may change for the goods and services that the country exports.

  Changes in supply may also have a noticeable effect upon the price of exports. If a number of countries experience an increased supply of a certain product, perhaps because weather conditions are favourable, then its price will fall. For example, record wine harvests in Australia led to a 9% fall in average prices in 2006. The effect of such a change on the TOT depends on the importance of overall exports of the good.

- Changes in relative inflation rates—if the inflation rates in one country are higher than in another then their export prices will begin to rise. Although this results in an improvement in the TOT, the country's exports will start to be less competitive.

- Changes in exchange rates—a change in the value of a country's currency will lead to a change in the price of exports relative to imports. The change in exchange rate may be through market forces, or as a result of government intervention in the foreign exchange market.

Long-run causes

Long-run changes in the TOT have various causes.

- Income changes—rising incomes, especially in developed countries, lead to an increase in demand for secondary and, especially, tertiary products, whose income elasticity of demand tends to be income elastic. This has an obvious effect upon the relative prices of the types of products. The TOT of developed countries, which produce more secondary and tertiary products, tend to improve relative to the TOT of developing countries, many of whom are much more dependent upon the exporting of primary products, whose income elasticity tends to be income-inelastic. In effect, there is a change in world trade patterns.

● Long-run improvements in productivity within a country will lead to a gradual deterioration of the TOT for that country because their real prices will not rise significantly. However, the country's exports would be more competitive on the international markets and so the result could be positive, if demand for the exports is elastic.

Elasticity of demand for imports and exports

As you now realize, the concept of elasticity is very important in economics. It is extremely relevant to our discussion of the TOT. We need to go back to a discussion about the price elasticity of demand for exports and imports in Chapter 27 to make an effective analysis of TOT changes.

Price elasticity of demand for exports

As we know, the price elasticity of demand for exports is a measure of the responsiveness of the demand for exports when there is a change in the price of exports. It is measured by the equation:

$$PED_{exports} = \frac{\text{Percentage change in demand for exports}}{\text{Percentage change in average price of exports}}$$

If the demand for exports is elastic, then a change in the average price of exports will lead to a greater proportional change in the demand for them. This would be good for a country where export prices were falling, since export demand would rise by proportionately more than the prices fell leading to an increase in export revenues. Most exports, certainly in the long run, face elastic demand, i.e. a value of $PED_{exports}$ that is greater than 1. However, many commodities (raw materials such as oil, copper, coffee, cotton, steel, rice, sugar, and rubber) tend to have inelastic demand.

● ● ● ● ● ● ● ● ● ● ● ● ● ● ● ● ● ●

Student workpoint 28.2

Be a thinker

Draw a revenue box diagram to show and explain the effect of falling average export prices on export revenues when demand for exports is inelastic. On the y-axis, write "Average price of exports".

Price elasticity of demand for imports

The price elasticity of demand for imports is a measure of the responsiveness of the demand for imports when there is a change in the price of imports. It is measured by the equation:

$$PED_{imports} = \frac{\text{Percentage change in demand for imports}}{\text{Percentage change in average price of imports}}$$

If the demand for imports is inelastic, then a change in the price of imports will lead to a smaller proportional change in the demand for them. This would not be good for a country where import prices were rising, since import demand would fall by proportionately more than the prices increased. Most imports, certainly in the long run, face elastic demand, i.e. a value of PED$_{imports}$ that is greater than 1. However, commodities tend to have inelastic demand.

Student workpoint 28.3

Be a thinker

Draw a revenue box diagram to show and explain the effect of rising average import prices on export expenditure when demand for exports is inelastic. Label the y-axis "Average price of imports".

How beneficial is an improvement in the terms of trade?

As noted earlier, an improvement in the TOT is not necessarily a good thing. We need to consider the effect of an improvement in the TOT on a country's current account balance. The outcome will depend upon the reason for the improvement. Possible reasons for improvement include the following.

An increase in demand for a country's exports

A number of factors may cause demand for a country's exports to rise. Consider the exports from country A. Prices in other countries may have risen, making country A's exports more competitive; incomes in importing countries may have risen, increasing their demand for imports and so increasing demand for country A's exports; and consumer tastes may have changed in favour of the goods and services that country A exports.

An increase in the demand for country A's exports is shown in Figure 28.1.

When the demand increases the average export price rises from P to P$_1$. The quantity of exports demanded and supplied increases from Q to Q$_1$. The higher export prices mean that the TOT have improved, and total export revenue rises from 0PxQ to 0P$_1$yQ$_1$. This will lead in turn to an improvement in the current account balance. We can say that:

● An improvement in the TOT, when caused by an increase in demand for exports, leads to an improvement in the current account balance.

Higher export prices caused by domestic inflation

Relative export prices may increase because a country is experiencing inflation that is higher than in the countries with which it trades. If this is the case then there will be an improvement in the TOT. Whether this improvement in the TOT leads to an improvement in the current account balance will depend upon the elasticity of demand for the country's exports. The situation is shown in Figure 28.2.

Figure 28.1 An increase in demand for exports

The demand curve for exports is normal and has the usual relationship with the MR curve and the TR curve. As we know from microeconomics, the value of price elasticity of demand on a demand curve falls as the price falls. There will be an elastic region of the demand curve and an inelastic region. These are shown in Figure 28.2.

If the demand for exports is inelastic, i.e. price is on the lower part of the demand curve, then an increase in price will lead to a proportionately smaller decrease in demand and so total export revenue will rise. As we see in the diagram, an increase in price from P to P_1 leads to an increase in export revenue from ER to ER_1. This will improve the current account balance.

Therefore we can say that:

● An improvement in the terms of trade, when caused by inflation, leads to an improvement in the current account balance when the demand for exports is inelastic.

If the demand for exports is elastic, i.e. price is on the upper part of the demand curve, then an increase in price will lead to a proportionately greater decrease in demand and so total export revenue will fall. As we see in the diagram, an increase in price from P_2 to P_3 leads to a fall in export revenue from ER_2 to ER_3. This will depreciate the current account balance. We can say that:

● An improvement in the terms of trade when caused by inflation leads to a depreciation in the current account balance when the demand for exports is relatively elastic.

When we compare this situation to the real world, we notice two things.

1 The price elasticity of demand for most exports tends to be elastic. For the majority of products sold on export markets, there is much competition between countries and so demand tends to be elastic. It is generally commodities that face inelastic demand, so it is likely that most countries will be on the elastic part of the demand curve for their exports.

2 Even if demand is on the inelastic part of the demand curve, if relatively high inflation rates continue then the price of exports will eventually move into the elastic region of the demand curve.

Overall, an improvement in the terms of trade due to inflation generally leads to a depreciation in the current account balance.

The significance of deteriorating TOT for developing countries

We know that there are vast differences among developing countries. Many developing countries, but certainly not all, are heavily dependent upon the exports of one or two commodities for their export revenue. This is illustrated in Table 28.2.

We see that for the first five countries listed the dependence upon the export of primary commodities as compared to the export of

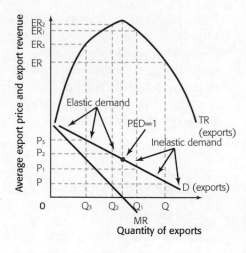

Figure 28.2 The demand for exports and export revenue

Country	Primary commodities			Manufactures			Total
	Unprocessed	Processed	Total	Low-skill	High-skill	Total	
Benin*	89.6	6.6	96.3	3.0	0.8	3.7	100
Chad*	94.9	1.4	96.3	0.6	3.2	3.7	100
Ethiopia*	82.7	6.5	89.2	5.7	5.1	10.8	100
Mali*	97.3	1.2	98.5	0.9	0.6	1.5	100
Uganda*	90.8	4.8	95.6	1.6	2.8	4.4	100
Angola**	97.6	1.9	99.4	0.2	0.3	0.6	100
Yemen**	91.4	8.1	99.4	0.2	0.3	0.6	100
Bangladesh†	9.5	0.3	9.9	87.8	2.4	90.1	100
Nepal†	6.3	1.8	8.1	88.7	3.2	91.9	100
Cape Verde‡	15.6	6.8	22.4	77.5	0.1	77.6	100
Maldives‡	32.2	16.1	48.4	48.7	2.9	51.6	100

Source: UNCTAD secretariat estimates

* Non-oil commodity exporting LDC † Manufactures exporting LDC

** Oil exporting LDC ‡ Services exporting LDC

Table 28.2 Share of primary commodities and manufactures in total merchandise exports, for selected LDCs, 1997–1999 (%)

manufactured products is very strong. For example, 94.9% of all Chad's merchandise export earnings come from the sale of unprocessed primary commodities. Uganda earns 90.8% of its merchandise export earnings by exporting primary commodities. Notice the difference between the first five countries and the next two, as noted in the key. The first five are known as "non-oil exporting LDCs", while Angola and Yemen are characterised as "oil exporting LDCs". There are two other categories of developing countries shown in the table. These are "manufactures exporting LDCs" such as Bangladesh and Nepal and "services exporting LDCs" such as Cape Verde and the Maldives. The problems facing different groups of LDCs come from different sources. We are focusing here on the problems facing those developing countries that are dependent on the export of non-oil commodities as some of the barriers to their growth and development are related to their terms of trade.

Did you know?

"As many as 43 developing countries depend on a single commodity for more than 20% of their total revenues from merchandise exports. Most of these countries are in sub-Saharan Africa or Latin America and the Caribbean and depend on exports of sugar, coffee, cotton and bananas. Most suffer from widespread poverty."

"Agriculture commodity prices continue long-term decline". Food and Agriculture Organization of the UN. 15 February 2005

4 International Economics

4 International Economics

Student workpoint 28.4

Be an inquirer

Create a table to list five countries that are dependent on a few (non-oil) commodities for a large proportion of their export revenues, the commodities they produce, and the share of export revenues earned from each of the commodities.

There has been a long-run downward trend in commodity prices for many years caused by a number of factors.

● There have been substantial increases in the supply of commodities, mostly caused by improvements in technology. For example, there have been huge improvements in agricultural yields over the last 100 years, caused by better fertilizers, high degrees of mechanisation, and scientific research into plant disease. Technology has also allowed for the discovery of more minerals and also for more efficient mineral extraction.

● The discovery of synthetic replacements for natural commodities, such as synthetic rubber, man-made fabrics, and plastics replacing metals, has contributed to the slow increase in demand for the natural commodities concerned.

● As developed countries have become richer and incomes have risen, the demand for commodities has not greatly changed, because their demand is income inelastic. At the same time, as incomes rise, the demand for manufactured goods and services has increased. Demand for such goods tends to be more income elastic. This means that the demand for commodities has not risen as much as the demand for other products.

● Agricultural policies in developed countries have had a damaging effect on world agricultural markets. Price support schemes in the EU and the US, for example, have led to relatively high prices there and over-production by domestic producers. These subsidies have also led to over-production. The over-production is then sold on the world markets, pushing down agricultural prices. For these reasons, developing countries often accuse the developed economies of 'dumping' agricultural products on the world market and so ruining their own agricultural industries.

● With huge leaps in technology over the last 50 years, many products have become smaller. For example, computers that once took up a whole room are now replaced by laptop computers of the same power; large tape recorders, the size of a suitcase, are now replaced by MP3 players the size of a cigarette lighter; and televisions, which were once housed in large cabinets, are now replaced by flat screens that require no such housing. This miniaturisation of many products and the improvement in plastics technology has led to a fall in the demand for the commodities that were traditionally used to make and package these products.

The effect of the above factors on the average price of commodities over time is shown in Figure 28.3.

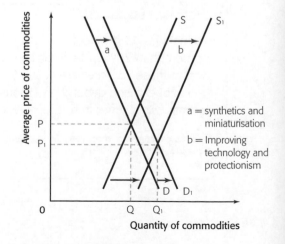

Figure 28.3 Falling world commodity prices

We would not want to imply that there has been a fall in demand for commodities. However, the combination of low income elasticity of demand, the increased use of synthetic substitutes, and miniaturisation have led to relatively small increases in demand, shown as a in Figure 28.3. Improvements in technology along with the agricultural policies in more developed countries have resulted in large increases in supply, shown as b in Figure 28.3. The result is that average commodity prices have fallen. This is highlighted in Figure 28.4.

Given that the TOT index is based on a weighted average of export prices, those countries that are dependent on commodities will see a fall in the index of their export prices and deterioration in their terms of trade.

The deterioration in their TOT results in depreciating current account deficits. This is because the demand for commodities tends to be inelastic. For example, although the demand for copper from Zambia is likely to be elastic as there are alternative sources of copper, demand for copper as a whole is inelastic as it is a necessary mineral in production with few substitutes. This can be said about most commodities. If you refer back to the revenue box diagram you drew in workpoint 28.2, you will see that the fall in average export prices when demand is inelastic results in a fall in export revenues.

We should also look at the effect on imports. With falling export prices, the price of imports has risen relative to the price of exports. The goods that developing countries need to import are necessities such as raw materials, components, and other capital goods. Because these are not available domestically and are required for economic growth, demand for them is inelastic. If you look back to the revenue box diagram you drew in workpoint 28.3, you will see that a rise in import prices when demand for import is inelastic results in an increase in import expenditure.

The deterioration in the TOT for developing countries that depend on commodities has several harmful consequences.

- Developing countries have to sell more and more exports in order to buy the same amount of imports. This is harmful enough, but in order to do this the developing countries then increase supply and this tends to push commodity prices down even more. We have a vicious circle.

- Many developing countries have high levels of indebtedness. Falling export prices and thus export revenue make it harder to service their debt. Indeed, in extreme cases, this leads to countries having to increase their borrowing and increasing their levels of indebtedness. This vicious circle links to the previous one. In order to pay back their debts, many countries have to increase their output of the commodities in which they have a comparative advantage. This increases the supply and drives the prices down.

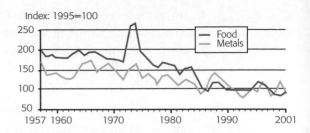

Figure 28.4 Falling commodity prices

● In order to increase the supply of commodities and gain more export revenue, some developing countries have overused their resources, resulting in negative externalities such as land degradation, desertification, soil erosion, and massive deforestation. This is clearly not sustainable in the long run.

While there is no doubt that the long-run trend in commodity prices has been downward over the last 50 years, there has been a short-run upward movement in the last few years, shown in Table 28.3.

Indices of primary commodity prices 1997–2005 (1995 = 100)							
Year	All primary commodities, weighted average (1)	Petroleum (2)	Non-fuel (3)	Edibles (4)	Agricultural raw materials (5)	Metals (6)	Industrial inputs (7)
1995	100.0	100.0	100.0	100.0	100.0	100.0	100.0
1997	102.4	112.0	95.4	100.7	91.7	89.8	90.6
1998	79.4	76.0	81.7	89.3	76.5	73.8	74.9
1999	87.5	104.5	75.8	77.0	77.4	73.0	74.8
2000	116.2	164.1	79.4	77.2	80.8	81.9	81.5
2001	105.6	141.4	75.5	76.0	76.8	73.9	75.1
2002	105.9	145.0	76.8	79.5	78.2	71.9	74.5
2003	119.7	167.9	82.1	83.6	81.1	80.6	80.8
2004	151.5	219.5	97.3	94.6	85.6	109.7	99.8
2005	195.7	310.1	107.3	96.1	86.9	138.7	117.4

Source: International Monetary Fund

Table 28.3 Real primary commodity prices (1997–2005)

From 1995 to 2001 there was a fall in the index of all primary commodities (column 1). Breaking the index into different categories of commodities, we see that the only increase in prices during the period was for petroleum prices (column 2), which itself experienced a fall from 1997 to 1998. Since 2001, however, there has been an upward movement in all commodity prices. To some extent petroleum will have heavily influenced the index, but it can be seen that since 2001 there have been upward movements in "Non-fuel" prices in general and "Edibles" and "Agricultural raw materials". Since 2002 "Metals" and "Industrial inputs" have also seen price increases, although they remain below their 1995 value. Increased commodity prices are largely a result of a growing world economy along with increased demand from rapidly growing economies such as China and India. Whatever the reasons, it may give some short-term help to commodity-exporting developing countries, although whether the commodity price increases will be sustained in the long run is uncertain.

The data also illustrate another problem for such countries. Commodity prices tend to be quite volatile. As a result, commodity-exporting countries are quite vulnerable to circumstances beyond their control. The fact that export revenues can fluctuate significantly can make it difficult for governments to plan effectively for the future.

At the outset, we emphasized that not all developing countries are the same, and we have focused on the problem facing countries that depend on commodities. If we look back at Table 28.2, we can also make a link between deteriorating TOT and another group of developing countries—the countries that are classified as manufactures exporting LDCs such as Bangladesh and Nepal. Both of these countries depend heavily for their export revenues on the export of low-skill produced textiles, whose prices are also dropping, so they also experience deteriorating terms of trade.

If we turn to one more group of developing countries, the oil exporters, we may assume that they have benefited from rising petroleum prices. Given the fact that demand for oil/petroleum is inelastic, we can conclude that their export revenues will have increased. Whether or not this has been translated into economic development is quite a different issue.

Examination questions

Short response questions

HL

1 Distinguish between the balance of trade and the terms of trade. *[10 marks]*

2 Explain how high inflation is likely to affect a country's terms of trade in the short run and in the long run. *[10 marks]*

3 Explain how a deterioration in a country's terms of trade will affect its trade balance if the demand for its exports and imports is elastic. *[10 marks]*

Essay question

1 a Explain what is meant by a deterioration in a country's terms of trade. *[10 marks]*

   b Evaluate the significance for less developed countries of a deterioration in their terms of trade. *[15 marks]*

Assessment advice: critical awareness

If you answer a question about developing countries, you really need to show critical awareness by noting that you are aware of the differences that exist among them. This should become more and more clear in the next chapters.

4 International Economics

29 Characteristics of developing countries

By the end of this chapter, you should be able to:

- explain and give examples of common characteristics of developing countries
- define and explain dependency ratios
- explain and give examples of the diversity that exists between developing countries.

Development economics is an extremely important part of the wider study of economics. In 1999, the United Nations estimated that 80% of the world's population of six billion people lived in poor countries. We have touched on development throughout this Course Companion, especially in Chapter 15 and in the chapters on international trade, and now we are going to consider the topic in more detail.

At the end of Chapter 15, you were asked to investigate the Millennium Development Goals and pick two countries to study in terms of their progress in meeting these goals. At the end of this chapter, you will be asked to continue that investigation so that you can build your own case studies of two developing countries.

You should already know the difference between economic growth and economic development (Chapter 15), but now, as a starting point to this section, we need to consider what makes a country a "developing country".

Common characteristics of developing countries

It would be useful to know if all developing countries displayed the same characteristics. If they do, then it would be easy to classify them and easier to solve the problems that they face. The development economist, Michael P. Todaro, produced a list of the common characteristics of developing nations[1]. He said that the common characteristics could be classified into seven broad categories.

1 *Low standards of living, characterized by low incomes, inequality, poor health, and inadequate education:* In developing countries, low standards of living tend to be experienced by the majority of the population. The main indicators of these low living standards are high poverty levels (i.e. very low incomes), high levels of inequality, very poor housing, low standards of health, high infant mortality rates, high levels of malnutrition, and lack of education.

2 *Low levels of productivity (output per person):* These are common in developing countries. The main causes are the low education standards within the countries, the low levels of health among workers, lack of investment in physical capital, and lack of access to technology.

5 Development Economics

[1] Michael P. Todaro, *Economic Development*, 7th edition, Addison Wesley Longman, 2000

3 *High rates of population growth and dependency burdens:* Developing countries tend to have crude birth rates that on average are more than double the rates in developed countries. The crude birth rate is the annual number of live births per 1,000 of the population. The world average in 2005 was 20.15, but in some developing countries it can be as high as 50 per thousand; for example, in September 2005 it was 51.33 in Niger and 49.99 in Mali. Most developed countries tend to have figures below 15 per thousand and some are well below, such as Japan, with 9.47 and Austria, with 8.81[2].

High crude birth rates in developing countries tend to be transformed into high dependency ratios. The high crude birth rates mean that there are a lot of young people under the age of 15 in developing countries. Those of working age, usually assumed to be 15 to 64, thus have to support a much larger proportion of children than does the work force in developed countries. However, interestingly, developed countries also have high numbers of the population over the age of 64, who also need to be supported by the work force. The dependency ratio is the percentage of those who are non-productive, usually those who are under 15 and over 64, expressed as a percentage of those of working age, usually 15 to 64. The equation would be:

$$\text{Dependency ratio} = \frac{(\% \text{ of population under 15}) + (\% \text{ of population over 64})}{(\% \text{ of population 15 to 64})}$$

Country	% aged under 15	% aged over 64	% aged 15–64	Dependency ratio
Australia	20.3	10.7	69.0	0.45
France	18.3	14.5	67.2	0.49
US	21.1	10.7	68.2	0.47
Bolivia	38.8	3.6	57.6	0.74
Botswana	38.2	2.6	59.2	0.69
Burkina Faso	47.7	2.3	50.0	1.00
Cambodia	38.3	2.8	58.9	0.70
Laos	41.7	2.9	55.4	0.81

Source: Adapted from Table 5 of UNDP Human Development Report 2005, (Columns 4 & 5—OUP 2007)

Table 29.1 Examples of dependency ratios in developed and developing countries (all figures are for 2003)

As we can see in Table 29.1, the three developed countries have dependency ratios of about 0.47 and they have significant percentages of the population over the age of 64 (and these are predicted to continue to grow). The developing countries have much higher dependency ratios and the main cause is the very high percentage of the population below the age of 15. The low percentages above the age of 64 serve to highlight the low levels of life expectancy in developing countries, as opposed to developed countries.

4 *High and rising levels of unemployment and underemployment:* Developing countries tend to have relatively high rates of unemployment, typically between 9% and 16% of the labour force. Although it is a difficult thing to measure accurately in a developed economy, let alone a developing economy, some estimated figures are shown in Table 29.2.

---

[2] Source: *World Factbook* 2005, CIA, US

Country	Unemployment rate %
Botswana	23.8
Brazil	9.0
Colombia	11.8
Georgia	12.6
Indonesia	11.8
Tonga	13.0

Source: The World Factbook, CIA, 2005

Table 29.2 Unemployment rates for selected developing countries

Although the unemployment figures in developing countries are problematic enough, there are three more groups that need to be considered. First, there are those who have been unemployed for so long that they have given up searching for a job and no longer appear as unemployed. Second, there are the hidden unemployed, those who work for a few hours in the day on a family farm or in a family business or trade of some sort, and so do not appear as unemployed. Then, lastly, there are the underemployed—those who would like full-time work but are only able to get part-time employment, often on an informal basis. It is when all of these groups are put together that the full extent of unemployment in developing countries can begin to be understood. It is impossible to be accurate, but it would be fair to say that in many developing countries the true rate of unemployment is over 40%. When we consider high birth rates, as discussed earlier, then the situation is only likely to become worse.

5 *Substantial dependence on agricultural production and primary product exports:* We have already discussed the over-dependence of developing countries on primary product exports in Chapter 28, when we were considering the significance of deteriorating terms of trade for developing countries.

6 *Prevalence of imperfect markets and limited information:* The trend in developing countries in the last 20 years has been towards a more market-oriented approach to growth. This has sometimes been promoted, or "encouraged", by international bodies such as the International Monetary Fund and the World Bank. However, this is possibly problematic, since while market-based approaches may work well in economies where markets are efficiently functioning, many developing countries face imperfect markets and imperfect knowledge.

Developing countries lack many of the necessary factors that enable markets to work efficiently. They lack a functioning banking system, which enables and encourages savings and then investment. They lack a developed legal system, which ensures that business takes place in a fair and structured manner. They lack adequate infrastructure, especially in terms of transport routes of all types, which would enable raw materials, semi-finished products, and final goods, to move around the country, and to be moved out of the country, efficiently and at relatively low cost. They lack accurate information systems for both producers and consumers, which often leads to imperfect information, the misallocation of resources, and misinformed purchasing decisions.

7 *Dominance, dependence, and vulnerability in international relations:* In almost all cases, developing countries are dominated by developed countries because of the economic and political power of the developed countries. In addition, they are dependent upon them for many things, such as trade, access to technology, aid, and investment. It is not really possible for economically small, developing countries, to isolate themselves from world markets. For these reasons, developing countries are vulnerable on the international stage, and are dominated by, and often harmed by, the decisions of developed countries over which they have no control. Some would argue that what is needed is for the developing countries to act as a bloc, rather like a trade union, in order to gain from "collective bargaining". We will consider this strategy in Chapter 32.

All of the above factors are characteristics of developing economies and are also hindrances to economic growth and, possibly, economic development.

Diversity among developing countries

As useful as a list of common characteristics is, we have to be aware that no two developing countries are the same. Developing countries display notable diversity in a number of areas.

1 *Resource endowment:* There is a tendency to assume that developing countries must be poorly endowed with resources, both physical and human. However, this is not necessarily the case. While it is common for the human resources to be undernourished and poorly educated and thus low-skilled (we may refer to this as low levels of human capital), endowment in terms of physical resources can vary immensely between developing countries. Angola possesses oil and diamonds, and yet is still very much a developing country. Chad had been considered a country that lacked physical resources, but the discovery of oil and subsequent production since 2003 may make a large difference to the country. Bangladesh, on the other hand, is very poorly endowed with physical resources and synthetic products have now replaced the one major resource that they did have, jute. It should be remembered, however, that a lack of physical resources does not necessarily mean that a country cannot be successful. Japan is not well endowed with physical resources, and Singapore has almost literally none, yet both countries have created "economic miracles" in the last 50 years.

2 *Historical background:* A large proportion of developing countries were once colonies of developed countries. However, the extent to which this has affected these countries varies greatly. Much depends upon for how long the countries were colonized and whether the eventual independence was given freely or whether it had to be fought for. It could be argued that some countries gained some positive outcomes from colonization, such as Singapore and Hong Kong, and some countries did not, such as Vietnam and Angola.

Colonized or not, there is no doubt that whatever developing countries we consider, there will be marked historical differences that will set the countries apart from each other socially, politically, and economically.

● ●

Student workpoint 29.1

Be an inquirer

Find out which European countries held colonies and make a list of the places that each country colonized. Better yet, if possible, get a world map and colour in the places that were colonized according to their colonial powers.

3 *Geographic and demographic factors:* Developing countries differ hugely in terms of geographical size and also in terms of population size. Some developing countries are truly huge, such as China, Brazil, India, and the Democratic Republic of the Congo, whereas others are very small in terms of land mass, such as Swaziland, Jamaica, and, especially, Nauru.

Did you know?

- The country Nauru is the world's smallest island nation.
- It covers 21 km^2.
- It is the smallest independent republic in the world.
- It is the only republican state in the world without an official capital.

Be knowledgeable

Now you find out more about Nauru!

In terms of population, it is a common mistake to assume that all developing countries have large populations. This is not the case. Developing country populations range from China (approx. 1300 million in 2003), India (approx. 1070 million in 2003), and Indonesia (approx. 217 million in 2003), three of the four most populated countries in the world, at one end of the spectrum, down to East Timor, Fiji, and Djibouti, who all have populations of less than one million people.

4 *Ethnic and religious breakdown:* Developing countries have a wide range of ethnic and religious diversity. High levels of ethnic and religious diversity within a country make it more likely that there will be political unrest and internal conflict. We have seen examples of this in Rwanda, Sri Lanka, Ethiopia, and Angola in the last 20 years. Examples of developing countries that are more ethnically and religiously homogeneous would be Egypt, Morocco, and Jamaica.

5 *The structure of industry:* It is widely assumed that all developing countries depend upon the production and exporting of primary products. While this may be true of many we should not forget the evidence that was presented in Table 28.2. Developing countries such as Ethiopia and Uganda may be typical of many in terms of primary product export dependence, but other countries, such as Bangladesh and Nepal, are exporters of manufactured products, and others, such as Cape Verde and the Maldives, are actually mainly exporters of services, in the form of tourism.

6 *Per capita income levels:* Although it is often thought that all developing countries have very low levels of income per capita, we should be aware that there are marked differences in per capita income from developing country to developing country. Table 29.3 shows a range of developing countries and their GDP per capita (PPP US$).

Country	HDI rank	GDP per capita (PPP US$)
Malaysia	61	9,512
Mauritius	65	11,287
Thailand	73	7,595
Jamaica	98	4,104
Yemen	151	889
Ethiopia	170	711
Sierra Leone	176	548

Source: Adapted from Tables 1 & 14 of UNDP Human Development Report, 2005

Table 29.3 GDP per capita (PPP US$) for selected developing countries in 2005

7 *Political structure:* Developing countries have very different political structures from each other. There are a number of structures:

● democracies, such as Brazil, Indonesia, and Mexico

● monarchies, such as Brunei and Tonga

● military rule, such as Myanmar and Pakistan

● single party states, such as China, Cuba, and Syria

● theocracies, such as Iran

● transitional political systems, where a country is in transition, often caused by conflict and civil war, and so cannot be classified, such as Haiti and Somalia.

Within each of these structures, there are of course many sub-structures. For example, democracies may be presidential systems, semi-presidential systems, parliamentary republics, or constitutional monarchies. The main point is that with developing countries being so diverse in their systems of government, it is very difficult to establish one-size-fits-all solutions to developmental problems.

In conclusion, we can say that while there are some common characteristics that are held by developing countries to a certain degree, there are also several significant differences. One must be very cautious in making generalizations that imply that all developing countries are the same.

5 Development Economics

student workpoint 29.2

Be an inquirer

Pick one country in the low HDI category, one country in the medium HDI category. Make notes on each of the characteristics described in this chapter for the two countries including:

- poverty level (% of population below the income poverty level of $2 a day)
- inequality (Gini index)
- infant mortality rate
- nutrition (% of population undernourished)
- literacy rate
- population growth rate
- dependency ratio
- unemployment rate
- resources endowment
- whether it was colonised, and if so, by which country
- land size
- population size
- the presence of ethnic or religious tension
- structure of industry
- per capita income.

You may well have some of this information from workpoint 15.4.

Examination questions

Essay question

1 a Explain two measures of economic development.   *[10 marks]*

b To what extent could it be argued that all developing countries share the same set of characteristics?   *[15 marks]*

Assessment advice: use examples

Don't forget real-world examples!

30 Sources and consequences of economic growth and economic development

By the end of this chapter, you should be able to:

- explain, and give examples of, sources of economic growth
- distinguish between, and give examples of, physical and social capital
- distinguish between, and give examples of, capital widening and capital deepening
- explain, and give examples of, consequences of economic growth
- explain, and give examples of, sources of economic development
- define, explain, and give examples of infrastructure.

There is often confusion between economic growth and economic development. In addition, just because something causes economic growth, there will not necessarily be an improvement in economic development. Indeed, it is possible that the quest for economic growth may even cause a reduction in economic development. We need to consider what are the sources of economic growth, what may be the economic consequences of that growth, and what are the main sources of economic development. In the following chapters, we re-examine many of the points introduced. Specifically, we will look at the barriers to growth and development and then the possible strategies to increase economic growth and improve economic development.

Economic growth

We should remember the distinction between potential growth and actual growth. Potential growth occurs when there is an outward shift in the PPC and a rightward shift in the LRAS curve. This is a measure of supply potential and is what we will consider in this section.

Sources of economic growth

These may be identified under four simple headings.

1 *Natural factors:* Anything that will increase the quantity and/or quality of a factor of production should lead to an increase in potential growth. Increasing the quantity of land available is not really very easy, although countries like the Netherlands and Singapore have done so by means of land reclamation. However, this will only have a very small effect upon total land area, and thus production capability, unless the land area is very small to start with, as is the case with Singapore. Using landfill methods, Singapore has increased its land area from 581.5 square kilometres in 1965, when it gained independence, to 697.2 square kilometres at the present time, an increase in land area of almost 20%. However, if its neighbour Malaysia were to gain the

same increase through landfill, 115.7 square kilometres, to add to its existing 329,847 square kilometres, this would represent an increase of 0.03% in land area!

Most countries will therefore attempt to improve the quality of their natural factors, rather than the quantity. The quality of land may be improved by fertilization, better planning of land usage, improved agricultural methods, and building upwards as opposed to outwards, as is the case in places like Hong Kong.

2 *Human capital factors:* The quantity of human capital may be increased either by encouraging population growth or by increasing immigration levels. However, the majority of developing countries would not be keen to increase population size and, even if they were, like Singapore, the process is very long-term.

Most emphasis is therefore put on improving the quality of the human capital. The main methods of doing this are improved health care, improved education for children, vocational training, and retraining for the unemployed. In addition, the provision of fresh water and sanitation can also very much improve the health and thus the quality of human capital.

3 *Physical capital and technological factors:* Economic growth may be achieved by improving the quantity and/or quality of physical capital. Physical capital includes such things as factory buildings, machinery, shops, offices, and motor vehicles. (Social capital includes schools, roads, hospitals, and houses.) The quantity of physical capital is affected by the level of saving, domestic investment, government involvement, and foreign investment. The quality of physical capital is improved by higher education, research and development, and access to foreign technology and expertise.

We identify two concepts here.

● *Capital widening:* This exists when extra capital is used with an increased amount of labour, but the ratio of capital per worker does not change. In this case, total production will rise, but productivity (output per worker) is likely to remain unchanged.

● *Capital deepening:* This exists when there is an increase in the amount of capital for each worker. This often means that there have been improvements in technology. Capital deepening will usually lead to improvements in labour productivity as well as increases in total production.

Physical capital enabling extraction, or improved extraction, of primary products, such as oil drilling, or improved mining techniques, may be very important in terms of economic growth, since it will, in effect, increase the quantity of a factor of production.

4 *Institutional factors:* A prerequisite for meaningful economic growth is the existence of certain institutional factors. These are factors such as an adequate banking system, a structured legal system, a good education system, reasonable infrastructure, political stability, and good international relationships. Some of these factors are also sources of economic development, as we will see later in this chapter.

Consequences of economic growth

Bearing in mind that consequences may be positive or negative, we can consider what might be the outcomes of higher levels of economic growth.

1 *Higher incomes:* Higher levels of economic growth lead to higher GDP per head of the population and this should, to some extent, improve the standard of living of the population. Of course, the end effect will depend upon how fairly the income is distributed. There is no doubt that higher GDP will benefit many, in terms of higher incomes, and so better living standards. However, it is possible that there will be a significant group that will see little, or even no, improvement.

2 *Improved economic indicators of welfare:* Historically, it is clear that economic growth has led to higher averages in terms of economic indicators of welfare, such as average life expectancy, average years of schooling, and literacy rates. However, this will once again not necessarily be the case for all sections of the population. We can illustrate this point by looking at selected countries in terms of their HDI values from 1975 up to 2003. Figures are shown in Table 30.1.

Country (HDI rank–2003)	GDP per capita Annual growth rate % (1975–2003)	HDI value 1975	HDI value 2003	HDI change (%)
Norway (1)	2.8	0.868	0.963	10.9
Singapore (25)	4.9	0.725	0.907	25.1
Bahamas (50)	1.3	0.809*	0.832	2.8
Thailand (73)	5.1	0.614	0.778	26.7
El Salvador (104)	0.2	0.592	0.722	22.0
India (127)	3.3	0.412	0.602	46.1
Mauritania (152)	0.4	0.340	0.477	40.3
Mozambique (168)	2.3	0.299*	0.379	26.8

Source: Human Development Report 2005

* 1980 values

Table 30.1 Economic growth and HDI change value (1975–2003)

In all of the cases in Table 30.1, there has been an improvement in the HDI value that corresponds with positive economic growth over the period. Although there are other factors that contribute to an improvement in the HDI value, apart from GDP per capita, it is fair to suggest that there appears to be evidence to show that one consequence of economic growth may be an improvement in welfare, measured by the HDI.

Student workpoint 30.1

Be a thinker

Figures for Venezuela, Algeria, and Niger, from the same source as Table 30.1, are:

Country (HDI rank—2003)	GDP per capita Annual growth rate % (1975–2003)	HDI value 1975	HDI value 2003	HDI change (%)
Venezuela (75)	−1.1	0.718	0.772	7.5
Algeria (103)	−0.1	0.506	0.722	42.7
Niger (177)	−1.8	0.236	0.281	19.1

What possible reasons may there be to explain the fact that although the GDP per capita annual growth rates were negative over the period, the HDI value still increased?

3 *Higher government revenues:* Even if the tax collection system is not very efficient, which is the case in many developing countries, increased GDP should see increased government revenues from taxation. If this is the case then the government will be in a better situation when it comes to the provision of essential services, such as education, health care, and infrastructure.

4 *Creation of inequality:* Many economists argue that economic growth, especially growth achieved through market-based initiatives, leads to increases in GDP but also increases in inequality. Put simply: the rich get richer and the poor get relatively poorer. Even if the poor get a little more money, the gap between the rich and the poor is said to grow, since the rich receive the majority of the gains. Over time this may be accentuated, and in developing countries the concept of a "trickle-down effect", where the rich spend more and some of this goes to the poor, does not seem to make much of a difference.

5 *Negative externalities and lack of sustainability:* In developed and developing countries the quest for economic growth, and economic growth itself, often leads to pollution, a negative externality. As incomes rise more people drive cars, enjoy plane travel, and buy goods that are imported across long distances. This behaviour creates negative externalities of consumption and production where the market prices of goods and services do not reflect the full costs to society, and to the environment. We can also link problems of deforestation, soil degradation, and reduction in bio-diversity to economic growth.

As economies grow, so does the demand for energy. Factories, power plants, and households all consume energy and to meet this demand, there have been huge increases in the burning of fossil fuels such as coal, oil, and natural gas. Along with rising pollution levels, the burning of fossil fuels results in huge emissions of carbon dioxide, the largest source of greenhouse gases and global warming.

Although different models produce different results, the conclusion of the 2001 Intergovernmental Panel on Climate Change was that the mean global temperature could increase by 1.4–5.8 degrees Celsius by 2100. Such warming may bring about some positive changes, but the warning signs of the negative consequences are frightening. Forests, coral reefs, and other ecological systems will be damaged as a result of their inability to adjust to changing temperature and precipitation patterns. The effects on humans will be severely felt in the developing countries.

- Access to safe water will become even more precarious. Even now more than one billion people do not have access to safe water.

- Tropical diseases may spread further north.

- Droughts will become more frequent and intense in Asia and Africa, and flooding will likely become a bigger problem in temperate and humid regions.

- Food production in the tropics and sub-tropics is likely to suffer. Food production could become easier in middle and high latitudes, but there is no guarantee that this will improve food security.

- Millions of people will be affected by rising sea levels. This includes coastal areas along with low-lying islands in the Caribbean Sea and Pacific Ocean.

The economist Herman Daly talks about "uneconomic growth", and has defined it as occurring "when increases in production come at an expense in resources and well-being that is worth more than the items made".[1] We can conclude that economic growth based on current consumption patterns is clearly not sustainable and is, in reality, uneconomic growth. In effect we are speaking about a kind of inter-generational inequity, or unfairness. Current generations are using up non-renewable resources and creating negative externalities of production and consumption that are likely to compromise the living standards of future generations.

Student workpoint 30.2

Be a communicator

Try to make a link between economic growth and one of the following three problems:

- deforestation
- soil degradation/desertification
- reduction in bio-diversity.

Sources of economic development

Some factors are not only sources of economic growth, but are also sources of economic development.

[1]Daly, H.E. September 2005. "Economics in a full world". *Scientific American*.

Education

Improvements in education improve the well-being of the population, both the educated themselves and society as a whole. That is, education provides external benefits. Although it leads to a more efficient work force, it actually does much more. Increased levels of education mean that people are better able to read and to communicate. This in turn makes discussion and debate more likely and, as a consequence, may lead to social change. Changing attitudes may achieve a number of developmental aims. The benefits are widespread, but include the following.

- *Improved role of women in society:* There is no doubt that women are empowered by education and that there are high correlations between women's education and child survival rates and fertility rates (the annual number of live births per 1000 women of child-bearing age). The role of women in society is hugely important in terms of development. As Amartya Sen says, "Nothing, arguably, is as important today in the political economy of development as an adequate recognition of political, economic and social participation and leadership of women."[2]

- *Improved levels of health:* Improved education levels, in particular literacy rates, improve levels of health in society. People, especially women, are able to communicate more fully and thus become aware of some of the hazards that face them and of some of the opportunities that exist. Individuals are able to read about, and be informed about, dangers such as HIV/AIDS, poor sanitary habits, and poor dietary habits. In addition, they are able to find out about the possibilities of such things as inoculations and water filtering.

Country (HDI rank)	Health expenditure (public and private) % of GDP	Life Expectancy Index	Education Index	GDP PPP (US$ billions)	Population (millions)
Norway (1)	9.6	0.91	0.99	171.9	4.6
Iceland (2)	9.9	0.93	0.98	9.0	0.3
Australia (3)	9.5	0.92	0.99	589.1	19.7
Canada (5)	9.6	0.92	0.97	970.3	31.6
Sweden (6)	9.2	0.92	0.99	239.6	8.2
Azerbaijan (101)	3.7	0.70	0.89	29.8	8.3
Algeria (103)	4.3	0.77	0.71	194.4	31.9
El Salvador (104)	8.0	0.76	0.76	31.2	6.6
Cape Verde (105)	5.0	0.76	0.75	2.4	0.5
Syrian A. R. (106)	5.1	0.81	0.76	62.2	18.1
Chad (173)	6.5	0.31	0.30	10.4	9.1
Mali (174)	4.5	0.38	0.23	11.6	12.7
Burkina Faso (175)	4.3	0.38	0.16	14.2	12.4
Sierra Leone (176)	2.9	0.26	0.35	2.9	5.1
Niger (177)	4.0	0.32	0.17	9.8	13.1

Source: Adapted from Tables 1, 5, 6 & 14 of UNDP Human Development Report, 2005 (All figures 2003)

Table 30.2 Health, education, GDP, and population data for selected countries

[2]*Development as Freedom*, Amartya Sen, OUP, 1999

Health care

Greater levels of health care, especially when combined with greater educational opportunities, will improve the levels of economic development. Although we realise that there are many factors that influence life expectancy, it would be fair to assume that there is a strong correlation between health care and life expectancy and the HDI figures would seem to bear that out. Look at Table 30.2.

Table 30.2 shows data for five high human development countries, five middle human development countries and five low human development countries. With the usual warning that there are many factors that affect a single outcome, let us consider some of the relationships. It is hardly surprising, but it appears that countries that spend a higher proportion of GDP on health care tend to have a higher life expectancy. This is apparent when we look at the specific comparison between Australia and the Syrian Arab Republic.

Australia spends 9.5% of $589.1 billion on its 19.7 million inhabitants. The Syrian Arab Republic, with a similar population, spends 5.1% of $62.2 billion on its 18.1 million inhabitants. Even though there are other factors in play, it is hardly surprising that life expectancy is considerably higher in Australia and that the Australian HDI ranking is much higher than that of the Syrian Arab Republic.

The close correlation throughout the table between the life expectancy index and the education index is also worthy of note, but may be difficult to fully justify with so many other variables to consider.

Theory of Knowledge

"There are three kinds of lies—lies, damned lies, and statistics."

(This quotation is attributed to Benjamin Disraeli and was popularised by Mark Twain.)

Why is this statement particularly meaningful in the field of economics?

Infrastructure

A full definition of infrastructure might be "the essential facilities and services such as roads, airports, sewage treatment, water systems, railways, telecommunications and other utilities that are necessary for economic activity". Improvements in infrastructure will lead to greater economic development. For example, better roads allow children to get to school, adults to get to market, and goods to get to potential buyers. Sewage treatment improves the lot of the population, if it is universal, as does an adequate water system. Any improvement in infrastructure will, in some way, improve the well-being of the people.

5 Development Economics

Political stability

Countries that have political stability are more likely to attract FDI and aid, and it is more likely that domestic savings and profits will stay in the country. Increased access to FDI may be more likely to contribute to increased growth than to development, but increased access to aid may increase development.

When there is political stability, citizens are more likely to have an input into the running of the country. Government planning is likely to be more structured and long-term, and the law is likely to be more enforceable. All of these elements should lead to higher living standards for the population.

Examination questions

Short response questions

1 How do education and health care create positive externalities?   *[10 marks]*

2 How is the provision of infrastructure important for both economic growth and economic development?   *[10 marks]*

Essay question

1 a Using a diagram, explain how it is possible for a country to achieve potential economic growth.   *[10 marks]*

   b Evaluate the consequences of economic growth.   *[15 marks]*

Assessment advice: linking syllabus areas

You could have answered this question much earlier in the course, but at this stage you should be able to see that it would be valuable to link it to the concept of economic development.

31 Barriers to economic growth and economic development

By the end of this chapter, you should be able to:

- explain, and give examples of, barriers to economic growth
- explain, and give examples of, barriers to economic development
- distinguish between relative poverty and absolute poverty
- define, explain, give examples of, and illustrate poverty cycles
- show awareness of the factors harming economic growth and economic development in a particular developing country.

Barriers to economic growth and economic development

It is widely agreed that there are many barriers to growth and development that hold back developing countries. It is perhaps easiest to understand them if they are separated into different categories; however, you should not lose sight of the fact that many of the barriers, although in different categories, are interconnected. You also need to be aware of the ways in which some barriers act as an obstacle to economic growth, some to economic development, and some to both.

Institutional and political barriers

Insufficient provision of education

One of the Millennium Development Goals is to "Ensure that by 2015, children everywhere, boys and girls alike, will be able to complete a full course of primary schooling". While progress has been made in the provision of education, particularly primary education, throughout the world, there are still more than 115 million children of primary school age that do not attend primary school. 80% of these children are in Africa or Southern Asia.[1] At the most basic level, the provision of education requires vast funding and this simply may not be available in sufficient quantities. Within a country there may be large disparities in the provision of education, with urban areas receiving more of the education funds than rural areas. There are also family economic conditions that prevent children from attending school; they may be needed to work within the home or farm, or they may be involved in external work as "child labourers". For the most part it is children from poor households, and from families where the mothers also received no formal education, who do not attend school. Enrolment in secondary schools tends to be far lower than primary schools, with the necessity of earning an income as the greatest obstacle to attending school.

[1] *The Millennium Development Goals Report*, The United Nations, New York, 2005

AIDS takes a harsh toll on education

The education crisis in sub-Saharan Africa is made worse by the impact of AIDS. In 1999 alone, nearly 1 million children in that region lost their teachers to AIDS. The cumulative effect of these deaths has been placing an untenable burden on many countries that already lacked sufficient trained teachers. When parents become ill with AIDS, children are often taken out of school to care for them, take on other household responsibilities or work to support the family. When parents die, children often leave school because of economic hardship. Tragically, education is all the more important at this time, because it provides a stable element in a child's life. Moreover, it is probably the single most effective way of preventing the further spread of HIV. Facts about how young people can protect themselves are increasingly being integrated into school curricula.

The Millennium Development Goals Report, The United Nations, New York, 2005

Insufficient health care systems

There has been much progress made by many developing countries in terms of the training of doctors and nurses, the building of hospitals and clinics, and the provision of public health services such as improved access to safe water and sanitation and the widespread availability of immunizations. Throughout the world infant mortality rates have fallen, life expectancy has increased, more children are immunized than ever before, and maternal mortality rates are falling. Nevertheless there are still significant shortcomings, particularly among the low-income countries. Table 31.1 provides some evidence of the disparities that exist. While it is a very small sample, its give us an idea of the figures involved.

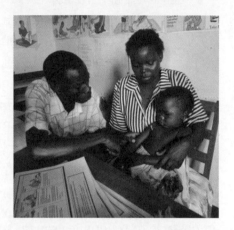

Country	Public health expenditure per capita (PPP US$)	One-year-olds fully immunized against measles (%)	Births attended by skilled health personnel (%)	Physicians (per 100,000 people)	Population with access to improved water source (%) 1990	Population with access to improved water source (%) 2002
Australia	2,699	93	100	249	100	100
Finland	1,943	97	100	311	100	100
Thailand	321	94	99	30	81	85
Bolivia	179	64	65	73	72	85
Namibia	331	70	78	30	58	80
Nigeria	43	35	35	27	49	60
Niger	27	64	16	3	40	46

Source: Adapted from Tables 6 & 7 of UNDP Human Development Report, 2005

Table 31.1 Selected health indicators

Lack of infrastructure

One of the greatest drawbacks for developing countries is their lack of infrastructure, which is essential for growth.

Infrastructure consists of the essential facilities and services such as roads, airports, sewage treatment, water systems, railways, telecommunications, and other utilities that are necessary for economic activity. We can identify different categories of infrastructure and some examples of these are shown in Table 31.2.

Category	Examples
Transport	● Roads ● Railways ● Seaports ● Airports ● Public transport ● Pavements
Public utilities	● Electricity ● Gas ● Water supply ● Sewers
Public services	● Police service ● Fire service ● Education service ● Health service ● Waste management
Communication services	● Postal system ● Telecommunications ● Radio and television

Table 31.2 Categories and examples of infrastructure

The lack of any of these facilities will harm the ability to achieve economic growth. If goods cannot be transported from one area of the country to another because of poor roads, or from one area of the country to a seaport for export, then trade, and thus growth, is restricted. If power supplies are intermittent and unreliable then production is harmed. If communication channels are poor or non-existent then the ability to coordinate economic activity is severely limited.

Limited infrastructure also hinders development prospects. Poor roads or public transport means that it may be difficult to get to a school to obtain an education (although it must be said that this is only one obstacle in terms of acquiring education). An underdeveloped radio and television network can make it difficult for people to find and participate in wider communities. The availability of gas and electricity is important to households for activities such as cooking and food preservation, while sanitation and safe water are vital for health to improve.

Weak institutional framework

Another large barrier to growth is the inadequacy of the institutional framework necessary to support and encourage economic activity. We can consider two main areas.

1 *The legal system:* In many developing countries, the legal system does not function well. Where this is the case, then there is no way to create and enforce contracts and there is no way to uphold property rights. Social scientists consider property rights to be essentially a "basket" of legal rights. This basket includes:

- the right to own assets, such as land or buildings
- the right to establish the use of our assets, such as adding to the building—for example, an owner might want to add sanitation to a house
- the right to benefit from our assets, such as renting out our land
- the right to sell our assets
- the right to exclude others from using or taking over our assets.

Property rights allow people to own and benefit from private property, so long as the law supports them.

If a person cannot guarantee his or her ownership of a property, then there is no incentive to improve that property, since it is possible that the property could be lost and the investment will have been wasted. If there are no enforceable property rights, as is the case in many developing countries, then investment and growth will be very much reduced.

2 *The financial system:* Developed and independent financial institutions are essential if economic growth is to be achieved, and these are often underprovided in developing countries. Most developing countries have dual financial markets. The official markets are small and tend to be dominated by foreign commercial banks who often have an outward-looking emphasis to their operations and restrict their lending to foreign businesses and the already established large manufacturing local businesses. The unofficial markets are not legally controlled and so are illegal. Their main operation is to lend money, usually at very high interest rates, to those who are desperate and poor enough to have to borrow it.

Saving is necessary to make funds available for investment and investment is necessary for economic growth. Saving is difficult enough in countries where there are high levels of poverty, but it is even harder if there is nowhere to save money that is safe and will give a good return. When there are weak or untrustworthy financial institutions, people with investment income tend to buy assets, such as livestock, or invest their money outside the country (capital flight).

Financial services are necessary if low-income people are to be able to manage their assets and to allow them to increase in value. The difficulties associated with saving and borrowing money are a significant barrier to economic growth and development. It makes it exceedingly difficult for low-income people to raise themselves out of poverty.

Ineffective tax structure and formal and informal markets

Tax revenue provides governments with the means to finance necessary public services, such as education and health care, and generally to improve the infrastructure of the country. However, this is very difficult to do if governments do not receive a great deal of tax revenue.

It is very difficult for governments to collect tax revenue in developing countries. We can consider reasons for this. First, as a result of tax exemptions, and inefficient or corrupt administration, it is estimated that less than 3% of the population in developing countries pay income tax, as opposed to 60%–80% in developed countries.[2] Second, corporate tax revenues tend to be low, since there is relatively little corporate activity in developing countries (although it is growing), and developing countries often offer large tax incentives in order to encourage domestic corporate activity and to attract FDI. Third, the main source of tax revenue in developing countries are export, import, and excise (customs) duties. These taxes are relatively easy to collect as they are paid when the goods pass through the country's border posts. However, it is only possible to gain significant tax revenue if the country is heavily involved in foreign trade. It is worth noting that the international trading system through the WTO, with its emphasis on liberalization of trade, may have negative implications for countries that earn significant revenue from tariffs. Finally, we have noted that developing countries have problems with the administration of their tax systems in terms of inefficiency, lack of information, and corruption. These elements, when combined, often mean that people are able to evade paying the taxes that they owe.

In Chapter 14 we met the concepts of formal and informal markets. In developing countries much economic activity takes place in informal markets. This is shown in Table 31.3.

Countries	Average size of the informal market (% of official GDP)		
Mostly developing countries:	1999/2000	2000/2001	2002/2003
Africa	33.9	37.4	41.2
Central and South America	34.2	37.7	41.5
Asia	20.9	23.4	26.3
Highly developed OECD countries	13.2	15.7	16.8

Source: The size of the shadow economies of 145 countries all over the world, Friedrich Schneider, University of Linz, Discussion Paper 1431, December 2004.

Table 31.3 Average size of the informal markets for developing and OECD countries in % of official GDP

The size of informal markets as a percentage of GDP in developing countries is far greater than in developed countries. It would also appear that the informal markets are growing in almost all countries in the world.

Large informal markets once again lead to much lower tax revenues for governments in developing countries. If the incomes of people are not recorded because they are earned in informal markets, then there will be no tax paid on such income. Lower tax revenues make it difficult for governments to promote growth and achieve development objectives. Furthermore, workers tend to be unprotected in the informal markets and are very poorly paid, with little job security, poor working conditions, and no social care. Productivity in the informal markets also tends to be very low; workers are often low-skilled migrants from rural areas, with little education, and low human capital.

[2] Michael P. Todaro, *Economic Development*, 7th edition, Addison Wesley Longman, 2000

Political instability and corruption

These are both barriers to growth and development. Political instability causes uncertainty and, at its most extreme, complete economic breakdown. Sudan, in Africa, is a relevant case. Civil wars from 1955 to 1972, and then from 1983 to 2005, together with a new civil war in the western region of Darfur, which began in 2003 and is still ongoing, have caused significant loss of life and displacement of the population. In addition, their neighbour, Chad, declared war on Sudan in December 2005. Such extreme political instability is bound to lead to very poor economic performance, high levels of poverty, and low standards of living for the majority of the population. The likelihood of attracting foreign investment, or even aid, becomes much smaller. A number of developing countries are experiencing civil wars as a result of ethnic and/or religious conflict or border conflicts. For example, since 1980 there have been ethnic- and/or religious-based conflicts in Afghanistan, Algeria, Côte d'Ivoire, Democratic Republic of the Congo, India, Indonesia, Iraq, Israel, Laos, Lebanon, Mexico, Myanmar, Nepal, Philippines, Russia, Rwanda, Senegal, Somalia, Sri Lanka, Turkey, and Uganda. The loss of life, damage to infrastructure, loss of investment and sometimes aid, and political instability have undoubtedly affected economic growth and development in these countries.

Corruption is defined here as the dishonest exploitation of power for personal gain. It poses a huge challenge to both growth and development. It tends to be most prevalent where:

1 governments are not accountable to the people, especially military governments

2 governments spend large amounts on large-scale capital investment projects

3 official accounting practices are not well formulated or controlled

4 government officials are not well paid

5 political elections are not well controlled, or are non-existent, i.e. there is no democracy

6 the legal structure is weak

7 freedom of speech is lacking.

Unfortunately, many of these conditions are to be found in a high proportion of developing countries, which may explain the high levels of corruption that can exist.

There are many forms of corruption includng bribery, extortion, fraud, patronage, and nepotism. The effects of corruption are likely to hinder growth and development with a number of causative factors.

1 Electoral corruption means that the wishes of the people are not heeded. This will put a government in place that has not been voted for by the majority. It is likely that such a government will not adopt policies to benefit the electorate.

2 Corruption of any sort reduces the effectiveness of the legal system. If people can "buy" their way out of trouble there may be an incentive to act illegally.

3 Corruption leads to an unfair allocation of resources. If contracts go to the highest bidder, as opposed to the most efficient producer, then there is a market failure and resources are being misallocated. It often sustains inefficient producers by shielding them from competition.

4 Bribes increase the costs of businesses, in cash terms and in terms of management negotiation time. This invariably leads to higher prices.

5 Corruption reduces trust in an economy. As a result, countries may find it harder to attract foreign investment, which will often be diverted to less corrupt countries.

6 Corruption increases the risk of contracts not being honoured and this, in turn, acts as a serious deterrent to investment, both internal and external.

7 Corruption means that officials will often divert public investment into capital projects where bribes are more likely. This tends not to be in important areas, such as education and health care, so it reduces the quality of government services for the population.

8 Corruption often means that officials turn a blind eye to regulations, such as those regarding construction or the environment. This can have a damaging effect on individuals and the country as a whole.

9 The monetary gains from corruption are often moved out of the country. This is a form of capital flight and it reduces the capital available for internal investment.

10 The constant paying of small bribes reduces the economic well-being of the ordinary citizen.

Some interesting research figures regarding bribery from Transparency International are shown in Tables 31.4 and 31.5.

Question: In the past 12 months, have you or anyone living in your household paid a bribe of any sort? Answer: Yes.	
31–50%	Cameroon, Paraguay, Cambodia, Mexico
11–30%	Ethiopia, Ghana, Guatemala, Lithuania, Moldova, Nigeria, Romania, Togo, Bolivia, Czech Republic, Dominican Republic, Ecuador, Greece, Indonesia, India, Kenya, Pakistan, Peru, Russia, Senegal, Serbia, Ukraine
5–10%	Argentina, Bulgaria, Bosnia and Herzegovina, Colombia, Croatia, Kosovo, Luxembourg, Macedonia, Malaysia, Nicaragua, Panama, Philippines, Poland, South Africa, Thailand, Turkey, Venezuela
Less than 5%	Austria, Canada, Costa Rica, Denmark, Spain, Finland, France, Germany, Hong Kong, Iceland, Ireland, Israel, Japan, South Korea, Netherlands, Norway, Portugal, Singapore, Switzerland, Taiwan, UK, Uruguay, USA

Source: Transparency International Global Corruption Barometer 2005

Table 31.4 Percentage of households making bribery payments in selected countries

5 Development Economics

Average amount paid in bribes per household per year, as a % of GDP per capita (2003)	
20%	Cameroon, Ghana, Niger
10–20%	India, Kenya, Moldova, Togo, Ukraine
10%	Bolivia, Dominican Republic, Guatemala, Lithuania, Mexico, Pakistan, Paraguay, Peru, Romania, Russia, Serbia

Source: Transparency International Global Corruption Barometer 2005

Table 31.5 Size of bribes as a percentage of GDP per capita

Unequal distribution of income

Although every country in the world has income inequality, it is fair to say that the gap between the rich and poor in developing countries is generally greater than that in developed countries.

High income inequality can be a barrier to growth for a number of reasons. First, there tend to be low levels of saving, because the poor save a very small proportion of their income. As we know, low saving means low investment and so low growth. Second, the rich tend to dominate both politics and the economy. This tends to mean that policies are followed that are more in their favour and so we do not have pro-poor growth. Pro-poor growth occurs when economic growth leads to a fall in some agreed measure of poverty. Third, high income inequality in developing countries tends to be marked by the rich moving large amounts of funds out of the economy (capital flight). Also, a large proportion of the goods purchased by the rich are foreign-produced and so their consumption does not help the domestic economy. Thus, although we usually link income inequality simply to a consequence of low levels of development, we can also see that it can act as a barrier to growth.

●●●●●●●●●●●●●●●●●●●●●●●

Student workpoint 31.1

Be an inquirer

Choose one of the developing countries that you investigated earlier and research the extent to which the following institutional and political factors hinder its economic growth and/or development:

● the provision of education and health care

● the extent and quality of infrastructure

● financial services/banking system

● legal system

● political stability

● extent of corruption.

International trade barriers

Overdependence on primary products, adverse terms of trade and the consequences of a narrow range of exports

While the share of manufactured goods produced by developing countries as a percentage of total world trade is growing, a number of developing countries are dependent on primary commodities for a significant share of their export revenues, as explained in Chapter 29. When commodity prices are rising, this may be beneficial to those countries. It will increase their rate of economic growth and if the revenues are used to finance spending on education, health care, and infrastructure, this can set off a positive cycle in terms of development and future growth. However, if the prices fall then the economies experience deteriorating terms of trade. Current account deficits will increase and it will be very difficult for countries to finance current expenditure and necessary imports. Unless they can change the pattern of their export trade, those countries that are dependent on a narrow range of primary exports will find it difficult to gain much growth through international trade.

Regardless of the types of goods exported, be they commodities, manufactured goods or even services like tourism, if a country is dependent on a narrow range of exports then it faces great vulnerability and uncertainty. For example, economic growth in a tropical country that is reliant on tourism revenues will be limited if the global tourist trade is damaged as a result of terrorism. It is also vulnerable to other forces outside of its control such as tsunamis and other environmental factors. Countries that were dependent on the export of a small range of low-skill manufactured goods, including textiles, were damaged when China joined the WTO and sharply increased the supply of textiles on world markets, driving down their prices.

Protectionism in international trade

Protectionism is any economic policy that is aimed at supporting domestic producers at the expense of foreign producers. We have already considered forms of protectionism such as tariffs, subsidies, quotas, and non-tariff barriers in Chapter 24. Protectionist measures by developed countries against the exports of developing countries may be very harmful. If the measures prevent developing countries from utilising their comparative advantages and exporting to developed countries, then developing countries will be limited in their ability to earn foreign exchange.

Protectionism in any market is damaging for developing countries, but it is especially the case in primary product markets. If we take the example of cotton, the US's 25,000 cotton farmers share almost $4 billion in government subsidies each year. This encourages farmers to produce more, forcing down the world price and exporting their surplus to developing countries that do not have the benefits of subsidies. This is immensely damaging for the developing country producers. The US currently does the same with maize, rice, and dairy products. Meanwhile, protected EU farmers over-produce and export sugar, cereals, and dairy produce, lowering world prices and damaging markets and local suppliers in developing countries. As these products are sold at lower prices than would be the case without subsidies it is argued that they are "dumped" in foreign markets. Small-scale farmers in developing countries are effectively deprived of the ability to earn a living, which is clearly a significant barrier to development.

Did you know?

According to Oxfam, "the rich world spends $1 billion a day subsidising its agricultural industries".

Visit www.maketradefair.com for excellent resources on this important topic.

An important related issue is tariff escalation, whereby the rate of tariffs on goods rises the more the goods are processed. An importing country therefore protects its processing and manufacturing industries by putting lower tariffs on imports of raw materials and components and higher tariffs on processed and finished products. In the most extreme cases, the developed countries import raw materials that have low tariffs on them, process the raw materials, adding value to the goods, and then export the finished goods. Tariff escalation creates a significant problem for developing countries in terms of their access to markets. There is little incentive to diversify away from producing raw materials to processing them as the higher prices due to tariffs will make their processed goods uncompetitive. Effectively, it can trap them as suppliers of raw materials. An example of tariff escalation on rice imports into the European Union is shown in Table 31.6.

	EU rice tariff, euros per 1000 kg (2002)
In the husk (paddy or rough)	211.00
Husked (brown)	264.00
Semi-milled or Milled	416.00

Source: EU Common Customs Tariff, Official Journal C 104A, vol 45, 30 April 2002

Table 31.6 Tariff escalation for rice in the EU, 2002

The tariff per 1000 kg of imported rice, still in the husk, is €211 but if the rice is husked then the tariff rises to €264, an increase of 21%. If the rice is semi-milled or milled, then the tariff rises to €416. This is a 57% escalation of the tariff from husked rice and a 97% tariff escalation from the raw material. Not surprisingly, the EU mainly imports husked brown rice, which accounts for approximately two thirds of its total imports of rice. Imports of semi-milled and milled rice are much lower, about one fifth of total rice imports.[3] This shows that the tariff escalation is successful in reducing the imports of the more processed good. The final processing of the rice along with the packaging and marketing are done in the EU. Since these add the highest value to the product in terms of the price at which it is sold, this is where the largest gains are to be made. Ideally, the developing country rice producers would like to diversify by investing in the processing stages, but the tariff escalation takes away the potential benefits. Tariff escalation is widely observed in the agricultural markets of meat, sugar, fruit, coffee, cocoa, and tobacco.

● ● ● ● ● ● ● ● ● ● ● ● ● ● ● ● ● ● ●

Student workpoint 31.2

Be an inquirer

Continue your investigation into your chosen developing country by researching possible international trade barriers that may be hindering its growth and development.

[3] EU Common Customs Tariff, Official Journal C 104A, vol 45, 30 April 2002

International financial barriers

Indebtedness

We shall look at the problems of debt in more detail in Chapter 33, so for now, we highlight the fact that indebtedness is a major barrier to growth and development for many developing countries. "Third world debt", as it has been known, and its huge annual debt repayments are a massive problem for many developing countries.

Capital flight

Capital flight occurs when money and other assets flow out of a country to seek a "safe haven" in another country. Developing countries have suffered greatly from this process ever since the 1970s. There are three main causes of capital flight and they are to be found in many developing countries.

First, there is the question of the safety of the domestic financial institutions. If citizens within a country do not feel that their capital would be safe in the financial institutions within that country then they will move it out of the country to somewhere that is more reliable.

Second, corruption in governments leads to siphoning off of funds, both domestic funds and investment from abroad, and then the removal of those funds out of the country to numbered accounts in other countries.

Third, currency instability encourages citizens to move money out of a country and into a more stable economy with a more stable currency.

Some also argue that the repatriation of profits by MNCs constitutes another type of capital flight. Certainly, the money sent out by the companies is money that cannot be used internally.

Capital flight has many damaging effects on the economies of developing countries. First, if money is outside of a country, then it cannot be used internally to develop that country. Second, if money is outside of a country, then it cannot be taxed and so the government loses potential tax revenue. Third, capital flight often reduces the ability of governments to pay decent wages to employees, which in turn forces the employees to turn to corruption and bribe-taking. Fourth, increases in capital flight lead to greater levels of poverty, which may lead to more social unrest and political instability.

In many cases, it is argued that developing countries lose more resources through capital flight than they do through debt repayment. For example, research in 2001 looking at capital flight for severely indebted sub-Saharan African countries between 1970 and 1996 concluded that Africa was a net creditor with the rest of the world in that the value of accumulated assets held outside of Africa through capital flight was greater than the total value of external debt.[4]

---

[4] Boyce and Ndikumana, 2001, "Is Africa a net creditor?" *Journal of Development Studies*, Vol 38, No. 2.

Another form of capital flight is human capital flight, often known as "brain drain". This is the emigration of educated and talented individuals from one country to another. The individuals usually leave in order to seek better employment opportunities and higher standards of living. This is typically found in professions where a university education is required, including scientists, engineers, doctors, and nurses. Emigration is sometimes forced by domestic unrest, lack of domestic opportunities, or health and safety hazards. For example, Iraq and Iran are said to be suffering heavily from human capital flight because of their political instability. Human capital flight represents an investment in higher education that will bring no return to the country where the education was funded. It also means that valuable personnel are not available within a country to promote its growth or development and results in less tax revenue to the home government.

On the other hand, people who leave developing countries to work abroad often send back money in the form of remittances. Such remittances can greatly benefit the families who receive the money.

Non-convertible currencies
Many developing countries have non-convertible currencies. These can only be used domestically and are not accepted for exchange on the foreign exchange markets. Most developing countries operate a fixed exchange rate system where the domestic currency is pegged to a more acceptable currency, often the US dollar, at a certain rate.

Non-convertibility means that trade is less likely to occur. Traders would be taking more of a risk dealing in a non-convertible currency and are likely to go elsewhere to conduct their business. The same is true of foreign investment.

Non-convertible currencies are often also over-valued at their official, pegged, exchange rate. This will usually mean that a black market for the convertible currency will arise and this may be very damaging for the economy. In some cases, the domestic currency will become almost unacceptable within the country, which damages local as well as international trade.

○ ○

Student workpoint 31.3

Be an inquirer
Continue your investigation by researching the extent to which capital flight and brain drain might be hindering growth and development in your chosen developing country.

Social and cultural barriers
There are a number of social and cultural barriers to growth and development in developing countries but it is difficult to be specific about the extent of their effect. It is an area that is, by definition, very subjective. We will now try to be objective and consider a few points that are relatively unarguable.

● Certain cultures disapprove of discussing matters relating to sex, especially with the young. This may lead to a lack of appropriate advice in countries where HIV/AIDS is reaching epidemic proportions, slowing progress in battling the spread of the disease. There is no doubt that in many developing countries, especially in Africa, HIV/AIDS is a very significant barrier to growth and development.

● If we take the countries that rank from 100 to 177 in the human development index, we find that in all but two of them women have a lower literacy rate, in all but 14 of them women spend less time at school, and in all of them the average estimated earned income for women is lower than that for men (usually substantially lower).[5] In many societies, religious, social, and cultural traditions have combined to make the role of women very different to that of men. Typically, they are expected to marry, raise children, work in the home, and cultivate family plots of land.

The deprivation of education is a barrier to development for women and the loss of the freedom to seek employment outside of the family is another.[6] It has been argued that the greatest untapped resource in the world is women. For this reason, many non-government organisations (NGOs) focus on women as a priority for development. Increasing the number of literate, educated women will also expand the labour force in a country, allowing its potential output to increase.

Student workpoint 31.4

Be an inquirer

To what extent is it possible to identify social or cultural issues as barriers to growth or development in the country you are researching?

 ### Theory of Knowledge

"Culture is the widening of the mind and of the spirit"
Jawaharlal Nehru (1889–1964) Indian Prime Minister.

It is often argued that cultural traditions and values hinder growth as they do not embrace the concept of change. However, governments that have forced the world's best practices to be adopted have often done so at the expense of their nation's cultural identity; their actions, while pro-growth, are in fact anti-development. Do you agree with this view?

---

[5] Source: Human Development Report 2005, UNDP
[6] Amartya Sen, *Development as Freedom*, OUP, 1999

Poverty trap/poverty cycles

Poverty is usually measured in two ways. First of all, there is relative poverty, which is comparative. A person is said to be in relative poverty if they do not reach some specified level of income. For example, a poverty level of 50% of average earnings may be set in a country and anyone who earns less than this figure would be deemed to be relatively poor. The level of relative poverty in a country will depend upon where the specified level of income is set and this in turn will often depend upon who is setting it. The government in a country would not like to see high levels of relative poverty in the media and so may set the level at 40% of average earnings. The opposition party may wish to embarrass the government and may set the level at 60% of average earnings. As we can see, the whole concept is relative.

The second measure is absolute poverty. The level for absolute poverty is measured in terms of the basic necessities for survival, and is the amount that a person needs to have in order to live. It is the level of income that is sufficient to buy items such as basic clothing, food, and shelter. This enables us to make comparisons across the world, but for this to be possible we must use purchasing power parity (PPP) exchange rates. The World Bank uses an absolute poverty line of US$1 per day, calculated using PPP exchange rates. If a person is below this level then they are considered to be in absolute poverty. The World Bank has also issued figures for US$2 per day. Table 31.7 shows figures for the six developing countries with the highest recorded poverty levels.

Population below income poverty line (%)		
Country	$1 a day	$2 a day
Mali	72.3	90.6
Nigeria	70.2	90.8
Central African Republic	66.6	84.0
Zambia	63.7	87.4
Niger	61.4	85.3
Madagascar	61.0	85.1

Source: Adapted from Table 3 of UNDP Human Development Report, 2005

Table 31.7 World Bank absolute poverty figures

Many of the barriers to growth and development are often connected in a cyclical fashion, which means that countries may be caught in a poverty trap. A poverty trap is any linked combination of barriers to growth and development that forms a circle, thus self-perpetuating unless the circle can be broken.

These traps may be illustrated by the use of a poverty cycle, also sometimes known as a development trap. An example of two poverty cycles is shown in Figure 31.1. On the left is a well-known poverty cycle that illustrates how low incomes perpetuate low incomes, thus harming economic growth. On the right we can see a different cycle, where low incomes perpetuate low incomes, but this time harming economic development.

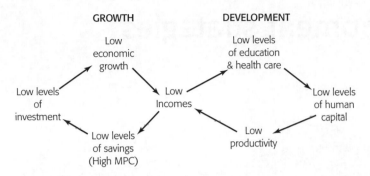

Figure 31.1 Examples of poverty cycles

student workpoint 31.5

Be a thinker

Devise circular poverty cycles beginning and ending with the following and suggest ways that the circles may be broken:

1 poor health

2 lack of technology

3 low consumption levels

4 HIV/AIDS

5 falling commodity prices

6 a barrier of your own choice.

Examination questions

Short response questions

1 Explain how a lack of property rights might be a barrier to growth in developing countries. *[10 marks]*

2 Explain how development **and** higher growth in developing countries may be achieved if more resources are directed towards the education of girls. *[10 marks]*

3 Explain how corruption can act as an obstacle to economic growth. *[10 marks]*

4 Explain how capital flight may be a barrier to economic growth. *[10 marks]*

5 Explain how brain drain may act as an obstacle to both growth and development in developing countries. *[10 marks]*

6 Explain how tariff escalation hinders economic development. *[10 marks]*

We will save questions involving the skill of evaluation until we have discussed growth and development strategies in the next chapter.

Assessment advice: growth or development?

When answering questions about developing countries, pay close attention to whether the question is asking about growth and/or development and structure your answer accordingly. Remember that we can never simply assume that growth will lead to development. There need to be government policies in place to ensure that if growth takes place, the benefits of the higher national income are directed towards the achievement of development objectives.

32 Growth and development strategies

By the end of this chapter, you should be able to:

- explain, give examples of, and evaluate different growth models
- explain, give examples of, and evaluate different growth strategies
- define and explain transfer pricing
- explain, and give examples of, different development strategies.

There is much confusion in development economics between models and strategies. When asked for strategies for development, students often offer models instead, and they are often growth models. We will try to simplify the situation by attempting to distinguish between growth models, growth strategies, and development strategies. As a general rule, growth models describe how growth has occurred and so suggest that this may be replicated. Growth strategies are economic policies and measures designed to gain growth, and development strategies are economic policies and measures designed to achieve human development, i.e. to improve the well-being of the people. Economic growth is not economic development, but if it can generate extra income for governments, firms, and people, then it may lead to development, depending upon how that extra income is used.

Growth models

Harrod-Domar growth model

Sir Roy Harrod in the UK and Evsey Domar in the US independently developed the Harrod-Domar growth model in 1939. Although its original purpose was to analyse the business cycle, the model has been used by economists to identify factors affecting the rate of growth of GDP.

In its simplest form, the model states that the rate of growth of GDP is determined by the national savings ratio and the ratio of capital to output in the economy. It can be stated as:

$$\text{Rate of growth of GDP} = \frac{\text{Savings ratio}^{1}}{\text{Capital/output ratio}^{2}}$$

So if the savings ratio in the country is 5% and the capital/output ratio is 2.5, then the country can grow at a rate of 2% per annum.

If the model is correct then we can say that the rate of growth of an economy may be increased by one of two things.

- *Increasing the levels of saving in the economy:* If savings are increased in the economy then our economic theory tells us that this can

---

[1] The marginal propensity to save.

[2] The expenditure on capital as a ratio of the output gained from capital. Thus it may be that it is necessary to spend $2.5 on capital in order to increase the national output by $1. Thus the ratio would be 2.5:1.

lead to an increase in investment. The increase in investment represents a greater stock of capital, which in turn should lead to greater output in the economy and greater income. Since a proportion of that increased income should be saved, we will have a circular situation, which should lead to increasing growth. This is shown in Figure 32.1.

Although the theory would appear to work, there are problems when it is applied to developing countries. In theory, all a country has to do is to increase the savings ratio. In our earlier example, with a savings ratio of 5% and a capital/output ratio of 2.5, we had economic growth of 2%. If the savings ratio is increased to 7.5% then economic growth will increase to 3%. However, raising the savings ratio in developing countries is not easy. Most developing countries have very low marginal propensities to save, as people spend the vast majority of their low incomes on consumption. Furthermore, if they do have spare income then they often spend it on assets, such as a small plot of land, or a bicycle, rather than put money into local banking systems that may not be that secure. In some cases, savings are sent out of the country in the form of capital flight. This combination of high consumption, poor financial infrastructure, and capital flight makes it difficult to increase the level of savings in developing countries.

- *Reducing the capital/output ratio in the economy:* If the capital output ratio can be reduced, i.e. the use of capital can become more efficient, this would increase the rate of economic growth. In our example, if the savings ratio stays at 5% but the capital/output ratio falls to 2, then the rate of growth rises to 2.5%.

However, increasing efficiency in this way is never easy and especially not so in developing countries. A shortage of educated and skilled labour (possibly made even worse due to "brain drain") implies that new capital will not be effectively used. In addition, a lack of managerial skills means that the organising factor will be weak, which is unlikely to result in improved efficiency. Research and development, which improve efficiency, are also likely to be under-funded, and access to foreign technology (another means of gaining efficiency) is expensive and so often not available to developing countries.

Structural change/dual sector model

The Lewis dual sector model was first conceived by W. Arthur Lewis in the 1950s and was later modified by other economists. Its main focus is on structural change and it attempts to explain how an underdeveloped economy moves from being a traditional agrarian economy, with a small manufacturing sector, to an economy where there is a more modern balance with a larger manufacturing and service sector.

The model starts from the assumption that there is a large agricultural sector with a surplus of labour, and a small, but productive, modern manufacturing sector. The surplus of labour in the agricultural sector is not productive and so moves to the manufacturing sector. They are attracted by wages that are higher than in the agricultural sector, but fixed because the supply of labour

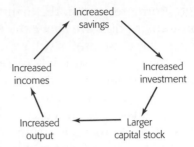

Figure 32.1 Savings and growth

is high. Entrepreneurs in the manufacturing sector will make profits because their prices are above the fixed wage rates. The theory assumes that these profits will be reinvested, which will increase the capital stock. This in turn will increase the productive capacity of the manufacturing sector and the demand for labour will grow. More workers will be employed from the surplus labour from agriculture and the profits of the entrepreneurs will once again increase and be reinvested. This process is assumed to continue until all the surplus labour has been employed in the larger manufacturing sector. A structural change has now taken place and the economy is no longer a traditional agrarian model, but is now an industrialized country. The model is illustrated in Figure 32.2.

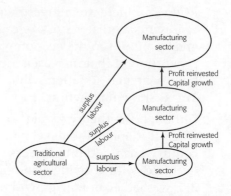

Figure 32.2 The Lewis dual sector model

 The Lewis model, in a rather simplified way, illustrates the process that took place during the industrial revolutions in many of the now developed countries. However, whether it can be used as a model for economic growth in developing countries is debatable. There are a number of weaknesses in the theory.

- The model assumes that entrepreneurs will keep adding capital that is the same as the original capital. However, it is likely that entrepreneurs would begin to invest in technologically advanced, more labour-saving capital and that this would reduce the increases in employment, severely slowing the process of growth.

- The model assumes that all profits are reinvested, but we already know that capital flight is a common occurrence in developing countries and it is likely that a large proportion of profits would leave the economy, thus reducing investment and again slowing the whole growth process.

- The model assumes that there is a pool of surplus rural labour. The situation in many developing countries actually indicates that there is more likely to be high unemployment in urban areas and little surplus of labour in rural areas, caused by rural–urban migration.

- The model assumes that wage levels in the manufacturing sector will remain constant. The growing existence of collective bargaining, imposed wage scales, and wages offered by foreign companies tends, however, to lead to rising wages, even where there is unemployment. This would reduce profit levels and the ability to reinvest.

Growth strategies

Export-led growth

Export-led growth is an outward-oriented growth strategy, based on openness and increased international trade. Growth is achieved by concentrating on increasing exports and export revenue, as a leading factor in the aggregate demand of the country. Increasing exports should lead to increasing GDP, and this in turn should lead to higher incomes and, eventually, growth in domestic markets as well as exporting ones. The country concentrates on producing and exporting products in which it has a comparative advantage of production.

In order to achieve export-led growth, it is assumed that a country will need to adopt certain policies. These include:

- liberalized trade; open up domestic markets to foreign competition in order to gain access to foreign markets in exchange

- liberalized capital flows; reduce restrictions on foreign direct investment

- a floating exchange rate

- investment in the provision of infrastructure to enable trade to take place

- deregulation and minimal government intervention.

This list illustrates the theoretical "package" of policies associated with export-led growth. In reality, countries that adopt an outward-oriented strategy do not necessarily adopt all of these policies.

Developing countries may attempt to export primary products and/or manufactured products (although some have tried to export services, usually in the form of tourism). We can consider the differences involved in using the export of primary or manufactured products as the engine for growth.

- Many developing countries depend upon the export of primary products in order to gain export revenue. However, the overall trend in primary product prices, with the exception of oil and some metals, has been downward for many years. This is due to increasing supply and relatively insignificant increases in demand, for a number of different reasons (see Chapter 28). This, combined with increased protectionism by developed countries, means that export-led growth based on the export of primary products is unlikely to be achieved.

- The focus of export-led growth is usually on increasing manufacturing exports. The success of countries such as Japan, South Korea, Hong Kong, Singapore, and Taiwan, known as the "Asian tigers", is usually used to illustrate the effectiveness of such a strategy. These countries exported products in which they had a comparative advantage, usually based upon low-cost labour, and were extremely successful in doing so. Over time, the type of product being exported by the majority of these countries has also tended to change from products that were produced using labour-intensive production methods, requiring low skill levels from the workers, to more sophisticated products, using capital-intensive production methods and more highly skilled workers. Improvements in education systems were essential for this.

 Although it would appear that export-led growth is an obvious way to gain success, this is not necessarily the case. There are a number of problems associated with export-led growth.

- The success of the "Asian tigers" since around 1965 has led to increased protectionism in developed countries against manufactured products from developing countries. Trade unions and workers in developed countries argued that they could not compete against the imports from low-wage developing countries and that this was unfair. They lobbied their governments to put tariffs and quotas on the lower-priced goods. Price increases as a result of tariffs effectively removed the comparative advantage of the exporting countries. Tariff escalation also reduced the ability of the developing countries to export processed goods and assembled products, forcing many to export primary products and low-skilled manufactured goods instead.

- Certain assumptions were made about the necessary conditions for export-led growth. If we look at the successful countries, these conditions were not necessarily met. Many economists would argue that the role of the state in successful export-led growth is vital and that minimizing government intervention is not the way forward. In the "Asian tiger" countries, governments played an important role by providing infrastructure, subsidizing output through low credit terms via central banks, and promoting savings and improvements in technology. In addition, governments adopted policies where they protected domestic industries that were not yet able to compete with foreign firms and promoted the industries that were ready for competition in export markets. This illustrates the "infant industry" argument for protection. This topic is one of great debate among development economists, and many argue that intervention is vital. Others argue that the state intervention in these economies actually slowed growth rates.

- If countries attempt to kick-start their export-led growth by attracting MNCs, there is always the fear that the MNCs may become too powerful within the country and that this may lead to problems. We will look at the role of MNCs and FDI later in this chapter.

- It is argued by some economists that free-market export-led growth may increase income inequality in the country. If this is the case, then economic growth may be achieved at the expense of economic development.

Research at the World Bank has identified countries known as "post-1980 globalizing economies". These are developing economies that have integrated more fully in the international economy through the processes of globalization such as trade liberalization and capital market liberalization. These become outward-oriented economies. The list of post-1980 globalizers includes such countries as Argentina, China, Hungary, India, Malaysia, Mexico, the Philippines, and Thailand. Average growth rates for these countries, "rich" countries, and developing countries that are not in the post-1980 globalizing group are shown in Table 32.1.

Types of country	Average annual growth rates (%)		
	1970s	1980s	1990s
Globalizing developing countries	2.9	3.5	5.0
"Rich" countries	3.1	2.3	2.2
Non-globalizing developing countries	3.3	0.8	1.4

Source: Dollar and Kraay. June 2001. *Trade, Growth and Poverty*. The World Bank. WPS2615.

Table 32.1 Growth rates for globalizing developing countries and others

Student workpoint 32.1

Be a thinker

What conclusions suggested by the data in Table 32.1 can be drawn about the link between economic growth in developing countries and the extent to which a country opens itself up to the global economy?

Import substitution

Import substitution is more fully known as import substitution industrialisation (ISI). It may also be referred to as an inward-oriented strategy. This states that a developing country should, wherever possible, produce goods domestically rather than import them. This should mean that the industries producing the goods domestically will be able to grow, as will the economy, and will then be able to be competitive on world markets in the future as they gain from economies of scale. Indeed, it is the opposite of export-led growth and is not supported by those economists who believe in the advantages of free trade based on comparative advantage.

In order for the strategy to work, there are some necessary conditions.

- The government needs to adopt a policy of organizing the selection of goods to produce domestically. Historically, this has been labour-intensive, low-skill manufactured goods such as clothing or shoes.

- Subsidies are made available to encourage domestic industries.

- The government needs to implement a protectionist system with tariff barriers to keep out foreign imports.

 There are a number of perceived advantages and disadvantages with ISI.

Advantages
- ISI protects jobs in the domestic market, since foreign firms are prevented from competing so domestic firms dominate.

- ISI protects the local culture and social habits by practically isolating the economy from foreign influence.

- ISI protects the economy from the power, and possibly bad influence, of multinational corporations.

Disadvantages
- ISI may only protect jobs in the short run. In the long run, economic growth may be lower in the economy and the lack of growth may lead to a lack of job creation.

- ISI means that the country does not enjoy the benefits to be gained from comparative advantage and specialization, so producing products relatively inefficiently when they could be imported from efficient foreign producers.

- ISI may lead to inefficiency in domestic industries because competition is not there to act as a spur to be efficient or to conduct research and development.

- ISI may lead to high rates of inflation due to domestic aggregate supply constraints.
- ISI may cause other countries to take retaliatory protectionist measures.

The main countries to adopt ISI strategies were in Latin America, including Argentina, Brazil, Mexico, Chile, and Uruguay. As former colonies gained their independence many also adopted inward-oriented strategies. These included India, Nigeria, and Kenya. These policies showed some success in the 1960s and 1970s, but the policies started to fail in the early 1980s. Government overspending and debt crisis led to an inability of governments to repay the loans they had taken and in the 1980s many of the countries were forced to go to the IMF for help.

The Washington Consensus

In 1989, the American economist John Williamson identified ten common reforms that were necessary for economic growth. The World Bank, the International Monetary Fund and the US Treasury Department agreed with this list and as a result, Latin American economies seeking economic help were encouraged to adopt such reforms. The policies were:

- fiscal discipline, that is, balanced budgets
- redirection of spending priorities from indiscriminate subsidies to basic health and education
- lowering of marginal tax rates and broadening of the tax base
- interest rate liberalization
- a competitive exchange rate
- trade liberalization
- liberalization of FDI inflows
- privatization
- deregulation
- securing of property rights.

 Because the reforms were common to the World Bank, the IMF, and the US Treasury Department, they became known as the Washington Consensus. By the end of the 20th century, the Washington Consensus was increasingly criticized by economists who were not supporters of such policies. The criticisms have formed the basis of what has come to be known as the anti-globalization movement.

This claims that reforms such as the Washington Consensus are just a way to ensure that MNCs have access to cheap labour markets in developing countries. In this way the MNCs can produce inexpensive products, which are then sold for high prices in developed countries. The MNCs make high profits and the workers in developing countries gain little. According to this view, the Washington Consensus has not led to high economic growth in Latin America. Instead there have been economic crises and increased debt, and such policies have led to increased income inequality and exploitative working conditions, thus working against the goal of economic development.

It is interesting to note that there seems to have been a movement towards the left in a number of Latin American countries, such as Venezuela, Bolivia, and Brazil, and these countries, along with Cuba, have been very vocal in their condemnation of the Washington Consensus. Argentina has, in the last few years, moved back towards an ISI approach to growth, which seems to have brought some economic success.

Foreign Direct Investment (FDI)

FDI is long-term investment by private multinational corporations (MNCs) in countries overseas. FDI usually occurs through MNCs building new plants or expanding their existing facilities in foreign countries. This is known as greenfield investment. Alternatively, MNCs merge with or acquire (buy) existing firms in foreign countries. There are approximately 70,000 multinationals operating internationally with 690,000 affiliates around the world.[3]
Table 32.2 provides some information about the largest eight multinational corporations, ranked in terms of their foreign assets.

Corporation	Home economy	Industry	Foreign assets (US$m)	Total assets (US$m)	Foreign employment	Total employment
General Electric	US	Electrical & electronic equipment	258,988	647,483	150,000	305,000
Vodafone Group plc	UK	Telecommunications	243,839	262,581	47,473	60,109
Ford Motor Co.	US	Motor vehicles	173,882	304,594	138,663	327,531
General Motors	US	Motor vehicles	154,466	448,507	104,000	294,000
BP plc	UK	Petroleum expl./ ref./distr.	141,551	177,572	86,650	103,700
ExxonMobil Corp.	US	Petroleum expl./ ref./distr.	116,853	174,278	53,748	88,300
Royal Dutch/ Shell Group	UK/ Netherlands	Petroleum expl./ ref./distr.	112,587	168,091	100,000	119,000
Toyota Motor Group	Japan	Motor vehicles	94,164	189,503	89,314	264,410

Source: UNCTAD World Investment Report 2005. Overview, Table 3, page 6

Table 32.2 The world's top 8 non-financial MNCs, ranked by foreign assets

There was a rapid increase in flows of FDI in the 1990s, a sign of the significant role that FDI has played in the integration of the world's economies and globalization. There was a sharp fall in global FDI flows in 2001 followed by three years of continuous drops, but they rebounded again in 2004, largely due to a strong increase in flows to developing countries. In 2004, the share of FDI flows to developing countries was 36% of all global inflows, up from 21.3% in 1999. China received 9.4% of all FDI inflows, while Africa as a whole received only 2.8%.[4] The United States is the largest recipient of FDI (14.8% of all inflows), followed by the United Kingdom and then China.[5]

---

[3] UNCTAD, *World Investment Report 2005*, Overview, page 4
[4] ibid, page 2
[5] ibid, page 2

MNCs are attracted to developing countries for a number of reasons.

- The countries may be rich in natural resources, such as oil and minerals. MNCs have the technology and expertise to extract such resources. For example, the top recipients in Africa are those countries with valuable natural resources: Angola, Equatorial Guinea, Nigeria, and Sudan.

- Some developing countries, such as Brazil, China, and India, represent huge and growing markets. If MNCs are located directly in the markets then they have much better access to the large number of potential consumers. With growing incomes, demand for all sorts of consumer goods is rising and MNCs wish to be there to satisfy the demand.

- The costs of labour are much lower than in more developed countries. Lower costs of production allow firms to sell their final products at lower prices and make higher profits.

- In many developing countries government regulations are much less severe than those in developed countries. This makes it easier for companies to set up but, more significantly, it can greatly reduce costs of production. Additionally, many developing country governments offer tax concessions to attract foreign direct investment. Over the last 15 years many countries, both developed and developing, have adopted policies that have been more and more favourable to foreign direct investment. In 2004, for example, more than 20 countries lowered their corporate tax rates in order to try to attract more FDI.

 We now consider the possible advantages and disadvantages that may arise for developing countries from receiving FDI from MNCs.

Possible advantages associated with FDI

- As we know from the Harrod-Domar model, a necessary condition for growth is increased savings and developing countries tend to suffer from a savings gap. FDI helps to fill that savings gap and thus may lead to economic growth.

- MNCs will provide employment in the country and, in many cases, may also provide education and training. This may improve the skill levels of the work force and also the managerial capabilities.

- MNCs allow developing countries greater access to research and development, technology, and marketing expertise and these can enhance their industrialization.

- Increased employment and earnings may have a multiplier effect on the host economy, stimulating growth.

- The host government may gain tax revenue from the profits of the MNC, which can then be used to gain more growth by investing in infrastructure, or to improve public services such as health and education to promote economic development.

- If MNCs buy existing companies in developing countries, then they are injecting foreign capital and increasing the aggregate demand.

- In some cases, MNCs may improve the infrastructure of the economy, both physical and financial, or they may act as a spur for governments to do so in order to attract them.

- The existence of MNCs in a country may provide more choice for consumers and lower prices. They may be able to provide essential goods that are not available domestically.

- MNC activities along with liberalized trade can lead to a more efficient allocation of world resources.

It is clear that there are vast gains to be made from FDI. This can be shown using China as an example. Although it is difficult to isolate FDI in terms of its effect on China's economic growth, it is reasonable to assume that it has played a significant role. Since 1978, China has actively tried to attract foreign investment as a way to stimulate economic growth. A significant proportion of China's exports are produced by foreign firms. Through joint ventures with foreign firms, Chinese firms have grown rapidly and successfully and China itself is now the source of a large outflow of foreign direct investment. As China grows, so does its demand for raw materials and much of Chinese FDI abroad is its investment in natural resources.

Possible disadvantages associated with FDI

- Although MNCs do provide employment, it is argued that they often bring in their own management teams, simply using inexpensive low-skilled workers for basic production and providing no education or training. This also limits the ability of host countries to acquire new technologies.

- In some cases it is argued that MNCs have too much power, because of their size, and so gain large tax advantages or even subsidies, reducing potential government income in developing countries. Along the same lines, it is argued that MNCs have too much power internationally. Their incomes and size allow them to exert too much influence on policy decisions taken in institutions such as the WTO.

- MNCs practise transfer pricing, where they sell goods and services from one division of the company to another division of the company in a separate country to take advantage of different tax rates on corporate profits. In this way, developing countries with low tax rates to encourage MNCs to invest reap little tax reward, and developed countries also lose out on potential tax revenue. Given that approximately one third of all international trade is made up of sales from one branch of a firm to another firm, this represents a potentially large loss of revenue to governments. Governments have rules to prevent firms from abusing their ability to use transfer pricing to minimize their tax payments, but these are difficult to monitor and enforce, particularly for developing country governments.

- It is argued that MNCs situate themselves in countries where legislation on pollution is not effective, and thus they are able to reduce their private costs while creating external costs. While this is good for the MNC, it is damaging for the environment of the host country. In the same way, MNCs may set up in countries where labour laws are weak or almost non-existent, allowing exploitation of local workers through low wage levels and poor working conditions.

5 Development Economics

- It is argued that MNCs may enter a country in order to extract particular resources, such as metals or minerals, then strip those resources and leave. There may be significant unrest as host country nationals see that the profits from their resources are being sent out of the country to foreigners.

- Economists have argued that MNCs may employ capital-intensive production methods to make use of abundant natural resources. This will not greatly improve levels of employment in the country. It is argued that the MNCs should use *appropriate technology*, where production methods are aligned to the resources available. Since developing countries usually have a large supply of cheap labour, the argument is that labour-intensive production methods would be more appropriate.

- In most cases where MNCs buy domestic firms, the owners of the firms being bought are paid in shares (stocks) from the MNC. This means that it is likely that the actual money will never be used in the developing country's economy.

- MNCs may repatriate their profits. This means that they transfer their profits out of the country back to the MNC's country of origin.

While most would agree that FDI is a positive factor for current economic growth the main concerns relate to the possible negative effects of MNCs on sustainable economic development. The extent to which FDI is able to contribute to this development depends very much on the type of investment and the ability of the host country governments to appropriately regulate the behaviour of the MNCs and use the benefits of the investment to achieve development objectives.

There have always been concerns related to MNC activity such as the possible exploitation of workers, the use of child labour, the inability of workers to form unions in some companies, and business practices that cause immediate or future environmental damage. With the increasingly fast flow of information through the media and the Internet and strong public interest groups acting globally, it is becoming difficult for MNCs to conceal activities that may contribute to these problems. They do not want to be perceived as being a cause of problems and are keen to promote their image in positive ways. As a result, firms are more and more likely to develop and publicize a set of policies to show that they are acting responsibly and ethically, and "doing their bit" to promote sustainable development. This is known as corporate social responsibility (CSR). Companies publish and promote their CSR policies through their annual reports, websites and advertising. The policies outline the firm's commitment to support human rights, employee rights, environmental protection, sustainable development, and community involvement. The extent to which such policies are consistently followed and the extent of their actual effect on workers, the workers' communities, and the environment is uncertain, but it is usually regarded as a step in the right direction!

Student workpoint 32.2

Be an inquirer

Research and write a brief report explaining the CSR policies of any multinational company. This is easily done by going to the website of the company. Warning—you will be viewing a one-sided report of their efforts!

Student workpoint 32.3

Be a thinker

Transfer pricing

Let us assume that there is an MNC called Wilkes International (WI) that operates in a developing country, X, and a developed country, Y. The corporate profit tax rate in country X is 15% and in country Y is 40%.

Situation 1

The firm produces its products in country X at an average cost of $250. It then sells the products to its own company in country Y at a price of $350. This is the transfer price. In country Y, the product is sold at a price of $450.

Calculate these outcomes:

- profit per unit in country X   _____
- profit per unit in country Y   _____
- total profit per unit   _____
- tax per unit in country X   _____
- tax per unit in country Y   _____
- total tax per unit   _____
- after tax profit per unit   _____

Situation 2

The firm decides to change its transfer price and to sell to its company in country Y at a price of $400.

Calculate these outcomes:

- profit per unit in country X   _____
- profit per unit in country Y   _____
- total profit per unit   _____
- tax per unit in country X   _____
- tax per unit in country Y   _____
- total tax per unit   _____
- after tax profit per unit   _____

Situation 3

The firm decides to change its transfer price and to sell to its company in country Y at a price of $450.

Calculate these outcomes:

- profit per unit in country X   _____
- profit per unit in country Y   _____
- total profit per unit   _____
- tax per unit in country X   _____
- tax per unit in country Y   _____
- total tax per unit   _____
- after tax profit per unit   _____

1 Explain what has happened to the amount of tax paid by WI as the transfer price has increased.

2 Explain what has happened to the after tax profit per unit.

3 Explain how transfer pricing affects the governments of countries X and Y.

Development strategies

Fairtrade organizations

In many developing countries many small-scale farmers and workers are unable to make a living income. Low world prices for primary products, high profits for middlemen, tariff escalation, and poor working conditions make life extremely difficult.

Fair trade schemes are an attempt to ensure that producers of food, and some non-food, products in developing countries receive a fair deal when they are selling their products. If consumers are aware of the harsh and often unfair conditions facing the farmers, then perhaps they may be willing to buy from producers who pay a fair price to the farmers.

Today, Fairtrade Labelling Organization International (FLO) coordinates Fairtrade labelling in 20 countries, including the Fairtrade foundation in the UK. The schemes aim to help small farmers and landless workers. Fair trade schemes have operated for over 50 years, but the real growth of the movement has come with the advent of Fairtrade labelling. This began in the Netherlands in 1988 when the Max Havelaar Foundation began to sell coffee from Mexico with the first Fairtrade consumer guarantee label.

This is a system where products can be certified if they meet the standards of the FLO, which gives them the right to display the International Fairtrade Certification Mark. This recognisable Mark means that consumers will be able to identify Fairtrade products, know that they are approved, and buy them knowing that the producer of the good was paid a fair price. FLO regularly inspects and certifies around 500 producer organizations in more than 50 countries in Africa, Asia, and Latin America, which results in fair trading conditions for approximately one million farmers, workers, and their families.[6]

A trading company wishing to qualify for the International Fairtrade Certification Mark must meet certain FLO criteria.

● The product must reach the trader as directly as possible with few, if any, intermediaries.

● The product must be purchased at least at the Fairtrade minimum price. This is a guaranteed price that covers production costs and provides a living income. It covers the cost of "sustainable production".

● The producer receives a premium if the product is certified as organic.

● The trader must be committed to a long-term contract, which in turn gives security to the producer.

● The producer has access to credit from the trader, upon request, of up to 60% of the purchase price.

● Where small farmers are involved the product must come from producers that are managed democratically. If the product comes

---

[6] www.fairtrade.net

from plantations then the workers must benefit from internationally recognized employment standards including trade unions, if they wish, and there must be no use of child labour.

- The producer must use sustainable farming methods to produce the good.

- The trader also pays a Fairtrade premium to the producer. The producers use these funds to aid local community development. The producers decide how the money will be spent, but it is usually used to promote health care, education, or other social schemes. The producers are accountable to the FLO for the appropriate use of the funds.

Fairtrade certified food products include bananas, cocoa, coffee, dried fruit, fresh fruit and vegetables, honey, juices, nuts/oil seeds and purees, quinoa, rice, spices, sugar, tea, and wine. Non-food products include cotton, cut flowers, ornamental plants, and sports balls.

Although the price might sometimes be slightly higher for Fairtrade certified products than non-Fairtrade products, it is clear that many consumers are willing to pay to contribute to better conditions for producers. Global sales of Fairtrade products were valued at just over €1.1 billion for 2005, an increase of 37% on 2004.[7] Fairtrade products are making their way into more and more shops and restaurants as firms become aware of the increasing popularity. Fairtrade, with its emphasis on granting a living income, giving security, demanding proper working conditions, encouraging sustainable production, and funding local community development, is clearly a strategy that leads to development as well as growth.

‘"The guarantee of the minimum price brings stability. We, producers, are not totally subjected to the law of supply and demand. We know that we will be paid at least US$69 the quintal. This guarantee makes it possible to plan long-term, to invest, to develop technical support, in one word, to develop our business," says Felipe Cancari Capcha, a producer from El Ceibo Cooperative, a Fairtrade cocoa producer in Bolivia.’

www.fairtrade.net.

Did you know?

You can buy Fairtrade footballs, rugby balls, and volleyballs. These are produced in three factories in Sialkot, Pakistan. This area is known as the capital of the export football trade.

Student workpoint 32.5

Be caring

Fairtrade organizations

Find out if there are Fairtrade products available in your country. If so, make a list of the products and where they can be purchased. Then be sure to try some—the chocolate is excellent!

---
[7] FLO News Bulletin, July 2006

Micro-finance

In developing countries, low-income people find it almost impossible to gain access to traditional banking and financial systems, since they lack assets to use as collateral, are often unemployed, and lack savings. If they can find a way to borrow money it is often at exorbitant interest rates. There is, however, a type of financial service that is geared specifically for them. This is known as micro-finance and provides financial services, such as small loans, savings accounts, insurance, and even cheque books.

The provision of small loans to individuals who have no access to traditional sources is known as micro-credit. A key element of original micro-credit schemes is that they did not originate in the developed world, but rather had their beginnings in developing countries. The first schemes began in the mid-1970s with projects such as Opportunity International (1972), ACCION International (1973), Muhammad Yunus/Grameen Bank (1974/76), FINCA International (1985), and The SEEP Network (1985).

Usually, the micro-credit loans are given to enable poor people to start up very small-scale businesses, known as micro-enterprises. These may include such things as roadside kiosks, bicycle repair services, market stalls, rice wine making, knitting, and woodworking. The loans give protection against unexpected occurrences and seasonal problems, and may help families to gain a regular income, start to build wealth, and so escape from poverty.

Women have tended to be the main recipients of micro-credit, for many reasons. It is thought that women are a better credit risk—they are more likely to pay back loans. Women are usually responsible for caring for children and so any reductions in a woman's poverty will translate into improvements for children. In many documented cases this has allowed for more poor children to go to school. When women take loans and can begin to earn an income their social and economic status is raised.

'*Any process of growth that fails to improve the welfare of the people experiencing the greatest hardship, broadly recognized to be women and children, has failed to accomplish one of the principal goals of development.*'
Michael P Todaro, Economic Development, *Addison Wesley Longman, 2000*

Student workpoint 32.6

Be an inquirer

Research and prepare a case study explaining any one example of an individual or a group of people who has benefited from a micro-credit loan.

Examination questions

Short response questions

1 Using the Harrod-Domar growth model, explain why there may be slow growth in developing countries. *[10 marks]*

2 Explain how Fairtrade is likely to contribute to economic development. *[10 marks]*

3 Explain how micro-credit can contribute to economic development. *[10 marks]*

Essay questions

1 a Explain the main characteristics of an export-led growth strategy. *[10 marks]*

  b Evaluate the view that economic growth and development are best achieved through the adoption of an outward-oriented strategy. *[15 marks]*

2 a Discuss three reasons for multinational company investment in developing countries. *[10 marks]*

  b Evaluate the role of FDI in promoting economic growth and development in developing countries. *[15 marks]*

Assessment advice: answering short response questions
Although short response questions 2 and 3 above do not specifically ask you to use a diagram, you are always encouraged to consider whether there might be an appropriate one that you could use. In this case a poverty cycle diagram could be helpful.

5 Development Economics

By the end of this chapter, you should be able to:

- define, explain, and give examples of different types of aid
- distinguish between humanitarian and development aid
- explain the workings of the World Bank Group and the International Monetary Fund
- explain, give examples of, and evaluate concerns about aid
- explain the role of NGOs in the development process
- explain, give examples of, and evaluate the problems of indebtedness in developing countries
- define, discuss, and evaluate market-led and interventionist growth strategies.

Aid

Aid, or foreign aid, is defined as any assistance that is given to a country that would not have been provided through normal market forces. Aid may be provided to developing countries for a number of reasons:

- to help people who have experienced some form of natural disaster or war
- to help developing countries to achieve economic development
- to create or strengthen political or strategic alliances
- to fill the savings gap that exists in developing economies and so encourage investment
- to improve the quality of the human resources in a developing country
- to improve levels of technology
- to fund specific development projects.

There are many ways to categorise aid, although we must immediately distinguish between official aid, which is aid that is organised by a government or an official government agency, and unofficial aid, which is organised by a non-government organisation (NGO), such as Oxfam. We can adopt two main headings to attempt to classify aid: humanitarian aid and development aid. There are also types of aid that come under both headings.

Humanitarian aid

Humanitarian aid is aid given to alleviate short-term suffering, which may be caused by such events as droughts, wars, or natural disasters. It can take a number of forms and usually comes under the heading of grant aid, which is short-term aid provided as a gift and does not have to be repaid.

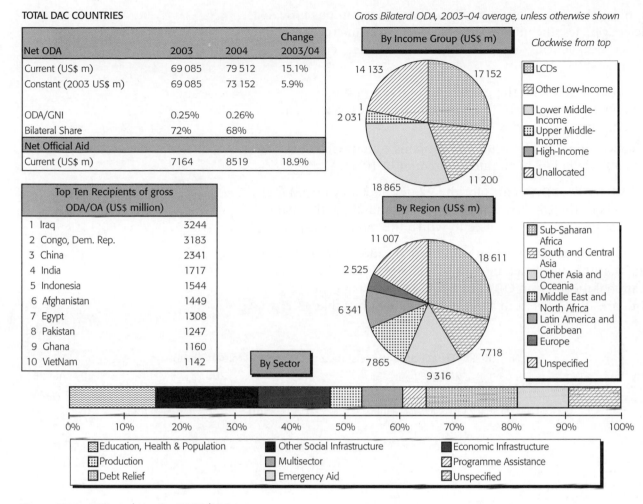

TOTAL DAC COUNTRIES

Net ODA	2003	2004	Change 2003/04
Current (US$ m)	69 085	79 512	15.1%
Constant (2003 US$ m)	69 085	73 152	5.9%
ODA/GNI	0.25%	0.26%	
Bilateral Share	72%	68%	
Net Official Aid			
Current (US$ m)	7164	8519	18.9%

Top Ten Recipients of gross ODA/OA (US$ million)	
1 Iraq	3244
2 Congo, Dem. Rep.	3183
3 China	2341
4 India	1717
5 Indonesia	1544
6 Afghanistan	1449
7 Egypt	1308
8 Pakistan	1247
9 Ghana	1160
10 VietNam	1142

Figure 33.1 ODA statistics for 2003/2004

Source: OECD, DAC. http//:www.oecd.org/

The three main forms of grant aid are:

- *food aid*: the provision of food from donor countries or money to pay for food, which also includes money given for the transport, storage and distribution of food

- *medical aid*: the provision of medical services and provisions from donor countries, as well as money to facilitate medical services

- *emergency aid*: the provision of emergency supplies, including temporary shelters, tents, clothing, fuel, heating, and lighting.

All of the above forms of grant aid may be classified as official aid or unofficial aid, depending upon their origin.

Development aid

Development aid is aid given in order to alleviate poverty in the long run and improve the welfare of individuals. Development aid is often referred to specifically as Official Development Assistance (ODA). This is aid provided by governments on concessional terms, sometimes as simple donations. It may be provided by individual countries, through their official aid agencies, or through multilateral organisations, such as the many branches of the United Nations.

The OECD's Development Assistance Committee (DAC) defines ODA as:

5 Development Economics

"flows to developing countries and multilateral institutions provided by official agencies, including state and local governments, or by their executive agencies, each transaction of which meets the following tests:

- it is administered with the promotion of the economic development and welfare of developing countries as its main objective, and

- it is concessional in character and contains a grant element of at least 25% (calculated at a rate of discount of 10%)."

Figure 33.1 shows ODA figures for the 22 developed countries that are members of the DAC over the years 2003 and 2004, the main recipients of this aid, and the uses to which the money was put.

In 1970, the United Nations General Assembly adopted a resolution agreeing that the developed nations would aim to spend 0.7% of their national incomes on ODA. In 2004, 34 years later, many countries are still far from this target, as is shown in Table 33.1.

Net Official Development Assistance in 2004 (Preliminary data)					
Country	2004		2003		% change 2003 to 2004
	ODA (US$m)	ODA/GNI %	ODA (US$m)	ODA/GNI %	
Australia	1,465	0.25	1,219	0.25	2.3
Austria	691	0.24	505	0.20	22.0
Belgium	1,452	0.41	1,853	0.60	−30.3
Canada	2,537	0.26	2,031	0.24	12.2
Denmark	2,025	0.84	1,748	0.84	3.5
Finland	655	0.35	558	0.35	5.9
France	8,475	0.42	7,253	0.41	4.3
Germany	7,497	0.28	6,784	0.28	−0.4
Greece	464	0.23	362	0.21	13.1
Ireland	586	0.39	504	0.39	2.2
Italy	2,484	0.15	2,433	0.17	−9.7
Japan	8,859	0.19	8,880	0.20	−4.8
Luxembourg	241	0.85	194	0.81	10.5
Netherlands	4,235	0.74	3,981	0.80	−4.0
New Zealand	210	0.23	165	0.23	8.2
Norway	2,200	0.87	2,042	0.92	−2.9
Portugal	1,028	0.63	320	0.22	187.5
Spain	2,547	0.26	1,961	0.23	14.5
Sweden	2,704	0.77	2,400	0.79	1.4
Switzerland	1,379	0.37	1,299	0.39	−3.0
United Kingdom	7,836	0.36	6,282	0.34	8.8
United States	18,999	0.16	16,320	0.15	14.1
Total DAC	78,568	0.25	69,094	0.25	4.6
Average effort		0.42		0.41	
EU countries	42,919	0.36	37,139	0.35	2.9
G7 countries	56,686	0.22	49,982	0.21	5.4
Non-G7 countries	21,882	0.45	19,112	0.46	2.2

Table 33.1 Net ODA figures for selected countries, 2004

Student workpoint 33.1

Be a thinker

1 Which countries met the UN aid target in 2004?

2 Which three countries gave the largest amount of aid relative to their GDP?

3 Which three countries gave the least amount of aid relative to their GDP?

Types of development aid

- *Long-term loans:* These are loans that are usually repayable by the developing country over a period of 10 to 20 years. The loans are known as concessional loans or soft loans, which are sometimes repayable in foreign currency, sometimes in the local currency, and sometimes in a mixture of both. The developing countries would prefer loans that are repayable in their own currency, since they would not then have to use valuable, and scarce, foreign currency. They tend to have very low rates of interest and to be repayable over a longer period of time than a standard commercial loan. These loans may come via official aid or non-official aid.

- *Tied aid:* This is grants or loans that are given to a developing country, but only on the condition that the funds are used to buy goods and services from the donor country.

- *Project aid:* This is money given for a specific project in a country and is often given in the form of grant aid that requires no repayment. The projects are often to improve infrastructure. One of the main suppliers of project aid to developing countries is the World Bank (see box on page 366).

- *Technical assistance aid:* This is sometimes included in project aid. There tend to be two aims. The first is to raise the level of technology in developing countries by bringing in foreign technology and technicians who can instruct on its use. The second is to raise the quality of human capital by the provision of training facilities and expert guidance. Foreign scholarships are also sometimes provided so that managers and technicians can study abroad.

- *Commodity aid:* This is grant aid given by countries to increase productivity in developing economies. It provides funds to purchase commodities including consumer items, intermediate inputs and industrial raw materials. For example, approximately 25% of the aid commitments to Bangladesh take this form, and provide necessary commodities such as edible oils, seeds, fertilizer, chemicals, cement, steel, pumps, and other equipment.

Most forms of development aid can be official or unofficial. In addition, there are two further ways of classifying official aid.

- *Bilateral aid:* This is aid that is given directly from one country to another.

● *Multilateral aid:* This is aid that is given by rich countries to international aid agencies, such as the World Bank Group's International Bank for Reconstruction and Development, the United Nation's Children's Fund, and the International Monetary Fund. It is then up to the agencies to decide where the aid is most needed and will be most effectively used.

The World Bank Group

The World Bank Group is a collection of five individual organisations. The World Bank was established, following the Bretton Woods Agreements in 1945. The main aims of the group are to provide aid and advice to developing countries, as well as reducing poverty levels and encouraging and safeguarding international investment. The overarching aim of the group is to promote economic development. The five organisations that make up the World Bank Group are as follows.

The International Bank for Reconstruction and Development (IBRD)

Founded in 1945, the IBRD grants loans to developing countries. The funds for these loans are generated by the issue of World Bank bonds in global capital markets. Repayment of the bonds is guaranteed by the member states and by the government of the borrowing country. Because of this the bonds are seen as very safe and the IBRD is able to get the funds at relatively low interest rates. Thus the IBRD can lend to developing countries at rates that are below the rates that the countries would have to pay if they borrowed the money themselves.

The loans are usually given to support specific projects that are aimed to promote economic development. Projects may include the provision of education, improvements in health care, improvements in agriculture, the reduction of pollution, or the improvement of a country's infrastructure. Loans are often conditional, which means that the recipient country may have to agree to follow certain policy changes if it is to receive the loan. For example, a loan to improve agricultural productivity may be tied to a guarantee to monitor and reduce environmental pollution.

The International Finance Corporation (IFC)

Founded in 1956, the IFC aims to promote private sector investment in developing countries, as opposed to public sector investment. IFC lends its own, and borrowed, funds to private customers to finance projects in developing countries. It is a profit-making institution and has never made a loss. The projects funded must be expected to have positive outcomes in terms of economic development. The IFC is also involved in giving technical assistance, both to companies and to governments.

The International Development Association (IDA)

Founded in 1960, the IDA gives interest-free loans, with repayment periods of up to 30 years, to the poorest of the developing countries. The lending is funded by contributions from member countries, and voting rights are based upon the size of each country's contributions, which has caused some concern.

The Multilateral Investment Guarantee Agency (MIGA)

Founded in 1988, MIGA promotes foreign direct investment in developing countries by selling political risk insurance to MNCs. This covers war, terrorism, the confiscation of assets by the government, and the freezing of funds within a country. MIGA is funded by the World Bank Group and its member countries.

The International Centre for Settlement of Investment Disputes (ICSID)

Founded in 1966, ICSID facilitates the settlement of investment disputes between member countries and individual international investors. Over 150 countries are now members of the ICSID.

 ## Concerns about aid

While it is generally agreed that humanitarian aid is a necessary and important contribution at times of short-term suffering, much research suggests that there appears to be no significant correlation between the level of aid given to a developing country and the growth of GDP. There are a number of concerns associated with aid as a means of reducing poverty.

In many developing countries the government in power may not necessarily have the welfare of the majority of the population at heart. This means that when aid is received it often goes to a small sector of the population when in many cases these are relatively wealthy city dwellers. Where there is extreme corruption aid often leaves the country almost as soon as it has come in.

Aid is sometimes given for political reasons rather than being given to countries where the need is greatest. It is argued that the developed countries tend to give aid to those countries that are of political or economic interest to them. One result of this is that the poorest people in the world actually receive less aid than people in middle-income countries. For example, Japan has often been accused of using huge aid packages to influence members of the International Whaling Commission (IWC). It gave 617 million yen (US $8.7m) to St Kitts and Nevis, the host of the 2006 IWC conference. It also gave approximately US$17 million to Nicaragua. Both countries voted with Japan to try to end the 20-year ban on commercial whaling.

It is generally agreed that tied aid is not as effective as untied aid. First, the developing country is not able to look for the least expensive goods or services but has to buy from the donor country, which may be more expensive. Second, it creates no employment or extra output in the developing country, since no expenditure takes place there. The imports may also replace domestic products, which may further harm domestic industries. Some economists have argued that tied aid is often politically motivated and is no more than a subsidy to industries in the donor country. The provision of tied aid has fallen in recent years and it has actually been made illegal in some countries. For example, the UK made tied aid illegal in June 2002.

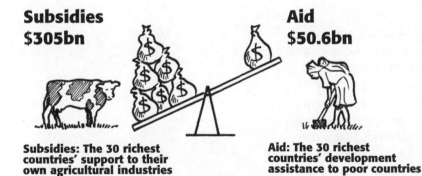

Subsidies $305bn

Aid $50.6bn

Subsidies: The 30 richest countries' support to their own agricultural industries

Aid: The 30 richest countries' development assistance to poor countries

While the short-term provision of food aid may be essential, long-term provision of large quantities of food may force down domestic prices and make matters worse for domestic farmers. It could be considered better for farmers to have a reduction in the subsidies given to farmers in the developed countries.

Continued dependency on aid may mean that there is little incentive to be innovative and that people develop a welfare mentality, where they feel that aid will always be there to help them.

Some argue that aid is often focused on the modern sector, industrialization, and may cause a greater gap in incomes and living standards between those in that sector and those in the traditional agricultural sector.

Aid is often only available if the country agrees to adopt certain economic policies. Donors may argue that aid will only be effective if it is given to countries that adopt what it considers to be "sound" economic policies and these often reflect the Washington Consensus (see Chapter 32) policies that emphasize the free market principles of liberalization, deregulation, and privatization to promote economic growth. It is argued that these policies might be more in the interest of the developed countries and multinational companies and not necessarily in the best interest of developing countries.

There is a suggestion that people in developed countries are beginning to suffer from "aid weariness". They are beginning to think that problems in their own economies may be more important than problems in other countries. This may start to reduce the flows of aid.

As we shall see in the next section, loan repayments on financial aid may lead to massive problems of indebtedness for developing countries.

However, allowing for all the concerns stated, we must not forget that in the poorest countries private investment is not an option and aid may be the only hope. Wars, an illiterate and uneducated workforce, corruption, and a lack of infrastructure mean that it is impossible to attract private investment. In these extreme cases, directly targeted aid, often from NGOs, may be the only viable option if growth and development are to be achieved.

Non-government organisations

NGOs have come to play a major role in international development. It is very difficult to generalize about NGOs as they are incredibly diverse—in size, orientation, outlook, nationality, income, and success. However, we can say that for the most part, the priority of NGOs is to promote economic development, humanitarian ideals, and sustainable development. Their work might be to provide emergency relief in cases of disasters or to provide long-term development assistance. Examples of international NGOs are Oxfam, CARE, Mercy Corps, Cafod, Greenpeace, Amnesty International, Global 2000, and Doctors Without Borders (*Médecins Sans Frontières*).

There are two main activities carried out by NGOs. They plan and implement specifically targeted projects in developing countries and they act as lobbyists to try to influence public policy in areas such as poverty reduction, workers' rights, human rights, and the environment. Some NGOs do one or another of these activities, and some do both, by actively raising funds and raising awareness of the issues. This can result in public pressure on governments that might affect the amount and type of official aid that is given. It may also influence the buying patterns of consumers in ways that contribute to better working conditions and the promotion of sustainable development.

As NGOs work directly in the field they can develop a much deeper understanding of the issues and challenges facing the poor than official aid donors may do. In this way, they can attack poverty directly. They often work in areas that official aid cannot reach and work with groups that might be isolated from official aid. Much of what is done by NGOs focuses on working directly with poor people to enhance their human capital. This may be done in a variety of ways such as literacy programmes, health education, AIDS prevention projects, agricultural extension, micro-credit schemes, immunization, and vocational training.

As noted earlier, many NGOs focus their attention on women in particular, and we have already recognised the value of raising women's incomes and status in achieving overall economic development.

Indebtedness

One of the major drawbacks to growth and development in developing countries is the level of debt repayments that these countries have to make on money that was borrowed previously.

In order to understand this situation we need to look at history and understand the "Third World Debt Crisis". Before the 1970s, the amount of borrowing by developing countries was low, and tended to be in the form of bilateral official aid at concessionary interest rates.

In 1973, the OPEC countries steeply increased oil prices, which led to a massive increase in oil revenues for the oil-exporting countries. These revenues, known as "petro-dollars", were deposited in Western commercial banks and interest rates started to fall sharply because of the large supply of available funds. The banks needed to lend the OPEC money to third parties in order to make profits. There was so much money now available that the usual borrowers did not take the full amount and so the banks offered loans to developing countries.

The developing countries started to borrow money from the Western banks, but these loans were made at market interest rates, not "soft" rates. They were also repayable in "hard" currencies not the currencies of the developing countries. Although the banks lent huge amounts of money they did not monitor what the money was being used for. Unfortunately, relatively little of the money borrowed was used for development purposes. Some went into large infrastructure projects that failed, approximately 20% of the money was spent on arms, and large amounts went into the private bank accounts of dictators, generals, and corrupt politicians.

5 Development Economics

Did you know?

In 1970, the world's 60 poorest countries owed $25 billion in debt. By 2002, this figure had risen to $523 billion. Africa's debt alone rose from $11 billion to $295 in this time.

Debts owed to multilateral institutions such as the IMF currently total around $153 billion, of which $70 billion is owed by the poorest countries.

Between 1970 and 2002, $550 billion was paid in both principal and interest. Despite this, there is still a $523 billion debt burden.

Although the borrowing by developing countries grew at an alarming rate, they managed to keep up payments during the 1970s, as there were high rates of inflation in the world so real interest rates were low. Also, world demand for their commodity exports was relatively high, as were the export prices, so they could earn enough revenue in hard currency to make their repayments.

However, in 1979 OPEC instigated another large increase in oil prices, which contributed to the start of a worldwide recession. This resulted in a sharp fall in the demand for commodities. For a variety of reasons, including lower commodity prices, developing countries found it hard, if not impossible, to make their loan repayments and in 1982 Mexico defaulted on its loans. In simple words, the Mexican government said that they could not "service their debt" that is pay back the loan and its interest. This threatened the whole international credit market—if one country did this what would happen if they all did?

Over the next few years, several countries followed Mexico in their inability to repay their debts and the International Monetary Fund (IMF) became instrumental in trying to solve what became known as the "Third World Debt Crisis" (see box on page 371).

The IMF lent funds to the developing countries that needed them, but would only do so if the countries in question adopted certain policies. These were known as Structural Adjustment Policies and would typically include such things as:

- encouraging trade liberalization by lifting restrictions on imports and exports
- encouraging the exports of primary agricultural commodities, known as "cash crops", and other commodities, such as minerals and metals
- devaluing the currency
- encouraging FDI
- privatization of nationalised industries

- reducing government expenditure in order to ensure that government budgets were balanced

- austerity measures, which reduced social expenditures

- charging for basic services, such as education and health

- removing subsidies and price controls

- improving governance, the process by which decisions are taken and policies are implemented, and reducing levels of corruption.

You will no doubt notice that these reflect the views of the Washington Consensus.

The International Monetary Fund (IMF)

The IMF was proposed at the Bretton Woods Agreements in 1944 and began financial dealings on 1 March 1947.

"The IMF is an organization of 184 countries, working to foster global monetary cooperation, secure financial stability, facilitate international trade, promote high employment and sustainable economic growth, and reduce poverty."
(Source: IMF)

The responsibilities of the IMF are set out in its Articles of Agreement as being:

- promoting international monetary cooperation

- facilitating the expansion and balanced growth of international trade

- promoting exchange stability

- assisting in the establishment of a multilateral system of payments, and

- making its resources available (under adequate safeguards) to members experiencing balance of payments difficulties.

The IMF uses three practices to meet its objectives. These are surveillance, technical assistance, and financial assistance. The IMF conducts an annual in-depth survey of each of its member countries and their economic performance. They then discuss, with the government of the country in question, the policies that are best suited to achieving stable exchange rates and economic growth. This is known as surveillance. These reports are normally published to encourage transparency.

The IMF offers technical assistance and training to its member countries, usually free of charge, in areas such as fiscal and monetary policy, exchange rate policy, banking and finance, and statistics.

When member countries are having problems in financing their balance of payments, the IMF can offer financial assistance in the form of loans. The IMF is funded by a system of "quotas", where each member country deposits money with the IMF. The size of the quota reflects each country's size in economic terms. The loans are made from these quotas. As a condition for receiving the loan, the IMF demands the implementation of a policy programme, agreed by the government of the country and the IMF. Support only continues if the policies are effectively carried out.

The policies were originally known as Structural Adjustment Policies (SAP). Now, in dealings with developing countries, the IMF uses Poverty Reduction Strategy Papers (PRSP), which detail a comprehensive economic, structural and social policy framework that is to be implemented to promote growth and reduce poverty in the country.

Working independently, and in partnership with the World Bank, the IMF provides concessional lending through the Poverty Reduction and Growth Facility, and the Exogenous Shocks Facility, and debt relief under the Heavily Indebted Poor Countries (HIPC) Initiative and the Multilateral Debt Relief Initiative.

5 Development Economics

The SAPs were heavily criticised by many development economists and by developing country governments. Although they may have helped in controlling inflation, improving the workings of the internal markets in the economy, lowering government budget deficits, reducing public ownership, and reforming exchange rate policies, it was also felt that there were heavy costs involved. These fell mainly on the very poor and included:

- a reduction in government-provided services, such as education and health care

- increasing unemployment

- a fall in real wage levels

- increased prices of essential products, as government subsidies were taken away.

As a result of the above, a significant number of developing countries experienced "de-development", indicated by increasing rates of malnutrition, declining school attendance rates, and increasing infant mortality figures. Although the SAPs may lead to long-term growth, it is often argued that the short-term costs to the very poor are simply too great.

At the present time many developing countries still have major problems with indebtedness. This has led to much international public debate about the importance of debt relief. Many argue that the debts of developing countries should be reduced or cancelled.

One reason given in favour of debt relief relates to debt servicing, the repayment of the original debt plus interest repayments. Some countries have only been able to afford to pay back interest, and not always all of it, so they have found that their debt has actually grown. For example, Nigeria borrowed $17 billion, has paid back $18 billion so far, and still owes $34 billion.[1] It has been argued that this escalation of the original debt is unfair.

Another reason is that the need to service debt means that governments are unable to spend money on other areas of the economy. This is a case of opportunity cost that has a detrimental effect on two fronts. First, it slows down economic growth. For example, governments do not have funds to invest in improving infrastructure. Second, it slows down development, because governments cannot afford to provide essential services. For example, Malawi spends more money on debt servicing than it does on the provision of health care.[2] Debt relief will release money, allowing governments to finance development objectives. This can be illustrated in a very simple diagram, similar to that of the production possibilities curve. If a government has a given amount of revenue, then it must choose between competing demands for the money. The demands include the requirement to service debt, invest in infrastructure, and invest in human capital through spending on education and health

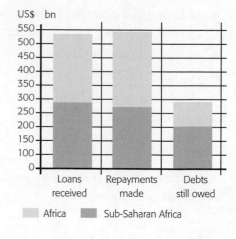

Figure 33.2 Africa's debts 1970–2002

---

[1] *Make Poverty History*, Geraldine Bedell, Penguin Books, 2005.
[2] Ibid.

care. If we take Malawi as an example, assume that the government is operating at point A on the "Spending Possibilities Line" shown in Figure 33.3. As you can see, it is spending more servicing its debt than it is on health care. If Malawi were granted debt relief, then it would be able to increase its spending on health care.

One of the main reasons put forward for debt relief is the issue of odious debt. Odious debt is a legal term and refers to debt that is incurred by a regime and is then used for purposes that do not serve the interests of the people. It is argued that much of the debt incurred by developing countries should be classified as odious debt. Dictators may have used much of the borrowed money for individual purposes and yet the people of the countries, having received no real benefits from the money, are now the ones that have to pay it back. The argument is that the lenders of the money, the Western commercial banks, international financial institutions, and developed countries were equally at fault in making the loans that they did. As such, they should not expect further repayment.

The development economist Susan George suggests that there are boomerangs associated with debt that come back to hit developed countries.[3] She suggests that debt creates problems for the developed countries in areas such as environmental damage, increased drug usage, higher taxes, higher unemployment, increased immigration, and increased levels of conflict. She argues that the developed countries themselves would thus benefit if debt were eliminated. It is also argued that debt relief would allow developing countries to experience better rates of economic growth. Rising incomes create more demand and this would benefit exporters in more developed countries. This is another reason suggesting why developed countries would also benefit from debt relief.

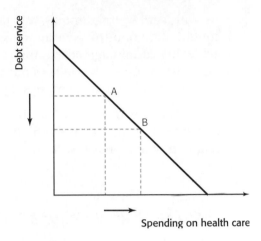

Figure 33.3 A government "Spending Possibilities Line"

Student workpoint 33.2

Be an inquirer

Choose one of Susan George's "debt boomerangs" to explain why developing country debt is also damaging to developed countries.

In 1996, the IMF and the World Bank launched a new programme. This was known as the Heavily Indebted Poor Countries (HIPC) Initiative. The programme was reviewed and modified in 1999. HIPC countries are those with the highest levels of poverty, which are undergoing international debt relief measures to reduce their external debts. The HIPC Initiative currently identifies 40 countries as being potentially eligible for debt relief. The majority of the countries are in sub-Saharan Africa.

---

[3] Source: *The Debt Boomerang*, Susan George, Pluto Press, 1992

5 Development Economics

As with earlier programmes, assistance under the HIPC Initiative is conditional upon the governments of the countries in question achieving certain agreed economic targets. These targets are still very much based upon the policies put forward in the Washington Consensus and have been the subject of much debate.

There appears to be no doubt that debt relief can be extremely effective in promoting growth and development. However, it is highly probable that it will not be enough on its own.

Student workpoint 33.3

Be an inquirer

Research one of the countries that has been designated as an HIPC to try to assess the extent to which it has benefited from debt relief.

Market-led v interventionist growth strategies

As we reach this final point in our study of Diploma Programme economics, we summarize the strengths and weaknesses of the two main approaches to growth and development: market-led strategies and interventionist strategies.

It should come as no surprise to you that there are two schools of thought. The discussion of the free market versus intervention runs throughout economics and has done so for over 250 years! Disagreements between Keynesian and classical economists, and neo-Keynesian and neo-classical economists, over macroeconomic policy in the twentieth century were mostly related to exactly this topic. All that has happened now is that the disagreement has taken on an international focus.

As we already know, market-led strategies are policies that are designed to minimize the role of the government and to maximize the free operation of supply and demand in markets. Examples of this would be export-led growth, growth through FDI, privatization of national industries, deregulation and the Structural Adjustment Policies and Poverty Reduction Strategy Papers of the International Monetary Fund and the World Bank. They are known by a number of names including free market policies, neo-classical policies, or neo-liberal policies.

Interventionist strategies are policies involving an active role by the government and manipulation of the workings of the markets in the economy. Examples of this would be import substitution, protectionist trade policies, exchange rate intervention, regulations, nationalization of industries, and government involvement in export markets to promote certain industries and their products.

It is fair to say that from the end of the second world war, and for about the next 30 years, there were various trends in terms of how to achieve economic growth and development over that time, but the main emphasis was government planning.

'In 2001, Tanzania was granted significant debt relief. As promised, this was directed to the priority sectors of education, health, water, rural roads and HIV/AIDS. Now the primary school population has increased by 66%; we have built 45,000 classrooms and 1,925 primary schools; we have recruited 37,261 new teachers between 2000 and 2004, and retrained another 14,852. At this rate we believe that the goal of universal basic education can be attained in 2006, nine years ahead of the 2015 target! ... Tanzania has shown dramatic improvements after getting partial debt relief. Clearly, much more can be done with total debt cancellation.'

Benjamin William Mkapa, president of the United Republic of Tanzania

However, there were no real examples of sustained growth and development from the countries involved, and also there were other problems that arose.

- Public sectors in these countries grew too large, leading to bureaucracy, over-staffing, and inefficiency. This, together with growing political instability, also provided the opportunity for the growth of corrupt practices.

- Nationalized industries, of which there were many, tended to be inefficient and thus loss-making. They also led to hidden unemployment.

- Government spending tended to be excessive, leading to large budget deficits, and thus the need for borrowing and for increasing the money supply.

- The increases in the money supply tended to lead to high levels of inflation.

- Much of the expenditure was on large infrastructure projects that saw little success.

In the 1980s, a movement towards more free market, supply-side-oriented governments in developed countries, such as the Reagan administration in the USA and the Thatcher government in the UK, saw a shift of emphasis in government policy in developed countries and a change of direction in thinking on the best way to achieve growth and development in developing countries.

As well as the change in economic policies in major developed countries, there were a number of other factors that influenced this change of direction.

- Following the Third World Debt Crisis, there were many developing countries that needed to borrow money from the IMF in order to avoid defaulting on their loans. The IMF would only grant loans if the countries adopted Structural Adjustment Policies that, as we know, were very market-based.

- The transition of the Soviet Union and its satellite states towards market-based economies, which started in the late 1980s, had two effects. First, it acted as a signal that planning was not a successful option in the quest for growth and development. Second, it removed financial support for a number of developing countries, which had been aligned with Eastern Bloc countries, forcing them to seek support elsewhere.

- The perceived success of the "Asian Tigers" such as Japan, Taiwan, Singapore, Hong Kong, and South Korea, who appeared to have adopted export-led growth and encouraged FDI, was significant in influencing thinking on the ways to achieve high levels of economic growth.

In the light of the above, developing countries were encouraged to reduce the role of the government in their economies and to adopt a more outward looking approach to achieving growth. In general terms, this included:

5 Development Economics

373

- freeing domestic markets, by eliminating price controls and subsidies, and increasing competition
- liberalising international trade, by eliminating trade restrictions, and encouraging FDI
- privatizing nationalized industries
- reducing government expenditure in order to eliminate budget deficits.

However, as we have moved into the new century, a number of concerns have been raised about the value of adopting a pure market-led approach.

Infrastructure is unlikely to be created through a market-based approach and developing countries simply do not have sufficient infrastructure to adopt a free market approach. Thus this requires planning for the future and government intervention.

Although the more developed countries promote trade liberalization, they themselves do not liberalize all their trade. Protectionism in developed countries makes it very difficult for the developing countries to compete on a fair basis. In recent years, led by the larger developing countries such as Brazil and India, developing countries have been cooperating with each other to have more influence in trade negotiations.

The success of the export-led Asian Tigers did not happen without government intervention. The governments in question were very interventionist in specific areas, especially in product markets that needed help and protection before they were able to export. They also were able to place great emphasis upon education and health care.

Although a more free market approach may lead to economic growth in the long run, there are without doubt short-run costs to the poorest people. In the short run, unemployment rises, as do the prices of essential products, and the provision of public services also falls. This will hit the poorest sector of the population more than anyone else, causing greater income inequality.

The adoption of free market strategies tends to concentrate attention and activities on the urban sectors of an economy and this tends to increase the divide between rural and urban areas, increasing the levels of poverty in rural areas and also leading to migration from rural areas to urban areas. This has created large area of slums on the edge of many major cities in developing countries.

Governments may adopt the concept of liberalized flows of capital, but a lack of political stability means that many countries are not in a position to attract the FDI necessary to achieve growth.

In the end, it is clear that the solutions will lie in a combination of different approaches and that the combination will need to be tailored to suit the needs of each individual country. Adopting a "one size fits all" policy will not be effective, as the IMF discovered with SAPs in the 1980s.

As a brief conclusion, we try to summarize some of the conditions that economists believe will be necessary for both economic growth and economic development to be achieved in developing countries.

- Trade justice—so that the developing countries are trading on a fair basis with the developed countries, not hampered by protectionist policies.

- Debt relief—to release funds that may be invested in physical and human capital.

- The free working of domestic markets, but only once the markets have achieved a competitive size and have sufficient support in terms of infrastructure, quality of the labour force, and technological and managerial expertise.

- The encouragement of political stability and good governance and the elimination of corruption.

- Effective, targeted, aid that leads to pro-poor growth—so that the aid given is directed at policies that will encourage economic growth that leads to a fall in poverty.

Examination questions

Short response questions

1 Explain why non-government organisations may be able to effectively promote economic development. *[10 marks]*

2 Distinguish between humanitarian aid and development aid. *[10 marks]*

3 Explain the possible benefits of debt relief to a developing country. *[10 marks]*

Essay questions

1 a Explain the characteristics of an IMF Structural Adjustment Plan (SAP). *[10 marks]*

  b Evaluate the effectiveness of a SAP for a country striving to achieve economic development. *[15 marks]*

2 a Explain the main characteristics of a market economy. *[10 marks]*

  b Evaluate the proposition that economic development is best achieved through the market system. *[15 marks]*

You be the journalist

Headline: Thousands line the streets urging the government to "drop the debt"

Economic concept: Debt relief

Diagram: Poverty cycle or government "spending possibilities line"

Data response exercise

Study the extract and data below and answer the questions that follow.

Tanzania

Tanzania is one of the poorest countries in the world. In spite of progress in certain areas, *per capita* income in 2004 is estimated to be at about US$282. Tanzania's economy is strongly dominated by agriculture, accounting for 45% of GDP and 85% of exports. This dependence has resulted in deteriorating terms of trade.

One of the key challenges in achieving sustainable improvements comes from rising numbers of HIV infections. Along with other worrying signs for **economic development** (see Figure 3), this is likely to have negative consequences for the productive labour force and hence growth.

Other key problems include inefficient land and labour markets, slow progress in the privatization of the gas, water and electricity industries, corruption in the administration and judicial system, and limited human and physical capacity.

The World Bank's board approved a Country Assistance Strategy (CAS) for Tanzania in June 2000. The focus of World Bank lending is on higher growth, poverty reduction, and institutional reforms to improve the quality of government. The strategy supports the priorities of the Tanzania government in its commitment to macroeconomic stability, renewed emphasis on rural development, greater openness in government, and increased private sector participation.

Adapted from original articles that appeared in *Human Development Report*, 2002 and *The World Development*, 2003

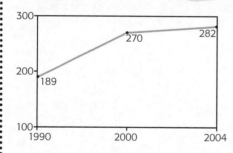

Figure 1 Gross domestic product (US$ per capita)

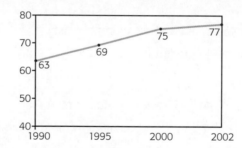

Figure 2 Literacy rate (percentage of adults)

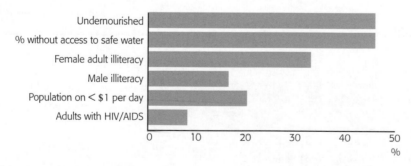

Figure 3 Poverty percentages

1 Define the following terms indicated in bold in the text:

   a economic development   *[2 marks]*

   b gross domestic product (GDP)   *[2 marks]*

2 Using an appropriate diagram, explain the effect of the improvement in the literacy rate on economic growth, as shown in the data. *[4 marks]*

3 Explain why the importance of agriculture in Tanzania may result in the change in the terms of trade suggested in the text. *[4 marks]*

4 Using the data and your knowledge of economics, evaluate measures that could be taken to achieve development in Tanzania. *[8 marks]*

N05 economics SL P2, q1

Data response exercise

Study the extract below and answer the questions that follow.

Africa's economic problems have a medical solution

Malaria kills three children per minute and this hidden global catastrophe affects Africa most. Currently, 300 million to 500 million cases occur each year, with severe cases resulting in death. Of the estimated 27 million people killed by malaria every year, 75% are African children under the age of five.

As the G8 countries (the world's eight leading industrialized countries) deliberate on a new approach for lifting African nations out of poverty, the leaders must look beyond increased aid and trade. Fighting disease must be a central part of economic strategy for Africa if countries are to achieve a significant boost in economic growth to reduce poverty and generate positive externalities.

Infectious diseases have crippled African efforts to achieve economic self-sufficiency and economic development for the last half century, well before the **indebtedness** crisis and the trade issues that have dominated G8 discussion on Africa.

If G8 leaders and others want to increase GDP in developing countries, they should consider that diseases such as malaria result in an enormous price for developing countries, not only in lives, but also in medical costs and lost labour, harming the economic well-being of entire families, communities and nations. Malaria keeps the poor in a continuous poverty cycle. According to a Harvard University study published in 2000, Africa's annual GDP would be US$100 billion more than it is today if malaria had been eliminated 35 years ago – many times more than all the development aid programmes to Africa in a year.

Meaningful **economic development** in Africa cannot occur if addressing infectious disease is seen as a secondary goal rather than a critical part of the new vision of economic stability. This will require that the people who implement a new economic plan for Africa must broaden their notion of what constitutes a successful macroeconomic strategy.

Adapted from original articles that appeared in *The Guardian Weekly*, 11–17 July 2002

1 Define the following terms indicated in bold in the text:

  a economic development *[2 marks]*

  b indebtedness *[2 marks]*

2 Using an appropriate diagram, explain how the provision of a malaria vaccine by the G8 countries would generate positive externalities for African nations. *[4 marks]*

3 Explain the link between the poverty cycle and disease. *[4 marks]*

4 Using information from the text and your knowledge of economics, evaluate the role of indebtedness in constraining economic development for African countries. *[8 marks]*

M05 economics HL P3, q5

34 Assessment advice and service opportunities

Preparing for your economics examinations

Hopefully, you will be able to start preparing for your exams well in advance. There are hundreds of approaches to exam revision, so we will not go into them here. However, there are several pieces of advice that we would like to share.

First, one thing that you have to do on *all* papers is define the key terms. Thus one element of your revision should involve making sure that you know accurate definitions of economic words. You should actively write out your own glossary and test yourself to ensure that you can remember the definitions.

Second, it is also recommended that you compile a collection of diagrams. Again, it is not enough to simply look at the diagrams in your notes or in your textbooks. You need to practise drawing them yourself, from memory, to ensure that you can include accurate labels and show the correct relationships between variables on the graphs. The key to remembering the graphs is to understand the story that they are telling.

Third, marks are awarded for the inclusion of examples wherever appropriate. Thus, as you are preparing your own revision notes, you are encouraged to note down current and relevant examples. For instance, if you are studying negative externalities of consumption, note the example of the external costs of smoking. If you are studying international trade barriers, then include an example such as the anti-dumping measures taken by the European Union against Chinese and Vietnamese shoes. If you are studying unemployment, then note some of the key facts about the country that you studied.

Fourth, a very important skill that the examination assesses is the skill of evaluation. We provide a separate explanation of this later in this chapter.

Revision notes should include definitions, diagrams, and examples.

Advice for all exam papers

This follows on from the information above. Marks are specifically given for defining the key terms, so make sure that you do this. At the very least, the economics words that are in the question must be defined.

Always draw diagrams where they are appropriate and draw as many diagrams as you need to make the points clear. Make sure you put *accurate* labels on the axes and all the curves and remember to show the correct relationships between the variables. Draw arrows to indicate the direction of changes in variables. Be sure to make reference to your diagrams in your writing.

The presentation of diagrams is very important. Use a ruler and draw your diagrams in pencil so that you can make corrections if necessary. Different colours are useful for showing shifts in curves (but not red, please, because examiners use red to correct the papers). Don't try to squeeze a diagram into a small space on the page. A small diagram may be difficult to interpret properly and it may be difficult to incorporate all the necessary information if it is too small.

Top mark bands include a reference to examples, so wherever remotely possible, include examples.

Standard level Paper 1 and Higher level Paper 1: the essay paper

For higher level students, this paper is worth 20% of the final grade. For standard level students, it is worth 25% of the final grade. There are four questions on this paper, and you are required to do one question in one hour.

All questions are divided into two parts. Part (a) is worth 10 marks and part (b) is worth 15 marks. You will be given five minutes of reading time before you can start writing, so this gives you time to carefully consider each question so that you can make the right choice. If there is not a full question that jumps out as the right one, carefully consider the marks available. It is more important that you are comfortable with part (b) because it is worth more marks.

In this paper, you want to be able to show that you have some in-depth understanding of one specific topic, but you will not do this if you have not read the question carefully. A very common error on this paper is that students don't read the questions carefully enough and write a lot of economic theory that isn't directly relevant to the question. Remember that it is the quality of the answer that is important, not the quantity!

It is a very good idea to make a plan before you start to write. You might think that there is not enough time, but a plan will help you to stay on track once you have started writing. You do not want to get sidetracked and lose your focus on the question. A plan can help you to manage your time properly and ensure that you cover the main points.

Ideally, parts (a) and (b) will be closely linked. It is suggested that you write an introduction in part (a) in which you set out what you are going to do in the whole answer. At the end of part (a), try to make a link to part (b). However, please be aware that parts (a) and (b) must be presented separately. Be sure you leave a space and note the (a) and the (b). Physically, the answer will appear in two separate sections. Because there is evaluation in part (b), a conclusion should come at the end. Although marks are not specifically given for an introduction and a conclusion as they might be in a languages exam, structuring your essay suitably will definitely lead to greater clarity, and this will help you to earn higher marks. As you proceed through the answer, keep checking to see that you are sticking to the question and not just trying to throw in all the economics you know!

In part (a), you will be asked to explain a particular economic concept or theory or to distinguish between related economic concepts. Here is a list of descriptors taken from the mark scheme to show you what is required for an excellent answer:

- clear understanding of the specific demands of the question
- relevant economic theory clearly explained and developed
- relevant terms clearly defined
- where appropriate, diagrams have been included and explained
- where appropriate, examples have been used
- no major errors.

In part (b) you will be asked to move beyond an explanation towards the evaluation of a particular economic policy or theory. You do not need to repeat the definitions that you wrote in part (a), but it is likely that there will be some new terms to define. If you have drawn diagrams in part (a) that are useful, then you can refer back to them, but it is likely that you will be extending the information in part (b) and so it may be more useful to redraw the diagrams and add the necessary information. For example, you might be asked to distinguish between demand-deficient and structural unemployment in part (a) and then asked to evaluate the policies that a government might use to reduce unemployment in part (b). It is likely that you will have drawn diagrams to support your answer in part (a), but you would need new diagrams to illustrate the solutions in part (b). The following list of descriptors is taken from the mark scheme and shows you what is required for an excellent answer:

- clear understanding of the specific demands of the question
- relevant economic theory clearly explained and developed
- relevant terms clearly defined
- where appropriate, diagrams have been included and explained
- where appropriate, examples have been used
- evidence of appropriate evaluation
- no major errors.

Higher level Paper 2: the short response paper

This paper is worth 20% of the final grade for higher level students. There are six questions on this paper and you are required to do three questions in one hour. Each question is worth 10 marks.

You will be given five minutes of reading time in which you are not allowed to start to write. This should give you enough time to select your three questions and begin to think about how you are going to answer them. Just as in Paper 1, it is extremely important that you read the questions very carefully so that you can make sure that you include the appropriate relevant theory.

The questions on this paper are similar to the part (a) questions on Paper 1. You will be asked to explain a particular economic concept or theory or distinguish between related concepts. You will not be asked to provide evaluation on this part of the examination. The general advice provided earlier is very important here. Every answer should include definitions of key terms, diagrams wherever appropriate, and relevant examples. You should consider these three items as a checklist and ask yourself whether you have included them all in each answer. Very occasionally, there is no appropriate diagram to be included, but do note that this is rare and you should always try to think of including at least one diagram. The mark scheme for the answers on this paper is the same as it is for the essay part (a) so you can refer to the previous page to see what you are aiming for in an excellent answer.

Clearly, as you have to answer three questions in one hour, you will have to work efficiently and manage your time properly. You should take 20 minutes for each answer. No matter how good they are, if you spend too long on the first and second questions, you will quite simply lose the opportunity to gain the marks on the third question. To help with their time management, many students keep their watches face up on their desk and make a note of the times at which they should move on to the next question. The best advice for this is practice—hopefully, your teachers will give you lots of tests to allow you to practise the skill of writing answers in 20 minutes!

Standard level Paper 2 and Higher level Paper 3: the data response paper

For higher level students, this paper is worth 40% of the final grade. For standard level students, it is worth 50% of the final grade. There are five questions on this paper, and you are required to do three questions in two hours. Each question is worth 20 marks.

All five questions will follow exactly the same format. There will be a set of data in the form of a piece of written text or in the form of numerical data (a table or graph) or a combination of text and numerical data. Each data response question has four sub-questions as described below.

- *Part (a):* You are asked to define two words that are in the text. Each definition is worth two marks. A very common problem here is that students often write far too much on the definitions, thus wasting valuable time.

- *Parts (b) and (c):* These sub-questions require you to apply a specific piece of economic theory and are worth four marks each. In the majority of cases, you will be asked to draw a diagram. Sometimes it will tell you which diagram to use, and sometimes this will be left up to you to decide. When you draw your diagrams, be sure to label the axes with the variables noted in the text. For example, if the text is about the price of chickens in China, then the y-axis label might be *price of chickens in yuan remnimbi*. On these sub-questions, you must carefully assess what the question is asking. You will be under time pressure and should not write more than necessary as it will cut into your time for the other questions. Always try to make use of the text to support your use of the theory. Use a decent amount of space for the diagrams and the explanations. Examiners do not like to see writing and diagrams squeezed into small spaces.

- *Part (d):* This sub-question asks you to use the information from the text and your knowledge of economics to evaluate something related to the text. This part of the question carries the most weight as it is worth eight out of the twenty marks. A key problem here is that students forget to use information from the text, even though the instructions specifically ask for this. Therefore, you are encouraged to use quotations or numerical data from the data in your answers. The section on evaluation that follows this should help you to know how you can be evaluative.

The five minutes of reading time are incredibly important here. You'll get a chance to skim all the questions to see which questions ask things you know about. Do not decide to do a question simply because you can define the two words given in part (a). It is more important that you can answer the last questions worth eight marks each. When you can begin to write, it is recommended that you annotate the text—underline, highlight, make notes in the margin—anything to make you familiar with the data.

Effective time management is also extremely important. You have to do three questions in two hours, which works out to 40 minutes per question. It might be helpful to write down the times at which you should move on to the next question and make sure that you stick to these or else you will not have enough time to complete three questions. If you have learned your definitions and diagrams effectively, then you should be able to move quite quickly through parts (a), (b), and (c), thus leaving yourself sufficient time to thoughtfully carry out the evaluation.

Evaluation

There are several places on your exam where you are asked to evaluate something. One place is the part (d) on the data response question and the other one is in part (b) of the essay. You should be aware that on the questions on HL3 and SL2, the highest mark bands are reserved for students who can illustrate the skill of evaluation.

What does evaluation mean?

Two dictionary definitions of evaluate are as follows:

- v: to examine and judge carefully; appraise
- v: to place a value on; judge the worth of something.

How can you evaluate?

It is not quite enough to simply finish a sentence that begins "On the other hand...", but it is a good start.

- *Compare advantages and disadvantages:* Perhaps the easiest way to evaluate is to explain the advantages or disadvantages of a particular economic issue or policy. This is a useful step in evaluation, but it isn't quite enough. In order to complete the process, you need to make conclusions about the relative weight of the advantages or disadvantages.

  Example 1: "This shows that there are several advantages of protectionism in international trade. However, in terms of global resource allocation, the disadvantages outweigh the advantages and justify the efforts of the WTO to liberalize international trade."

Example 2: "As the diagram shows, the clear disadvantage of a minimum wage is that it can increase unemployment. However, the advantage of a minimum wage is that it ensures that workers earn a reasonable wage, and this may outweigh the increase in unemployment."

- *Prioritise the arguments:* After giving a list of points, you could make a conclusion in which you state which one is the more (or least) significant or important point and then explain why.

  Example 1: "The most important argument against protectionism in international trade is that it represents a global misallocation of resources. This is because when countries erect protectionist barriers, they are supporting inefficient domestic producers at the expense of more efficient producers in foreign countries that are exploiting their comparative advantage."

  Example 2: "The least effective way to effectively reduce the negative effects of smoking is to increase taxes. This is because the demand for cigarettes is inelastic and the increase in price due to taxes is likely to result in a proportionately smaller fall in quantity demanded. However, the government may earn high tax revenues which can be used to pay for the external costs and finance no-smoking campaigns."

  Note that in each case, it is not enough to say which is the most important; you also need to explain why.

- *Long run vs. short run:* It is quite possible that the short-run consequences of an economic policy or event might be different from the long-run consequences. If you distinguish between the two time frames, you will be evaluating.

  Example 1: "In the short run, abnormal profits can be earned in perfect competition. However, in the long run this is not possible. The existence of abnormal profits, perfect information, and lack of barriers to entry means that industry supply will increase, driving down the price taken by individual firms so that only normal profits may be earned."

  Example 2: "In the short run, it may be possible to justify the infant industry argument as it is possible that, protected by tariffs, some firms will develop the economies of scale necessary to be internationally competitive. However, the danger is that in the long run, the industry will not become internationally competitive due to the lack of effective competition."

- *Consider the issue from the points of view of different stakeholders:* What is a stakeholder? One dictionary definition is as follows: "a person or group that has an investment, share, or interest in something".

  In terms of economic theory, examples of stakeholders could be domestic producers, consumers, foreign producers, high-income people, low-income people, or the government.

  Example 1: "A high exchange rate may be *good for consumers* because it makes imported goods less expensive and forces domestic producers to be more efficient so that they compete with the less expensive imports. On the other hand, it is clearly a *disadvantage for those domestic producers* who suffer from the competition from imports which become less expensive with the higher value of the currency."

Example 2: "Supply-side policies may be very good in terms of creating a more flexible labour force and achieving economic growth. However, they may lower the standard of living of workers who may suffer from deregulation of the labour laws."

Internal assessment

Every IB Diploma Programme Economics student completes a portfolio containing four "commentaries" of between 650 and 750 words each. You select your own articles from the print media and write a commentary in which you apply economic theory to the real-world example discussed in the article. Ideally, the four commentaries are written as the course progresses, as you learn more and more economic theory. The four commentaries must come from at least three sections of the syllabus.

The portfolio as a whole is worth 25% of the final grade for standard level students and 20% of the final grade for higher level students. Assessment of the portfolio is identical for both groups and is based on five criteria. These mirror the skills that are emphasized in the examinations, but without the time pressure of an exam! The criteria are listed and briefly explained in Table 34.1.

Criterion	Title	What is expected?	Marks available
A	Rubric requirements	Each commentary must be within the word count and the portfolio as a whole must address at least three of the five syllabus sections.	2
B	Organisation and presentation	The articles must come from four different sources. The commentaries should be well-presented, should include appropriate diagrams, and should be properly referenced.	4
C	Use of economic terminology	Throughout the portfolio, appropriate economic terminology is employed and definitions of key words are provided.	5
D	Application and analysis of economic concepts and theories	Throughout the portfolio, relevant concepts and theories have been identified and applied or analysed well.	5
E	Evaluation	Throughout the portfolio, there is evidence of appropriate evaluation of the economic concepts and/or theories.	4

Table 34.1 Internal assessment criteria

It is not possible to provide the full assessment details in this companion so it is absolutely vital that students are given access to the full IB document about internal assessment in economics. This includes sample commentaries that will help the students have an understanding of the end result. Included in the guide are valuable checklists, frequently asked questions, and further hints for students.

The first step in approaching the task of writing a commentary is to find a suitable current article. Nowadays, the bulk of articles come from Internet sources and there are a number of search engines that are useful in finding appropriate articles. Ideally, you will find articles that highlight the theory that you have just finished studying. This way, the material will be fresh, and hopefully you will have been discussing relevant examples in class. Table 34.2 provides some examples of words that can be used on search engines to generate articles on topics once they have been studied.

Topic covered	Possible search words or phrases
Theory of the firm (Section 2)	Monopoly power, price-fixing, collusion, competition commission, competition watchdog
Market failure (Section 2)	External costs, air pollution, water pollution, road-pricing, cigarette taxes, alcohol taxes, sustainable development
Macroeconomics (Section 3)	Consumer confidence, interest rate changes, aggregate demand, unemployment, inflation
International trade (Section 4)	Trade disputes, tariffs, subsidies, quotas, VERs
Exchange rates and balance of payments (Section 4)	Value of the euro (or any other currency), current account deficit, trade deficit,
Development (Section 5)	Aid, MNCs, Fairtrade, micro-credit, agricultural subsidies, debt, foreign direct investment

Table 34.2 Suggestions for finding articles

You should *not* take the first article that you find. You should read through several and take your time to select the one that allows you to write down relevant definitions, apply the theory through the use of graphs and written explanation, and illustrate evaluative skills. Short articles, concerned with real economic matters, are recommended. The article that you choose may be written in any language, but you are required to provide a translation of the article if it is not in the working language of your school. This allows you to choose one in your own language, but will give you some extra work. Please note that as part of the requirements, you must choose the four articles from four different sources.

One danger in the writing of commentaries is that students often simply summarise or paraphrase their article. This is not the correct approach. You might provide a brief introduction in which you summarize what the issue is about, but the bulk of the commentary must include definitions, diagrams, analysis, and evaluation.

As with any of the assessment carried out in economics, it is very important to include diagrams. Just as in any data response exercises that you do, make sure that you label the axes accurately and use the relevant data from the text. For example, if the article is about sugar subsidies to European farmers, don't just write "price" on the y-axis, write "price of sugar in euros". If there are any figures in the text, then try to use them on the diagrams.

The presentation of your portfolio will be enhanced if you adopt a common format throughout the portfolio. That is, use a common font, size, and style for each of the commentaries. According to the IB guidelines, a standardized cover sheet that includes the following information must accompany each commentary:

● the title of the extract
● the source of the extract

- the date of the extract
- the word count of the commentary
- the date the commentary was written
- the section(s) of the syllabus to which the commentary relates.

Once the final portfolio is complete, your teacher should provide you with a standardized form known as the Portfolio Cover Sheet that is to be placed on the front of your portfolio. Your teacher will then mark the portfolio, and submit the marks to the IB. These marks will be subject to moderation by an external examiner who will be sent a sample of portfolios from your school.

The extended essay

An extended essay in economics provides you with the opportunity to undertake in-depth research in economics in an area of personal interest. It gives you the opportunity to develop research skills, to apply economic theory to real-world situations, and to analyse and evaluate the outcomes of your research. The outcome of the research should be a coherent and structured analytical essay, which effectively addresses the particular research question.

Perhaps the most important information available to you when you write your extended essay, regardless of the subject area, are the IB assessment criteria. Quite simply, no matter how good a writer you are, if you are not aware of the specific guidelines and assessment criteria published by the IB, then you are not likely to write a successful essay. In fact, we often compare the assessment criteria to a recipe. If you are trying to cook something new, then you should follow a recipe to achieve best results. Please note that new extended essay criteria will apply from 2009 onwards. The advice given here is relevant to the old and new criteria.

How you should choose your topic

First of all, you should choose something that interests you. However, more importantly, you must choose a topic that allows you to apply the economic theory that you learn in the course. While there is a lot more to economic theory than simply the material that is in the IB course, you do not want to have to do a lot of extra learning on the side! Perhaps the best reason for choosing and expanding on a topic covered in class is that this will ensure that you are choosing an appropriate economics topic.

In choosing your topic, you will need to think of the research that you are able to do. If at all possible, try to think of topics where you can gather some primary data, either through questionnaires, surveys, or interviews. Having said this, there are highly successful essays that are based on useful secondary data, particularly statistical data. The key is that the topic chosen should provide opportunities for some critical analysis of the data collected.

After choosing your topic, the most important task is to develop your research question (RQ). This should definitely be able to be phrased as a question, but it should not be a yes/no question. Nor should it be a double question, such as "Do the petrol stations in Haastown operate in an oligopoly and, if so, do they collude?"

You should also avoid asking questions that are too historical in nature, such as "What were the effects of the supply-side policies of Ronald Reagan?" While analysis that makes a comparison over time may be very good, you should avoid going back farther than 10 years into the past. The danger with choosing something that has taken place in the past is that the essay is likely to be a descriptive summary of secondary sources that have already considered the topic and it is unlikely that you will be able to use your own economic analysis. Your question must be capable of being answered through the application of economic concepts and theories.

It is incredibly important that you narrow the focus of your essay to ask something that is very specific in its scope. In doing this, you should be able to demonstrate some detailed economic understanding and critical analysis. Do not choose a question that investigates the impact of an economic event or policy on a whole economy, e.g. "What are the effects of the World Cup on the German economy?" is far too large in scope.

The following examples of titles for economics extended essays are intended as guidance only. The pairings illustrate that focused topics (indicated by the first title) should be encouraged rather than broad topics (indicated by the second title).

● What market form characterises the petrol supply industry in my area of Madrid? *is better than* What is the market structure of the Spanish petroleum industry?

● What is the effect on unemployment in the fast food industry in Graz of the recent imposition of a minimum wage in Austria? *is better than* What has been the effect of the minimum wage on unemployment in Austria?

● To what extent has the fall in the exchange rate of the US dollar affected the tourist industry in Carmel, California? *is better than* How has the fall in the exchange rate of the US dollar affected the US economy?

● What has been the economic effect of water privatization on the farming industry in my region of Zambia? *is better than* How has the privatization of water affected Zambia?

Every school has its own timetable for the completion of the extended essay, but it is hoped that you will have plenty of time to change your focus if it turns out that you have asked a question that you are unable to answer because there is simply not enough information.

When writing your essay, it is vital that you integrate relevant economic theory with the evidence obtained through the research. It is not appropriate to deliver several pages of theory as a separate section of the essay. Any theory that you present must be presented in the context of your research question. Additionally, you should not try to expand your essay by including irrelevant material or information that you cannot directly link to the question. It should be evident throughout the entire essay that the research question is being answered. A valid and persuasive argument needs to be developed in a clear and structured way with some awareness that there may be alternative viewpoints. You should also attempt to show critical awareness of the validity of your information and the possible limitations of your arguments. Very importantly, the essay should clearly note any assumptions that have been made in setting out the argument and reaching the conclusions.

You will be "measured" by your ability to use the language and concepts of economics. All important terms that are included should be defined and the concepts should be explained. This will be enhanced through the use of diagrams that, as always, must be accurately labelled. The diagrams should reflect the evidence acquired through your research. Thus if you are doing an essay on local house prices, the diagram should illustrate the domestic currency and should include some actual numbers.

One of the criteria measures the presentation of your essay. This refers to several things and these are described clearly in the assessment criteria. It includes a measure of the physical layout of the essay with the required elements such as a table of contents and page numbering. It considers your ability to compile an appropriate bibliography and cite the sources of all the information that you have used. There are several different methods for doing this. The key is that you adopt one of the accepted standardized methods and stick to it. Please be sure that as soon as you start your research you keep a very detailed list of all the material that you use so that you can put it all together in the bibliography. It is very difficult to track down resources several months after you have used them. This is particularly the case for any Internet sites that you use. Be sure to note the full address, the date accessed, and the title of any articles that you use. Also included in the criteria for presentation is a measure of its appearance, so do your best to make sure that you produce a final essay that you can be proud of! This includes appropriate headings and neatly and accurately presented graphs and tables.

An element that must be included in an extended essay that you are probably not familiar with is something called an abstract. An extended essay abstract is essentially a 300-word summary of the essay. It must include the research question, the scope of the investigation setting out what exactly how the question is going to be answered, and it must also contain the conclusion.

The essay must also include a clear conclusion and you are advised to set this out under a separate heading. In your conclusion, you should summarize the main points and provide the final answer to your research question, noting possible limitations to the validity of your research. Make sure that you do not introduce new information.

Please remember that the extended essay assessment criteria are a valuable recipe for you. Be sure to read the criteria very carefully in order to maximize your chances of success.

Extended essay checklist

- Is the essay within 4,000 words?
- Is there a contents page?
- Are all pages numbered?
- Is there an abstract?
- Is the research question clearly stated in the early part of the essay?
- Are all necessary terms defined?
- Are the diagrams neatly presented with accurate labels?
- Are references and footnotes used appropriately and fully?
- Are the references set out consistently?
- Does the bibliography include all, and only, the works of reference consulted?
- Does the bibliography specify author/s, title, date of publication, and publisher for each reference?
- Has a standardised and accepted method been used to present the bibliography?
- If there is an appendix, does it contain only relevant information?
- Has the conclusion been clearly indicated?
- Has the research question been answered? (!)

Service opportunities

As economists, you might decide to take the opportunity to raise awareness of the economic implications of world issues in your school community. There are several days throughout the year that have been designated to recognize important issues and challenges facing the world's people and environment. You could use these days as focal points to look at the economic implications for the stakeholders involved.

You might set up a permanent club to carry out the task throughout the year or work independently when issues that interest you arise. If you do pursue such activities, it may be useful for you to record them as part of your CAS programme as you will be working to raise awareness of the issues.

Activities to highlight the issues and share your findings might include:

- displays/exhibitions in the hallway
- computer-assisted presentations to an assembly of your peers or other schoolmates
- newsletters
- events to publicize the issues

The official international days are listed below. Attached are brief suggestions of possible links to economic theories. In each case, country case studies could be carried out to illustrate the issue or problem.

- 21 September *International day of peace*; the costs of war in terms of the damage to the factors of production and potential output.

- 17 November *International literacy day*; the importance of literacy in terms of raising human capital; correlation between literacy rates and growth and development.

- 1 December *World AIDS day*; the economic costs of HIV-AIDS.

- 10 December *Human Rights day*; the significance of the respect for human rights in the process of development.

- 8 March *International women's day*; the importance of the education of girls and women; varying levels of unemployment among men and women; the role of women in micro-credit schemes.

- 22 March *World day for water* and *world biodiversity day*; external costs of economic growth; the importance of clean water for health and economic development.

- 24 March *World tuberculosis day*; the effects and the costs of the continuous presence of the illness in developing countries.

- 31 May 31 *World no tobacco day*; the external costs of smoking; the direct costs of smoking; a comparison of measures taken around the world to reduce the costs of smoking.

If there are no official days designated, you can still declare a day, or week to promote a particular issue. For example, some schools establish a "Fairtrade Week" to promote Fairtrade products and spread awareness of the Fairtrade movement. You might run your own "Make Trade Fair", "Drop the Debt" or "End Poverty Now" campaigns. These are all campaigns that have been carried out by international non-government organizations and they have resources available to students who would like to raise awareness of global issues (see www.oxfam.org).

Index